D1480421

Metatheorizing
in Sociology

Lexington Books Series on Social Theory

George Ritzer, editor

**Emotions and Violence: Shame And
Rage in Destructive Conflicts**
Thomas J. Scheff and Suzanne M. Retzinger

Metatheorizing in Sociology

By

George Ritzer
University of Maryland

Lexington Books
D.C. Heath and Company/Lexington, Massachusetts/Toronto

Library of Congress Cataloging-in-Publication Data

Ritzer, George.
  . Metatheorizing in sociology / by George Ritzer.
     p. cm.
  Includes bibliographical references and index.
  ISBN 0–669–25008–2 (alk. paper)
  1. Sociology—Methodology. 2. Metatheory. I. Title.
  HM24.R4937 1991
  301'.01—dc20   90–47068
                                                                                CIP

Published simultaneously in Canada
Printed in the United States of America
International Standard Book Number: 0–669–25008–2
Library of Congress Catalog Card Number: 90–47068

The paper used in this publication meets the minimum requirements of American National Standard for Information Sciences—Permanence of Paper for Printed Library Materials, ANSI Z39.48–1984. ∞™

Year and number of this printing:

91 92 93 94 10 9 8 7 6 5 4 3 2 1

To Pop
whose decidedly more mundane concerns made
metatheorizing (and everything else) possible.

Contents

Preface

T his book was written in the midst of the coming of age of meta-theorizing in sociology. As we will see, there is an explosion of interest in this area as we enter the 1990s. One of my goals here is demonstrate that sociological metatheorizing is blossoming. My other goals include a definition of this still-emergent area and a demonstration of at least some of the things that it has to offer to sociology in general and to sociological theory in particular.

This book represents the culmination of work I began almost two decades ago on the paradigmatic status of sociology. It has a somewhat unusual history, for I began my work in this area with a set of specific metatheoretical concerns and have only more recently begun to understand and deal with the broader context of those interests.

The objective of my initial metatheoretical work was to make sense out of sociology, especially sociological theory, largely in the 1960s, by examining its paradigmatic structure (chapter 6). My views on that paradigmatic structure led to a sense of the need for, and then to the first steps in the construction of, an integrated sociological paradigm (chapters 7 and 8). Later, I analyzed metatheoretically developments in sociological theory: the rise of microsociological theory in the 1970s (chapter 9); the boom in interest in the micro-macro (and agency-structure) linkage in the 1980s (chapter 10); and the more general concern with theoretical syntheses as we move into the 1990s (chapter 11). In addition to looking at recent theoretical developments, I also looked back at the early history of sociological theory with the intent of uncovering one of its underlying architectonics (chapter 4). Analysis of the work of Max Weber on rationality (as well as that of the neo-Weberians) led to the creation of a new theoretical idea: hyperrationality (chapter 5). Along the way, I also turned my attention to theoretical developments within two subareas in sociology: the sociology of work and socioeconomics (chapter 12).

Only lately have I come to see these specific concerns as part of the nascent field of metatheorizing in sociology. In recent years I have been reflecting on the nature and variety of such metatheoretical work. The result of my ruminations is contained in the introductory chapter and Part I of this book (chapters 1–3) in which I describe metatheorizing in general as well as its three major types. Part III (chapters 13 and 14) is devoted to the lessons to be learned by metatheorists from other disciplines and presents some general thoughts on metatheorizing in sociology and its coming of age in the 1990s. Thus, I have progressed from a series of specific metatheoretical studies to a general sense of the parameters and importance of metatheorizing in sociology. The atypical sojourn described here is undoubtedly the result of the fact that the general field of meta-theorizing was undefined when I began my work years ago. It is my hope that this book offers such a definition and illustrates a few of the many things that can be done with a metatheoretical orientation as well as the many contributions that metatheorizing has made, and will make, to the development of sociology.

It is no accident that a good portion of this book was written during various stays in Europe. Europe is a comfortable environment in which to work on abstract theoretical and metatheoretical issues. While, as we will see in this book, American theorists often react negatively to meta-theoretical work, their European counterparts accept it as an essential and integral part of their intellectual craft. The last stages of my analysis of the paradigmatic status of sociology were completed in 1975 while I was on a Fulbright-Hays Fellowship and serving as a visiting professor at Erasmus University, Rotterdam, The Netherlands. My work on the inte-grated sociological paradigm was completed during a year-long (1980–81) stint as fellow-in-residence at the Netherlands Institute for Advanced Study in Wassenaar. A substantial portion of the present book was com-pleted in 1989 at The Swedish Collegium for Advanced Study in the Social Sciences in Uppsala, where I was fellow-in-residence. I would like to thank all these institutions for providing a fertile ground for metatheoretical work. Of course, most of the thinking, research, and writing for this book was done at the University of Maryland which, while it lacks old-world charms, has provided me with a supportive context in which to devote myself to metatheoretical issues. Finally, and as usual, I would like to thank my wife who has had the superhuman strength to tolerate, and even support, my propensity to metatheorize.

Many of the chapters in this book have not been published previously (chapters 2, 3, 4, 5, 13, and 14), but others have been (or will be) pub-lished elsewhere. However, the latter have been modified here, in many cases dramatically, in order to create a coherent book, as well as to update them where necessary. The following is a list of chapters that were pre-viously (or soon will be) published (in whole or in part) and the titles and locations of the original publications:

Introduction: "Metatheorizing in Sociology." *Sociological Forum* 5 (1990): 3–15.

Chapter 1: "Sociological Metatheory: A Defense of a Subfield by a Delineation of Its Parameters." *Sociological Theory* 6 (1988): 187–200; "Collins Does Metatheory (Again) and He Does It (Pretty) Well." *Symbolic Interaction* 12 (1989): 81–84.

Chapter 6: "Sociology: A Multiple Paradigm Science." *American Sociologist* 10 (1975): 156–67; "Paradigm Analysis in Sociology: Clarifying the Issues." *American Sociological Review* 46 (1981): 245–48.

Chapter 7: *Toward an Integrated Sociological Paradigm.* Boston: Allyn and Bacon, 1981; "Of Levels and Intellectual Amnesia." *Sociological Theory* 7 (1989): 226–29.

Chapter 8: "Emile Durkheim: Exemplar for an Integrated Sociological Paradigm?" (with Richard Bell). *Social Forces* 59 (1981): 966–95; *Toward an Integrated Sociological Paradigm.*

Chapter 9: "The Rise of Micro-Sociological Theory." *Sociological Theory* 3 (1985): 88–98.

Chapter 10: "The Micro-Macro Linkage: Threats to an Emerging Consensus." In *Frontiers of Social Theory: The New Syntheses,* edited by George Ritzer. New York: Columbia University Press, 1990; "Agency-Structure and Micro-Macro Linkages: Crossroads in Contemporary Theorizing." In *Social Theory and Human Agency,* edited by Bjorn Wittrock. Forthcoming, 1991.

Chapter 11: "The Current Status of Sociological Theory: The New Syntheses." In *Frontiers of Social Theory.*

Chapter 12: "The Sociology of Work: A Metatheoretical Analysis." *Social Forces* 67 (1989): 593–604; "Socioeconomics: In Tune, But Out of Touch, with Recent Sociological Theory." *Work and Occupations* 17 (1990): 240–245; "A Metatheoretical Analysis of Socioeconomics." *Mid American Review of Sociology* 14 (1990): 27–43.

Metatheorizing
in Sociology

Introduction:
Metatheorizing in Sociology

There is strong antipathy, at least on the surface, among many sociological theorists to abstract (Stinchcombe 1986) and grand (Hirsch, Michaels, and Friedman 1987) theorizing. Opponents argue that the abstraction of sociological theory should be greatly circumscribed and that theories should be derived from, and remain close to, the social world. This hostility is surprising because sociological theory, by its very nature, must be abstract, at least to some degree. It is also surprising because it comes from theorists; one would expect empiricists and practitioners to be hostile to the abstraction of sociological theory, but not theorists. After all, there is a need for at least some portion of the sociological community to think abstractly: if not theorists, who will function at this level?

This hostility to abstraction is related to an even stronger animosity among theorists toward those who analyze other theories, either theoretically or empirically. Such work is seen as doubly abstract: the study of abstract theories yields even more abstract results. Most sociological theorists are quite willing to allow sociologists to turn their theoretical arsenal and empirical tools on social and ideational phenomena *but* not on sociological theory. Clearly, however, sociological theory *is* a social and intellectual phenomenon that is, in turn, affected by a wide range of other social and cognitive phenomena. Thus, sociological theory, like any other social and ideational entity, can and should be studied theoretically and empirically.

In spite of the criticisms, the vast majority of theorists do, in fact, spend a good deal of time studying sociological theory in various ways. Some do this quite self-consciously in systematic efforts to deepen their understanding of various aspects of sociological theory. Others reflect on extant theories as a way of laying the basis for their own theories. Still others reflect on theory in order to get at basic principles that transcend theory.

As an example, let us focus for the moment on those who study theory as a basis for developing their own theories. Most such theorists (and this is true of most empiricists as well) in sociology do not spend large portions of their time studying the social world directly. Relatively few theorists develop and refine their theories while they study assembly-line workers or other denizens of the "real" world. Some may develop their theories as they analyze empirical data they have collected themselves. Others theorize on the basis of data collected and reported by other sociologists. Some may develop their theories, at least in part, on the basis of a careful study of, and reaction to, the work of other theorists. Still others may develop their theories by utilizing theoretical ideas drawn from other fields: economics, philosophy, psychology, etc. I suppose there are even those who practice "cerebral hygiene" (which we usually associate with Comte and Spencer[1]) and whose theories emerge out of a kind of immaculate conception. The fact is that it matters little *where* the theories come from; what counts is whether they make sense and whether they help us understand, explain, and make predictions about the social world. Close contact with the social world *may* yield such theory, but so *may* intense involvement with the ideas of our theoretical predecessors and contemporaries. Similarly, such involvement can yield a deeper understanding of sociological theory as well as useful perspectives that overarch sociological theory.

My goal in this book is to describe and make the case for *metatheorizing*,[2] the systematic study of sociological theory, as an independent and significant endeavor, albeit one that is intimately involved in sound theoretical and empirical work. Most theorists (and other kinds of sociologists as well) do a great deal of metatheorizing. Thus, this book is not proposing something new, but rather is giving explicit recognition to something that has been a reality in sociology since its inception. My secondary objective is to help metatheorists come "out of the closet."[3] Too often, those who metatheorize have been subjected to vitriolic attacks, especially by fellow theorists (who themselves are often unwitting practitioners of this traditional form of work in sociology). There is nothing reprehensible about metatheorizing; some of the most important classic thinkers (Marx, Weber, Durkheim, Parsons) were, and many key contemporary theorists are (Habermas, Collins, Giddens, Alexander), avid metatheorists.

As I stated above, and will explain in much greater detail later (chapter 2), metatheorizing lies at the base of much of sociological theory. If that is true, then what is the distinction between a metatheorist and a theorist? To put it (too) strongly, a metatheorist is one who studies sociological theories of the social world, while a theorist is one who studies the social world more directly in order to create (or employ) sociological theory. However, despite this seemingly neat distinction between metatheorist and theorist (and they are ideal types), the categories overlap to a great extent. For example, most of those we consider metatheorists also study the social world[4] and most of those classified as theorists[5] also study theoretical works. Furthermore, both theorists and metatheorists study documents. The theorist often examines documents derived from the social world while the metatheorist usually analyzes documents produced by theorists. Finally, and perhaps most importantly, substantial metatheorizing often precedes, and helps lead to, advances in social theory.

I must distinguish between those who seek to lay down the prerequisites for doing theory before theory is developed and metatheorists who take developed theories as their subject matter (Turner 1991). In most other fields metatheorizing (and *all* forms of metaanalysis) is done *after* theories have been developed. Such metatheorizing may seek a better understanding of those theories, or it may seek to create new theory, or it may seek to create an overarching theoretical perspective. However, in Turner's view,[6] most metatheorists in sociology do not study extant theory, but rather seek to create *a* metatheory (i.e., an overarching perspective) that in their view must be articulated *before* adequate theory can be developed. That is, "advocates of meta-theory usually emphasize that we cannot develop theory until we have resolved these more fundamental epistemological and metaphysical questions" (Turner 1991). Turner concludes, quite rightly in my opinion, that "such meta-theorizing has put the cart before the horse" (1991, 9). Not only is such metatheorizing misplaced, but it leads us into an arena of substantial difficulty and irresolvable controversy. Because of these and other problems, metatheorizing, as the term is used in this book, is not a process that occurs *before* theory is developed in order to lay down its prerequisites. Rather, metatheorizing is a process that occurs *after* theory has been created and takes that theory itself as the object of study.

Paul Furfey (1953/1965, 8) in *The Scope and Method of Sociology: A Metasociological Treatise* claims to have introduced the term *metasociology,* of which metatheory is clearly a part. Furfey (1953/1965, 9) defines *metasociology* as a science distinct from sociology; that is, sociology takes as its subject matter the social world, "whereas the subject matter of metasociology is sociology itself."[7] This definition is in accord with the more specific approach to metatheory I take in this book. That is, theory focuses on the social world, while metatheory takes theory as its subject matter. However, it is useful to take a closer, critical look at the details of Furfey's ideas because it will help us to clarify the meaning of *metasociology* and *metatheory.*

While he made an important beginning, Furfey has an orientation that involves a questionable approach to metasociology (and metatheory, in particular), an approach that has been attacked explicitly by Turner. Furfey *is* guilty of undertaking the kind of metasociology criticized by

Turner.[8] In spite of the way he defines the term, Furfey's metasociology does *not* involve the study of sociology, but instead is a set of principles that is prior to, and presupposed by, sociology. He begins with the debatable assumption that sociology *is* a science and proceeds to argue that metasociology has three tasks to perform for the field. First, it is to develop criteria for distinguishing scientific from nonscientific sociological knowledge. Second, and reminiscent of Durkheim (but more than a half century later), metasociology is to differentiate between phenomena that are and are not relevant to the field of sociology. Third, "metasociology is to provide practical procedural rules for applying in actual sociological research the two sorts of criteria mentioned" (Furfey 1953, 14).

Furfey's (1953, 17) work is dominated by his view that sociology is a science and metasociology is "an auxiliary science which furnishes the methodological principles presupposed by sociology." In Turner's terms, Furfey is here putting the cart before the horse. Metasociology should *not* provide a service to scientific sociology (or, for that matter, antiscientific sociology) but rather should take sociology as a subject of study.[9] Where I part company with Turner is over the type of metasociology, particularly metatheorizing, that takes sociology as its subject of study. Turner has more sympathy for this type of metasociology, but even here he concludes that metatheorizing bogs us down in unresolvable philosophical controversies. Turner's criticisms here rest on practical grounds: metatheorizing prevents us from getting on with theorizing. While this *may* be the case, I will argue in this book that a careful study of extant sociological theories can be a great aid in gaining a greater understanding of theory, creating transcendent perspectives, and creating and developing theories.[10] For instance, a number of examples come to mind of metatheorizing that proved highly useful in theory creation, including Marx's study of Hegel, the Young Hegelians, the French Socialists, and the political economists; Parsons's detailed analysis of Weber, Durkheim, and Pareto; and Alexander's similar work on Marx, Weber, Durkheim, and Parsons.

I also differ with Furfey over the idea that metasociology (and implicitly metatheorizing) is a field distinct from sociology. To my mind, metasociology in general, and metatheorizing in particular, are parts of sociology, subareas within the larger field.

In spite of Furfey's position, and Turner's critique of his orientation, the overwhelming majority of metasociological and metatheoretical efforts have *not* sought to predefine the field, but instead have studied what actually transpires in the field. Gouldner (1970) labels this kind of work the "sociology of sociology," or, more specifically, "reflexive sociology."[11] Without getting into the "radical" rhetoric[12] that characterizes (and badly dates) *The Coming Crisis of Western Sociology* (1970) and Gouldner's specific thoughts on reflexive sociology, I am quite satisfied with his position that "first and foremost, a reflexive sociology is concerned with what sociologists want to do and with what, in fact, they actually do in the world" (Gouldner 1970, 489). More specific to the narrower aims of this book, Gouldner (1970, 46) is interested in getting at the "sub-theoretical level, the 'infrastructure' of theory." He is quite clear about the relationship between metatheory and metasociology: "My concern with a theory of social theories is only part of a larger commitment to a 'sociology of sociology' " (1970, 488). Gouldner's sociology of sociology, and more particularly his "theory of social theories," is much closer to the approach taken in this book than Furfey's metasociology. However, as we will see, metatheorizing does not merely involve theorizing about theory: it also includes empirical studies of theories and theorists.[13]

Indeed, Gouldner had earlier done such an empirical study in *Enter Plato: Classical Greece and the Origins of Social Theory* (1965). Gouldner traced the roots of Plato's theory to the social structure and culture of Athens. In addition, he offered "a critical case study of Plato as a social theorist" (1965, 168). He was interested not only in gaining a deeper understanding of Plato's theory, but also in deriving from such an analysis lessons relevant to contemporary theory. In the context of his discussion of Plato, Gouldner offered a good description of his metatheoretical approach: "Some social scientists are interested in studying industrial workers; some study physicians; and still others, drug addicts and prostitutes. I happen to be curious about social theorists, as part of a sociology of social science" (1965, 170–71).

Sociologists in general, and sociological theorists in particular, are not the only ones to do metaanalysis, that is, to reflexively study various aspects of their own discipline. Others who do such work include philosophers (Radnitzky 1973), psychologists (Gergen 1973, 1986; Schmitt et al., 1984), political scientists (Connolly 1973), other social scientists (see the various essays in Fiske and Shweder 1986), and historians (White 1973). Some of these efforts are quite similar to at least some types of metaanalysis in sociology, while others differ considerably from the types of work done in sociology. The key point is that the reflexive study of one's own discipline is not the exclusive province of sociology.

Beyond the fact that metaanalysis is found in other fields, it is also true that various kinds of sociologists, not just metatheorists, do such analyses. We can group the various types of metaanalysis in sociology under the broad heading of *metasociology,* which we can define as the systematic study of sociology in general and of its various components: substantive areas (e.g., Hall's [1983] overview of occupational sociology), concepts (Porpora's [1989] analysis of the concept of "structure"), methods (*metamethods;* e.g., analyses by Coleman [1986b] and Bailey [1987] of the micro-macro problem in social research; Brewer and Hunter's [1989] effort to synthesize methods; Noblit and Hare's [1988] work synthesizing qualitative methods), data (*meta-data-analysis*[14]; e.g., Hunter, Schmidt, and Jackson 1982; Fendrich 1984; Wolf 1986; Polit and Falbo 1987; Hunter and Schmidt 1989) and theories. It is the latter, *metatheorizing*, or the systematic study of sociological theory, that will concern us in this book.

A wide variety of work can be included under the heading of sociological metatheorizing. What distinguishes work in this area is not so much the process of metatheorizing,[15] although it may vary greatly in a variety of ways, but rather the nature of the end products. In my view, there are three varieties of metatheorizing, with each largely defined by differences in their end products. The first type, *metatheorizing as a means of attaining a deeper understanding of theory—*M_U, involves the study of theory in order to produce a better, a more profound understanding of extant theory (Ritzer 1987, 1988a). M_U is concerned, more specifically, with the study of theories, theorists, and communities of theorists, as well as with the larger intellectual and social contexts of theories and theorists. The second type, *metatheorizing as a prelude to theory development—*M_P, entails the study of extant theory in order to produce new sociological theory (Ritzer 1989a). The third type, *metatheorizing as a source of overarching theoretical perspectives—*M_O is oriented to the goal of producing a perspective, one could say *a* metatheory, that overarches some part or all of sociological theory. All three types involve the systematic study of sociological theory; they differ mainly in terms of their objectives in that study (Ritzer 1990d).

The third type of metatheorizing (M_O) is not identical to the kind of overarching metatheory (O_M) (e.g., Furfey's positivism) rejected earlier in this chapter. In fact, O_M does not even fit my definition of metatheorizing because it does not occur after theory has been created and take that theory as a subject of study. M_O, like the other two types of metatheorizing, occurs *after* theory has been developed, while O_M occurs *prior to* the development of theory. Thus, M_O is derived from theory rather than imposing itself on theory. In this sense, M_O is the preferable approach because it at least allows us to assess the process by which the transcendent perspective is created. In the case of O_M we have no way of ascertaining the validity of the process through which the overarching perspective came into existence.

Nevertheless, in spite of differences in how they reach their objective, both M_O and O_M produce overarching theoretical perspectives. In so doing, they share the likelihood that they will, as Turner suggests, embroil us in a series of irresolvable controversies. In chapter 3 I will examine six examples of M_O, O_M, as well as mixed types that produce positivistic, dialectical, and postpositivistic perspectives that transcend sociological theory. Needless to say, supporters of one of these types of overarching perspectives are likely to reject, or at least be extremely uncomfortable with, the other types. Overarching perspectives whether they precede or come after theory are likely to be highly controversial and often counterproductive. Thus, I will argue that M_O, while it is not without utility, may be the least productive of the three major types of metatheorizing.

In spite of their inherent problems, there has been a tendency to equate the third type of metatheorizing (M_O), as well as O_M, with metatheorizing as a whole. This is because they, unlike the other two types of meta-theorizing (M_U, M_P), produce *a* metatheory in the sense of a perspective that stands above sociological theory. While it is distinguished by this end product, M_O involves essentially the same kind of metatheoretical proc-esses as the other two types (M_U and M_P). As we will see, some sociologists do engage in M_O, but many more do M_U and M_P. Since all three are legitimate forms of metatheorizing, it would be much too restrictive to equate M_O with the field of metatheorizing as a whole. Furthermore, as I mentioned above, M_O is the most problematic of the three types of meta-theory. As to O_M, the approach that comes before theory has been created, it poses, as we have seen, even greater difficulties. Thus, the production of overarching perspectives, as well as those perspectives themselves, con-stitute only a very small and highly controversial portion of sociological metatheorizing.

The three varieties of metatheorizing are, of course, ideal types. Ac-tual cases are usually marked by considerable overlap in the objectives of particular metatheoretical works. Nevertheless, those who do one type of metatheorizing tend to be less interested in achieving the objectives of the other two types. Thus, for example, those who seek the creation of tran-scendent perspectives tend to be less interested in achieving a deeper un-derstanding of theory or in new theory creation than those who engage in these latter types of metatheorizing directly. Of course, there are soci-ologists who at one time or another have done all three types of meta-theorizing. For example, Alexander (1982–83) created overarching perspectives in the first volume of *Theoretical Logic In Sociology* (1982), used them in the next three volumes to achieve a better understanding of the works of the classic theorists, and in more recent works has sought to help create neofunctionalism as a theoretical successor to structural functionalism (Alexander 1985b; Alexander and Colomy 1990).

Metatheorizing (and more generally metasociologizing) is intimately related to several extant subfields within sociology. For example, it has much in common with the sociology (and philosophy) of science. How-ever, the sociology of science is clearly more general than the sociological study of sociological theory as a specific scientific endeavor. Furthermore, many would contest the applicability of the sociology of science to soci-ological theory because of their view that sociology is not a science. There is more to sociology than its scientific aspects. In taking extant theory as its subject, metatheorizing need not make the assumption that sociological theory is scientific or that it is part of a scientific discipline. Nevertheless, to the degree that it is applicable to sociology, metasociologists have much to learn from the sociology (and philosophy) of science. In fact, ideas drawn from the sociology (e.g., invisible colleges, scientific networks) and philosophy (e.g., paradigms, scientific research programs) of science have played a central role in metasociology and metatheorizing.

Metatheorizing also has much in common with the sociology of knowledge, although the latter too is much more general than meta-theorizing—there are certainly many other forms of knowledge than so-ciological knowledge. Furthermore, sociological theory is more than knowledge (e.g., schools, networks) and in that sense is broader than the sociology of knowledge. Again, in spite of the differences, metatheorizing has gained much from the sociology of knowledge.

Still another subfield with which there is overlap is the history of sociological theory. In my view, most histories of sociological theory in-volve metatheorizing, especially M_U. The objective of such histories is a more profound understanding of theory. There are, however, histories, or at least parts of some of them, that are interested in historical issues per se and because of this the history of sociological theory cannot be sub-sumed under metatheorizing. On the other side, not all metatheorizing involves historical analysis. In fact, all three types of metatheorizing can focus on contemporary sociological theory. Thus, I think metatheorizing is far broader than the history of sociology, although historians of soci-ological theory obviously go into historical issues in much greater depth than most metatheorists.

Thus, while metatheorizing overlaps with the sociologies of science and of knowledge and the history of sociology,[16] in some senses it is narrower than them and in other senses it is broader. This means that metatheorizing cannot subsume, or be subsumed by, these other fields and must be considered an independent subfield.

Earlier in this chapter I mentioned those who are critical of abstract sociological theory and grand theory. It should come as no surprise that metatheorizing, which is even more abstract than theory or even grand theory, has itself come under substantial attack. However, most of these attacks are general and unfocused. Most critics have an unclear and un-differentiated sense of metatheorizing. Their criticisms cannot be taken seriously because they fail to specify exactly what type of metatheorizing they are attacking. While they seem to think that they are indicting all metatheorizing, it is clear, given the three types outlined above (as well as the rejected form [O_M]), that their criticisms are far narrower in scope.

Jonathan Turner (1991, 9; see also Turner 1985) is critical of meta-theorizing largely on pragmatic grounds because, in his view, it "often gets bogged down in weighty philosophical matters and immobilizes the-ory building. . . . meta-theory often stymies as much as stimulates theoretical activity because it embroils theorists in inherently unresolvable and always debatable controversies." Later, Turner describes metatheory as "interesting but counterproductive" and contends that those who propound it "never get around to developing theory" (1991, 24).

Turner is really criticizing those who seek to lay down prerequisites to adequate sociological theorizing (O_M) rather than those who do any of the three types of metatheorizing. If Turner is critical of any of the latter, it is of M_O because overarching perspectives emerge from analyses of extant theory. It is likely that such overarching perspectives plunge us into a series of irresolvable controversies. However, these works do come after theory has been created and in this sense Turner would be satisfied with them. Turner is far less likely to be critical of the other two types of metatheorizing. Neither M_U nor M_P involve us in irresolvable controversies. Few sociologists would be critical of the objective of attaining a deeper understanding of extant theory or of developing new theory (indeed the latter is what Turner [1989] often seeks to do). A particular understanding and a specific new theory might be controversial, but such controversies can be resolved by analyzing and discussing the steps involved in the attainment of a given understanding or the creation of a particular theory. Furthermore, both *are* productive, of greater understanding of theory in the former case and of new theory in the latter case. Thus, it is clear that Turner (1990a) is not critical of all types of metatheorizing and he may well not be critical of any of the three types to be discussed in this book.

In a now infamous review of a book (Alford and Friedland 1985) in political sociology, Theda Skocpol (1986) makes it clear that in her view what is good and useful in that subfield is substantive theory and research. She describes the Alford and Friedland work, pejoratively, as "five hundred pages of nothing but metatheory" (Skocpol 1986, 10). She attacks the authors for "pigeonholing" the work of political sociologists; for arguing for the need for an integrated theory that draws from every pigeonhole but never specifies what it is about; for arguing that different types of approaches fit best at different levels of analysis; and for ignoring the fact that the best work in political sociology has dealt with the interrelations among such levels. She hopes that Alford and Friedland will return to substantive work in political sociology, but in the meantime "may the good lord protect other political sociologists from wandering into the dead end of metatheory" (1986, 11–12). The use of the phrase "dead end" here, as well as in the title of her review essay, imply clearly that Skocpol sees *no* productive role for metatheorizing within sociology.

Skocpol's critique of metatheorizing, like that of Turner, lacks specificity. What she is being critical of, in my view, is M_U and *not* the other two types of metatheorizing. Alford and Friedland practice M_U since their objective is to review work in political sociology in order to achieve a more profound theoretical understanding of it (as well as of the polity). Skocpol believes that such a deeper understanding comes not from thinking about the theoretical work of others, but from substantive investigations in the political world. I believe that Skocpol would find the other two types of metatheorizing less likely to be "dead ends" because they produce either new theory (M_P) or overarching theoretical perspectives (M_O). Furthermore, I am far from being convinced that M_U is a dead end. In fact, I think such work can be, and has been, highly important to the development of sociological theory. A better understanding of extant theory is invaluable in the development of new theory.

Perhaps the most interesting critique of metatheorizing comes from Randall Collins (1986a). At first, Collins associates metatheorizing with the overarching perspective of antipositivism. This, implicitly, involves an attack on M_O and/or O_M. However, Collins quickly moves to a much broader critique:

> It is not surprising to me that metatheory does not go anywhere; it is basically a reflexive specialty, capable about making comments on other fields but dependent on intellectual life elsewhere that it can formalize and ideologize . . . or critique. That is why so much of the intellectual work of today consists of commentaries on works of the past rather than constructions that are creative in their own right. (1986a, 1343)

Collins, unlike Turner and Skocpol, is, I think, indicting implicitly all three types of metatheorizing, although he lacks a differentiated sense of the field. Like Turner and myself, Collins is critical of those (in this case the antipositivists) who seek to lay down prerequisites for the field.[17] His critique is more general than that of Turner and Skocpol since he is attacking metatheorizing, or all work that takes extant theory as the object of study. However, the implication is that Collins is most critical of M_U because it is the least creative of the three types of metatheorizing. The other two types of metatheorizing are clearly creative of new theory or overarching perspectives, and hence Collins would find them far more acceptable. In spite of his seemingly general critique of metatheorizing, Collins proceeds in the same essay to do what he condemns most (M_U) and undertakes a metatheoretical analysis of a variety of works of the (recent) past.

Perhaps the most telling response to the critics discussed above is to point out that they themselves, like most sociological theorists, do a great deal of metatheorizing. Given their criticisms, one would assume that none of these notables had ever uttered a metatheoretical word. However, even a cursory review of their work indicates significant metatheorizing. This is not the place to go into a full-scale review of the works of Turner, Collins, and Skocpol; a few examples will have to suffice.

Turner has done all three types of metatheorizing at one time or another in his work. Some examples of M_U include attempts to analyze and critique structural functionalism (Turner and Maryanski 1978), neo-functionalism (Turner and Maryanski 1988a), and the history of American sociological theory (Turner 1990b). Most of his work on positivism would be included under the heading of M_O. However, this is being charitable to Turner and accepting the idea that his positivism is derived from his study of sociological theory. If, however, Turner's positivism was developed prior to his study of theory, and is a prerequisite to theory, then he is guilty of creating the kind of approach (O_M) of which he (and I) is highly critical. In fact, Turner's vocal adherence to a strict positivistic perspective *does* plunge us into the kind of irresolvable controversies (e.g., with antipositivists, postpositivists) that he is so concerned about. Turner has also done M_P, including an effort to piece together a micro theory of motivation out of the contributions of a number of micro theoretical traditions (exchange theory, interactionism, ethnomethodology, structuration theory, and the theory of interaction ritual chains) (Turner 1987); the fifth edition of his theory text which, like the others, attempts to derive hypotheses from a variety of contemporary theories (Turner 1991); and a similarly oriented book aimed at the development of elementary principles derived from work, mainly theoretical,[18] in the area of social stratification (Turner 1984). Turner makes his use of M_P clear in the conclusion of the chapter in his stratification book devoted to prior theories: "In this chapter, I have reviewed some of the weaknesses in the literature on stratification. . . . Yet, there have been numerous important contributions to theorizing about stratification processes. . . . I will borrow from Marx, Weber and Spencer; I will recast dramatically the functional argument; and I will use many elements of Lenski's synthesis" (1984, 55). Turner also makes a more general case for M_P, or what he calls "theory cumulation": "We selectively take the ideas of others and extend them in some way, producing a theoretical argument that is more powerful than the one with which we began. Unfortunately, we do not do enough of this kind of activity" (1989, 9–10).

As for Collins, among his recent works are efforts to review and build theoretically upon the work of theorists like Weber (Collins 1985), Goffman (Collins 1986c), and Mead (Collins 1989b). Even his best-known theoretical works on conflict (Collins 1975, 1990) and interaction ritual chains (Collins 1981c, 1981b, 1987b) are based heavily on an analysis and critique of the work of theoretical predecessors (e.g., Marx, Weber, Durkheim, Goffman, Garfinkel, etc.) within those traditions. Thus, Collins is one of our most prominent practitioners of M_P. I have already noted how he did M_U in a paper purportedly critical of metatheorizing. He also does M_O as, for example, in his work (Collins 1989a) outlining and defending his view that sociology must be a science, albeit a more broadly defined positivistic science that avoids some of the excesses of Turner's positivism.[19]

Skocpol is the least metatheoretical of this triumvirate, but a portion of her major work, *States and Social Revolution* (1979), is a metatheoretical analysis (M_P) of various theories of revolution. Indeed, Skocpol's preface to that book makes her metatheoretical intentions abundantly clear:

> Developed through critical reflection on assumptions and types of explanation common to most received theories of revolution, the principles of analysis sketched in the first chapter of the book are meant to reorient our sense of what is characteristic of—and problematic about—revolutions as they actually have occurred historically. Then the remainder of the book attempts to make the program of Chapter 1, a calling for new kinds of explanatory arguments, come alive in application. (1979, xi)

This is a remarkable position for someone who, as we saw above, came to label metatheory a "dead end" (Skocpol 1986). Chapter 1 of *States and Social Revolutions* is an avowedly metatheoretical endeavor involving a critique of extant theories of revolution and an effort to develop an alternative theory on the basis of that critique. The remaining "empirical" (comparative/historical) chapters are merely meant to make the derived theoretical program "come alive."[20]

Thus, it is clear that the major critics of metatheorizing do a great deal of this kind of work themselves. If this is true of such critics, it seems obvious that metatheorizing is ubiquitous among sociological theorists. Such well-known contemporary theorists as Habermas, Giddens, and Alexander do a considerable amount of metatheorizing; it may well be the case they do more metatheorizing than theorizing. In fact, it appears that while theorists have always been inclined toward metatheorizing, today's theorists do a great deal more of it than the classic theorists. While there is much merit in metatheorizing, it might become a problem if our dominant theorists do increasingly more metatheorizing and correspondingly less theorizing about the social world. In line with the criticisms voiced (and largely rebutted) earlier in this chapter, such perspectives *are* in danger of growing too abstract and too removed from the social world.

This book, then, is about a ubiquitous form of sociology, a form that has been widely, albeit largely implicitly, practiced. It is also a form of sociology that has been often, and wrongly, maligned. One objective of this book is to make the practice of metatheorizing more explicit. I hope that by making it explicit, future practitioners will be able to consciously develop and refine metatheorizing. Another function of making metatheorizing more explicit is that it will allow critics of the practice to refine their criticisms, if they still wish to make them. The continuing development of metatheorizing in general, as well of its various subtypes, will make it much more difficult to simply dismiss the field out of hand. Critics will need to come to grips with the field in general as well as with its various subtypes. They will need to specify the forms of metatheorizing of which they are critical, and why they are critical of them. The propensity to criticize may come to be mitigated by the fact that the critics will realize that they themselves are frequently metatheoreticians.

Another hope I have is that metatheoretical work will come to be accepted in its own right. Frequently, metatheoretical work is dismissed because it is "not theory," that is, because it is not about the social world, but rather about theory. But metatheory is not theory and it should be judged on its own grounds. The study of theory is an acceptable, even desirable, type of sociological work that can be distinguished, at least in part, from theory. Those who do sound metatheoretical work are contributing to sociological theory (and empirical research as well) in a variety of ways and thereby, indirectly, to a better understanding of the social world.

Notes

1. I could say that what we have here are bad practitioners of metatheory. Spencer (1904, 289), in his autobiography, describes how he had read only the first few pages of Kant's *Critique* and had read no books in psychology or philosophy. Spencer was apparently not much of a reader and was content to pick up what he could from casual conversations and popular publications. In other words, Spencer was not a serious student of other theoretical works. He was a metatheorist (he certainly did not bother to venture into the field to collect data); he was just not a very good one. Turner and Maryanski (1988b) would disagree with this characterization of Spencer, but it seems to me that the thrust of their work is that Spencer was a better empiricist than he was a metatheorist.

2. Thus, this book is not about metatheory which, as we will see, is one possible end product of metatheorizing, but about the *process* of metatheorizing which may have several end products. This constitutes one change from my early work on this issue (Ritzer 1987, 1988b) where I discussed metatheory rather than metatheorizing.

3. This idea, of course, was first applied to homosexuals. In fact, there are a number of similarities between homosexuality and the practice of metatheorizing. For example, both homosexuals and metatheorists have been judged in negative terms and practitioners have been stigmatized for their activities.

4. For example, while most of my work is metatheoretical, I have done work using Weberian theory to analyze society in general (Ritzer 1983), the professions (Ritzer 1975b), and the medical profession in particular (Ritzer and Walczak 1988).

5. For example, as we will see in chapter 2, that sophisticated theorist of capitalist society, Karl Marx, did a great deal of metatheorizing.

6. While I too see this kind of work as problematic, I do not agree that the majority of metatheorists do it.

7. Furfey (1953/1965, 8) also is cognizant of metatheory which he sees, unlike this author, as dealing with the "logic of a theory."

8. I also think that most of the authors in Fiske and Shweder's *Metatheory in Social Science: Pluralisms and Subjectivities* (1986) are guilty of this charge.

9. This is in line with Harvey's definition of metascience, following Radnitzky (1973), as "research into science . . . coming 'after' science, or 'about' science" (1987, 271).

10. In fact, Turner (1991) himself does this type of metatheorizing when, for example, he uses his study of sociological theories to generate a wide range of hypotheses.

11. For a comparison of Gouldner's "reflexive sociology" and Bourdieu's "auto-analysis," see Swartz (1990).

12. *The Coming Crisis in Western Sociology* is a product of the late 1960s. Gouldner sympathizes with the radical movements of that period both in and out of sociology, and thus tends to take positions that sound naive and antiquated today.

13. In fact, as we will see in chapter 2, Parsons (1937/1949, 697) describes his own work of this genre as an "empirical monograph." Merton (1968:4), another key figure in the history of metatheoretical work, argues in a similar fashion that the works of classical theorists are "crucial source materials."

14. I have labeled this (somewhat awkwardly) as meta-data-analysis in order to differentiate it from the more generic metaanalysis. In meta-data-analysis the goal is not to study methods, but to seek ways of cumulating research results across research studies. In his introduction to Wolf's *Meta-Analysis*, Niemi defines metaanalysis as "the application of statistical procedures to collections of empirical findings from individual studies for the purpose of integrating, synthesizing, and making sense of them" (Niemi, in Wolf 1986, 5).

15. While I focus here and in this book on the end products of metatheorizing, similar work is needed on the process of metatheorizing, especially the methodologies employed by metatheorists.

16. See chapter 13 for a discussion of some of the things that metatheorizing has to gain from these subfields.

17. As we will, Collins (1989a) does just what he is critical of here when he outlines a proscience position for sociology.

18. Turner recognizes his comparative lack of involvement with the empirical literature: "critics will decry . . . the lack of an extensive literature review of empirical findings" (1984, 207).

19. In outlining such an M_0 position Collins is likely to create (again) an unresolvable controversy involving his position and that of the more extreme positivists and hermeneuticists.

20. The bulk of *States and Social Revolutions*, however, is a comparative/historical analysis of various societies. As is the case in all such research, Skocpol's data base is secondary historical *documents*. One might well ask why the analysis of historical documents is acceptable, but the study of theoretical documents is such a heinous endeavor? To put it another way, much of metatheorizing *and* much of Skocpol's empirical work involve documentary analysis.

I
Varieties of Metatheorizing

My objective in part I of this book is to outline the general nature of metatheorizing in sociology. Each of the chapters in this part deals with one of the three major types of metatheorizing. Chapter 1 focuses on metatheorizing in which the objective is to gain a deeper understanding of sociological theory (M_U). Chapter 2 deals with metatheorizing in which the goal is the creation of new sociological theory (M_P). Chapter 3 analyzes metatheorizing (M_O) in which the end product is a perspective (a "metatheory") that overarches sociological theory, perhaps all of the social sciences, or even all disciplines of all types.

1
Metatheorizing as a Means for Attaining a Deeper Understanding of Sociological Theory

Varieties of M$_U$

There are several well-defined varieties of metatheorizing in which the objective is to attain a more profound understanding of extant sociological theory (M$_U$). All these subtypes involve the formal or informal study of sociological theory. A fourfold table utilizing the dimensions *internal-external* (Smelser 1989) and *intellectual-social* yields a typology that deals exhaustively with the varieties of M$_U$.[1] *Internal* refers to things that exist within sociology, while *external* deals with phenomena that are found outside of sociology but that have an impact on it. By *intellectual* I mean anything that relates to the cognitive structure of sociology: theories, metatheoretical tools, ideas borrowed from other disciplines, and so on. *Social* refers to the sociological structure of sociology: schools, the effect of individual background factors on sociologists, the impact of the larger society, and so forth. Figure 1–1 is the fourfold table that is created when we crosscut the internal-external and intellectual-social dimensions.

Four cautionary notes are in order before I proceed. First, the two dimensions (internal-external; intellectual-social) are continua with no hard and fast dividing lines between the poles of each. Second, the four types of M$_U$ developed by crosscutting these continua are not rigidly distinct from one another. In other words, specific metatheoretical works may, as we will see, bridge two, three, or even all four types of M$_U$. Third, the enumeration of kinds of work to be discussed under each heading will likely require expansion in the future as other kinds of work under each heading evolve. Fourth, we should not reify the typology to be discussed below; its utility is in helping us to understand the diverse types of work going on in M$_U$. Thus, other typologies may be developed that could prove even more useful in analyzing M$_U$.

Internal-Intellectual

The first, and by far the largest, body of work in M$_U$ is derived from Thomas Kuhn's (1962, 1970b) philosophy of science (as well as that of

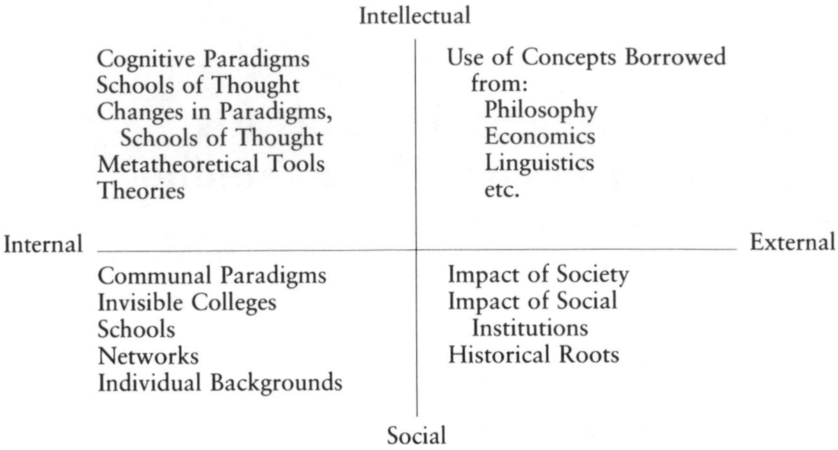

Intellectual

Cognitive Paradigms	Use of Concepts Borrowed
Schools of Thought	from:
Changes in Paradigms,	Philosophy
Schools of Thought	Economics
Metatheoretical Tools	Linguistics
Theories	etc.

Internal ———————————————————————————— External

Communal Paradigms	Impact of Society
Invisible Colleges	Impact of Social
Schools	Institutions
Networks	Historical Roots
Individual Backgrounds	

Social

Figure 1–1. Major Types of M_U

others—e.g., Lakatos 1978[2]), and attempts to identify the major paradigm(s) in sociology. Although Kuhn's paradigms encompass both intellectual and communal (social) components, most sociologists working within the Kuhnian tradition have emphasized the cognitive aspects. At a cognitive level, paradigms are sometimes equated with theories (Friedrichs 1970, Effrat 1972, Leinhart 1977, Colclough and Horan 1983, Rosenberg 1989), sometimes with groups of theories (Eisenstadt and Curelaru 1976; Strasser 1976), and sometimes with a variety of cognitive components including theories and/or methods (Ritzer's [1975c, 1975d] "social facts," "social definition," and "social behavior" paradigms that encompass both theories and methods;[3] Albrow's [1974] distinction, focusing on methods, between the "dialectical" and "categorical" paradigms; Platt's [1986] more specific effort to study the linkage between structural-functional theory and the survey research method).

Many of the works discussed above and derived from Kuhn's approach have themselves spawned considerable thought and research. For example, Ritzer's multiple paradigm schema has elicited a number of empirical tests (e.g., Snizek 1976; Picou, Wells, and Nyberg 1978; Friedheim 1979; Platt 1986; Fuhrman and Snizek 1987), theoretical extensions (Staats 1976; Ritzer 1981b), applications (Falk and Zhao 1989; Rosenberg 1989), heated critiques (Eckberg and Hill 1979; Bealer 1990), debates (Hill and Eckberg 1981; Ritzer 1981a; Falk and Zhao, 1990), and so on. These extensions are as much a part of M_U as the original works on the cognitive structure of sociology.

Efforts to map the cognitive structure of sociological theory are not restricted to those inspired by Kuhn. Examples of non-Kuhnian efforts to map the cognitive structure of sociological theory include H. Wagner's (1964) distinction between "structural-functional" and "interpretative-interactional" orientations and D. Wagner and J. Berger's (1985) differentiation among theoretical contexts: orienting strategies, unit theories, and theoretical research programs.

Also to be included in the non-Kuhnian cognitive strategy is the "schools of thought approach" (Sorokin 1928; Martindale 1960). This is distinguished from the communal approach (to be discussed under the internal-social heading) by the fact that a school of thought is a larger, more far-flung group of theorists most of whom have little or no personal contact with one another.[4] They are tied together by their common identity with a particular theoretical orientation.

The metatheoretical approaches discussed above tend to be static orientations identifying what Harvey (1987) calls "meta-scientific units": extant paradigms, idea systems, schools of thought.[5] These approaches have been criticized for their static character (Harvey 1982) and they have led to an approach in which calls are made, and efforts undertaken, to develop a more dynamic approach to the underlying structure of sociological theory (Wiley 1979; Wagner 1984; Wagner and Berger 1985). The focus here is on what causes paradigms, idea systems, schools of thought (Harvey 1987) to change, grow, decline, etc. Included here would be various aspects of the history of sociology (e.g., works like that of Shils [1970] on the general history of sociology, or more specific works like Lengermann's [1979] study of the founding of the *American Sociological Review*).

A very different internal-intellectual approach involves the development of general metatheoretical tools with which to analyze existing sociological theories and to develop new theories. Included here would be Gouldner's (1970) use of concepts like "background assumptions" and "domain assumptions" to analyze the underlying structure of sociological theory, Kalberg's (1983) effort to get at the underlying "architectonic"[6] of at least a portion of Weber's work, efforts to deal with "levels" of analysis[7] within sociological theory (Edel 1959; Blau 1979; Berger and Chaffee 1988; Wiley 1988; Ritzer 1989c; Wiley 1989), and more specific attempts to analyze "micro-macro" linkages in sociology (Wagner 1964; Wallace 1969; Kemeny 1976; Collins 1981b, 1981c, 1987a, 1987b, 1988; Ritzer 1981b, 1988a, 1990b; Alexander, Giesen, Munch, and Smelser 1987). It is the latter metatheoretical tool which, at the moment, is attracting the most attention in the field; it will be utilized in this book, particularly in chapters 9 and 10.

The last body of M_U work to be discussed in this section is also far and away the most common: the reexamination of sociological theories as well as the work of sociological theorists. The list here is almost literally endless, but some recent examples include Camic's (1987) reexamination of the methods of the early Parsons, Marske's (1987) look at Durkheim's "cult of the individual," Hilbert's (1987) subjectivistic interpretation of Weber's views on bureaucracy, Elster's (1985) micro interpretation of Marx, and at least a portion of Collins's (1989b) analysis of Mead.[8] Such work is characterized by direct and careful examination of a theory in order to shed new light on it. This work is generally unfettered by the kind of metatheoretical paraphernalia (e.g., "paradigms," "levels," "micro-macro linkage") discussed above and instead looks quite directly at the theories themselves.

Internal-Social

The main internal-social approach is also indebted to Kuhn (as well as to others, such as Price [1963] and Crane [1969], and their notion of "invisible colleges") and emphasizes the communal aspects of various sociological theories. The tendency in this approach is to focus on relatively small groups of theorists who have direct links to one another. Of utmost importance are the various approaches that have sought to identify the major "schools" in the history of sociology (Wiley 1979; Tiryakian 1979, 1986; Besnard 1983a, 1983b; Bulmer 1984, 1985). The greatest amount of work and the strongest documentation exists on the Chicago and Durkeimian schools, but some sociologists doubt whether there have been any true "schools" in the history of sociology.

Also worth noting here is a related, but more formal approach, to the study of the ties among groups of sociologists. For example, Mullins (1973, 1983) used a network approach to identify the major "theory groups" in sociology.

As with the paradigm concept, work on schools has now created an independent, developing body of scholarship. For example, Tiryakian's work on schools has led to a variety of efforts to critique, clarify, and extend his ideas (e.g., the various essays in Monk 1986 and Harvey 1987).

Another internal-social metatheoretical approach involves turning to the sociological theorists themselves and examining, among other things, their training, their institutional affiliations, their career patterns, their positions within the field of sociology, etc. (Gouldner 1970). The view here is that these and many other experiences shape a sociologist's theoretical orientation. As Gouldner puts it, "much of theory-work begins with an effort to make sense of one's experience" (1970, 484). Of importance here are the biographies (e.g., the various works on C. Wright Mills: Horowitz 1983; Tilman, 1984) and autobiographies (Homans 1984) of sociologists.

External-Intellectual

The third M_U orientation involves turning to other academic disciplines for ideas, tools, concepts, theories, and the like that can be used in the analysis of sociological theory. Paradigm analyses in sociology obviously owe a great debt to philosophy and the ideas of Kuhn, Lakatos, and others. Currently, much theoretical work is being done in sociology using economics as a model (e.g., Coleman 1987; Gerstein 1987). One other example of this orientation is found in the efforts to look at sociological theories as forms of discourse and to analyze them using an array of linguistic tools (Brown 1987, 1990). Sociologists in general, and sociological theorists in particular, are seen as using rhetoric in order to persuade others of the adequacy of their approaches. Thus, sociological rhetoric, especially sociological theory, can be studied using the same linguistic tools used to study everyday forms of discourse. Sociological theory is seen, from this perspective, as *not* being a privileged form of disclosure.

External-Social

Finally, the external-social approach (also suggested by Gouldner) involves shifting to the more macro level to look at the larger society and the nature of its impact on sociological theorizing. For example, Tiryakian (1979) suggests that we look at the national setting,[9] the sociohistorical setting, the relationship between sociology and various institutions, the relationship between sociology and its funding agencies, sociology as an institution and the process of institutionalization (Shils 1970), as well as sociology as a profession. In his essay on external influences on sociology, Smelser (1989) examines cultural influences, trends in the larger society, the influence of science, and the impact of the polity. Very suggestive in this realm is the work of Michel Foucault (1965, 1975, 1979) and his thoughts on the historical roots of the human sciences (including sociology) as well as the power-knowledge (especially sociological knowledge) linkage.[10]

The Four Types of M_U: A Case Study

The four types of M_U are depicted above as being discrete and appearing in separate works. However, it is possible for all types of M_U to be found in the same work.[11] I will now look at Collins's (1989b) recent essay on Mead as such a work.[12] The irony of using one of Collins's work as a metatheoretical model is that, as we saw in the introduction, Collins

(1986a, 1989a) has been a vocal critic of metatheorizing. It might seem outrageous to critically examine his essay on Mead as a model of M_U, but that is precisely what I intend to do. In this essay, and elsewhere in his work, Collins offers clear examples of metatheorizing.[13]

It is evident that in his essay on Mead, Collins is doing much of what he is criticizing metatheorizing for (see the introduction). His essay is dependent on Mead's work (and that of others such as Durkheim and Goffman); it does critique it; it is in a sense an extended commentary on Mead and his work. However, it is also creative in attempting to offer a new sociology of the mind; indeed it is a model of the fact that metatheoretical works can be highly creative. Collins is a critic of metatheorizing at the same time he is doing some of its best contemporary work.

In this section I intend to examine Collins's essay from the point of view of the four types of M_U. The first type, internal-intellectual, involves the study of cognitive factors internal to the field. Here Collins is not doing what many metatheorists do and looking at such phenomena as paradigms or "schools of thought," but he is doing what metatheorists *most often* do: offering a detailed examination of a theory. In this case, of course, Collins is taking a close look at Mead's ideas and he is also trying to link them (especially Mead's theory of the mind) to the ideas of other theorists including Durkheim (solidarity) and Goffman (interaction rituals), as well as to his own work on interaction ritual chains.

The study of internal-social factors, the second type of M_U, involves looking at sociological phenomena internal to the field such as schools, "theory groups," and the backgrounds of sociological theorists themselves. Collins does a good deal of this kind of analysis. Among other things, Collins looks at Mead's family background and "family connections," his religious ties, his publication pattern (including his writing block), and his "intellectual connections" with major thinkers, such as his sponsorship by John Dewey and his observations in John Watson's laboratory. Collins indicates that these internal social factors had a major impact on Mead's thought system.

Turning from internal to external phenomena, Collins does relatively little with external-social factors (sociological factors external to the discipline), although he does mention the early twentieth-century political context, Mead's reform activities, the changing American university system, and his clashes with the president of the University of Chicago. Collins does much more with external-intellectual factors (cognitive factors external to the discipline), although this is a little tricky since it is a bit unclear in this case which are the internal and which are the external fields. The ambiguity stems from the lack of institutionalization of sociology, Mead's academic position in a philosophy department, and the early subsumption of psychology by philosophy. Although Mead ultimately came to be best known as a sociologist, technically he was a philosopher and Collins focuses on his place within that field. If we take philosophy as the internal field, then the external fields are the developing disciplines of psychology and sociology and the focus is on the relationships and tensions within and between these fields. Collins does look at the relationship between Mead's ideas and those that had developed and were developing in the "external" fields of psychology and sociology.

Thus, to his great credit, Collins covers (implicitly) all of the M_U bases. While most of those who do M_U do a specific type, or even subtype, of analysis, Collins looks at Mead's work utilizing all major M_U perspectives. In this sense, Collins's essay on Mead is an exemplary piece of M_U. But use of these same types of M_U will also allow us to see some weaknesses in Collins's analysis.

In fact, Collins's strength is also his metatheoretical weakness. That is, he covers all types of M_U, but since his study is merely an essay (albeit a long and complex one) one comes away feeling that many things have been covered superficially and many other metatheoretical issues have been overlooked entirely. On the internal-intellectual dimension, the main weakness is the highly limited treatment of Mead's (and other) theories. One leaves the essay also wishing that there were more than the few offhand comments on the relationship between Mead's theories and those of Herbert Blumer and other later symbolic interactionists. Turning to internal-social factors, Collins's comments here, while provocative, are hardly the last word on Mead's psyche, his family life, his friendship patterns, the strain that helped cause his death, and so on.[14] In the external-intellectual domain, it is clear that much more could be said about the ties between philosophy[15] and religious ideas, psychology and sociology. Finally, on the external-social issue, the most notable omission, and it is a huge one, is a treatment of the sociohistorical context in which Mead lived and worked.

To insist that Collins do all of this in a paper, or even in a book, is obviously ridiculous. Collins has offered a laudable sketch of what can be done in terms of understanding and extending Mead's theory of the mind. But as this discussion makes clear, Collins would need to add a great deal more before he had anything approaching a definitive metatheoretical analysis of Mead (as well as an adequate theory of the mind).

Collins is not merely doing an exercise in M_U. He is also, and perhaps more importantly, using his metatheoretical analysis of Meadian theory and its weaknesses to do M_P by building a broader theory by combining Mead's ideas with ideas from Durkheim, Goffman, and Collins's own work. In so doing, he is demonstrating that metatheoretical analysis is one of the key ways of creating new theoretical perspectives. Collins's theories here, as elsewhere, come out of metatheoretical analyses. Collins's theoretical ideas did not stem from a study of the empirical world; rather they flowed out of the study and critique of Mead's theory and the attempt to combine some of its salvageable components with ideas drawn from other sociological theorists. This is not the only way to create sociological theories (induction from empirical research would be another way), but it is a perfectly respectable way of producing a sociological theory. The issue is not where Collins (or anyone else) got his theoretical ideas, but whether they make sense and whether they are useful in explaining and predicting social life.

I would also recast a portion of Collins's argument and contend that creative theorists are (often) sophisticated metatheorists. Collins's way of saying this is to point out that creative intellectuals occupy key positions in the intellectual debates of their day, are very knowledgeable about them, and are therefore able to recombine them in creative ways. To my mind *that is* M_P, or at least good M_P, and we can argue that sound metatheorizing can lead to creative theorizing. In fact, I think Collins is an excellent example of a sound metatheorist who is using that work as a base to do creative theorizing.

I close this section with a somewhat different metatheoretical point. On other occasions, I and others (e.g., Giddens 1984; Porpora 1989) have been critical of Collins for his tendency toward micro-reductionism (see chapter 9). To his credit, in this work Collins—although he continues to focus on the micro level (in this essay, the mind)—offers a number of useful openings to macro-level phenomena. One can only hope that as Collins continues his metatheoretical journeys he will venture more into the linkages between micro- and macro-level phenomena and ultimately to the generation of a more integrative micro-macro theory of the mind as well as of other social phenomena. In fact, we will see in chapters 10 and 11 that Collins is indeed moving, at least part way, toward a more integrated micro-macro conception of the social world.

Criticisms and Responses

In this section we move back from the specific case study of Collins's work on Mead to M_U in general. My focus here is on some of the major criticisms of M_U and what responses, if any, can be made to the critics. One of the things this delineation of the four subtypes of M_U makes clear is how difficult it is to offer global criticisms of metatheorizing. Not only do critics face these four subtypes of M_U, but they also must contend with the other two main types of metatheorizing, M_P and M_O, as well. If, in fact, metatheorizing can be divided into three broad types, and M_U into four subtypes, which of them, if any, are the critics of the field attacking?

Clearly, the critics need to be much more specific if we are to take their ideas seriously.

One of the most general criticisms of metatheorizing is that it tends to be ideological, especially in offering pro-, anti-, or postpositivistic ideologies. The varieties of M_U outlined above are probably no more or less ideological than most other types of sociological analysis. In the main, the works discussed above are nonideological efforts to arrive at a deeper understanding of sociological theory. M_O and especially O_M (the rejected effort to create an overarching perspective before theory is developed) are more open to the charge of being ideological.

Turning more specifically to M_U, critics often complain that it has little to offer other than a series of "pigeonholes" into which various theories or sets of theories are to be (uncomfortably) stuffed. The implicit message is that great violence is being done to theories and little or nothing is gained by pigeonholing them. Critics imply that the metatheorist oversimplifies and has little or no sense of the great subtlety of sociological theories. If this criticism has any validity, it is with reference to some (but not all) of the internal-intellectual and internal-social metatheories[16] that delineate cognitive and communal paradigms, schools, schools of thought, etc. Even if one is willing to assume that nothing else is accomplished in these works but pigeonholing, it must be asked whether this is such a nonproductive activity? While not among the greatest accomplishments of M_U, categorizing various types of theories can be a useful activity that might allow us to see some surprising similarities (e.g., between structural-functionalism and conflict theory) as well as to uncover some unsuspected dissimilarities (e.g., between symbolic interactionism and exchange theory). Categorization systems *can* be useful. More importantly, most metatheorists who develop categorization systems go well beyond that limited task and deal with changes, interrelationships, conflicts, etc., within and among various sets of theories. For example, in addition to "pigeonholing" structural functionalism and conflict theory within the social facts paradigm, I (see chapter 6) discuss their relationship, how conflict theory grew out of a reaction to structural functionalism, and how in addition to the similarities there are important differences between structural functionalism and conflict theory, with structural functionalism focusing on the order among social facts and conflict theory focusing on conflicts and tensions among social facts.

Another basic criticism of M_U is that it is not an independent field, but depends on the work of theorists to provide it with the material with which it works. While this is certainly true of those metatheorists who analyze theories, it is not true of others who study such things as networks, backgrounds of individual theorists, and the relationship between sociological theory and the larger society. Even where metatheorists study theories and are dependent on them, similar dependencies characterize most other types of sociology. Most researchers base their hypotheses on the theoretical, conceptual, and empirical work of their predecessors; a review of the literature precedes most pieces of research. More importantly, few contemporary researchers collect their own data; they tend to rely on extant data sets, data collected by the federal government, and so on. Many theorists spend much more time analyzing and critiquing the work of other theorists (that is, doing M_P) than they do theorizing about the social world. Researchers, theorists, *and* metatheorists are *all* dependent on the work of others to provide them with the bases for their own work. To put it another way, they all tend to rely on documents provided to them by others.

Related to the above is the argument that M_U is largely a critique of the work of others. While some M_U involves a critical analysis of sociological theories, most of it involves the *study* of theories and/or theorists. Furthermore, M_U is at least as likely to be constructive and to offer positive direction to sociological theorists.

Related to the dependence critique is the argument that because metatheorists are more dependent, they are less "creative" than other sociologists. However, creativity is not to be judged by the materials used, but by the results produced. It would be impossible to show that metatheoretical work is somehow less creative than other work in sociology. Furthermore, with most research dominated by "normal science" and minute additions to extant bodies of knowledge, and with no contemporary theorists creating idea systems to rival those of the early giants in the field, it would be difficult to document a high level of creativity in the other areas of sociology.

As we saw in the introduction, perhaps the most basic objection to metatheorizing in general is made on pragmatic grounds. It is seen as enmeshing us in unresolvable debates that prevent us from getting on with the business of extending and developing theories, elaborating and testing hypotheses, and collecting data and expanding our substantive knowledge of the social world. This is the criticism of M_U that is most difficult to take seriously. For one thing, it applies mainly to M_O and O_M and not to M_U. For another, the opposite argument could easily and convincingly be made: it is the failure of contemporary theorists (and researchers) to make much progress that is breathing more and more life into M_U. Furthermore, if a miniscule proportion of the sociological community wants to devote itself to the "rarefied" atmosphere of work in M_U, how does that serve to impede the work of the vast majority of other sociologists? They are free to ignore the work of metatheorists; indeed, it seems unlikely that many sociologists are avid followers of the most recent developments in metatheory. Most sociologists go about their work with little or no handwringing over the issues raised by metatheorists. The assumption behind this critique seems to be that earthshaking progress is being made in other areas of sociology and if only metatheorists would stop metatheorizing, then progress would occur at an even more rapid pace. Needless to say, it is hard to accept this view of the current state of sociology, or of what it would be like if those who do M_U were magically transformed into theorists, methodologists, or researchers.

Still another general criticism of metatheorizing is that it is too general, vague, and abstract. On one level, this means that it is hard to translate metatheoretical abstractions into the more concrete concerns of sociological theorists and researchers. To put it another way, sociological theorists and researchers can find little utility in metatheorizing. At another level, metatheorizing is seen as even more remote from, and irrelevant to, the real social world. These criticisms are far more germane to M_O (and O_M) than they are to M_U. However, concepts that are an integral part of M_U, like paradigms, levels of reality, discourse and the intricacies of Foucaldian theory, among others, all seem of little relevance to helping us understand drug addiction, respond to the AIDS threat, or deal with the possibility of nuclear war. It is certainly the case that such concepts are remote from sociological research (and even some theory) and the day-to-day social world. However, that is precisely where they are *supposed* to be. Those who do M_U are often determinedly abstract, but they usually do their work in the hope that others will be able to translate their ideas so that they will be usable by sociological researchers and applicable to the social world. In most cases this is little more than a faint hope. Sometimes it is the fault of metatheorists themselves whose work is often too jargonistic, overly complex, or simply wrongheaded. Sometimes it is the fault of those who translate the ideas of the metatheorists or apply them to research and/or the social world. And sometimes it is the fault of the researchers or the analysts of the everyday social world who fail to grapple seriously with ideas derived from M_U.

Another criticism of M_U is that it is overly formalistic. This would be most true of those efforts to categorize sociological theories into paradigms, schools, and schools of thought, as well as the attempts to develop metatheoretical tools with which to analyze sociological theories. I am a bit mystified by the charge of formalism since, if anything, most of sociology (including M_U) suffers from far too little formalism. In any case, even if we accept the charge of formalism in terms of these types of M_U, it certainly does not apply to all types of M_U.

In this section I have responded to most of the major criticisms leveled at M_U. I do not mean to imply that M_U is without problems. In fact, I will touch on some of those problems in the next section, but in the context of a positive statement about the future direction of M_U.

Future Directions in M_U

One would hope and predict that in the future M_U and the other types of metatheorizing—and more generally metasociology—will continue to develop and contribute further to the day-to-day activities of sociologists.

One of the many important functions that M_U can perform is to increase the "theoretical self-consciousness" of sociologists by making the various intellectual and social factors that lie at the base of their work more explicit and more amenable to critical analysis. While all sociologists can profit from M_U in this sense, theorists have the most to gain. Many theorists are so deeply enmeshed in their particular orientation that they are unaware of the kinds of things that concern metatheorists and that have an impact on their theorizing. Sociological theorists (indeed all sociologists) can become more theoretically self-conscious by becoming more knowledgeable about the cognitive structure of a theory and its similarities to, and differences from, the cognitive structures of other theories; of the community (or "school") whose members share the theory; of the broader school of thought in which the theory is embedded; of the changing nature and context of the theory; of how individual- and societal-level factors affect theories and theory choices; and of the rhetorical aspects of sociological theories. Greater self-consciousness should, in turn, lead to greater understanding of one's own theory as well as of competing theories, more self-criticism, and ultimately to improvements in sociological theory and, more generally, sociology.

We should soon see advances within each of the major subtypes of M_U as well as the proliferation of other subtypes of M_U. A particularly promising area for future work concerns the linkages and relationships among the various types of M_U.

A most pressing need is for work on the linkage between the cognitive and communal aspects of a paradigm. These two areas of M_U have run a parallel course for some time with only occasional and limited efforts at dealing with their interrelationships. Tiryakian (1979, 230), for example, seems to assume a one-to-one relationship between the cognitive and the communal dimensions in discussing the relationship between "the school and its paradigm," and later of the "intrinsic relation between a school and an SRP [scientific research program]" (Tiryakian 1986, 420). However, it is clearly debatable whether every school has a cognitive paradigm (or SRP) and conversely whether a cognitive paradigm must be tied to a school. We need some serious thought and research on the relationship between the cognitive and communal dimensions.

Many other issues suggest themselves when we open up the arena of the relationship between the cognitive and the communal components. For example, we would want to know much more about how groups of sociologists create and/or expand upon sociological theories. Some attention should be devoted to internal group processes and how they might lead to theoretical schisms and ultimately to theory proliferation. On the other side, we would want to examine how the nature of a theory affects the character of the group. And, shifting the focus to linkages to another type of M_U, we will need to examine how communal and/or cognitive aspects of a theory affect whether it will expand into a broader school of thought. Once a theory has moved beyond a community and become a broader school of thought, we will need to examine whether it is destined to change dramatically. For example, must a theory become flaccid as it drifts away from its intellectual center? Shifting to still another subtype of M_U, we will need to look at how communal and cognitive elements relate to the changing nature of sociological theories.

Another set of questions involves the relationship between the varieties of M_U dealing with the internal-social (communal, individual) and external-social (societal) factors that affect sociological theories. The most obvious issue is how the interaction of personal biography, intellectual community, and social context affects the kind of theory an individual sociologist is drawn to, as well as the way in which he/she might be inclined to alter the theory.

However, the arena in which I think we are likely to see the most work in the future is on the development, refinement, expansion, and application of M_U tools, the tools used to think about and analyze sociological theories. I have in mind here such tools as "levels of analysis" in general, and the micro-macro and agency-structure linkages in particular, the objective-subjective continuum (Wallace 1969; Ritzer 1981b; Couch 1987), and the "architectonic" undergirding the work of sociological theorists. Let me briefly illustrate (and anticipate chapters 7 and 10) what can be done and remains to be done with this type of metatheorizing by showing how the idea of levels of analysis in general, and more particularly the micro-macro continuum, can be used metatheoretically to better understand ongoing developments in sociological theory.

When thought about in these terms, we can make sense out of much of what took place in sociological theory in the 1980s. Kemeny (1976) argued that in the mid-1970s few sociologists were conscious of the micro-macro distinction and its importance to sociology. Only a decade later, however, many new theoretical perspectives are informed, explicitly or implicitly, by a sense of levels of analysis in general, and the micro-macro linkage in particular (Alexander, Giesen, Munch, and Smelser 1987). This is made manifest, among many other places,[17] in Bourdieu's (1977) work on the "habitus" and the dialectical relationship between objective structures and structured dispositions, Gidden's (1984) "structuration theory," Habermas's (1984, 343) integration of "action theory and systems theory," Ritzer's (1981b) work on an integrated sociological paradigm, Collins's (1981b, 1981c, 1987a, 1987b, 1988) attempt to delineate the micro-foundations of macro-level phenomena, and Hechter's (1983a; Friedman and Hechter 1988, 1990) effort to integrate rational choice theory with more macro sociological issues. The metatheoretical analysis of their work using the micro-macro schema allows one to see the centrality of this continuum in their work and to see an underlying commonality in theoretical works that on the surface seem to be very different. Furthermore, these theoretical works on the micro-macro linkage promise to enrich this metatheoretical approach and, in fact, many of them (e.g., Giddens's [1984] excursus on the micro-macro issue) are at least in part metatheoretical in their own right.

Another important issue is the relationship between the micro-macro tool and other metatheoretical tools. Many of the other tools (e.g., agency-structure, nominalism-realism, methodological individualism-holism, atomism-holism [Bealer 1979]) are similar to the micro-macro continuum. But, they are rarely identical to it. Work is needed on the precise relationship among these continua, but the greatest need in my view is for work on the relationship between the micro-macro and the objective-subjective continua. It seems clear that the objective-subjective continuum[18] is one of the most often used in sociology. There are various ways to think about this continuum: constant-change, objective world-subjective comprehension of the world, material-nonmaterial, etc. However it is conceptualized, a clear distinction exists between the objective-subjective continuum and the micro-macro continuum. Once clearly distinguished, the issue of the relationship between these two continua comes to the fore.

Interestingly, many sociologists do not keep the two continua distinct theoretically or empirically, nor do they interrelate them carefully. For example, at a theoretical level Giddens sees such macro theories as structural-functionalism and structuralism as objective and such micro theories as symbolic interactionism and phenomenology as subjective. But some macro theories are also highly subjective (e.g., structural functionalism with its emphasis on norms, values, and culture), and some micro theories are also highly objective (e.g., symbolic interactionism's interest in action and interaction). That is, some macro theories and some micro theories have an interest in *both* objective and subjective phenomena.

An example of this same problem, but at an empirical rather than a theoretical level, is found in Mayhew's (1980, 1981) structuralism in which he equates macro with objective phenomena (social organization, networks) and micro with subjective phenomena (values, attitudes). Micro-macro and objective-subjective are no more coterminous empirically than they are theoretically. There are objective social phenomena at the macro level (e.g., the state) and the micro level (e.g., interaction patterns), just as there are subjective phenomena at the macro level (norms and values) and at the micro level (consciousness). The micro-macro and objective-subjective continua cannot simply be reduced to one another theoretically or empirically but the complex interrelationship among them needs to be thought through and studied empirically.

Up to this point I have focused on a number of issues that are internal to M_U. On most of these, there is at least some body of work on which to build. However, there is another large area in which future work is needed and which is almost totally unexplored. That is, the relationship between M_U and the other major types of metatheorizing (M_P and M_O),[19] as well as the relationship of all types of metatheorizing to other types of metaanalyses within sociology—that is, metasociology in general and metamethods in particular.[20] A number of analysts have addressed the relationship among various components of the sociological enterprise. For example, Ritzer (1975c, 1975d) and Snizek (1979) have analyzed the linkage between theory and methods within broader paradigms, Platt (1986) has examined a more specific theory-methods relationship, and Coleman (1986b) has addressed the implications of various choices on theories and methods. More generally, much more work is needed on the relationship among metaanalyses of theory, methods, concepts, values, and many other components of the sociological enterprise.

Another important issue is the relationship between sociological M_U and similar analyses in other fields (e.g., political science, psychology). At one level, work is needed on the relationship between M_U in these various fields. At another level, it is already clear that sociologists can play a central role in metaanalyses in other fields. That is, sociological M_U is peculiarly able to develop metaanalytical tools that can be applied not only to itself, but to most, if not all, other fields.[21] To put it another way, in all fields such self-analysis involves explicitly and implicitly a sociological approach. In doing their analyses of their own field, sociologists who do M_U are in the process creating and refining the techniques needed for metaanalyses in all other fields.[22] More specifically, *all* of the types and subtypes of M_U analysis outlined earlier in this chapter can be applied to all other academic fields. This is perhaps the most exciting aspect of the development of M_U in sociology. Approaches being used in the study of sociological theories can be used in the study of theories in an array of other fields. Sociologists are well situated to do these studies and in the process to refine their metaanalytical tools. Furthermore, sociology has the potential to become the repository of a range of M_U (and other metaanalytical) tools that can be used throughout the academic world.

Another factor in the distinctive role to be played by sociologists in metaanalysis is sociology's unsettled state as a science. In Kuhnian terms, since there is no single, dominant paradigm, there is relatively little normal science in sociology. The result is considerable self-consciousness, self-criticism and self-analysis. In other words, there is considerable M_U. While other social sciences share with sociology this unsettled character, they lack the distinctive capacity to create the needed tools. Most natural sciences also do not produce such tools; furthermore, the natural sciences generate less self-analysis because of their more "settled" paradigmatic status. Thus, not only do sociologists who practice M_U have the distinctive tools to do such analyses, but the present, unsettled nature of their field has led them to do these analyses and, in the process, to develop and refine the needed tools.

Let me close with one other intellectual arena in which there is a great need for additional work. Work in M_U owes a great debt to work in other fields, most notably the philosophy of science (the work of Kuhn, Lakatos, and many others). Metatheorists who do M_U need to continue to mine these fields (and others—see chapter 13) and, at the same time, may begin to make important contributions to them. Within sociology, there are strong ties between M_U and such other subfields as the sociology of science, the sociology of the professions, the history of sociology, and the sociology of knowledge. Here, too, one would expect increasing reciprocal inputs in the future.

There is clearly no end to the potential future directions for M_U in particular and metatheorizing in general. Suffice it to say that M_U (and the other types of metatheorizing) came of age in the sociology of the 1980s and the future offers a range of possibilities for its enrichment (as well as the development of the other types of metatheorizing). More importantly, enriched metatheoretical tools will lead to a greater understanding, and further development, of sociological theory, sociology as a whole, as well as an array of other fields.

Notes

1. I would like to thank Shanyang Zhao for suggesting this kind of differentiation. Jonathan Cole and Stephen Cole (1973) employ a similar fourfold table of influences on scientific development utilizing identical internal-external and intellectual-social dimensions to develop their typology.

2. For one metatheoretical effort influenced by Lakatos and his notion of a "scientific research program," see Tiryakian 1986.

3. For a discussion of my work on paradigms as well as on an integrated sociological paradigm, see chapters 6, 7, and 8.

4. This distinction is made by Tiryakian (1979).

5. This label can also be affixed to the "schools" approach to be discussed shortly.

6. See chapter 4 for a utilization of this tool.

7. See chapter 7 for a discussion of levels of analysis.

8. As we will soon see, Collins also does M_P in this essay.

9. A recent example of this is Vidich and Lyman's *American Sociology* (1985).

10. For more on the applicability of Foucault's ideas to metatheory, see chapter 13.

11. While I will use Collins's (1989b) essay on Mead as my example of this, there are others. Implicit in Lamont's (1987) analysis of Derrida are all four types of M_U: internal-intellectual (e.g., Derrida's ideas and their linkage to ideas dominant in literary criticism), internal-social (e.g., the school in which Derrida studied, the journals in which he published), external-intellectual (e.g., the intellectual climate in France), and external-social (e.g., the intellectual community in France and the absence of a similar community in the United States). To take another of Collins's (1987a) essays, similar coverage is found in his analysis of German idealist philosophy in which he examines internal-intellectual (e.g., the various philosophical idea systems), internal-social (e.g., the philosopher's network of personal connections; the "theory group"), external-intellectual (e.g., hostility to ideas derived from the university), and external-social (e.g., the political context) phenomena.

12. To be precise, Collins's essay focuses on the roots of Mead's ideas in philosophy (*not* sociology). Metatheory can be used to analyze theories within philosophy (as well as other fields; see, for example, Lamont's [1987] essay on Derrida and linguistics) just as it can be used to study theories within sociology.

13. As a matter of fact, a good portion of what is usually thought of as sociological theory is, in fact, metatheory. Good examples of this are Parsons's *The Structure of Social Action* and Alexander's *Theoretical Logic in Sociology*. I would like to thank Gary Fine for pointing out to me that Mead also produced a monumental piece of metatheory, *Movements of Thought in the Nineteenth Century*.

14. Collins, himself, admits that he is hampered by a lack of a "thorough intellectual biography of Mead" and Collins, of course, is certainly not providing one within this limited context.

15. In a few pages Collins attempts an overview of the history of turn-of-the-century philosophy.

16. And it has nothing to do with the external-intellectual and external-social types of metatheory.

17. In the following enumeration, I am conflating work on agency-structure with work on the micro-macro linkage. As we will see in chapter 10, there are important differences between these two literatures.

18. Objective-subjective is more of a duality, but there are mixed types in the middle such as culture, which combine objective and subjective elements.

19. I will deal with this relationship in chapter 14.

20. In political science, Connolly has defined a similar task: "I approach theoretical self-consciousness as I attain awareness of previously unexamined assumptions at the center of my theory, as I attend to its conceptual contours and to test the procedures it supports, as I probe the inner connections among these three dimensions and explore the normative implications of the entire system"

(1973, 34). It is clear that Connolly is attempting to link theoretical assumptions, concepts, methods, and normative implications.

21. For example, Connolly (1973), a political scientist, does an avowedly sociological analysis of political science.

22. For a recent collection of essays that outline a similar role for psychology in "metascience," see Barry Gholson, William R. Shadish, Jr., Robert A. Neimeyer, and Arthur C. Houts, *Psychology of Science: Contributions to Metascience* (Cambridge: Cambridge University Press, 1989).

2
Metatheorizing as a Prelude to Theory Development

The main theme of this chapter is that most sociological theorists have done a significant amount of metatheorizing as a prelude to theory development (M_P); in other words, metatheorizing has been (and continues to be) an appropriate and a significant source of sociological theory.[1] I will show that most of our best-known theorists were and are metatheorists. It is time that sociological theorists acknowledge the fact that metatheorizing has had, and *should* have, a key role to play in the development of sociological theory (and of sociology as a whole). In describing the ubiquity of M_P I will indicate many of its positive contributions to the development of sociological theory. However, my discussion will also lead to the conclusion that there may be an excessive reliance on M_P by contemporary sociological theorists and that such dependency has been increasing over time. The chapter will close with some thoughts on dealing with the excesses while retaining the strengths of metatheoretical analysis.

The Ubiquity of Metatheorizing as a Prelude to Theory Development

Let us look at the work of some of the major theorists in the history of sociology in order to see the extent to which their theories are based on M_P.

I will begin with the work of Karl Marx. In my view, Marx developed his theory of capitalism much more metatheoretically than on the basis of an in-depth empirical study of the realities of capitalist society. That is, much of Marx's published work involves the careful study of the work of other thinkers. Marx fashioned his theories by critiquing those ideas and putting them together in novel and creative ways.

For example, in *The Economic and Philosophic Manuscripts of 1844*, Marx (1932/1964) develops his perspective on the basis of a detailed and careful analysis and critique of the works of such political economists as Adam Smith, Jean-Baptiste Say, David Ricardo, and James Mill; such philosophers as G. W. F. Hegel, the Young Hegelians (e.g., Bruno Bauer), and Ludwig Feuerbach; such utopian socialists as Etienne Cabet, Robert Owen, Charles Fourier, and Pierre Proudhon; and a variety of other major and minor intellectual schools and figures. It seems safe to say that almost in its entirety *The Economic and Philosophic Manuscripts* is a metatheoretical treatise in which Marx develops his own ideas out of an engagement with a variety of idea systems.

What of Marx's other works? Are they more empirical? Less metatheoretical? In his preface to *The German Ideology* (Marx and Engels 1845–46/1970), C. J. Arthur describes that work as comprised mainly of "detailed line by line polemics against the writings of some of their [Marx and Engels] contemporaries" (1970, 1). In fact, Marx himself describes *The German Ideology* as an effort "to set forth together our conception as opposed to the ideological one of German philosophy, in fact to settle accounts with our former philosophical conscience. The intention was carried out in the form of a critique of post-Hegelian philosophy" (1859/1970, 22). *The Holy Family* (Marx and Engels 1845/1956) is, above all, an extended critique of Bruno Bauer and the Young Hegelians, and of their propensity for speculative "critical criticism."[2] In their foreword, Marx and Engels make it clear that this kind of metatheoretical work is a prelude to their coming theorizing: "We therefore give this polemic as a preliminary to the independent works in which we . . . shall present our positive view" (1845/1956, 16). In the *Grundrisse* Marx (1857–58/1973) chooses as his metatheoretical antagonists the political economist David Ricardo and the French socialist Pierre Proudhon (Nicolaus 1973). Throughout the *Grundrisse* Marx is struggling to solve an array of theoretical problems, in part through a critique of the theories and theorists mentioned above and in part through an application of ideas derived from Hegel. In describing the introduction to the *Grundrisse,* Nicolaus says that it "reflects in its every line the struggle of Marx against Hegel, Ricardo and Proudhon. From it, Marx carried off the most important objective of all, namely the basic principles of writing history dialectically" (1973, 42). *A Contribution to the Critique of Political Economy* (Marx 1859/1970) is, as the title suggests, an effort to build a distinctive economic approach on the basis of a critique of the works of the political economists.

Even *Capital* (1867/1967), admittedly one of Marx's most empirical works since he deals more directly with the reality of the capitalist workworld through the use of government statistics and reports, is informed by Marx's earlier metatheoretical work and contains some metatheorizing of its own. In fact, the subtitle, *A Critique of Political Economy,* makes the study's metatheoretical roots absolutely clear. However, Marx is freer in *Capital* to be much more "positive," that is, to construct his own distinctive theoretical orientation. This freedom is traceable, in part, to his having done much of the metatheoretical groundwork in earlier works.

Furthermore, most of the new metatheoretical work is relegated to the so-called fourth volume of *Capital,* published under the title *Theories of Surplus Value* (Marx 1862–63/1963; 1862–63/1968). The latter is largely composed of extracts of the work of the major political economists (e.g., Smith, Ricardo) as well as critical analyses of them by Marx. In sum, it is safe to say that Marx was, to a very large extent, a metatheorist, perhaps the *most* metatheoretical of all classical sociological theorists.

Max Weber was a somewhat less overt user of M_P; he was also somewhat more empirical than Marx in the sense that he engaged in historical, cross-cultural research.[3] Nevertheless, in many places Weber was openly metatheoretical. This is particularly true in his "methodological" works where he developed his ideas on the basis of a critical analysis of the work of others. Such an approach is explicit in the title of one work, *Roscher and Knies: The Logical Problems of Historical Economics* (Weber 1903–6/1975) and less clearly labeled in, but also true of, *The Methodology of the Social Sciences* (Weber 1903–17/1949).

In his introductory essay, Guy Oakes (1975) points out that while *Roscher and Knies* had been published in segments in journals, Marianne Weber reprinted the entire work as the first volume of what she called *Gesammelte Aufsatze zur Wissenshaftslehre.* According to Oakes, the "word 'wissenschaftslehre' might also be translated as 'theory of science'—in the sense of a theory which is about science—or 'metascience' " (1975, 2). Oakes sees this monograph as Weber's "first explicit attempt to undertake metatheoretical work" (1975, 5). Oakes apparently does not use the term "metatheoretical" in the same way it is used in this book; his use of the term seems closer to the idea of metascience mentioned above. Nevertheless, *Roscher and Knies* is clearly metatheoretical in the sense of the way the term M_P is used in this chapter.[4] Oakes argues that Weber saw value in his metatheoretical work because it could help lead to "theoretical progress" in the sociocultural sciences, a view in accord with the one taken in this chapter. Oakes's description of Weber's procedure in *Roscher and Knies,* as well as in his other methodological works, is quite close to the practice found in most M_P texts:

> Weber develops his own solution to problems in the course of a critical analysis—sometimes laboriously detailed, often quite sketchy[5]—of positions he rejects. Weber describes, explains, analyzes, criticizes, revises, occasionally uses, and most often refutes the results of others. Following this work of exposition, analysis, and criticism. . . . Weber attempts to show how the *Methodenstreit*[6] can be resolved. (1975, 24)

The key point to be noted is that Weber's engagement with the ideas of others allowed him to develop his own position. Again, M_P can lead to creative new ideas.

The Methodology of the Social Sciences is less overtly metatheoretical than *Roscher and Knies*. Nevertheless, one of the three main essays in that book, "Critical Studies in the Logic of the Cultural Sciences," is largely an extended analysis of the work of Eduard Meyer. Here, Weber develops many of his own ideas in the course of a critical dialogue with Meyer's work. In addition to explicit metatheoretical consideration of the work of Meyer and others (e.g., Schmoller) in *The Methodology of the Social Sciences,* as well as elsewhere, Weber carries on a fruitful metatheo-retical debate with Marx and the Marxists. In fact, regarding this topic, one could only wish that Weber had been a better metatheorist as far as his analysis of Marx is concerned. There is no evidence in Weber's work of a sustained critical reading and analysis of Marx's work. Thus, he often works with caricatures of Marx's ideas (probably derived secondhand from the Marxists). Weber's own theoretical ideas might have been richer had he done a better metatheoretical job with Marx's work.

What about Weber's historical works? Are they not wholly or mostly theoretical analyses of empirical data? They do involve the theoretical analysis of empirical data in the sense that Weber's main data base was secondary sources that deal with various historical developments rather than overtly theoretical works. But little evidence indicates that Weber did much original historical research himself. Weber relied on secondary sources, whether they were theoretical or empirical/historical. In both cases Weber built his theory on the basis of an analysis and critique of the work of others. In some cases he relied on theoretical documents, in other cases on empirical documents, but in all cases he analyzed *documents* to de-velop his approach. There are important differences between theoretical and empirical documents, but the analysis of either is still far removed from the direct study of the empirical world. Weber was, at times, a theorist relying on secondary data and at other times a metatheorist (of the M_P type), but he was *never* an empiricist who developed his theory on the basis of first-hand study in the real world.

Turning to Durkheim, I think it fair to say that he is closer to Marx than Weber as a practitioner of M_P, even though he too did considerable work based on historical (and anthropological) documents (as well as statistical data). His Latin thesis (1893/1960) dealt with the work of Mon-tesquieu, especially *The Spirit of Laws,* and is an overtly M_P work. On the basis of a study of his work, Durkheim sees Montesquieu as a pre-cursor of his own effort to discover the laws of social behavior, to develop a science of society.[7] *The Rules of Sociological Method* (1895/1964) is less concrete and direct, but it too is clearly an example of M_P. Durkheim sought to develop his sense of sociology by distancing it from psychology, philosophy, and the various notions of sociology implicit in the work of people like Tarde, LeBon, Comte, and Spencer. Durkheim fashioned his own sense of sociology in the process of engaging in an intellectual dialogue with other thinkers,[8] *not* out of a direct engagement with the empirical world. But Durkheim did seek to deal with this problem by turning his attention to an empirical study, *Suicide* (1897/1951), in which he sought to "test" his theoretical orientation.[9] As laudable as this effort may be, it seems clear that the theory was first developed metatheoretically and then applied to empirical reality. Durkheim even did a number of metatheoretical analyses in *Suicide* such as his critique of various alternative explanations of suicide, including the imitation theory of suicide offered by his adversary, Tarde.

On the surface, *The Division of Labor in Society* (1893/1964) appears to be a historical study of the transition from mechanical to organic solidarity, but in reality its perspective was shaped more by M_P concerns. As Lukes puts it:

> There were, however, three particular theories of which Durkheim was most clearly aware in developing the thesis of the *Division of Labour:* those of Comte, Spencer and Ferdinand Tonnies. By reacting against them (as he interpreted them), he was able partially to work out his relationship to the various intellectual traditions which they respectively employed: French positivism and authoritarianism; English utilitarianism and *laissez-faire* liberalism; and German state socialism. (1973, 140)

Later, Lukes says that "*The Division of Labour* . . . sought to develop an explanation of social solidarity in industrial or 'organized' societies that was consistent with Durkheim's objections to Comte, Spencer and Tonnies" (1973, 146–47). Only a limited amount of empirical research (again a secondary analysis of the work of other researchers) was reflected in *The Division of Labor* and, in fact, Lukes makes the point that "At this stage in his career, he [Durkheim] had not come upon the growing body of ethnographic literature that was to transform his ideas and dominate his later work" (1973, 159). By the time he wrote *The Elementary Forms of Religious Life* (1912/1965) much more ethnographic research was available, particularly on Australian aborigines, on which Durkheim could base his conclusions. Of course, Durkheim did not go to Australia; he relied instead on the work of a variety of ethnographers. But while this work could not be described as theoretical, it is not devoid of M_P analyses.[10]

Turning to more recent theory, the pervasiveness of M_P is even more clearcut. Take the major twentieth-century American theorist, Talcott Parsons. Parson's *The Structure of Social Action* (1937/1949) may be the purest example (except, perhaps, for the work of the neo-Parsonsian, Jeffrey Alexander) of M_P. Most of *The Structure of Social Action* is devoted to a serious study of the work of Alfred Marshall, Vilfredo Pareto, Emile Durkheim, and Max Weber.[11] And Parsons uses that metatheoretical work to begin to lay out his own action theory. The roots of Parsons's work lie not in the empirical world, but in what in his view were the convergent ideas of the theorists mentioned above.

In fact, Parsons was explicit about his M_P approach. He describes *The Structure of Social Action* as an *"empirical* monograph" and indicates that the phenomena under scrutiny "happen to be the theories that certain writers have held about other phenomena. . . . the theories that have been discussed is just as much a question of fact as any other, to be verified by the same method, that of observation. The facts in this case have reference to the published works of these writers" (1937/1949, 697). But Parsons is not content simply to analyze extant theories; his study "has also done some explicit theorizing on its own account" (1937/1949, 697; for similar viewpoints, see Merton 1968). In the preface to the second edition of *The Structure of Social Action* Parsons makes a similar point in reflecting on the work over a decade after its publication: "This was a convenient vehicle for the clarification of problems and concepts, of implications and interrelations. It was a means of taking stock of the theoretical resources at our disposal. . . . The clarification gained from this stocktaking has opened up possibilities for further theoretical development of sufficient scope so that its impetus is as yet by no means exhausted" (1937/1949, B).

Only two years after the publication of the revised edition of *The Structure of Social Action,* in the part of *Toward a General Theory of Action* (1951) written by Parsons and Shils (with the assistance of Olds), the authors make the metatheoretical roots of the revised theory of action perfectly clear in the very first footnote, which follows the first four words of text: "The present exposition of the theory of action represents in one major respect a revision and extension of the position stated in Parsons's *The Structure of Social Action.* . . . particularly in the light of psychoanalytic theory, of developments in behavior psychology, and of developments in the anthropological analysis of culture" (Parsons and Shils 1951, 53).

Between the publication of *The Structure of Social Action* in 1937 and his works on the theory of action published in the early 1950s, Parsons amended and changed his theoretical orientation. It *may* be that those changes were the result of changes in the social world, but it is *certainly* the case that his theoretical ideas changed over the years as Parsons metatheoretically engaged the ideas of a variety of theorists, including the psychiatrist Sigmund Freud,[12] the anthropologist Franz Boas,[13] and the behaviorist Edward Tolman. Above all, Parsons elaborated his theory on the basis of a metatheoretical reanalysis of his own work as well as the criticisms of that work. Thus, for example, late in his life Parsons (1966, 1971) shifted to evolutionary theory on the basis of his own analysis of the shortcomings of his earlier work as pointed up by the critics.[14] Parsons makes this clear in one of his earlier works on change: "I should address myself to the problem of social change. I am very happy to do this, both because of the intrinsic importance of the subject and because its place in my own work has been the subject of considerable concern, even controversy. Furthermore, I have been devoting more explicit attention to this field recently than before, and some of the things I have to say are, I think, new" (1961b, 219).

Alfred Schutz was a contemporary of Parsons, but one with a very different theoretical orientation. Like Parsons, Schutz formed his theories on the basis of a metatheoretical engagement with the ideas of his intellectual predecessors, most notably Max Weber, Edmund Husserl, and Henri Bergson. Also like Parsons, Schutz wasted no time in making clear the M_P roots of his own phenomenological sociology. The preface to the original, 1932 edition of *The Phenomenology of the Social World* opens as follows:

> The present study is based on an intensive concern of many years' duration with the theoretical writings of Max Weber. During this time I became convinced that while Weber's approach was correct and that he had determined conclusively the proper starting point of the philosophy of the social sciences, nevertheless his analyses did not go deeply enough to lay the foundations on which alone many important problems of the human sciences could be solved. Above all, Weber's central concept of subjective meaning calls for thoroughgoing analysis. (1932/1967, xxxi)

Schutz's critical analysis of Weber's sense of meaning is based on his study of the work of Husserl and Bergson: "Of central importance for this investigation are the studies of Bergson and Husserl on the internal time-sense. Only in the work of these two thinkers, especially in Husserl's transcendental phenomenology, has a sufficiently deep foundation been laid on the basis of which one could aspire to solve the problem of meaning" (1932/1967, xxxii). That is precisely what Schutz seeks to do in his own theorizing. Chapter 1 of *The Phenomenology of the Social World* is devoted to a critical review and analysis of Weber's pertinent ideas and chapter 2 introduces the relevant ideas of Bergson and Husserl. As the latter chapter unfolds, and throughout the remainder of the book, Schutz develops his distinctive theoretical orientation. However, throughout the book Schutz often returns to critical analyses of the ideas of his theoretical predecessors, especially Weber and Husserl. Furthermore, in later essays Schutz (1962, 1964, 1966) not only reanalyzes the ideas of these theorists, but also extends his own theories in a critical dialogue with the work of an array of other theorists, including Max Scheler and Jean-Paul Sartre.

As we turn to the more contemporary scene, theorists, if anything, have grown even more prone to doing M_P. I will begin my discussion of contemporary theorists with the work of the sociologist who has been labeled "Parsons, Jr.,"[15] Jeffrey Alexander. His four-volume work, *Theoretical Logic in Sociology* (1982–83), is self-consciously modeled after Parsons's *The Structure of Social Action*. In the first volume Alexander lays out his metatheoretical ideas, including his intention to use as one of his key metatheoretical tools the idea of "multidimensionality" (another key tool is "action-order"). By "multidimensionality" Alexander means, among other things, that a theory rejects a one-dimensional focus on either material (conditional) or ideal (subjective) factors and instead is concerned synthetically with the impact of both types of factors. Having laid out in volume 1 his sense of multidimensionality, Alexander turns in the next three volumes to M_P in the form of a detailed critical analysis of the work of Marx, Durkheim, Weber, and Parsons from the point of view of such a sociology. Although all these theorists are found wanting from a multidimensional point of view, Alexander clearly finds much to recommend in the Parsonsian perspective. This leads Alexander to structural functionalism, to his support for a neofunctionalist orientation, and ultimately to his effort to create a neofunctionalist theory (Alexander 1985b, Alexander and Colomy 1990). Thus, Alexander's route to his own theoretical orientation is based on his metatheoretical analysis of the work of the major figures in the history of sociology.

Alexander and Colomy (1990) make it clear that neofunctionalism is not merely an extension of structural functionalism, but is a new theoretical orientation. They are endeavoring to overcome the weaknesses in structural functionalism, particularly as it was articulated by Parsons, by fusing it with ideas from a number of other theoretical traditions.

In one forum or another Anthony Giddens has dealt with virtually every major theorist and theory. In the course of these M_P endeavors Giddens has created his own theoretical orientation, structuration theory, a perspective that achieved its most complete articulation in *The Constitution of Society* (1984). This work is the least metatheoretical (and the most theoretical) of Giddens's efforts (although it does include a number of M_P excurses), but it is itself the product of the many M_P works done by Giddens over more than two decades.

In many of his earliest works Giddens examined metatheoretically the work of his theoretical predecessors as a prelude to the delineation of his own theory. Take, for example, the opening lines of the preface to his book on Marx, Durkheim, and Weber, *Capitalism and Modern Social Theory:* "This book is written in the belief that there is a widespread feeling among sociologists that contemporary social theory stands in need of radical revision. Such a revision must begin from a reconsideration of the works of those writers who established the principal frames of reference of modern sociology . . . Marx, Durkheim and Max Weber" (1971, vii). In this book, and in other early works, Giddens was content to reanalyze the work of earlier theorists,[16] but he soon moved on to the more creative metatheoretical endeavor of using such reviews as a base to develop and refine his own theoretical ideas.

One of the earlier places in which this more creative metatheorizing is made manifest is in *New Rules of Sociological Method* (1976). The book is essentially a critical review of both interpretive and institutional sociologies in which both are found to have something to offer, but both are also found to be weak in a number of respects. While interpretive sociologies have little to contribute on macro-structural constraints, institutional sociologies (e.g., Durkheim, Parsons, Marx) do not deal adequately with the way actors constitute the social world. It is out of the strengths and weaknesses of these traditions that Giddens begins to develop his structuration theory in which structures are seen as both enabling actors and constraining them. The book closes with Giddens's effort to enumerate some new rules of sociological method, rules self-consciously developed to overcome liabilities in Durkheim's original rules.

Giddens has used this same strategy in a number of books and articles. To take one example: in *A Contemporary Critique of Historical Materialism* (1981) Giddens says that although he will be critical of Marxian theory, "my concerns are by no means wholly critical or destructive; in diverging from Marx I want to propose the elements of an alternative interpretation of history" (1981, 3). Giddens's use of the critical analysis of Marx's theory (as well as that of many others) to develop his own theoretical perspective is made clear in the introduction to *The Constitution of Society:* "This book . . . might be accurately described as an extended reflection upon a celebrated and oft-quoted phrase to be found in Marx. Marx comments that 'Men [let us immediately say human beings] make history, but not in circumstances of their own choosing.' Well, so they do. But what a diversity of complex problems of social analysis this apparently innocuous pronouncement turns out to disclose!" (1984, xxi).

Finally, let us look briefly at Jurgen Habermas as a practitioner of M_P. It is almost impossible to enumerate all of the sociological theorists and philosophers that Habermas has studied, critiqued, and built upon en route to his own communication theory. Included in the list are Kant, Hegel, Marx, Weber, and an array of first-generation critical theorists (e.g., Marcuse). Of all of these, it seems clear that the most important influences are Habermas's critical reflections on the work of Marx and Weber. While these continue to be important, in his most recent work

(1984, 1987) Habermas has extended his M_P domain to include critical analyses of the work of Schutz, Parsons, Mead, and Durkheim. Note how Habermas introduces volume 2 of *The Theory of Communicative Action* and, in the process, introduces us to the new M_P concerns to be taken up in this volume:

> Whereas the problematic of rationalization/reification lies along a "German" line of social-theoretical thought running from Marx through Weber to Lukacs and Critical Theory, the paradigm shift from purposive activity to communicative action was prepared by George Herbert Mead and Emile Durkheim. Mead . . . and Durkheim . . . belong, like Weber . . ., to the generation of the founding fathers of modern sociology. Both developed basic concepts in which Weber's theory of rationalization can be taken up again and freed from the aporias of the philosophy of consciousness: Mead with his communication-theoretic foundation of sociology, Durkheim with a theory of social solidarity connecting social integration and system integration. (1987, 1)

These new directions in Habermas's M_P concerns lead us to an important general point: *major changes in sociological theories are often portended by a shift in M_P concerns.* The systematic analysis of the work of a new theorist, or set of theorists, is likely to be followed by changes—some subtle, some dramatic—in the theory of the analyst.

This discussion of a wide range of classic and contemporary theorists who did a great deal of metatheorizing as a prelude to developing their own theories generates an important question: are there any major theorists who do little or no metatheorizing in developing their theories? There are: the two major examples are Georg Simmel and Erving Goffman.

Simmel is disinclined, in his various essays on types of interactants and forms of interaction, to cite the works of intellectual predecessors, let alone deal with them in any systematic fashion. The same is true of his massive *The Philosophy of Money* (1907/1978). Bottomore and Frisby note: "Simmel's writing, like poetry, requires no footnotes. None are provided in *The Philosophy of Money* and almost no works are cited in the text" (1978, 5). Metatheorizing plays a far smaller role in Simmel's work than in that of any of the classical theorists discussed previously.

In Goffman's major work, *The Presentation of Self in Everyday Life* (1959), he does cite the work of a number of sociological theorists (e.g., Simmel, Durkheim), but Goffman does not do a serious study of their work as a prelude to his own theorizing. Rather, he is prone to use their work for illustrative purposes. They have no privileged status over the other sources of Goffman's illustrations; in fact, there are many more citations to the empirical studies of Chicago sociologists than there are to the work of theorists. The work of ex–major league baseball umpire Babe

Pinelli is cited more often (4 times) than the work of Durkheim (3 citations) or Simmel (2 references).

It is interesting that Simmel and Goffman emerge as two of the theorists who are least likely to do M_P. They are more inclined to launch directly into theorizing than to first go through their metatheoretical "paces." This makes their work harder to evaluate; the strength of an M_P work (e.g., did the author get the ideas right? cite the right sources? and so on) is far easier to evaluate than "straight" theory. This fits with the curious positions that both Simmel and Goffman have in the history of sociological theory. Controversy over the questions of whether they were good theorists and whether their theories are important continues to cloud their reputations. While some observers see them as major theorists (e.g., Collins [1986c] on Goffman; see also Giddens [1987]), others regard them as intellectual "lightweights." They may be regarded as lightweights precisely because they usually disdained the required M_P work. Furthermore, since they do little M_P and much straight theory, it is very difficult to evaluate their work. Evaluations are based much more on esthetic tastes in theory and, as is well known, such tastes vary widely.

Explicit and Implicit Metatheorizing

The preceding discussion has been based on whether the theorist engages in the explicit study of intellectual predecessors. However, it is likely that those theorists, like Simmel and Goffman, who do not explicitly metatheorize, implicitly metatheorize. Furthermore, it is also likely that those who do not do a great deal of explicit analysis of the social world do such analyses implicitly. Much of Marx's work may have been explicitly devoted to metatheoretical studies, but it seems certain that those analyses were influenced and guided by Marx's implicit observations and studies of the capitalistic society in which he lived. The differentiation between explicit and implicit metatheorizing and analyses of the social world allows me to offer a more complex model of their interrelationships. Figure 2–1 depicts this relationship.

The bulk of this chapter has been devoted to explicit metatheorizing, but it is clear that at least some theorists do implicit metatheorizing. Both explicit and implicit metatheorizing contribute to the development of theory. Not discussed in this chapter, but also very important, is the fact that explicit and implicit analyses of the social world contribute to theory creation. A fuller analysis of theory creation would need to take all of these ideas into consideration.

There are a number of more general implications to be drawn from figure 2–1. All of the relationships flow in both directions; that is, all of

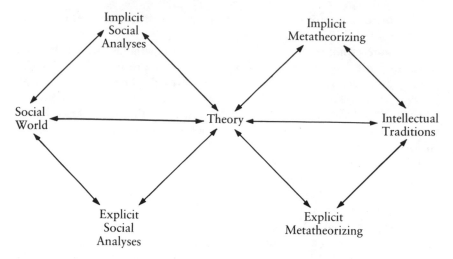

Figure 2–1. The Relationship Between Implicit and Explicit Social Analyses and Metatheorizing[17]

the elements are dialectically related to one another. Thus, for example, while we are mainly interested here in the impact of metatheorizing (implicit and explicit) on theory, it is clear that theory, in turn, affects the kind and nature of metatheorizing. Similarly, social analyses (implicit and explicit) not only affect theory, but theory has an impact on social analysis. This is not the place to go into all of the permutations and combinations suggested by figure 2–1, but it is clear that this task is worth doing.

Another issue is the relative weight of each of the arrows in particular works of theory construction. If one concentrates on one of the arrows, does that inevitably mean that the amount of attention devoted to other arrows is either reduced or eliminated?

Finally, the center of figure 2–1, and of the process, is theory. But are we talking about a single type of theory? Could it be that we have two broad types of theory here, one shaped by metatheoretical work and the other by (empirical) analyses of the social world? Or, that perhaps what we have is a continuum with the varying points along it determined by the relative input of metatheorizing and social analysis? While both extremes might be acceptable, could it be argued that *the* most desirable theories represent a reasonable balance of metatheoretical and social analytical inputs?

As in all such depictions, figure 2–1 includes a number of artificial distinctions. For example, in actual theoretical work, metatheoretical (both explicit and implicit) and social analytic (again, both explicit and implicit) approaches are usually conducted in concert with one another. In fact, it could be argued (again) that the very best theoretical works involve substantial amounts of both metatheoretical and social analyses.

Reflections on M_p

It seems abundantly clear that most major classical and contemporary sociological theorists were and are practitioners of M_p and that their metatheorizing played and plays a key role in the development of their social theories. Furthermore, this metatheorizing has produced a number of sociological theories that have been, and continue to be, useful in understanding the social world. It is likely that even better theories would be produced if those theories were also derived from a more serious empirical study of that world. However, most of the critics of metatheorizing are not themselves actively engaged in studying the social world and in helping to determine whether such study pays off in "better" social theories.

While in this chapter I have taken a strong position regarding the thesis that metatheorizing often provides the base for theoretical development, the fact is that the examples I have cited probably understate the case. That is, my focus has been mainly on works that are explicitly metatheoretical, but in many theoretical writings the metatheoretical work has been only implicit. By this I mean that the author has shaped his/her theoretical ideas in an unspoken and unwritten dialogue with the work of other theorists. The most notable case is Weber's largely implicit dialogue with Marx. While Weber is, at times, clear about his debate with Marx, much more often the reader is left to sense that Weber is writing with Marx (and the Marxists) in mind. More generally, I believe that such implicit metatheoretical dialogues are the norm in the history of sociological theory. These implicit dialogues are far less desirable than explicit engagements with other theories. If the engagement is only implicit, the reader must guess at what is transpiring and will be unable to assess the adequacy of the author's interpretation of other theories.

Although this chapter comes at the issue in an entirely different way, it does underscore the oft-observed serious gap between theory and empirical research. The fact is that most often theorists develop their approaches in an intellectual dialogue with other theorists. For their part, most empiricists engage in a dialogue with other empiricists, a dialogue that often appears in the review of the literature that precedes most research studies.[18] This is not the first effort to argue for the need for more cross-fertilization of theory and research, but it is, I think, the first to come to this conclusion by way of an analysis that demonstrates that most theorists are metatheorists. I do not think theorists ought to stop metatheorizing, nor do I think there is anything inherently wrong with M_P. What I do believe is that at least some sociological theorists, while continuing to rely on metatheorizing, should entertain the possibility of doing more theorizing that is tied (preferably explicitly) to research in the social world.

A critic of sociological theory might say that this chapter underscores the self-referential, incestuous character of sociological theory. Sociological theorists seem much more likely to derive their ideas from the work of other theorists than from empirical research or observations of the social world. I am, to some degree, sympathetic with this perspective. While there is nothing wrong with developing theory on the basis of metatheoretical reflections, theory would be improved if it was more engaged with empirical research and the social world.

This raises the question of whether sociological theorists do too much metatheorizing in preparation for the development of their own theoretical orientation. I think that the answer to this question is yes, especially in light of the fact that modern theorists (e.g., Alexander, Giddens, Habermas)[19] seem even more inclined to metatheorizing than their predecessors were. Metatheorizing is a legitimate prelude to theorizing, but it is not the only one and should not be used to the exclusion of all others (e.g., induction from empirical reality). It would be dangerous for sociological theory to develop total, or near-total, dependency on metatheorizing. Yet that seems to be what is occurring.

Why the increasing reliance on metatheorizing? For one thing, as the years pass there is more and more theory to pore over *before* one can develop one's own theory.[20] For another, the nature of the academic review process pushes theorists more and more in the direction of large doses of metatheorizing. The reason is that it is relatively easy to assess the adequacy of a theorist's metatheorizing. A reviewer can assess whether an analysis of a theorist or set of theorists is adequate. The reviewer can determine whether authors have gotten their metatheorizing "right": whether the interpretations are accurate, the right sources have been used, etc. However, it is much more difficult to assess the adequacy of theory presented without metatheoretical background (hence the controversy over the theories of people like Simmel and Goffman). How does a reviewer assess the adequacy of such a theory? Without the requisite metatheoretical markers, most reviewers have little to go on in assessing the quality of a theory. Without such markers, the easiest course is to raise a series of objections against the theory and recommend against its publication.

While the case has been made throughout this chapter that metatheorizing can lead to creative theorizing, it could be argued that a slavish reliance on metatheorizing can be a straightjacket that limits or prevents creative theorizing. Creative theory can be impeded by an inability to move beyond the metatheoretical analysis of the work of others, by an excessive need to get one's metatheorizing "right," by being overly influenced by the work of predecessors, and so on. Since there seems to be more dependence on metatheorizing today than in the past, it may be that the pendulum is swinging and metatheorizing is beginning to have more negative effects and fewer positive impacts on creative theorizing.

Having reviewed the best M_P in the history of sociology, I am in a position to offer some conclusions about how to do it well. First, metatheorizing should be explicit rather than implicit. Explicit metatheorizing allows the reader to know exactly where the theorist is coming from and enables the reader to check on the accuracy of the metatheoretical work, if the reader so wishes. Conversely, implicit metatheorizing is more likely to leave the reader unclear about the roots of a theory and unable to check the veracity of M_P. Second, metatheorizing should be systematic rather than haphazard. One of the things that separates great theorists from poor ones is the systematic character of their metatheorizing. Third, those who do M_P must subordinate their metatheorizing to their ultimate goal of developing and refining sociological theory. It is all too easy to get involved in the minutia of detailed metatheorizing and lose sight of the theoretical objective.[21] This can serve to hamper greatly a theorist's creativity.

In sum, we have seen that metatheorizing as a prelude to theory creation is ubiquitous in classical and contemporary theory, that it can be the base of creative theorizing, but that if it is not done judiciously, metatheorizing can severely hamper creative theorizing.

Notes

1. For that matter, there is nothing "wrong" with developing theory on the basis of empirical research, or any other way.

2. In fact, the book is subtitled "Against Bruno Bauer and Co."

3. It is likely that Weber's more empirical orientation is one of the factors that led American sociologists to favor Weber's work more than Marx's work.

4. And even as Oakes means it (theorizing about science), *Roscher and Knies* involves one type of metatheoretical analysis (M_U).

5. Oakes is implying here that at times Weber is sometimes not a very good metatheorist.

6. The *Methodenstreit* was, of course, a major methodological controversy of Weber's day.

7. Durkheim (1918/1960) did a similar metatheoretical work on Rousseau and his *Social Contract*.

8. Another example of this is Durkheim's book *Socialism* (1928/1962), which

is more about theories of socialism, especially Saint-Simon's, than it is about the social reality of socialism.

9. In which he examined various documents containing statistics on suicide rates.

10. See, for example, chapter 5 in *The Elementary Forms of Religious Life*, in which Durkheim critically examines a number of other theories (e.g., Tylor, Frazer) of totemism.

11. As well as of a variety of philosophical traditions—e.g., utilitarianism, positivism, empiricism, etc.

12. In fact, in the preface to the second edition of *The Structure of Social Action*, Parsons discusses the need to do a "full-dress analysis of Freud's theoretical development seen in the context of the 'theory of social action' " (1937/1949, B).

13. Although Parsons (1937/1949,C) does not see Boas "of comparable *theoretical* stature" to Freud, Durkheim, or the other major thinkers he analyzes.

14. In terms of his metatheoretical work, I have not even mentioned Parsons forays into M_U in his frequent essays on the general state of sociological theory such as "The Prospects of Sociological Theory" (Parsons 1954b) and "The Present Position and Prospects of Systematic Theory in Sociology" (Parsons 1954a). Also worth mentioning is Parsons's role as the initial editor of the original *American Sociologist* which was founded as a major outlet for metasociological work.

15. This is Sica's (1983) description of Alexander.

16. In *Central Problems in Social Theory* Giddens says of his work: "Some ten years ago, I conceived the project of examining the residue of nineteenth-century European social theory for contemporary problems of the social sciences. Virtually all my work since that date has been concerned with developing that project. . . . These ideas [early theories] must be radically overhauled today: any appropriation we make from nineteenth-century social thought has to be a thoroughly critical one" (1979, 1).

17. I would like to thank Gyorgy Peteri for suggesting this model and my graduate students for suggesting various ways of improving it.

18. Reviews of literature are a kind of metasociology. It strikes me that they are often done far too casually and haphazardly. Sociologists need to develop a better, more explicit sense of what elements go into a good literature review.

19. In addition, we have already seen in the introduction that some of the major critics of metatheorizing (Turner, Collins, Skocpol), themselves important contemporary theorists, are very strongly metatheoretical in their orientation.

20. This can be interpreted positively as the fact that there is more theoretical knowledge to build upon or negatively as reflecting theoretical insecurity and the need to "touch all the theoretical bases" before going on to develop one's own theory.

21. This is not to say that all metatheorists must avoid total immersion in metatheorizing. In fact, M_U *requires* such a total commitment. However, in M_U the goal is not the creation of new theory, but the better understanding of extant theory.

3

Metatheorizing as a Source of Perspectives that Overarch Sociological Theory

This chapter focuses on the third type of metatheorizing, M_O, in which the study of theory is oriented to the goal of producing a perspective—one could say a metatheory—that overarches some part or all of sociological theory.[1] A number of works, in addition to the ones discussed in this chapter, involve this third major type of metatheorizing. Three recent examples are Friedman and Hechter's (1988, 211) effort to outline the "overarching metatheoretical perspective" that is derived from and informs rational choice theory, Levine's (1989) attempt to find the roots of his preferred metatheory, "methodological pluralism," in the work of Georg Simmel and Gibbs's (1989:1) effort to define "control" as a notion that "transcends all [sociological] perspectives."

While I have argued earlier that the first two types of metatheorizing are often very useful, I, and others (e.g., Turner 1985, 1991), have contended that this third type is frequently far less constructive. One objective in this chapter is to take a detailed look at a few key examples of efforts to produce perspectives that transcend theory in an attempt to uncover just what it is about this type of metatheorizing that is often so unproductive or even counterproductive.

In addition to focusing on M_O, this chapter will also deal with a similar approach (O_M) in which an overarching perspective is posited without doing any prior metatheoretical work. M_O involves the study of theory in order to produce an overarching perspective while O_M produces an overarching perspective without such study. In a formal sense, O_M is *not* a style of metatheorizing since it does not fit the definitional requirement of occurring *after* theory is created. O_M is often the kind of counterproductive work that leads us into interminable and irresolvable controversies. Nevertheless, work of this type exists in sociology and, given its similarity to M_O, it is instructive to look at it in this chapter and to compare it to M_O. Furthermore, in a specific work M_O and O_M may be combined and/or it may be difficult to ascertain whether the overarching perspective precedes, or is derived from, a body of theory. Thus, M_O and O_M are ideal types, but in the real world of sociology we will find mixed types that seem to have elements of both.

The works to be examined offer a wide range of overarching perspectives. Some seek to transcend sociological theory, others search out perspectives that overarch part or all of sociology, while still others attempt to transcend not only sociology but an array of social sciences and other disciplines as well. Thus, the first group seeks to produce metatheories, the second metasociologies, and the third meta–social sciences or metadisciplines. However, whatever their scope, all of these metatheories involve a direct or indirect attempt to develop a perspective that transcends sociological theories.

In this chapter I will examine two examples of M_O: Walter Wallace's (1988) "disciplinary matrix" and George Ritzer's (1979, 1981b) "integrated sociological paradigm"; two cases of O_M: Paul Furfey's (1953/ 1965) positivistic metasociology and Llewellyn Gross's (1961) "neodialectical" metasociology; and two mixed types: Jeffrey C. Alexander's (1982–83) "general theoretical logic for sociology" and Edward W. Lehman's (1988) presuppositions and models (derived from Alexander) of the state.

Wallace's and Ritzer's work fit into the category of M_O because their transcendent perspectives are derived from a careful study of sociological theory. In contrast, the work of Furfey and Gross are examples of O_M because they do not derive their overarching orientations from a study of sociological theory, but rather posit them as approaches that precede and inform sociological theory (and sociology in general). Finally, the perspectives of Alexander and Lehman represent mixed types since they do both. Their adoption of a multidisciplinary approach represents O_M, while their focus on action and order is derived more from an M_O approach. In spite of these differences, for the purposes of the ensuing discussion I will treat all six together as works that produce overarching theoretical perspectives. At the close of the chapter I will return to the issue of the implications of whether a work represents M_O, or O_M, or a mixed type.

The works of Furfey, Wallace, and Gross are so broad that they are better seen as producing perspectives that overarch all of sociology and not just transcend sociological theory. However, they either explicitly or implicitly include a perspective that overarches sociological theory. Ritzer's work involves the creation of a more limited metasociological perspective, one that seeks to transcend a more circumscribed, but still large, portion of sociology. Alexander's general theoretical logic is still more limited in that its objective is to overarch sociological theory rather than all, or part, of sociology. Finally, Lehman offers the most bounded of the perspectives discussed here since he seeks the creation of a perspective that transcends the theory of only a single social institution: the polity.

In spite of their metatheoretical differences, as well as the differences in scope, these six efforts have at least two things in common: they take as their objective the production of an overarching perspective and they have been (or will be) largely unproductive and/or counterproductive. What is it about such works that makes them so problematic?[2]

The first difficulty with such work is that it assumes, by definition, that sociological theory, or at least a substantial portion of it, can be subsumed under a single overarching perspective. Moreover, metatheorists who do this kind of work have a tendency to argue that they are offering the "right" transcendent perspective and that all other approaches, including those that argue that there can be no such overarching orientation, are "wrong." Work of this type thus systematically and gravely underestimates the amount of diversity within sociology in general, and within sociological theory in particular. Because of this deep and pervasive diversity, there is little or no immediate possibility of coming up with a single, "right" transcendent perspective.

Furfey, for example, begins with the assumption that sociology *is* a science. This was clearly a debatable assumption in 1953 and it continues to be debatable today. There was, and is, a wide range of views within the field over whether sociology is, can, or even should be a science. Even among those who accept the idea that sociology can be thought of as a science, substantial disagreement exists over what is meant by the term "science" (Collins 1989a). Many in the latter group would disagree with Furfey's positivistic image of a science.

Metasociology, to Furfey, "transcends" sociology by laying down the rules for the science of sociology. In fact, metasociology is seen by Furfey as a distinct science "which furnishes the methodological principles presupposed by sociology" (1953/1965, 17). Sociology is a positivistic science and it requires the services of another positivistic science, metasociology. Clearly, many sociologists reject the idea that sociology is a science, let alone one in need of the services of still another science. This is positivism heaped upon positivism.

A similar problem is found in Wallace's much more recent disciplinary matrix for sociology. First, Wallace pulls no punches on the overarching character of his disciplinary matrix:

> This chapter sets forth a matrix of concepts aimed at making the essential constituents of *all* orientations, paradigms, theories, propositions, hypotheses, and findings (indeed *all* empirical statements of *any kind*) that have *ever been* current, or that are likely *soon to become* current, in sociology plainer and more systematically useful for understanding, constructing, criticizing, and testing theory, and research—both pure and applied. (1988, 23; my italics)

In short, Wallace's disciplinary matrix overarches everything that all sociologists (theorists and empiricists) have done or will do in at least the near future. This is a breathtaking claim and it is clear that at least a few sociologists might feel that their concerns are not adequately covered by this (or any!) disciplinary matrix.

This result is made even more likely by the fact that Wallace, like Furfey, assumes that sociology is a natural science and that such a science needs an agreed-upon disciplinary matrix. Again, however, many would disagree with the idea that sociology is a science, or at least the kind of science described by Wallace. Those who do not accept Wallace's views on sociology as a science are unlikely to seek shelter under the overarching umbrella of his disciplinary matrix.

Interestingly, as breathtaking as Wallace's claims are for his disciplinary matrix within sociology, it turns out that he has an even more ambitious (and debatable) agenda for it. That is, he believes that it transcends not only sociology, but all of the social sciences *and* sociobiology.

> if we want the fullest possible knowledge of social phenomena, we must eventually understand the *overarching* [my italics] principles of *sociality* that underlie[3] all the social sciences—including anthropology, economics, geography, history, political science, social psychology, sociology, and also the several fields that investigate social phenomena among non-human organisms (i.e., all or parts of ethology, entomology, ecology, behavior genetics, comparative psychology, primatology, microbiology, and marine biology—fields that will be referred to collectively here as "sociobiology").
>
> The disciplinary matrix proposed here, while formally limited to sociology (solely because of limits in the author's disciplinary competence and not because of any supposed intrinsic barrier between sociology and the other social sciences) is also tentatively set forth as applicable to *all* the social sciences, and therefore as a conceptual basis for their eventual unification into a single multifaceted discipline. (1988, 28)

It could be said that Wallace is endeavoring to construct not just a metatheory, or even a metasociology, but a meta–social science. Since many sociologists will be uncomfortable with his overarching perspective, it seems very likely that the wide array of social scientists and sociobiologists will find it even more discomforting. While sociology is clearly diverse, that diversity pales in comparison to the differences among the various social sciences, to say nothing of the differences between the social sciences and the sociobiologies.

Turning to Gross's work, we find a very different, and even more overarching, perspective. While Gross calls his neodialectical approach a metatheory, it seems clear in my terms that it is much broader than that. Furthermore, it is also clear that neodialectics is offered as an alternative to positivism as a metasociology. For example, Gross argues that a neodialectical "framework would bring to the forefront of attention the crucial role played by imagination, conjecture, serendipity, and nondemonstrative inference" (1961, 127). Such terms, and such an orientation, are obviously at odds with the conventional positivistic orientation. Gross clearly believes that his neodialectics is no less "right" than positivism (e.g., of Furfey and Wallace), but just as clearly there are many sociologists (including Furfey and Wallace) who would reject Gross's approach.

It is evident that Gross's neodialectics is meant to overarch all of sociology, but Gross goes even further than Wallace and sees it transcending not just the social sciences and sociobiology, but *all* sciences and *all* disciplines: "Thus, neodialectic appears to offer the widest possible foundation from which 'analytical theory construction' may appraise the formal and empirical content of science. It provides a metatheoretical framework from which the propositions of every *science or discipline,* including sociology, may be selected and reviewed" (1961, 135). It is certain that, at the minimum, the large number of positivists in sociology, to say nothing of those in all other sciences, would have considerable difficulty accepting neodialectics as a transcendent orientation.

Next, there is my own integrated paradigm (see chapters 7 and 8), which, because it overarches a number of aspects of sociology, including theories and methods, is also better described as a metasociology than a metatheory (although it clearly includes a metatheory). Like Gross's perspective, it accepts the importance of dialectics, but in a much narrower way. I am interested in the dialectical relationship among and between levels[4] of social analysis and not in dialectics as a metasociology. Like all of the other metatheorists, I created an integrated paradigm with a transcendent character, but it is far more limited in its ambitions than the others. Unlike Wallace and Gross, I have no sense that an integrated paradigm can transcend other social sciences, to say nothing of overarching all sciences and disciplines, as Gross suggests. Furthermore, and unlike all the others, my integrated paradigm does not even transcend all of sociology. Thus, it is my view that there continues to be room for extant paradigms (see chapter 6) within sociology; the integrated paradigm is merely designed to supplement these paradigms.

In spite of its more limited goals, the integrated paradigm is clearly a metasociology and is therefore subject to the criticism that it is too general and underestimates the diversity of those who might adopt such an approach. For example, it emphasizes the dialectical relationship among levels of social analysis, but others may want to deal with those relationships differently. Furthermore, it is based on the assumption that the integrated paradigm is the right approach, at least for those who are interested in the relationship among and between levels of social analysis.

Again, many sociologists may not regard the integrated paradigm as the best approach to the study of the interrelationships among such levels. Moreover, many sociologists are uncomfortable with the whole idea of thinking about social reality in terms of "levels."

While Furfey and Wallace clearly feel that the "right" metatheory lies in a positivistic direction, Gross and Ritzer move toward an anti- or a nonpositivistic direction with their interest in dialectics. Alexander points to still a third path, which he too clearly feels is right, of developing a "postpositivistic" perspective that deals with some of the problems of positivism without going too far in the direction of the antipositivistic (i.e., dialectical) perspectives that pose a whole other set of problems.

Alexander offers a "general [i.e., "overarching"] theoretical logic for sociology" (1982, 1). Alexander declares: "In the present work . . . the decision has been made to focus attention on the most general level of the sociological continuum . . . the level of 'general presuppositions' " (1982, 36). Alexander's overarching concern with multidimensionality seeks to avoid the extremes of theoretical and empirical work by calling for a relatively equal mix of the two. Furthermore, multidimensionality involves an "alternation of freedom and constraint" (Alexander 1982, 74), as well as an effort to avoid the extremes of idealism and materialism. This leads Alexander to his two general propositions. The first involves the problem of action, or "the particular nature of norms and motivation" (1982, 70). The second involves the problem of order, or "how a plurality of such actions become interrelated and ordered" (1982, 90). Action and order involve general theoretical propositions and "*[e]very* social theory inherently combines an answer to the problem of action with an answer to the question of how a plurality of such actions become interrelated and ordered" (1982, 90).

But multidimensionality, in its various senses, is likely to prove controversial. At one level, some sociologists will clearly argue for the primacy of empirical or theoretical work. At another level, many sociologists will reject an overarching concern with action and order. Just to take one example, Giddens (1984, xxxvii) has problems with all work derived from the Parsonian focus on action and order because it is weak at the micro-levels, especially "the knowledgeability of social actors, as constitutive in part of social practices." He does "not think that *any* standpoint which is heavily indebted to Parsons can cope satisfactorily with this issue at the very core of social theory."

Lehman (1988, 821) explicitly focuses on the creation of an "ultimate overarching model" for political sociological theory. Lehman is building upon the work of Alexander on multidimensionality and action and order. Lehman (1988, 807) is quite explicit about the need to search for the " 'right' metatheory" (i.e., an overarching perspective) and he clearly feels that a perspective derived from Alexander's approach is "right" for political sociology. But the search for the "right" overarching metatheory is, as always, destined to plunge sociology into a series of controversies and unresolvable debates. The fact is that many political sociologists are unlikely to accept Lehman's overarching metatheory as the correct one. Those who hold to other general, overarching metatheories are likely to come up with very different perspectives on political theory. And this says nothing about the many political sociologists who reject the whole idea of a perspective overarching the field.

Lehman imposes a two-pronged metatheory on political sociology. First, at the presuppositional level, Lehman starts with Alexander's action and order, argues that they are too general for political sociology, and employs as presuppositional analogs the ideas of power and viability. At the model level of Alexander's continuum of theoretical to empirical work, Lehman insists on the use of multiple levels[5] and organizational features. While not offering all the answers, this overarching perspective is somehow capable of generating the "key questions," formulating and testing decisive hypotheses, and so on. My guess, however, is that many political sociologists will take issue with Lehman's metatheory as well as with his sense of what the key questions and hypotheses in the field are.

A second major criticism of these overarching approaches is their vagueness. This is true to some degree of all of the examples offered here, but it is most descriptive of Gross's neodialectical metasociology. In fact, Parsons (1961a), in a comment on Gross's essay, makes this same point. For example, he talks "of the difficulty of pinning him [Gross] down on any clear issues." Parsons also argues that although "speaking of the need for an improved theoretical framework, Gross does not give any clear conception of what it should be, or of its functions in the development of a scientific discipline" (1961a, 136). Furfey is vague on the nature of metasociology as a science, a science distinct from sociology, but which provides services to it. Ritzer's integrated paradigm is vague about the precise character of the four major levels of social reality (macro-objective, macro-subjective, micro-objective, micro-subjective) that make up the integrated paradigm as well as on the nature of their dialectical relationship.

Wallace appears to be the most sensitive to the problem of vagueness and he seeks in almost laborious detail to lay out the various components of his disciplinary matrix. We are treated to one 2x4 table that, it is purported, "systematically subsumes *all* descriptions of social phenomena to be found in the sociological literature" (1988, 35; my italics). Another 2x6 table gives us "*all* the explanatory-predictive variables to be found in the sociological literature" (1988, 39; my italics). Finally, still another figure offers us an exhaustive list of the causal images in sociology. Not only do we get a set of figures, but also textual material that ranges widely in sociology to give us a detailed sense of each of the main components of each figure.

In spite of all of this exhaustiveness, one comes away from this effort with a lingering sense of vagueness. On the one hand, a seemingly endless list of components do not seem to add up to a clear sense of the overarching disciplinary matrix. On the other hand, when Wallace tries to deal with each of the components by drawing on an array of work by sociologists, classic and contemporary, the reader still emerges feeling that no single component has been dealt with exhaustively and satisfactorily and that each remains vaguely defined. Wallace's net is cast so widely and his objective is so broad that it is impossible to produce a work that possesses anything approaching full specificity and clarity.

As to vagueness in Alexander's overarching perspective, even as ardent a supporter as Lehman recognizes that "Alexander's definition of multidimensionality is somewhat elusive" (1988, 809). At various points Alexander discusses multidimensionality in terms of avoiding the extremes of theoretical and empirical work, idealism and materialism, and action and order. Multidimensionality has a series of shifting meanings that make it a very elusive idea, especially for an idea that is designed to transcend sociological theory.

In his own use of multidimensionality, Lehman, like Alexander, is quite slippery. For example, Lehman discusses Skocpol's (1986) work in terms of multidimensionality. In her work it means, in Lehman's view, the use of more than one perspective and a concern for the relationship among different levels of analysis. But as Lehman interprets Alexander, multidimensionality means a two-directional flow of scientific work (metaphysical [theoretical]-empirical) and "a preference for two or more parameters [e.g., conflict and consensus] in the generation of metatheoretical frameworks and skepticism about presuppositions and models that elaborate only a single factor" (1988, 809–10). At the minimum, crucial differences exist between Lehman's sense of multidimensionality and Skocpol's, with which Lehman seeks to align himself. Skocpol's levels differ from Lehman's parameters, and she is silent on the issue of the two-dimensional flow of scientific work. Furthermore, given the multiple and somewhat different meanings of multidimensionality found in Alexander's work, important differences between Lehman's and Alexander's sense of multidimensionality emerge. It is difficult to build a clear overarching perspective on the back of a perspective that itself is admittedly "elusive."

The third major criticism of transcendent works of the type discussed here is that they do not help sociologists get on with their work, be it empirical or theoretical. As we saw earlier, Turner (1985, 1991) has taken the lead in making this kind of criticism. While Turner is prone to indict metatheorizing in general (even though, as he now admits [Turner 1990a], he himself clearly does a kind of metatheorizing), his criticisms are most appropriately aimed at metatheorizing that seeks to create an overarching sociological perspective.

Some critics argue that overarching metatheories exist at such a high level of generality that they ignore, or are difficult to translate into, the day-to-day concerns of practicing sociologists. How in practical terms is the theorist and/or the empiricist to *use* Furfey's positivistic metasociology or Wallace's disciplinary matrix, Gross's neodialectical approach or Ritzer's integrated paradigm, or Alexander's and Lehman's multidimensionality? Parsons explicitly criticizes Gross on these grounds: "The other side of this picture, which Gross almost altogether ignores, is the importance of getting on with the central tasks of the field itself. The two central tasks are clearly empirical research on theoretically-significant problems, and theory-building in the specifically technical sense" (1961a, 139). Thus, sociology's grandest "grand theorist"—and, as we have already seen, a metatheorist of note, himself often accused of being far removed from the concerns of practicing sociologists—finds Gross's neodialectics too remote for even his tastes.

Impracticality is related to still another criticism of overarching approaches, that they are not just remote from the concerns of practicing sociologists, but actively hamper their efforts to get on with their empirical and theoretical business. Again, Parsons targets Gross: "Indeed it seems to me that Gross's formula of emphasizing neodialectics is not only not likely to be very fruitful but may positively impede progress" (1961a, 139). Parsons, however, traces this problem to the particulars of Gross's neodialectical orientation: "The simple reason for this is that making a primary principle of continual confrontation with alternatives at all levels is incompatible with giving any one line of analysis a fair trial" (1961a, 139).

A more general variant on this criticism indicates that *all* M_O hinders the progress of sociology. Turner (1991, 9) is a major spokesperson for this viewpoint. This seems to be clearly true of the six examples marshalled in this chapter. Two of them adopt a disputable positivistic orientation; two utilize an even more controversial dialectical approach; and two employ a postpositivistic position. "Positivism," "dialectics," and "postpositivism" are red flags for many sociologists and their use *is* likely to embroil us in unresolvable controversies over their basic assumptions and utility in sociology. "Positivism," "dialectics," and "postpositivism" are, in Turner's terms, "weighty philosophical matters" and debate over them, while fascinating, is unlikely to provide a simple conclusion.

Thus, I have offered four basic criticisms of overarching approaches, criticisms that I feel help to explain the failure of these efforts to have much influence on sociology. Given these problems and failures, the issue is whether there is a place in sociology for such overarching perspectives. While I have far less sympathy for this form of metatheorizing than all the others, my answer would be a qualified "yes." At a minimal level, such efforts do the field little harm. Such work is clearly of interest to a limited number of metasociologists; the rest of the discipline is free, as it often does, to largely ignore such efforts. More strongly, these works do raise the broadest kinds of issues in a field, dominated by normal science, which is ever-more likely to be drawn in the direction of minutia. While I would not want all sociologists addressing these broad issues, it is clearly useful for a few metasociologists to do so. While I may not want everyone to be obsessed with these issues, I would not want them to be totally ignored either.

However, the strongest case to be made on behalf of these overarching approaches is that just because such transcendent perspectives seem out of reach now does not mean that they will always be unattainable. Many sociologists hold out the hope (dream) of a single overarching "disciplinary matrix" and many social scientists in general fantasize about the day when their disciplinary differences will be replaced by a single, transcendent social scientific perspective. What appear to be unbridgeable differences today may seem like a discipline's immaturity from the point of view of those living a century from now. From that vantage point, today's reviled metatheorists may seem like prophets whose dreams have been redeemed by history. Those who dared to work at the broadest level of analysis may be celebrated, while those who did sociological minutia may be damned for bogging us down in an unending series of meaningless empirical, theoretical, and methodological problems. It is *the latter* who may come to be seen as having impeded the "real" work of sociology and as having blocked its progress.

I do not want to go too far in this defense of overarching approaches. My own view is that future generations, like today's, will probably find this work to be largely unproductive or counterproductive. Nevertheless, I do not think that such work is harmful to the discipline. Furthermore, it is important that a few people keep the broadest possible orientations before the sociological audience. These general perspectives allow specialized sociologists to see the broader context in which their work is embedded.

But what of the different types of overarching approaches: M_O, O_M, and mixed types? Are they all equally defensible? In my view, the strongest case can be made for M_O. Those who are interested in an overarching perspective can assess its sources in works of the M_O type. Before deciding to accept or reject an overarching perspective, students of an M_O work can trace its development, discover whether any errors were made along the way to its creation, and attain a better understanding of just what is involved in it. In contrast, overarching perspectives derived from O_M works are laid out first with little or no background on their theoretical roots. The result is that students of such a work must decide whether to accept or reject its overarching perspective more on aesthetic, political, and emotional grounds than on a careful assessment of the factors that went into its creation. Aesthetics, politics, and emotions always play a role in selection of an overarching perspective, but in the case of O_M that is sometimes *all* one has to go on in deciding whether to make an intellectual commitment. For these reasons, I would judge M_O superior to O_M as a way of creating overarching perspectives in sociology.

A good test of this conclusion is to be found in the mixed types exemplified in the work of Alexander and Lehman. The ideas on a multidisciplinary orientation stem from an O_M approach and my guess is that most sociologists will have a hard time deciding whether to accept them, and, if they accept them, what to do with them. But the ideas of action and order, as well as power and viability, have explicit roots in an array of theoretical works, thus sociologists will have a clearer sense of where those ideas come from, whether to accept them, and what to do with them. Therefore, in the mixed types, it is my guess that the overarching ideas derived from M_O work will be far more influential than those derived from work of the O_M variety.

In sum, while far stronger cases can be made for M_U and M_P, the case in favor of M_O is by no means trivial. All three types of metatheorizing, then, have important roles to play in sociological theory.

Notes

1. There has been a tendency to equate this type of work with metatheorizing, but in my view it is only one of three main types of metatheorizing. While it is concerned with the production of a metatheory, the other types of metatheorizing have very different objectives (greater understanding, production of new theory). Furthermore, as we will see in this chapter, M_O is the most problematic of the three types of metatheorizing.

2. And they have been unproductive. For example, in the 21 years between 1966 and 1986, Llewellyn Gross's essay, which was the lead article in the September 1961 issue of the *American Journal of Sociology*, was cited only nine times, less than once every two years!

3. One might ponder how such principles can both *overarch* and *underlie* the social sciences. Actually, there probably is an important issue here that needs to be sorted out. That is, does such a metatheory transcend (implying merely a commonality of interest) or undergird (implying some basic principles that structure an array of perspectives) the social sciences (or some other disciplinary entity).

4. For more on levels of social analysis, see chapter 7.

5. The way in which he uses levels is another weakness in Lehman's work. He identifies four "levels" starting at the "bottom" with the public and moving "up" to organizations, political parties, and the state. What is lacking here is any acknowledgement of the now voluminous literature of the micro-macro linkage (see chapter 10) (which is clearly implied in Lehman's analysis) and levels of social analysis (see chapter 7).

II
Studies in Metatheorizing

In part II I will present case studies of each of the three main types of metatheorizing. Although I deal mainly with a number of M_U analyses of sociological theory, two examples of M_O and one example of M_P are also offered. Several M_U tools are deployed and then utilized in a series of historically specific analyses of the state of sociological theory generally, as well as within two subareas within sociology: the sociology of work and socioeconomics. Two chapters are largely concerned with one example of M_O: the integrated sociological paradigm. Finally, one chapter is devoted to an example of M_P in an effort to develop a theory of hyperrationality on the basis of a metatheoretical study of the Weberian and neo-Weberian theory of rationality.

The preponderance of chapters devoted to M_U does not reflect the greater importance of this type of metatheorizing, but rather the fact that I have devoted more attention to this type of metatheorizing than to M_P and M_O. In fact, if I had to assess relative importance on this issue, M_P would emerge as the most important type since it produces new theory. On the other hand, M_U is likely the most common form of metatheorizing and furthermore the other two types imply that M_U, at least to some degree, is undertaken in order to yield a new theory or metatheory.

In chapter 4 the M_U idea of an architectonic, defined briefly as an underlying structure of sociological theory, is developed. It is then employed in an analysis of the work of three classic sociological theorists, Marx, Weber, and Simmel, as well as of one contemporary theorist, Peter Berger. I demonstrate that a highly similar architectonic undergirds these substantively very different theories. I also suggest that a limited number of such architectonics lie at the base of most of sociological theory.

Chapter 5 offers an example of M_P in the development of a theory of hyperrationality derived from a careful study of the work of Weber and the neo-Weberians on rationality. The chapter not only shows the utility of M_P, as well as the continuing vitality of Weberian theory, but it closes with an ideal-typical characterization of hyperrationality. My hope is that this new concept, derived metatheoretically, will prove useful in future empirical and theoretical work.

Chapter 6 looks at sociology in general, and sociological theory in particular, as it existed primarily in the 1960s. The M_U tool of a paradigm is used to demonstrate that sociology in the 1960s was a multiple paradigm science. Three major sociological paradigms are detailed. Theoretically, this multiparadigmatic status marked the end of the earlier (1940s and 1950s) hegemony of structural functionalism. There was a flowering of sociological paradigms as well as of a far greater number of theories that were subsumable under one of the three major paradigms.

Chapter 6 closes with a call for a new, more integrated sociological paradigm. That call is picked up in chapter 7 in the context of a discussion of levels of analysis in sociology. The idea of levels is shown to have been central to understanding sociology's multiple paradigms as well as to the idea of an integrated sociological paradigm (M_O). A schematic outline of such an integrated paradigm is offered.

Chapter 8 looks at the works of Emile Durkheim and Karl Marx as possible exemplars for an integrated sociological paradigm. While Durkheim's work is found wanting from this point of view, my examination does cast new light on it. Karl Marx's work is found to be an appropriate exemplar for an integrated sociological paradigm.

Chapter 9 looks at sociological theory primarily in the 1970s and describes the rise of various micro-level theories (e.g., phenomenology, ethnomethodology, exchange theory) and the corresponding decline of macro-level theories like structural functionalism and conflict theory. While sociological theory, as we have seen, had been dominated in the 1940s and 1950s by macro-level theory (especially structural functionalism), and structural functionalism retained much of its power in the multi-paradigmatic 1960s, in the 1970s there was a strong surge of interest in the micro-level theoretical alternatives.

While the history of sociological theory from the 1940s through the 1970s had been dominated by macro- and micro-level theoretical extremism, the 1980s witnessed an enormous growth of interest in theories that integrated micro- and macro-level concerns. Chapter 10 deals with this development as well as with the threats that exist to it from micro- and macro-extremists. Chapter 10 will also discuss the parallel development in European theory known as the effort to link agency and structure. In Chapter 11 I deal with sociological theory at the close of the 1980s and the beginning of the 1990s. Here there is a movement toward more general syntheses than simply micro-macro integration. A wide range of synthetic efforts are described and theoretical syntheses are seen as dominant in sociological theory as we move into the 1990s. These developments, along with the micro-macro integration of the 1980s, suggest that a firm basis for an integrated sociological paradigm may now be developing.

Overall, chapters 9–11, as well as 4 and 6, demonstrate the utility of metatheorizing (M_U) for understanding specific epochs in the history of sociological theory. Furthermore, it allows us to discern a longer-term trend away from extremism in sociological theory and to more synthetic efforts (Ritzer, 1990a).

Finally, in Chapter 12 I turn to more specific applications of metatheorizing. I look at developments in two subareas in sociology, the sociology of work and socioeconomics. In the sociology of work I show that there is a strong correspondence between developments in it and in sociological theory in general. Most notably, a growing interest in micro-macro linkage issues occurred in the sociology of work at the same time that this topic was booming in sociological theory. However, the two developments occurred side-by-side and were largely invisible to one another. I argue that sociologists of work and sociological theorists have much to gain from one another. The metatheoretical concepts of a paradigm and micro-macro theoretical linkage are employed in the discussion of socioeconomics. I show that socioeconomics is not a new paradigm and that it suffers from a lack of input from recent theoretical developments in micro-macro (and agency-structure) linkage.

4

The Early History of Sociological Theory: The Delineation of an Underlying Architectonic

This chapter is based on my conviction that the works of a number of seemingly diverse classical sociological theorists share a limited number of architectonics (defined for the moment as underlying structures). By employing architectonics as an M_U tool, we can gain better insight into the real similarities and differences among classic sociological theorists. Beyond this, and perhaps more importantly, architectonics can give us a firm understanding of the various bases used—in the past, present, or future—to systematically erect sociological theories of social phenomena.

This chapter is an effort to delineate *one* of the most important architectonics in sociological theory. It is clear to me that a number of other architectonics exist; I will hint at the natures of a few of them in the closing pages of this chapter. A major utility of this kind of work will lie ultimately in studies of comparative architectonics. At this point, I can only suggest what such comparative work might look like.

The importance of the architectonic that will be delineated in this chapter will be demonstrated by the fact that it will be shown to undergird a significant portion of the work of three of the most important theorists in the history of sociology: Karl Marx, Max Weber, and Georg Simmel.[1] In addition, in order to demonstrate the breadth of the applicability of the architectonic, it will also be applied to the more contemporary work of Peter Berger and Thomas Luckmann, *The Social Construction of Reality*.[2] This is not an exhaustive list of those whose work can be analyzed using such an architectonic; others (e.g., Gerth and Mills 1953) are easily identified.

While of crucial importance to an understanding of the works of the theorists mentioned above, this architectonic does not undergird the entirety of their work. Furthermore, there is considerable variation in the degree to which it informs the work of these thinkers. Thus, for example, while I believe it lies at the base of much of Marx's work, it is largely confined to those aspects of Weber's work devoted to the economy and bureaucracy. Despite such variation, the fact that it underlies a significant portion of the work of these thinkers shows a continuity among a range of theorists who are not often thought to be linked so strongly.

The term "architectonic"[3] has been used by the Weberian scholar Stephen Kalberg (1983) to mean "the underlying themes," "the comprehensive analytic," the "universal-historical" analytic that penetrates Weber's "entire opus." I too associate architectonic with underlying themes: a comprehensive, universal-historical analytic. While I borrow the term "architectonic" from Kalberg, I must here note important differences between the way in which he uses the concept and the way in which I use it. For one thing, Kalberg's objectives are narrower than mine. While Kalberg's sole objective is to identify Weber's architectonic, my goal is to identify a more general sociological architectonic that undergirds the work of a number of (especially) classical sociological theorists. For another, even within Weber's work my objectives are broader than Kalberg's. His goal is to "identify major theoretical possibilities for economically-oriented action at the level of civilizational analysis" (Kalberg 1983, 256). He admits that this is "*one small step* toward a reconstruction of Weber's entire historical sociology of comparative civilizations" (1983, 255; my italics). In contrast, rather than identify a small portion of a very detailed architectonic, I have attempted to identify in broad terms the parameters of Weber's architectonic.[4]

Although she does not use the term architectonic, an effort that bears a strong resemblance to the one undertaken here, at least as far as the analysis of Marx is concerned, was made earlier by the philosopher Carol C. Gould (1978). Gould's basic description of Marx's "social ontology," or his "metaphysical theory" of social reality is, as will be seen, very close to the image of the architectonic developed in this chapter:

> Such a metaphysical theory would give a systematic account of the *fundamental entities and structures of social existence*—for example, persons and institutions—and of the nature of social interaction and social change. Such an ontology is only *implicit* in Marx's work. Nevertheless, my thesis is that his concrete analysis of capitalism and of the stages of social development *presupposes such a systematic ontological* framework. Thus, for example, Marx's account of the transition from precapitalist societies to capitalism, his theory of surplus value, his analysis of technological development and his outline of the communal society of the future *cannot be adequately understood apart from . . . his fundamental philosophical ideas about the nature of social reality and the systematic interrelations among those ideas.* (Gould 1978, xi–xii; my italics)

Although Gould's analysis of Marx is similar to the analysis of his ideas presented below, there are significant differences. As a philosopher, she is led in some very different directions than those taken by a sociologist. Thus, while some elements of Marx's social ontology identified by Gould are similar to the elements of his architectonic outlined here, others (e.g., freedom and justice) are significantly different or encompassed by broader concepts (e.g., praxis, emancipation). Furthermore, Gould seeks simply to identify Marx's social ontology, while I seek to uncover a more general sociological architectonic. Thus, while there are some efforts that presage my own, they are far narrower in scope than my attempt.

It could be argued that the approach taken here parallels Marx's own orientation to the study of capitalism.[5] Marx (1857–58/1973, 247, 509, 595, 639) sought to probe beneath the surface economic appearances of capitalism (e.g., money, wages, profits) to examine the underlying economic structure of capitalism (e.g., capital, value, surplus value) (Godelier 1972, 3). I seek to probe beneath Marx's analysis of the underlying economic structure of capitalism (as well as the theories of Weber, Simmel, and Berger and Luckmann) to examine the sociological architectonic that undergirds and informs it. In other words, a sociological architectonic does inform Marx's analysis of the hidden economic structure of capitalist society. One could say that this sociological architectonic informs Marx's analysis of the underlying economic structure and that the two together guide his analysis of the surface economic structure.[6] More generally, it can be argued that the same architectonic is at the base of Weber's theory of the iron cage of rationality in the economy and the bureaucratic structures of Occidental society, Simmel's theory of the tragedy of culture involving the growing gap between individual and objective culture, and Berger and Luckmann's theory of the social construction of reality.

A Sociological Architectonic

The sociological architectonic of concern to us here consists of six basic components. It begins with a set of fundamental assumptions about the nature of human beings and their thoughts and actions. This first element of the sociological architectonic can be called a *philosophical anthropology*. Brubaker, in his work on Weber, defines a philosophical anthropology as the "conception of the essence of human being, of what it is that distinguishes human life from other natural processes" (1984, 92). Not all sociological architectonics have a philosophical anthropology, and of those that do some differ in their specifics from the philosophical anthropology of concern here. In this particular philosophical anthropology it is assumed that people are endowed with the ability to think, and that action and interaction are largely based on this capacity.

Second, this architectonic assumes a process of *institutionalization*, a series of steps whereby the thoughts, actions, and interactions of people are transformed into larger social structures and social institutions.

Third, it assumes that in at least some cases people lose control over the larger structures and institutions that emerge out of thought, action, and interaction. This loss of control over macro-level phenomena is most often thought of as *reification*.

Fourth, once larger structures and institutions take on a reified existence, the architectonic assumes that it is likely that these creations will come to exert control and *domination* over the people who created them both historically and on a continuing basis.

Fifth, the existence of reified structures that dominate individuals is seen as creating the likelihood that they will have *adverse consequences* on the individuals who exist within those structures.

Sixth, there is a concern in this architectonic for how people can achieve *emancipation* from these reified structures and their adverse effects.

Given these six elements of one sociological architectonic, the goal in the rest of the chapter is to systematically examine the way in which it informs the work of Marx, Weber, Simmel, and Berger and Luckmann.

Philosophical Anthropology

The basic element of Marx's sociological architectonic is his concept of *praxis* (encompassing his—actually Feuerbach's—earlier idea of *species being*). It can be argued that *everything* that is sociologically (and economically) meaningful in Marx's work is derived from his conception of praxis (Henry 1983, 14). The concept of praxis not only informs the manuscripts of 1844, but also the notebooks of 1857–58 and the later writings on capital. Praxis is *more basic* to Marx's work than his fundamental economic concepts.

In the end, economics in Marx's work is subordinated to his sociology.[7] The admittedly enormous body of work done by Marx on the economy represents a specific application of his sociology; his work on capital is a case study utilizing his sociology. Marx focused on the economy because it was, by far, the dominant institution in capitalist society. In fact, this dominance was a problem that had to be overcome. The point I wish to make is that the nature of capitalism, *not* the nature of his architectonic, led Marx to focus on the economy.[8] That sociological architectonic could have been, and could be, as easily focused on the family, religion, or any other (predominant) institution.[9] This perspective is consistent with one taken by Engels (e.g., 1890/1972, 642) in various writings.[10]

As I indicated above, the focal concern in Marx's philosophical anthropology is with praxis, although it is important to discuss the earlier concept of species being. Species being,[11] at least in its most developed form, has *never* fully existed historically. It is a *potential,* the fulfillment of which has always (at least to the present time) been thwarted by the conditions of material life. Thus, in looking for a full expression of species being one cannot look to some "fictitious primordial condition" (Marx 1932/1964, 107). Capitalism, while denying species being, provides the material conditions necessary for the future full expression of species being. As Heller put it: "capitalism creates needs that are 'rich and many-sided' at the same time as it impoverishes men" (1976, 47). In the future communist society people will be able to "bring their species powers out of themselves" (Marx 1932/1964, 73; see also Barbalet 1983, 47, 53).

In earliest times, people were too busy desperately trying to survive to be able to approach anything like a full expression of species being. They were able to develop and express only a limited number of needs (Marx 1857–58/1973, 398). The ability of people to think, their consciousness, was limited and amounted to little more than animal, "sheep-like," consciousness (Marx and Engels, 1845–46/1970, 51). In spite of limited needs and limited abilities to think, people needed to act.[12] Indeed, they had to act in order to acquire the food, clothing, and shelter they needed to survive (Marx and Engels 1845–46/1970, 48). The production[13] of material life cannot be accomplished by isolated individuals, but requires cooperation with other people; in other words, production requires social relationships (Marx 1857–58/1973, 84). Out of human action and interaction consciousness is shaped. "Consciousness is, therefore, from the very beginning a social product, and remains so as long as men exist at all" (Marx and Engels 1845–46/1970, 51). Out of people's activities, social relationships, and production of material life comes an expansion of consciousness (Marx 1857–58/1973, 494). There is, then, a dialectic between activities, social relationships, products, and consciousness. In his effort to separate himself from German Idealism, Marx gave priority to material (activities, relationships, products) factors over ideal (conscious) factors.

While Marx gave the material world priority, he certainly did not ignore the ideal domain of consciousness. Among the characteristics associated with consciousness by Marx are the ability to choose, to plan, to concentrate, to be flexible and purposive, and to set the self off mentally from the action being taken (Ollman 1971). McMurty (1978) argues that to Marx the special property of human nature is its creative intelligence: the ability to raise a structure in one's imagination and then to erect that structure in reality. McMurty (1978, 23) calls this distinctive human capacity "projective consciousness."[14] But projective consciousness is not enough; people are endowed with the need to express that consciousness in "creative *praxis*" (McMurty 1978, 32).

In sum, species being involves an interrelated set of ideas about people, their actions, thoughts, social relationships, and the world they create and that, in turn, creates them. It encompasses Marx's philosophical anthropology, his philosophical presuppositions about the nature of human beings.

Yet, as Marx's work progressed, he used the philosophical concept less and less, although he retained its essential ideas. Barbalet (1983), for example, sees a shift as early as *The German Ideology* (1845–46/1970) away from an essentialist conception of man (species being) and toward an empirical view of man in *praxis;* rather than referring to species being (with its bothersome combination of historical and ahistorical components[15]), Marx focuses on "real individuals" in action. Nevertheless, his discussion of praxis is informed by his earlier notion of species being. Whereas in the Feuerbachian notion of species being intuition is the essence of reality, for Marx that essence lies in practice.

We can conceive of praxis as productive activity (Meszaros 1970, 78) carried out in conjunction with other people. Thus, involved in the idea of praxis is action, interaction (Lefebvre 1968, 34), production, and consciousness (Avineri 1968, 138). In other words, in its essential components, praxis is indistinguishable from species being. But while species being is a philosophical concept, praxis is ontological.[16]

Let us turn now to Weber. Weber bases his architectonic on a philosophical anthropology (what Brubaker [1984, 49] calls his "philosophical psychology") of *action* that is very similar to Marx's ideas on praxis (and species being). Kalberg sees Weber's four types of action (traditional, affectual, wertrational, and zweckrational) as "universal capacities of *Homo sapiens,*" "anthropological traits of man" (1980, 1148). Involved in Weber's (1921/1968, 1:4) conception of action, is the ability to think[17] (Weber 1903–17/1949, 40), and to link that thought to action and interaction: "We shall speak of 'action' insofar as the acting individual attaches a subjective meaning to his behavior—be it overt or covert, omission or acquiescence. Action is 'social' insofar as its subjective meaning takes account of the behavior of others and is thereby oriented in its course."[18] While all action involves subjective meaning, motive ("a complex of subjective meaning . . . ground for the conduct in question" [Weber 1921/ 1968, 1:11]), and the ability to think, rational action is distinguished by the capacity to consciously regulate or control (Kalberg 1980), to deliberately plan (Brubaker 1984, 92), action. Here is the way Weber describes rational mental processes and their linkage to action:

the acting person weighs, *insofar as he acts rationally* (my italics) . . . the "conditions" of the future development which interests him, which conditions are "external" to him and are objectively given as far as his knowledge of reality goes. He mentally rearranges into a causal complex the various "possible modes" of his own conduct and the consequences which these could be *expected* to have in connection with the "external" conditions. He does this in order to decide, in accordance with the (mentally) disclosed "possible" results, in favor of one or another mode of action as the one appropriate to his "goal." (1903–17/1949, 165)

In contrast, those who engage in nonrational action act blindly on the basis of affect or tradition; their actions are not controlled by conscious processes. In other words, much of Weber's philosophical anthropology is embedded in his work on rational action: zweckrationality and wertrationality. In sum, Weber's work, like Marx's, is premised on a philosophical anthropology that links thought, action, and interaction.

Despite this general similarity, crucial differences separate the philosophical anthropologies of Weber and Marx. For one thing, while Marx's philosophical anthropology is richly developed, Weber's is comparatively undeveloped with bits and pieces scattered throughout his work. As Brubaker put it in terms of Weber's ideas on rational action, they are "terse, undeveloped, fragmentary" (1984, 49). Moreover, while Marx's actors create things, Weber's are largely endowed with thinking ability, self-consciousness, intentionality, meaning, and motives. The result is that Weber's actors, while endowed with the capacity to act and interact, do not seem to have the same capacity as Marx's actors to *create* things. I will return to this idea and its implications in the section on institutionalization.

Simmel's philosophical anthropology (Oakes 1984, 15) is manifested throughout his work, but usually in an indirect way. In the range of essays devoted to forms of interaction and types of interactants Simmel clearly operated with the assumptions that human beings possess creative consciousness and this consciousness lies at the base of their ability to act, interact (especially through exchange, which "is the purest and most developed level of interaction" [Simmel 1907/1978, 82]), and create the larger society. While Simmel believed that consciousness allowed people to create their social worlds, he also believed that it gave them the ability to reify social reality, to create the objects that enslave consciousness. As Simmel said, "Our mind has a remarkable ability to think of contents as being independent of the act of thinking" (1907/1978, 65). While Simmel bases his work on a sense of creative human consciousness, "he does not try to discover or to explain what goes on in the mind itself" (Aron 1965, 5–6). On the other hand, Simmel was quite interested in social action and interaction and devoted considerable attention to the forms that they might take.

Simmel's philosophical anthropology is expressed nowhere better than in his sense of *individual culture*. Individual culture encompasses, among other things, the ability to think, act, create, and objectify. In other words, individual culture is intimately linked to *objective culture*. Through individual culture people produce objective culture and objective culture, in turn, shapes and expands individual culture. However, the crucial problem for Simmel is that objective culture can become detached from, and come to control, individual culture.

Finally, we come to Berger and Luckmann's *The Social Construction of Reality* (1967). We should not be surprised to learn that the philosophical anthropology that underlies that work is consistent, at least in part, with the philosophical anthropologies discussed in this section. The authors explicitly state that their "anthropological presuppositions are strongly influenced by Marx" (Berger and Luckmann 1967, 17). They also acknowledge their debt to Weber and his interest in the subjective meaning of action. Although affected by the ideas of Marx and Weber (and Simmel, among many others), Berger and Luckmann are most heavily influenced by phenomenology. But the powerful influence of phenomenology still leaves Berger and Luckmann with a philosophical anthropology of thoughtful individuals who act, interact, and create social reality that is quite consistent with the one discussed in this section. However, as we will see later, the phenomenological influence pushes Berger and Luckmann in some crucially different directions on other elements of the architectonic.

Berger and Luckmann see people as unique in the animal kingdom. Their uniqueness stems from people's "world-openness." Their sense of human nature lies in this openness, or the plasticity of instincts, and not in any fixed structure that determines social life. Thus, people construct their own nature rather than being determined by it. Basic to that nature is human consciousness. Influenced by phenomenology, Berger and Luckmann see that consciousness as intentional rather than as a mental substratum; that is, consciousness is always consciousness *of something*. As a result of the influence of phenomenology, every aspect of Berger and Luckmann's work focuses on consciousness. They recognize various kinds of consciousness, but the most important is the consciousness of everyday life. Action and interaction are determined by consciousness. Of all of the realms of interaction, it is face-to-face interaction that is most important because the actors are in the presence of each other's subjectivity. That subjectivity is also expressed, as we will see in the next section, in the things that people produce.

Also inherent in Berger and Luckmann's sense of "human nature" is human sociability: "Man's specific humanity and his sociality are inextricably intertwined" (Berger and Luckmann 1967, 51). People cannot develop as human beings without social relationships. People cannot produce a human environment in isolation from other people. In other words, "Men *together* produce a human environment, with the totality of its sociocultural and psychological formations" (Berger and Luckmann 1967, 51).

Institutionalization

Built into Marx's notion of praxis (as well as his idea of species being[19]), but worth separating out for our purposes, is the concept of *objectification*. As Ollman says, "Man's productive activity [praxis] . . . is objectified in his products in all societies" (1971, 143). By "objectification" Marx is referring to the fact that people must produce the objects (food, clothing, shelter, etc.) that they need in order to survive. While we often associate economic phenomena with the process of objectification, we can also think of the family structure, religious institutions ("spiritual goods" [Heller 1976, 28]), organizations, and governments (among others) in the same way (Marx 1932/1964, 136). This extended meaning of objectification is close to what we now think of as *institutionalization* in contemporary sociology.

People, through their thoughts and actions, and in concert with other people, produce the objects (economic and otherwise) that they need in order to survive. In other words, objectification is an inherent part of praxis (and species being). The objects that people produce, in turn, act back upon them, helping to expand human capacities. This ongoing process continually accelerates with more and more varied objects eliciting extended human capacities. People and the objects they produce are dialectically related (Marx 1867/1967, 177).

In praxis, at least in its potential form, objectification is a natural process; it is not a problem; it does not create problems. In fact, objectification is a positive process in a variety of senses, including the fact that we produce "objects which confirm and realize . . . individuality" (Marx 1932/1964, 140). People express their essential powers, they express themselves, in the objects that they produce.

However, the process of objectification, like praxis in general, can be perverted.[20] For example, in capitalism objectification, at least within the economy, is reduced to production. ("Man objectifies himself in production" [Marx 1857–58/1973, 89].) Within the capitalist economy production becomes "the predominant moment" (Marx 1857–58/1973, 94). On the one hand, this means that the process of objectification within other institutions becomes stunted and subordinated to economic production.

On the other hand, the process of objectification within the economy is itself limited. That process comes to be defined by the nature of the relationship between capitalist and proletariat. In the production process it is the proletariat that objectifies and it is the capitalists that control the objects (commodities) produced. Thus, the proletariat loses control over its objects; indeed, it loses control over the entire process of objectification. These objects (products), as well as the market for them, come to have a separate and external existence, a life of their own. In effect, the process of objectification becomes separated from the other elements of praxis. People are no longer able to express themselves in the process of objectification. Instead, man "loses his way among the products of his own efforts, which turn against him and weight him down, become a burden" (Lefebvre 1968, 8).

While Weber had a clear sense of objects[21] and, more generally, of institutions, one of the crucial problems in his work is often thought to be that he lacked a clear sense of objectification or institutionalization. As I pointed out above, Weber's actors often do not seem to create anything, with the result that they appear to lack the capacity for institutionalization (or objectification). In Levine's view, Weber lacked "a viable theory of institutionalization, such that he did not have at his disposal a ready and precise way of distinguishing the term 'objective' in the sense of *valid* from 'objective' in the Durkheimian sense of supra-individual or institutionalized" (1981, 11). Udehn (1981, 131) puts this issue in slightly different terms by arguing that there is a conflict between Weber's "individualist and subjectivist methodology" (in my terms, his philosophical anthropology) and his work on the development of rational structures in the Occident.

Although it is true that Weber's architectonic is weak on institutionalization (at least in comparison to Marx's), it must not be assumed that the process is ignored entirely. There is at least one notable place in which Weber has a sense of objectification that is very close to that of the other thinkers discussed in this chapter:

> An inanimate machine is mind objectified. Only this provides it with the power to force men into its service and to dominate their everyday working life as completely as is actually the case in the factory. Objectified intelligence is also that animated machine, the bureaucratic organization, with its specialization of trained skills, its division of jurisdiction, its rules and hierarchical relations of authority. (1921/1968, 1402)

Furthermore, the processes of objectification and institutionalization appear in several strategic areas of Weber's work. One crucial area is in his discussion of the routinization of charisma. Clearly, the process by which the extraordinary abilities of the charismatic leader are turned into day-to-day authority involves institutionalization. Under this heading we can also include the transformation of the authority of the prophet into a permanent congregation and of the sect (a group of charismatic individuals) into a church.

Also of note is Weber's concern with the institutionalization of formal (as well as substantive and theoretical) rationality. According to Kalberg, formal rationality does not "remain simply amorphous sociocultural regularities of action . . . [but] are institutionalized as normative regularities of action in 'legitimate orders', organizations, traditional . . . and rational-legal . . . forms of domination, types of economic structures, ethical doctrines, classes and strata" (1980, 1161). In contrast, practical rationality does not lead to institutionalization, but is confined to the "domain of routine, everyday, pragmatic difficulties" (Kalberg 1980, 1161).

Finally, I should note Weber's discussion of the transformation from nonstatutory norms to customary law that indicates a clear concern with both objectification and institutionalization:

> The psychological "adjustment" arising from habituation to an action causes conduct that in the beginning constituted plain habit later to be experienced as binding; then with the awareness of the diffusion of such conduct among a plurality of individuals, it comes to be incorporated as consensus into people's semi- or wholly conscious "expectations" as to the meaningfully corresponding conduct of others. Finally, these consensual understandings acquire the guarantee of coercive enforcement by which they are distinguished from mere "conventions." (Weber 1921/1968, 754)

In spite of these and other examples of a concern for objectification and institutionalization in Weber's work, it seems clear that these processes are less well-developed there than they are in Marx's work. This difference in the treatment of institutionalization is of significance in understanding the differences in the specific architectonics (and substantive theories) of Marx and Weber.

Simmel's actors are closer to Marx's than to Weber's in that they are clearly endowed with the capacity to create their social worlds. In other words, Simmel does have a sense of objectification. At one level, objectification is clearly implied by the notion of objective culture. That is, it is through the process of objectification that people produce objective culture. For example, Simmel (1921/1968, 11, 42) talks of "the spiritual dynamic" and "the creative processes of the soul" that create objective culture. At another level, however, objectification lays the groundwork for the development of an objective culture that grows more and more remote from individual culture. Thus, objectification is a normal process and a process that enables individual culture to grow and expand. However, objectification inevitably leads to a massive expansion of objective culture and a growing gap between it and individual culture.

Simmel (1907/1978, 174) sees "the interaction between individuals [as] the starting point of all social formations." But out of interaction emerges macro-level phenomena: "Further development replaces the immediacy of interacting forces with the creation of higher supra-individual formations, which appear as independent representatives of these forces and absorb and mediate the relations between individuals. These formations exist in great variety; as tangible realities and as mere ideas and products of the imagination" (Simmel 1907/1978, 174). In other words, interaction produces social objects that can take the form of what we today would call either social structures or social institutions.

As far as Berger and Luckmann (1967, 52) are concerned, "externalization" is "an anthropological necessity." People must produce things, most importantly the social order in which they live. What people externalize may take subjective or objective forms; when they take objective forms we are talking about objectivation (Berger and Luckmann 1967, 60). Berger and Pullberg (1965, 199–200) clarify this process by differentiating between "objectivation" and "objectification." *Objectivation* is the process by which human subjectivity is embodied in objective products. In other words, there is a sense in Berger and Pullberg of the production of objective reality. However, not only is the production of objects anthropologically necessary, but so too is *objectification* which (in their work) is the process by which people distance themselves from these objects so that they can take cognizance of them, so that the products can become objects of consciousness. Thus, externalization for Berger and his coauthors has both an objective and a subjective component, but, as we will see, it is the subjective aspect that interests them most.

Reification

The perversion of objectification within capitalism, *reification*, is the third element of Marx's sociological architectonic. Ollman (1971, 143) clearly links the perversion of objectification with reification when he argues that what distinguishes objectification in capitalism is that man's products have a separate existence and become a power on their own confronting man. The term "reification" is usually associated not directly with Marx, but with the neo-Marxist Georg Lukacs (1922/1968, 135). Reification can be conceived of as a process whereby people lose control over the "objects" that they created, come to believe that those objects have a natural life of their own that is fixed and immutable, and come to be controlled by those objects. In objectification people control objects; in reification objects control people. People express themselves in the process of objectification; they deny themselves in the process of reification.

Although Marx does not use the term *reification*,[22] the phenomenon appears in his work in a variety of places. The most notable source of the idea of reification is in Marx's work on the *fetishism of commodities*.[23] This is the process by which laborers in capitalism lose sight of the fact that it is their labor that gives commodities their value. They come to believe that value arises from the natural properties of the things themselves, or that value is conferred on commodities through the impersonal operation of the market. In effect, it appears that things themselves, or the relationship among things in the marketplace, are the source of value. "A definite social relation between men . . . assumes, in their eyes, the fantastic form of a relation between things" (Marx 1867/1967, 72).[24]

The process of the fetishism of commodities, as well as the resulting commodities and the marketplace for them, are an example of reification occurring within the economy. But there is more to reification within the economy than the fetishism of commodities. For example, Marx (Marx and Engels 1845–46/1970, 54) describes a reified division of labor[25] within capitalist society and has an even broader sense of a reified economy (Marx 1857–58/1973, 307, 831; see also, Gould 1978, 156–57). But Marx (cited in Bender 1970, 176) goes even further than this, arguing that reification occurs in other institutions such as the state (as well as religion [Barbalet 1983, 147]). Finally, and most generally, Marx (Marx and Engels 1845–46/1970, 53) seems to have a world/historical conception of reification. Thus, Marx is not restricted to the fetishism of commodities; underlying his work is a general conception of reification.

As I made clearer earlier, Weber does not have a strong, explicit sense of objectification (or institutionalization), but it is certainly at least implicit in his architectonic because his actors, like Marx's, end up being confronted by the problem of reification.[26] Reified structures can only come about as a result of the perversion of the process of institutionalization. The idea that Weber deals with reification is well recognized by sociologists. Swingewood, for example, says that in "Weber's discussion rationality and technology have become reified" (1975, 107). Mitzman (1969, 176) argues that in many places Weber does "a sociology of reification." Weber's image of the reified world becomes clearest in his ideas on the "iron cage" of rationality in the economy and bureaucracy. Take the following statement by Weber on the rationalized economy of the Occident: "Capitalism is today an immense cosmos into which the individual is born, and which presents itself to him, at least as an individual, as an unalterable order of things in which he must live" (1904–5/1958, 54).

The capacity of Simmel's actors to objectify leads, as we have seen, to the production of *objective culture*. Although objective culture need not be reified, the problem in the modern world is that it does take on a reified existence. Simmel describes the structure of the reified society in these words: "They [the elements of culture] acquire fixed identity, a logic and lawfulness of their own; this new rigidity inevitably places them at a distance from the spiritual dynamic which created them and which makes them independent" (1921/1968, 11). Swingewood notes that for Simmel "the social world was a world dominated by reification" (1975, 87).

Oakes (1984) describes reification in Simmel's work as both a process and a state of cultural development. He sees four stages as necessary for the development of reified structures. First, the actor must objectify, specifically by producing cultural artifacts. Second, this set of cultural artifacts "becomes a relatively independent entity, self-contained, self-perpetuating, and developing according to its own immanent principles" (1984, 12). Third, this objective culture grows increasingly remote from the individual culture that created it. Fourth, and finally, "the development of this form outstrips the ability to master or control it" (1984, 12). In a reified world, people are controlled by objective culture rather than exerting their control over it.

Berger and Luckmann's actors also reify social reality. Reification is intimately related to the processes of objectivation and objectification. As we saw, objectivation involves the production of the objective world and "as soon as an objective social world is established, the possibility of reification is never far away" (Berger and Luckmann 1967, 89). Once the world has become objectivated, and people have objectified it, reification can occur as the world "loses its comprehensibility as a human enterprise and becomes fixated as a non-human, non-humanizable, inert facticity" (Berger and Luckmann 1967, 89).

Reification, like most of Berger and Luckmann's other concepts, is defined *subjectively* as "the apprehension of human phenomena as if they were things, that is, in non-human or possibly supra-human terms . . . such as facts of nature, results of cosmic laws, or manifestations of divine will" (Berger and Luckmann 1967, 89). Berger and Pullberg (1965, 200) directly link reification to alienation: *"reification is objectification in an alienation mode."* As we will see, Berger and Pullberg define alienation, following Marx, as the breakdown of the interconnection between producing and the product. Thus, actors are taking cognizance of objects that are separate from them; that have acquired the character of "things." For Berger and Luckmann, reification is *not* the process by which objects acquire the character of "thinghood," but rather the cognitive process by which actors *think* of these things as objective facts. "It must be emphasized that reification is a modality of consciousness" (Berger and Luckmann 1967, 89). Once they have reified the world, people forget that they created the world and that they can re-create it, they lose control over it, and they see themselves as products of the world rather than producers of it.

Domination

In Marx's work, in one sense, it is the capitalists who come to control and benefit from the reified economic structures of capitalist society. The capitalists are able to dominate the proletariat because the workers must sell the capitalists their labor time in order to gain access to the means of production (reified structures) (Gould 1978, 157). The domination of the proletariat by the capitalists is closely related to exploitation.[27] The capitalists *exploit* the workers because they appropriate at least part of the products of the proletariat without recompense. The capitalist only pays for part of a day's labor (enough to keep the laborer and his family alive), but gets a full day's work. The rate of surplus value (the amount of surplus labor divided by the amount of necessary labor) is "an exact expression of the degree of exploitation of labour-power by Capital, or the labourer by the capitalist" (Marx 1867/1967, 218; see also Marx 1857–58/1973, 646). Marx also depicts the domination and exploitation of the proletariat by the capitalists in a more graphic manner: "Capital is dead labour, that vampire-like, only lives by sucking living labour, and lives the more, the more labour it sucks" (Marx 1867/1967, 233). This domination and exploitation by those who control the reified structures of capitalism leads to alienation. "Indeed, exploitation and alienation are the same process viewed from two sides: the first from the side of capital and the second from the side of labor" (Gould 1978, 145).

But while it is possible to discuss domination in terms of the relationship between capitalist and proletariat, there is another and perhaps sociologically more important form of domination embedded in Marx's work. This form is the domination of *both* proletariat *and* capitalists by the reified structures of society. While he sometimes writes as if capitalists do things *to* workers, more often he makes clear that both classes are embedded in a coercive system that compels them to act in certain ways (Marx 1867/1967, 309–10, 592). Marx indicates that it is not just the proletariat that is affected by reified structures: "(and this applies to the capitalist) all is under the sway of *inhuman* power" (1932/1964, 156).

Weber makes it clear that his reified system exerts domination over people: "It forces the individual, in so far as he is involved in the system of market relationships, to conform to capitalist rules of action" (1904–5/1958, 54). Later, in the *Protestant Ethic,* and even more strongly, Weber says: "the tremendous cosmos of the modern economic order . . . is now bound to the technical and economic conditions of machine production which to-day determine the lives of all the individuals who are born into this mechanism, not only those directly concerned with economic acquisition, with *irresistible force"* (1904–5/1958, 181; my italics). More specifically, he described bureaucracies as systems of domination that are "escape proof," "practically unshatterable," and from which the individual bureaucrats could not "squirm out" once they were "harnessed" in them. Weber wrote of bureaucracies in these terms:

> Objectified intelligence is also that animated machine, the bureaucratic organization, with its specialization of trained skills, its division of jurisdiction, its rules and hierarchical relations of authority. Together with the inanimate machine it is busy fabricating the shell of bondage which men will perhaps be forced to inhabit some day, as powerless as the fellahs of ancient Egypt. (1921/1968, 1402)

While Marx saw domination stemming from both individual capitalists and reified systems, Weber emphasized the domination of the latter. However, like Marx, Weber (1904–5/1958, 54–55) saw the reified system of capitalism as coercive over *both* workers and capitalists.

Simmel too not only had a sense of reification, but also of actors dominated by reified structures: "Society transcends the individual and lives its own life which follows its own laws. It, too, confronts the individual with a historical, imperative firmness" (1908/1950, 258). Coser argues that these structures "confront the individual as if they were alien powers" (1965, 5). Heberle argues that for Simmel society is "an interplay of structural factors in which the human beings appear as passive objects rather than as live and willing actors" (1965, 117). Frisby writes of the "reified objective culture" within which "each individual's opportunity for creativity and development becomes increasingly restricted" (1984, 108). Thus Simmel, as well as numerous commentators on his work, have pointed to his concern for the domination of individuals, of individual culture, by an increasingly reified objective culture.

Berger and Luckmann's actors are dominated by objective structures and institutions. For example, social institutions "control human conduct by setting up predefined patterns of conduct" (Berger and Luckmann 1967, 55). Not only is control exerted by the institutions themselves, but they also tend to develop mechanisms of social control that further dominate people. In their work on domination, Berger and Luckmann are borrowing from Durkheim and thinking of social facts (e.g., social institutions) as external to and coercive on people. Thus, there is a sense in Berger and Luckmann in which actors are dominated by objective structures, but of greater importance is the domination exerted by their own reified consciousness.

Adverse Consequences

To Marx, the major adverse consequence of the existence of reified structures is *alienation*. Following Ollman (1976), I define alienation as the breakdown of the natural interconnectedness that is praxis (and species being[28]). This separation is clear in a number of places in Marx's work (e.g., Marx 1857–58/1973, 489). In capitalism, people are separated from their praxis: productive activity (and nature), their products, other people, and their species being. Alienation has disastrous consequences for people; it is a condition that is in many ways the antithesis of praxis (Marx 1867/1967, 350, 360, 508). The individual "does not affirm himself but denies himself, does not feel content, but unhappy, does not develop freely his physical and mental energy but mortifies his body and ruins his mind" (Marx, 1932/1964, 110). As a result of alienation, instead of engaging in distinctively human praxis, people are reduced to the status of lower animals (Marx 1932/1964, 111).

What causes alienation and the disastrous consequences outlined above? The domination of reified structures (and the exploitation practiced by those [capitalists] who control reified structures) that interpose themselves between people and productive activity, products, other people, and themselves. Among the reified structures within the economy discussed by Marx are capital, commodities, the market, private property,[29] the division of labor, social class, etc. Meszaros makes this same point using somewhat different terms: "Man's productive activity cannot bring fulfillment because the institutionalized second order mediations [division of labor, private property, exchange] interpose themselves between man and his activity, between man and nature, and between man and man" (1970, 83).

As I discussed earlier, Marx's concern with the economy led him to focus on reified economic structures, domination, and the alienation produced by them. However, since people can and do reify noneconomic structures, it is possible to talk of alienation in other social institutions (e.g., the state, religion). Furthermore, reified structures are not restricted to modern capitalist societies: they existed in precapitalist societies. Finally, reified structures can be thought of as existing in contemporary communist and socialist societies since modern man has disassociated reification from the capitalist economy in particular and the economic institution in general.

While alienation is certainly not the focal concern for Weber that it is to Marx, Weber was clearly interested in alienation (Swingewood 1975, 87) and, more importantly, in the adverse consequences for individuals of the reified structures of rationalized society. At one level, Weber took pains to show that alienation existed in institutions (e.g., the military) other than the economy. At another level, Weber's interest in the individual within the rational society can be seen as a concern for the adverse effects of such a society on people. Weber clearly has a sense of the actor as capable of distinctively human thought, but that thinking process is limited, if not destroyed, by the structures of capitalist society. Thus, for example, Weber argues that rational calculation within bureaucracies "reduces every worker to a cog in this bureaucratic machine and, seeing himself in this light, he will merely ask how to transform himself into a somewhat bigger cog" (1921/1968, liii). In other words, the wide range of thought open to humans is reduced to a concern with how to get ahead in the bureaucratic system. " 'Specialists without spirit, sensualists without heart; this nullity imagines that it has attained a level of civilization never before achieved' " (1904–5/1958, 182).

The domination of individuals by reified structures is linked in Simmel's work, as it is in Marx's and Weber's, to the problem of adverse consequences (Swingewood 1975, 87). For example, Simmel says of "the objective culture" that "the diversity and liveliness of its content attain their highest point through a division of labour that often condemns the individual representative and participant in this culture to a monotonous specialization, narrowness and stunted growth" (1907/1978, 199). Such a view is strikingly similar to what Weber has to say about the negative impact on people in the rationalized society and what Marx says about the alienated individual in capitalism.

Simmel's most general point is that the growth of individual culture cannot keep pace with the expansion of objective culture. Rather than being produced and controlled by people, objective culture comes to have a life of its own that increasingly produces and controls people. This could be termed a process of "cultural alienation" (Frisby 1984, 107). Instead of being naturally connected to objective culture, people come to be increasingly separated from, and dominated by, it. In other words, the natural interconnection between individual and objective culture is progressively severed in the modern world. As Simmel put it: "Thus far at least, historical development has moved toward steadily increasing *separation* between objective cultural production and the cultural level of the individual (1908/1971, 234; my italics).

Although Berger and Luckmann eschew dealing with the concept of alienation because of the confused way in which it had come to be dealt with in the contemporary literature, Berger and Pullberg do deal with alienation and, as we have already seen, in a manner very similar to the way in which the concept was dealt with by Marx. According to Berger and Pullman: *"By alienation we mean the process by which the unity of the producing and the product is broken"* (1965, 200). We could hardly be closer to the Marxian definition of alienation, especially as it is defined by Ollman in terms of breakdown of natural interconnectedness.

Emancipation

The final component of this general sociological architectonic, and Marx's in particular, is *emancipation*.[30] As I have detailed from Marx's work, through a perversion of the natural process of objectification, people have produced reified structures (in capitalism, in particular) that have served to dominate (and exploit) and alienate them. The political goal for Marx is the overcoming of these reified structures: the emancipation of people from the domination of reified structures. The community that would be created "does not rule over the individuals and is nothing in itself beyond the concrete individuals in their social relation to each other" (Gould 1978, 166). This would serve to eliminate alienation ("the human condition in the pre-communist stage" [Barbalet 1983, 53]) and reunite people with their products, productive activities, other people, and themselves. In other words, the goal of emancipation is *praxis (species being)*. "Human emancipation will only be complete when the real, individual man . . . has become a species being" (Marx cited in Bender 1970, 66). Another way of saying this is that the goal of emancipation is communism,[31] which is "The first real emergence, the actual realization for man of man's essence and of his essence as something real" (Marx 1932/1964, 187). In Avineri's view, "Marx's postulate about the ultimate possibility of human self-emancipation must be related to his philosophical premise about the initial creation of the world by man" (1968, 65). In other words, communism cannot be understood without understanding praxis and species being.

The clear implication is that people have yet to engage in praxis and become species beings; they can only achieve that state in the future. Praxis can only be attained by building on the achievements of capitalist society, overcoming the reified structures that are an inherent part of capitalism, and creating a society without exploitation, alienation, and reified structures (Marx and Engels 1845–46/1970, 50, 86).

One of the specific reified structures to be destroyed is the arbitrary and oppressive division of labor, leaving people free to pursue their interests to the best of their ability (Marx and Engels 1845–46/1970, 108,

109). However, not all structures can or should be abandoned. For example, people cannot abandon the technological advances produced by capitalist society because these advances themselves help make praxis possible for the first time. While these technologies are needed, they cannot be allowed to become reified in a future society. Technologies need to be controlled by people and subordinated to their species needs.

Like Marx, Weber is concerned not only with the problem of the adverse consequences of a reified society, but also with the emancipation of people from the source of this problem.[32] However, emancipation represents a far greater intellectual problem for Weber than for Marx. Nevertheless, Weber (cited in Mitzman 1969, 978) urges that people fight against the bureaucratic machine "in order to preserve a remnant of humanity from this parcelling-out of the soul, from this exclusive rule of bureaucratic life ideals." More specifically, he urges that professional politicians "be the countervailing force against bureaucratic domination" (Weber 1921/1968, 1417). On the other, more general level, he urges people to live by an ethic of responsibility in which ends are chosen by wertrationality and means by zweckrationality. Only in this way can individuals live a "truly human life within the modern rationalized world" (Brubaker 1984, 110). But while Weber details these and other ways of struggling for emancipation, he does not seem to recognize the possibility of any meaningful success.

Thus, while Marx foresees the overthrow of the structures of capitalist society, Weber is not nearly as optimistic as Marx about the structures of the rationalized society. In fact, Weber is strongly pessimistic about the possibilities of emancipation. This is manifested in his view that "the future belongs to bureaucratization" (1921/1968, 1401). More generally, he felt that the kind of socialist revolution envisioned by Marx would only serve to heighten the level of rationalization. This pessimism about the possibility of emancipation led Weber (cited in Gerth and Mills 1958, 128) to conclude: "Not summer's bloom lies ahead of us, but rather a polar night of icy darkness and hardness, no matter which group may triumph externally now."

Simmel is closer to Weber than Marx on the issue of emancipation in that he saw the problems of reification and its adverse consequences as inherent to the nature of human life (Weingartner 1959; Aron 1965, 139). Furthermore, in the modern world he saw an increasing tendency of objective culture to expand at the expense of individual culture. There is little hope of emancipation because Simmel saw the modern world becoming an "iron cage" of objective culture. Simmel also shared with Weber a pessimism about socialism, which he felt would only serve to heighten cultural alienation rather than help to alleviate the problem.

Finally, Berger and Luckmann's thoughts on emancipation are

embedded in their ideas on "alternation." This is the possibility of the transformation of subjective worlds "in which the individual 'switches worlds' " (Berger and Luckmann 1967, 157). In other words, since the problems of reification and its adverse consequences (as well as their sources) are subjective, emancipation from them will come in the form of a subjective transformation. Berger and Pullberg talk more concretely about the sociohistorical situations that make "de-reification," or doubting the taken-for-granted, possible. First, natural or man-made catastrophes can lead to the disintegration of social structures and, as a result, of taken-for-granted worlds. Second, culture contact can lead to culture shock and a questioning of the way in which people perceive the world. Third, those individuals or groups who are socially marginal have a proclivity toward de-reification. Whether emancipation comes from alternation or de-reification, it is clear that it lies in subjective change.

Conclusions

This, then, is the sociological architectonic that undergirds a significant portion of the work of Marx, Weber, Simmel, and Berger and Luckmann. That architectonic, which is potentially applicable to *any* institution and to *any* social structure in *any* society, as well as to entire societies, involves the relationship among *philosophical anthropology, institutionalization, reification, domination, adverse consequences,* and *emancipation.*

Now, I do not want to press this architectonic similarity too far. There *are,* as we have seen, important differences between the specific architectonics of Marx, Weber, Simmel, and Berger and Luckmann. For example, Weber's actors often lack the ability to objectify that is possessed by Marx's actors. Simmel (and Weber) take a pessimistic view on the issue of emancipation, while Marx is optimistic about the possibility of emancipation. Berger and Luckmann's architectonic is purely subjective while that of Marx integrates subjective and objective dimensions. In spite of these important differences, there clearly *are* striking similarities in the architectonics discussed in this chapter.

On a more general metatheoretical (M_U) level, there is the issue of the utility of comparative architectonics. On the surface, the substantive sociologies of Marx, Weber, Simmel, and Berger and Luckmann seem very different. It is difficult to say what it is that serves to unify their sociologies of capitalism, rationalization, cultural domination, and knowledge. However, when one strips away these substantive concerns, one is able to see the underlying similarities in sociological approach. While increasing the ability to see underlying similarities is one use of sociological architectonics, this approach also allows us to get at basic sources of differences among sociological theorists. Among the theorists discussed here, major theoretical differences between Marx and Weber are traceable to differences in their philosophical anthropologies. Furthermore, because Marx's actors objectify, they are endowed with the capacity to destroy the structures they create. Because Weber's actors are largely lacking in the capacity to objectify, they are doomed to living life in the iron cage. Thus, an architectonic is useful *both* for uncovering underlying similarities in superficially different theories and for tracing the sources of the differences in these theories.

This chapter has been restricted to theorists who can be subsumed largely under a given architectonic. It seems clear, however, that theorists such as Durkheim, Mead, Garfinkel, Goffman, and Homans operate with very different architectonics. What is needed is M_U work oriented to uncovering the architectonics of thinkers such as these. The analysis of a wide range of architectonics, once we know them, should allow us to get a truer sense of the basic similarities and the truly fundamental differences within sociological theory. We may even be able to come up with a limited number of basic types of architectonics. If we do, my view, as I have tried to show throughout this chapter, is that the bulk of the work of Marx, Weber, Simmel, Berger and Luckmann, and many others is informed by the same architectonic.

How might other architectonics differ from the one delineated here? A genuine answer to this question is far beyond the scope of this chapter. In order to get at this question, I would need to identify and delineate the other sociological architectonics. Lacking such elaboration at this point, all I can do is suggest a few of the ways in which other sociological architectonics might differ from the one outlined above.

While the architectonic discussed here is based on a philosophical anthropology of people who think, act, interact, and create, other architectonics may not operate, explicitly or implicitly, with a philosophical anthropology. Still other architectonics may have a philosophical anthropology that does not endow people with the ability to think, may relegate that ability to insignificance, and/or may not link thinking ability to peoples' actions and interactions.

The architectonic of concern here emphasizes institutionalization, the process by which large-scale structures and institutions emerge out of micro processes. Other architectonics may not accept the existence of macro-level phenomena; may reject the idea that larger structures and institutions emerge out of these micro processes; or may begin at the structural and institutional levels without linking them to the micro levels.

The architectonic outlined in this chapter not only accepts the emergence and reality of macro-level phenomena, but also the fact that these structures and institutions can come to have lives of their own that control, rather than are controlled by, the people who created them. Other architectonics that do not accept the idea of emergence also reject the notion of reification. In addition, some architectonics may accept the idea of emergence, but reject the possibility of reification.

In the architectonic analyzed in these pages, the emphasis is on the way reified structures dominate people. In other architectonics, such reified structures may not exist and therefore cannot dominate people. In still other architectonics people are not dominated, or if they are, it is by other people rather than by reified structures.

The emphasis in the architectonic discussed here is on the adverse effect of reified structures on people. In other architectonics the focus may be on how larger, nonreified structures positively affect individuals.

Since the emphasis in the architectonic discussed above is on the negative effects of reified structures on people, there is a parallel interest in emancipating people from such structures. In other architectonics that emphasize the positive effects of structures on people, the concern may be with increasing the control of such nonreified structures over individuals, not emancipating them from that control. In still other architectonics, the problem may be the emancipation of people from the control of other people, not from the control of reified structures.

Finally, it must be said that other architectonics have been discussed in terms of the dimensions of the architectonic outlined here. It is highly likely that these other architectonics have a range of other dimensions that have not even been suggested by the architectonic of concern to us here.

Returning to the more general theme of this book, this chapter can be seen as an effort to demonstrate the utility of one M_U tool, the architectonic, as well as a series of subsidiary tools like philosophical anthropology, for enhancing our understanding of the work of some of the leading classical sociological theorists.

Notes

1. This correspondence in the work of Marx, Weber, and Simmel finds support in the work of Habermas (1987, 1) who sees them as part of a " 'German' line of social-theoretical thought" dealing with the "rationalization/reification" problematic. As we will see, the latter problematic is an essential aspect of the architectonic to be outlined here.

2. This discussion will be supplemented with an analysis of a paper Berger coauthored with Stanley Pullberg that was designed as a precursor to the *Social Construction of Reality*. In fact, Pullberg was to have been one of the coauthors of that book. See Peter Berger and Stanley Pullberg, "Reification and the Sociological Critique of Consciousness," *History and Theory* 4:196–211.

3. The term architectonic (like other terms used here [e.g.: philosophical anthropology]) has been used in many different ways in philosophy. See the many definitions in the *Compact Edition of The Oxford English Dictionary*. 1987. Ed. by Robert Burchfield. Oxford University Press, 1:434.

4. Also by way of contrast, it is worth noting that I use *architectonic* as a noun to denote underlying structure and not, like Cohen (1981, xliii), as an adjective meaning an approach that is static, not dynamic. Furthermore, there is no contradiction between an architectonic and dynamism; the architectonic I will present *is* processual.

5. However, while Marx is doing theoretical work on social reality, I am doing a metatheoretical analysis of sociological theory. While the realities of capitalism were Marx's data, my data are the various theories.

6. Mandel makes at least part of this explicit when he argues that "Underlying Marxist economic theory is an anthropological paradigm: man is a social animal; the human species can only survive through social labor" (1983, 189). As we will see, Marx's (philosophical) anthropology, embodied in his ideas on praxis (and species being), is one component, the most basic aspect, of his sociological architectonic.

7. For a similar view, see Mazlish 1984, 117–118.

8. In other words, the position taken here is in accord with those who argue that Marx was *not* an economic determinist (e.g., Meszaros 1970, 118; Ollman 1971, 9).

9. This implies that the dominance of *any* institution constitutes a problem for society. While Marx could have focused on other institutions, it is notable that he did not. As Worsley says, "It is significant that Marx's greatest intellectual achievement is *Capital*, a study in political economy, and that he never produced any parallel study of non-economic institutions, or a systematic *sociology* of society (or even of any particular society) as a whole" (1982, 53).

10. However, to be frank, it is *inconsistent* with many statements made by Engels (and Marx) that reflect economic determinism. See Worsley (1982, 47–51) for a discussion of some of the vacillations of Marx and Engels on this issue.

11. There is little dispute that the concept of species being lies at the base of Marx's early works, especially the manuscripts of 1844. More controversial is the assertion that it informs the later work. But in the *Grundrisse* (1857–58/1973), Marx not only uses the term "species being" (p. 243), but uses other terms that reflect the basic concept (e.g., the workers' "creative powers" [p. 307]). In discussing the individual in a classless society in the *Grundrisse* (p. 51), Marx writes of "all-sided, full, rich development of needs and capacities." In *Capital*, vol. 1, the term *species being* does not appear, but the concept is clearly there in, among other things, Marx's (1867/1967, 167, 508) discussion of labor and labor power. Thus, in my view, the idea of species being informs the entire range of Marx's economic works. However, as we will see, the concept of praxis comes to subsume the idea of species being. It is in the concept of praxis that we find Marx's philosophical anthropology.

12. As Ollman makes clear, the concepts of activity, work, and creativity are interrelated in Marx's work. While they may be separated in capitalism, "in communism, as far as possible, all activity and work is creative" (1971, 105).

13. Marx adds production to Feuerbach's conception of consciousness, emphasizing "production as conscious life activity" (Barbalet 1983, 54).

14. McMurty (1978, 30–31, 35) clearly sees Marx's notion of species being, or more specifically "projective consciousness," as part of Marx's architectonic since he sees it as underlying, or being the ground for, his entire work.

15. Walliman (1981, 11) differentiates between the biological and social/ historical aspects of species being. More specifically, Heller (1976, 28) differentiates between "natural" needs and "socially produced" needs. This duality leads to interpretive difficulties. Thus, on the one hand, Avineri (1968, 71) can talk of everchanging human nature, while Ollman (1971, 76) is led to emphasize the fact that Marx has "a conception of man outside of history." These views *can* be reconciled (Geras 1983) by arguing that there are universal human characteristics (e.g., thought, action, interaction, production), but their specific manifestations are shaped by the nature of the given historical epoch. However, although a reconciliation was possible, Marx obviously felt it best to move away from the notion of species being and toward praxis.

16. Many observers echo the position taken here on the centrality of the concept of praxis in Marx's work (e.g., Meszaros 1970, 79; Rockmore [in Henry 1983, ix]; Lefebvre 1968, 8, 34).

17. In fact, Weber is not mainly interested in mental processes per se, but in how they are translated into patterns of social action (Kalberg 1980).

18. In fact, to Weber "the specific task of sociological analysis [was] . . . the interpretation of action in terms of its subjective meaning" (1921/1968, 8).

19. For example, Heller linked the concept of need associated with species being and objectification: "Marx considered the object of need and the need itself to be always interrelated. . . . Types of need are formed in accordance with the objects toward which they are directed" (1974, 28).

20. The 1844 manuscripts are ambiguous on this topic. At times, objectification itself is seen as leading to problems, but later it is clearer that the problems stem from the form taken by objectification in capitalism (Nicolaus 1973, 50).

21. Although I am arguing that Weber had a clear sense of objective structures, there are many places in his work (e.g., Weber 1903–17/1949, 99; Weber 1921/1968, 13, 14) where Weber discusses objective structures as if they were nothing more than the sum of micro processes. Many Weberian scholars (e.g., Kalberg 1980) interpret his work in this way. Other observers walk a tightrope on this issue. For example, Cohen admits that Weber does not "focus on the desiccated short-term strands of social action undertaken by discrete individuals. Rather he devotes the largest part of his analyses to patterns of action within and between large-scale institutions, modes of domination, and cultural ways of life" (1981, xxix).

22. Although it sometimes appears in translations as an appropriate word for what Marx is describing.

23. In fact, Ollman (1971) equates the fetishism of commodities and reification.

24. Elsewhere, Marx makes similar points. See, for example, Marx 1857–58/1973, 157, 161; 1867/1967, 72.

25. Walliman (1981) places great emphasis on this reified structure; see also Rattansi 1982.

26. As on the issue of objectification, there are many places where Weber (e.g., 1921/1968, 27) explicitly rejects the idea of reification and reified structures.

27. According to Worsley, Marx "put at the heart of his sociology—as no other sociology does—the theme of exploitation" (1982, 115).

28. As Barbalet puts it, the "concept of 'alienation', . . . is a derivative of the concept 'species being' in so far as the meaning of alienation can be understood only in terms of man's divested species-being" (1983, 53).

29. Ollman argues that " 'private property' is Marx's most general term for the objects produced by alienated labor, and encompass all the products that come out of the capitalist society" (1971, 159).

30. Barbalet links the idea of emancipation to alienation: "All theories of alienation entail a concept of the transcendence of alienation" (1983, 102). Similarly, Swingewood says: "Freedom from alienation thus becomes indissolubly bound to total revolution" (1975, 93).

31. According to Berki, communism is "the *only thing* that is important about Marx's thought" (1983, 1).

32. Still another parallel between Marx and Weber is the linkage between their philosophical anthropologies and their political philosophies. While Marx wanted to create a society in which praxis (species being) is possible, Weber wanted a society that had room for a "personality" endowed with dignity, integrity, and autonomy (Brubaker 1984).

5
Hyperrationality: An Extension of Weberian and Neo-Weberian Theory*

O ur objective in this chapter is to demonstrate the utility of M_p by carefully analyzing and building upon the work of Max Weber and a number of neo-Weberians in order to push Weberian theory in a new direction. The concept of *hyperrationality* developed in this chapter is consistent with the ideas of Weber and the neo-Weberians, although it represents a clear extension of that set of ideas.[1] In extending Weberian theory we are, following Merton (1965), "standing on the shoulders of giants" in order to go beyond the horizons set in their own work. Weber's ideas (as well as those of his interpreters) are treated as living legacies to be expanded and to be rendered capable of addressing social realities not envisioned by Weber (and perhaps not even envisioned by more contemporary Weberians).

While we could focus on many other aspects of Weber's work (see chapter 4), our concern is with what many consider the overarching themes in his *substantive*[2] work: rationality and the rationalization process. To adopt such an interest is to reject many of the arguments of Weber himself, as well as those of many neo-Weberians, that there is no overarching theory in Weber's work. In order for us to take the view that there *is* an overarching theory of rationality in Weber's work, we adopted some positions taken explicitly by Weber (and his followers) but rejected many others.[3] At times Weber rejected the idea of a general theory, but at other times he seemed to argue that he offered such a theory and that its focus was rationality and rationalization. We do not intend to suggest that the idea that such a theory is embedded in Weber's work is the only valid interpretation of Weberian theory, but it certainly is *one* of them. We will demonstrate this viewpoint through a metatheoretical analysis of the work of Weber and the neo-Weberians.

One source of the concept of hyperrationality, and the one that will be the focal concern of this chapter, is Weberian and neo-Weberian theory of rationality. We will demonstrate that hyperrationality is a logical and defensible extension of that theory. There is a second source for this idea,

---

*This chapter was co-authored by Terri LeMoyne.

but it will only be touched on in this chapter because of our metatheoretical focus. That second source is the contemporary social world, especially the post–World War II development of Japanese industry.[4] The concept of hyperrationality flows from *both* a study of Weberian theory *and* the examination of the dramatic growth of Japanese industry.

Weber's theory of rationality focused on what he viewed as the unique characteristics of the Occident of his day. However, a new set of uniquely rational characteristics has appeared in Japanese industry (and Japanese society in general) that Weber did not anticipate and that is not completely described by the Weberian concept of rationality. This "new" uniqueness requires a new theoretical concept, *hyperrationality,* to help us understand its sociological importance. It could be argued that our objective here is to create a new ideal type: hyperrationality. This is certainly acceptable, even desirable, from the point of view of Weberian methodology since new developments often require new or revised ideal types.

Why this particular ideal type? In the best Weberian tradition, the focus on hyperrationality has been chosen because of its "value relevance." In other words, it was selected because of its importance from the point of view of the "evaluative ideas which dominate the investigator and his age" (Weber 1903–17/1949, 84). Also following Weber, the focus must be on a given "sphere of life" (or social institution) because of its value relevance as well as because it is difficult, if not impossible, to look at the society as a whole. Few issues are of greater importance to the American economy (and to sociologists of the economy) than an understanding of Japan's economic success and its implications for the future of the American economy.

According to Weber, "European and American social and economic life is rationalized in a specific way and a specific sense. The explanation of this rationalization . . . is one of the chief tasks of our discipline" (1903–17/1949, 34). Such an analysis remains important today, but given the rise of Japanese industry, it is also necessary to analyze the "specific way" and "specific sense" in which Japan's industries have been rationalized. That specific way and that specific sense *is* hyperrationality. In other words, Japanese industry has rationalized in a manner that is different from the rationalization of Occidental industry.

This shift to a focus on Japan has some precedent in Weber's own work since Weber often analyzed rationalization processes in the Orient. In fact, Levine argues that "he can be viewed as crediting the Orient for having developed heights of rationality in some respects superior to those reached in the Occident" (1981, 9). Along these lines, it can be argued that contemporary Japanese industry has now progressed so far that it can no longer be described by the term *rational;* a new theoretical concept—hyperrationality—is needed to adequately describe it.

While Weber made a few isolated comments specifically about Japan, he did not single Japan out for full-scale treatment as he did China and India. Thus, "Weber did not develop a systematic analysis of Japanese society" (Tominaga 1989, 139). However, Tominaga, building on Weber's work and contributing his own insights into Japan, has argued that Japan provided a more favorable ground for the rationalization process than China. This favorable atmosphere allowed Japan to import, through "cultural diffusion," Western rationality. However, as we will see, Japan did not stop with the importation of Western rationality, but went on to develop its own distinctive hyperrational system.

The ultimate objective in this chapter is to create an ideal type of hyperrationality. One route to this end, and the main concern in this chapter, is through an analysis of the major concepts in Weberian theory related to the broad idea of rationality. These concepts will be utilized, but we will put them together in a new way, to help create the concept of hyperrationality. Thus one source of hyperrationality is conceptual. The second source is empirical. That is, the concept comes not just from past conceptual work, but also from the current historical realities of Japanese industry. In this sense, an "historically saturated typology" is being created. The idea of hyperrationality can be judged in terms of how well it is derived from both a set of conceptual ideas and the empirical realities of Japanese industry. However, the ultimate judgment lies in the concept's utility in empirical research. As Kalberg points out, "the formation of clear concepts [is] simply the unavoidable first step in undertaking a sociological analysis" (1980, 1177). Following Weber (1903–17/ 1949), the concept of hyperrationality should be used to compare, for example, American and Japanese industries, to look for divergences and similarities, to describe them, and to attempt to understand them causally.

Hyperrationality: The Conceptual Roots

Weber's voluminous work, especially as it relates to the issue of rationality (and the process of rationalization), is very difficult to analyze. Among the many reasons for this difficulty, two stand out. First, Weber clearly has a number of different subtypes of rationality in mind, and while he sometimes carefully labels the subtype that he is dealing with, more often he simply uses the generic term *rationality* and the reader is forced to try to deduce which type of rationality he is discussing at a given point in his text. Second, while Weber overtly eschews an overarching theory of rationalization, it is possible to discern one in his work. Without entering into the many debates over these issues, this chapter is premised on two positions: (1) Weber had a multifaceted conception of rationality that is well-defined by the neo-Weberian differentiation among four subtypes: practical, theoretical, substantive, and formal rationality; (2) an overarching theory of the rationalization of the West (and the failure of the rest of the world to rationalize) is embedded in his work and that theory can be extended to the hyperrationalization of the modern world, especially regarding Japan and its industrial system.

Let us begin with the four subtypes of rationality. We accept the typology developed almost simultaneously by Kalberg (1980), Levine (1981), and Habermas (1984, 168–72), although it is buttressed, as will be shown, by our independent reading of Weber. Other typologies may be developed and supported by a review of Weber's work, but the one employed here is useful given the purposes of this chapter and accords well with Weber's own statements about rationality.

Practical rationality is to be found in mundane, day-to-day reality and involves the "worldly interests" of the individual (Weber 1904–5/1958, 77). The actor accepts the world as it is and seeks to deal with its difficulties in the most expedient way possible (Kalberg 1980, 1152). In practical rationality, the actor pursues a "practical end by means of an increasingly precise calculation of adequate means" (Weber 1958, 293). Elsewhere Weber contends that practical rationality involves "the methodical attainment of a definitely given and practical end by means of an increasingly precise calculation of adequate means" (1958, 293). Practical rationality is to be found in all historical epochs and in all societal settings. While everyone is capable of practical rationality, the business classes ("merchants and artisans") have been its distinctive carriers (Weber 1958, 279). Later, Weber describes the carrier as the "civic strata" and describes its rationality as having "been based upon technological or economic calculations and upon mastery of nature and of man, however primitive the means at their disposal" (1958, 284). This contention about primitive means makes it clear that practical rationality has existed throughout history.

Weber draws a clear distinction between practical and theoretical rationality:

> We have to remind ourselves in advance that "rationalism" may mean very different things. It means one thing if we think of the kind of rationalization the systematic thinker performs on the image of the world: an increasing theoretical mastery of reality by means of increasingly precise and abstract concepts. Rationalism means another thing if we think of the methodical attainment of a definitely given and practical end by

means of an increasingly precise calculation of adequate means. (1958, 293)

While practical rationality is to be found in the mundane world, theoretical rationality involves an attempt to transcend that haphazard world by according it some sort of logical meaning. Unlike practical rationality which directly involves action, theoretical rationality involves "an increasingly theoretical mastery of reality by means of increasingly precise and abstract concepts" (Weber 1958, 293). Logical deduction and induction, the attribution of causality, and the arrangement of symbolic meanings are all part of theoretical rationality. While practical rationality must be useful, the products of theoretical rationality need not be of utility (Weber 1921/1978, 1:67). Like practical rationality, theoretical rationality is found in all epochs and in all societies, but unlike practical rationality not everyone is capable of theoretical rationality. Intellectuals "have always been the exponents of a rationalism which in their case has been relatively theoretical" (Weber 1958, 279). While intellectuals tend to be the "carriers" of theoretical rationality, others are capable of this type of rationality as well.

Substantive rationality involves the choice of means to ends guided by some broader set of human values. A good example is to be found in Calvinism where one feels as if one is "fulfilling a duty" in finding the best means to an end (Weber 1904–5/1958, 177). Calvinism is a specific form of asceticism which Weber sees as an attempt "to rationalize the world ethically in accordance with God's commandments" (1958, 291) (or as "God-willed [1958, 332]). More specifically, Calvinism is a form of inner-worldly asceticism that is characterized by "methodical and rationalized routine activities of workaday life in the service of the Lord" (1958, 291). Such a value system compels us from without, but it is also internalized in the actor who "wants" to fulfill the demands of the value system (e.g., "The Puritan *wanted* to work in a calling" [Weber 1904–5/1958, 181]).

Focusing more specifically on *economic* substantive rationality, Weber defines this as "the degree to which the provisioning of given groups of persons (no matter how delimited) with goods is shaped by economically oriented social action under some criterion (past, present, or potential) of ultimate values. . . . regardless of the nature of these ends" (1921/1978, 2:85).

Weber also sees substantive rationality operant in law. He discusses the substantive rationality of administration and judiciary practiced by the patrimonial prince in which utilitarian and social ethical blessings are bestowed upon the prince's subject "in the manner of the master of a large house upon the members of his household" (1958, 298). This is contrasted to formally rational law in which trained jurists "have carried out the rule of general laws applying to all 'citizens of the state' " (1958, 299). By this differentiation, Weber appears to mean, at least in part, that substantive rationality is much more arbitrary than *formal rationality* because the latter is codified in generally applicable laws while substantive law exists solely in the realm of unwritten values. Thus, Weber says that the bureaucracy strives for the "removal of the completely arbitrary disposition of the 'chief' over the subordinate official" (1958, 242). However, the key is not its arbitrariness, but rather the fact that substantive law is dominated by values:

> But the contrast to "substantive rationality" is sharpened, because the latter means that the decision of legal problems is influenced by norms different from those obtained through logical generalization of abstract interpretations of meaning. The norms to which substantive rationality accords predominance include ethical imperatives, utilitarian and other expediential rules, and political maxims, all of which diverge from the formalism of the "external characteristics" variety as well as from that which uses logical abstraction. However, the peculiarly professional, legalistic, and abstract approach to law in the modern sense is possible only in the measure that the law is formal in character. . . . Only that abstract method which employs the logical interpretation of meaning allows the execution of the specifically systematic task, i.e., the collection and rationalization by logical means of all the several rules recognized as legally valid into an internally consistent complex of abstract legal propositions. (1921/1978, 2:657)

It seems clear that it is not the nature of the values that matters to Weber (they can be "ethical, political, utilitarian, hedonistic, feudal, egalitarian, or whatever" [1921/1978,1:85]), but that choices are guided by a value system. What, then, differentiates a rational value system from a nonrational value system? What makes a value system rational is the fact that is involves a set of *consistent* value postulates. As with the preceding types of rationality, substantive rationality can be found in all historical epochs and in all societies.

Unlike all of the other types of rationality, formal rationality, in Weber's view, occurs only in the modern world and only in the Occident. In formal rationality, the best means to an end is chosen on the basis of universally agreed-upon rules, regulations, and laws (Kalberg 1980, 1158). Although found in a variety of settings (e.g., the capitalistic economy in general as well as in such specific aspects of capitalism as the money economy and double-entry bookkeeping, the factory, modern Western law, etc.), the paradigm case of formal rationality is the bureaucracy in which what people do is determined by "laws or administrative regulations" (Weber 1958, 196). Individual choices are guided by rules rather than the values that determine action in substantive rationality. The result is action devoid of human values such as the bureaucratic official who behaves in a "spirit of formalistic impersonality . . . without hatred or passion, and hence without affection or enthusiasm" (Brubaker 1984, 21). Similarly, Weber (1921/1978, 1:165–66) describes the formal rationality of Western capitalism. Within the capitalistic economy Weber argues that "the functionalized world of capitalism certainly offers no support for any such charitable orientation" (Weber 1921/1978, 1:585) and further that "matter-of-fact considerations that are simply non-ethical determine individual behavior" (Weber 1921/1978, 2:1186). In modern law, issues of ultimate justice are ignored and the emphasis is placed on the application of "definitely fixed legal concepts in the form of highly abstract rules" (Weber 1927/1984, 277). Formally rational law becomes a gapless system of legal propositions. In the private realm, we see the dominance of contracts, which are needed by formally rational businesses. Brubaker offers a good summary view of formal rationality: "Common to the rationality of industrial capitalism, formalistic law and bureaucratic administration is its objectified, institutionalized, supra-individual form: in each sphere, rationality is embodied in the social structure and confronts individuals as something external to them" (1984, 9). Thus, while the values behind substantive rationality can be internalized in actors so that they "want" to act in a certain way, in formal rationality they cannot be internalized so that people are "forced" to act in the desired manner (Weber 1904–5/1958, 181).

The development of bureaucracies furthers formal rationalization in other sectors of society. For example, Weber argues that the "modern development of full bureaucratization brings the system of rational, specialized and expert examinations irresistibly to the fore" (1958, 241). Also enhanced is the value of certificates and diplomas acquired through such examinations. Thus, the educational system is heavily affected by the advance of bureaucratization and formal rationalization.

The bureaucracy is far from the only place in which Weber saw the triumph of formal rationality. Another is the modern capitalist factory which, in turn, was heavily influenced by the formally rational military and its "discipline." He sees the organizational discipline in the modern factory as completely formally rational. Weber sees the height of this kind of formal rationality in the American system of scientific management:

> With the help of suitable methods of measurement, the optimum profitability of the individual worker is calculated like that of any material means of production. On this basis, the American system of "scientific management" triumphantly proceeds with its rational conditioning and

training of work performances, thus drawing the ultimate conclusions from the mechanization and discipline of the plant. The psycho-physical apparatus of man is completely adjusted to the demands of . . . the tools, the machines—in short, it is functionalized, and the individual is shorn of his natural rhythm through the functional specialization of muscles and through creation of an optimal economy of physical effort. (1921/1978, 2:1156)

While Weber clearly has a multifaceted sense of rationality, he argues that in the West formal rationality comes to overwhelm the other three types. This is clearest in the case of the defeat of substantive rationality by formal rationality (Cohen 1981, xxvi). For example, in his work *The Protestant Ethic and the Spirit of Capitalism,* Weber sees Calvinism as a specific example of substantive rationality that helped give birth to the formal rationality of modern capitalism. Calvinism was a substantively rational system in which a coherent set of values led the individual to behave as a nascent capitalist. However, once the formally rational system of capitalism was set in motion, it no longer needed the substantive rationality of Calvinism. As Weber put it, "victorious capitalism, since it rests on mechanical foundations, needs its [Calvinism's] support no longer" (1904–5/1958, 181–82). (Weber also uses machine imagery to describe the bureaucracy: "that animated machine . . . busy fabricating the shell of bondage" [1921/1978, 2:1402–3]) Not only did capitalism no longer need Calvinism, but it pushed it into the realm of the irrational. Furthermore, formal rationality served to destroy substantive rationality in general, and religious substantive rationality in particular. In other words, formal rationality served to demystify and disenchant the modern world. On the issue of formally rational bureaucracies, Weber argues: "The march of bureaucracy accordingly destroyed structures of domination which were not rational in this [formally rational] sense of the term. Hence we can ask: What were these structures?" (1921/1978, 1:102). The structures that were destroyed were forms of domination such as patriarchalism and patrimonialism. These can be seen as substantively rational in the sense that they are characterized by norms derived from tradition rather than the enacted norms of formally rational bureaucracies.

On a more general level, Weber sometimes talks as if formal rationality will eventually leave little room for any other type of rationality (or, for that matter, for anything else): "Thus, discipline inexorably takes over ever larger areas as the satisfaction of political and economic needs is increasingly rationalized. This universal phenomenon more and more restricts the importance of charisma and of individually differentiated conduct" (Weber 1921/1968, 3:1156). While charisma is often used in Weber's work for nonrational, or even antirational, action, "individually differentiated conduct" could apply to the other three types of rationality. That is, each of the other types exerts less control over the actor and each allows for greater differences from one individual to another than formal rationality.

While Weber is less explicit about the destruction of practical and theoretical rationality, it seems clear that his image of the iron cage of formal rationality leaves little place for either in the modern world. The rules and regulations of formally rational systems dictate what is to be done. As a result, there is little room or need for people to practically figure out the best means to an end. Similarly, there is little need for people to theoretically order situations since that order is provided by the formally rational system.

While Weber does not develop a notion of hyperrationality, he does discuss the relationships among subtypes of rationality in a variety of ways. At some points he is concerned with the conflict among these subtypes, while at others he is interested in possible coexistences among these subtypes. Thus, Kalberg discusses "the manner in which types of rationality *combine* or *struggle* against one another in history in separate rationalization processes" (1980, 1146; our italics). While we have some things to say about the conflicts, our main interest given our concern with hyperrationality (which involves the coexistence of all four subtypes of rationality) is with Weber's thoughts on the various possibilities for coexistence.

Looking at substantive rationality and its conflicts first, the immediacy of practical rationality comes into conflict with the broader orientation of substantive rationality. As Weber puts it, "the conflict between empirical reality and [substantive rationality's] conception of the world as a meaningful totality, which is based on the religious postulate, produces the strongest tensions in man's inner life as well as in his external relationship to the world" (1921/1978, 1:451). Substantive rationality can also come into conflict with theoretical rationality, as, for example, in the case of the tendency for the substantive rationality of salvation religions to "directly or indirectly" call for the " 'sacrifice of the intellect' in the interests of a trans-intellectual, distinctive religious quality of absolute surrender and utter trust" in God (Weber 1921/1978, 1:567). Finally, of course, and of paramount concern to Weber, is the conflict between substantive rationality and formal rationality. Thus, Kalberg concludes: "Formal rationalities have stood in the most direct antagonism to many substantive rationalities" (1980, 1157). For example, in discussing the relationship between a formally rational capitalist economy and the substantive rationality of Calvinism (and its ethic of brotherliness), Weber (1958, 331) argues that such an economy follows "its own immanent laws" and grows less likely to have "any imaginable relationship with a religious ethic of brotherliness." Elsewhere, Weber contends that "the people filled with the spirit of capitalism today tend to be indifferent, if not hostile, to the Church" (1904–5/1958, 70). Turning to modern politics, Weber argues that "every ethical religion must, in similar measure and for similar reasons, experience tensions with the sphere of political behavior" (1921/1978, 1:590). The matter-of-factness of formally rational political behavior appears "to an ethic of brotherliness to be estranged from brotherliness" (1958, 335). In law, Weber contends that substantive justice will inevitably conflict with the "formalism and the rule bound and cool 'matter-of-factness' of bureaucratic administration" (1921/1978, 1:220–21).

Most of Weber's explicit attention to conflict is devoted to a discussion of the struggles between substantive rationality and the other rationality types. However, conflicts among these other rationality types are implicit in his work. The mundanity of practical rationality clashes with the abstraction of theoretical rationality and the creativity involved in practical rationality comes into conflict with the rule-governed character of formal rationality. The abstract search by people for answers about the world around them in theoretical rationality is likely to be stifled by the rules and regulations of formally rational systems.

Weber's thoughts on the conflicts among rationality types are important here for two very different reasons. First, they show, albeit in a negative way, that there *are* relationships among the rationality types. Second, they represent a body of ideas that need to be overcome in order to get at the idea of hyperrationality. That is, if these conflicts are inevitable and insurmountable, then there can be no coexistences among subtypes of rationality, and, if this is so, then there can be no such thing as hyperrationality. However, Weber himself shows that they can be overcome by offering a series of ideas on the coexistence of the various types of rationality.

Unfortunately, Weber's ideas on coexistence are neither as clear nor as explicit as his thoughts on conflict among rationality types. One exception is found in his ideas on the relationship between theoretical and practical rationality in which he concludes, in spite of the conflicts, that "ultimately they belong inseparably together" (1958, 293). More specifically, the use of abstract ideas can help effect the "methodical attainment of a definitely given and practical end by means of an increasingly precise calculation of adequate means" (1958, 293). In making sense of the world around them, intellectuals surely are of help in the solution of practical problems. Another exception is found in Weber's thoughts on the linkage between substantive and practical rationality where he argues that "to the extent that an inner-worldly religion of salvation is determined by distinctly ascetical tendencies, it always demands a practical rationalism, in the sense of the maximization of rational action as such" (1921/1978, 1:551). On the relationship between practical and formal rationality, Weber writes that the development of economic rationalism "though it is partly dependent on rational technique and law, it is at the same time determined by the ability and disposition of men to adopt certain types of practical rational conduct" (1904–5/1958, 21). On theoretical and substantive rationality, Weber claims that "the destiny of religions has been influenced in a most comprehensive way by intellectualism and its various relationships to the priesthood and political authorities" (1921/1978, 1:500). Weber implies a linkage between theoretical and formal rationality in lawmaking and lawfinding in arguing that "they are formally irrational when one applies in lawmaking and lawfinding means which cannot be controlled by the intellect, for instance when recourse is had to oracles or substitutes therefor" (1921/1978, 1:656).

Most strikingly, even formal and substantive rationality can coexist in Weberian theory. Weber writes that "formal and substantive rationality, no matter by what standard the latter is measured, are always in principle separate things, no matter that in many (and under certain very artificial assumptions even in all) cases they may coincide empirically" (1921/1978, 1:108). Specifically, Weber states that substantive values can exist within formally rational capitalism if there is the "provision of a certain minimum of subsistence for the maximum size of the population" (1921/1978, 1:108). When this occurs, and Weber claimed that it had within the last few decades of his lifetime, "formal and substantive rationality coincide to a relatively high degree" (1921/1978, 1:109). In discussing sacred law, Weber argues that the Occidental church combined formal legal technique with substantive legislation and moral ends (1921/1968, 2:829). Finally, Weber implies a coexistence of practical, substantive, and formal rationality when he argues that entrepreneurs must possess a "radical concentration on God-ordained purposes; the relentless and practical rationalism of the asceticist; and methodical conception of matter-of-factness in business management" (1916/1964, 247).

Thus, while Weber does not develop a full-scale sense of the mutual interrelatedness of all four types of rationality, he clearly recognized a variety of coexistences. It is by extending Weber's limited thoughts on coexistence that we can begin to get at the concept of hyperrationality. In doing so, the sense in Weber's work that formal rationality will ultimately and inevitably triumph over the other three types needs to be rejected. It seems clear that Weber did not foresee a future in which all four types of rationality would coexist and feed off one another to produce a level of rationality unseen in his day.

In this section, we have offered a demonstration of the roots of the idea of hyperrationality in Weberian theory. However, this new theoretical concept was created not only on the basis of a metatheoretical (M_p) study of the work of Weber and the neo-Weberians, but also out of an analysis of contemporary Japanese industry. We found that the Weberian hypothesis that formal rationality would triumph over the other types did not hold in the case of Japanese industry. Rather, the Japanese appear to have created an industrial system in which all four types of rationality coexist and feed off one another to produce a hyperrational industrial system.

Hyperrationality: The Case of Japanese Industry

Formal Rationality

While it certainly had indigenous examples of formal rationality (see below) that predated the American occupation of Japan after World War II, a number of formally rational ideas and systems were imported into Japan at the close of the war in an effort to make it more self-sufficient economically.[5] Japanese industry adopted the ideas of W. Edwards Deming and J. M. Juran, both American experts in statistical quality control, in particular their efforts to control production in general, and quality in particular, through the quantification of as many factors as possible. (In fact, quantification is one of the crucial dimensions of a formally rational system [Ritzer 1983]). Overall, the importation of Western formal rationality provided a shortcut to the modernization of industry; resulted in the saving of enormous amounts of time and money; provided a powerful incentive to set up new factories; and made it possible for these factories to be quickly provided with the most up-to-date technologies.

The late importation of these ideas (the West had been utilizing them for many decades) and systems into a society that already had strong substantive, theoretical, and practical rationality helps to explain why formal rationality did not triumph over these other forms. It was the formal rationality that was largely foreign, and while it was adopted, it was forced to accept and accommodate itself to the other types of rationality.

Japanese industry has not contented itself with the importation of Western formal rationality. It has its own indigenous forms, most of which have been developed in recent decades. One formally rational structure in existence prior to the importation of Western formal rationality, and which helped to allow it to prosper on Japanese soil, was the Ministry of International Trade and Industry (MITI) (Johnson 1982). In brief, MITI is a formally rational bureaucratic structure that has the (formally rational) responsibility of overseeing Japan's industries in order to be sure that their individual and collective success maximizes the interest of the nation as a whole. In effect, the objective of MITI is to organize in a rational manner the entire structure of Japanese industry (Vogel 1979, 72). Among other things MITI encourages long-range planning. Long-term thinking at MITI involves the extension of formal rationality to future planning. This gives Japan an enormous advantage over American industry where formal rationality has been employed largely in the service of short-term maximization. With MITI, the Japanese have, in effect, created a second formally rational system with its own bureaucratic branches, sectors, and hierarchical levels to oversee the formally rational industrial and business sector.

Another distinctively Japanese formally rational development is the "Just-in-Time" (JIT) system. The JIT system involves producing and delivering finished goods just in time to be sold, subassemblies just in time to be assembled into finished products, fabricated parts just in time to go into subassemblies, and purchased materials just in time to be transformed into fabricated parts. One could say that the Japanese produce small quantities just in time, while, in contrast, industries in the United States produce large quantities "just in case" (Schonberger 1982, 16). The JIT system is clearly more formally rational than the Western Just-In-Case system (JIC). For example, the greater calculability associated with JIT leads to lower inventories and greater profits.

Finally, there are the bureaucratic systems that are integral to Japanese manufacturing. In many ways these systems are more bureaucratic, more formally rational, than Western bureaucracies. For example, one must have had the "right" education, including attendance at one of the imperial universities, in order to qualify for a position within these organizations. Entry into the organizations is governed by tough entrance examinations that *all* prospective employees must take. All those who are hired in a specific job track must move through the hierarchy together as a group and at the same pace. All of these workers are regularly rotated to a variety of different positions and departments. In these and other ways, Japanese bureaucracies are more formally rational than their Western counterparts which exercise far less control over individuals and permit much more individual variation in movement through the system.

This high degree of formal rationality paradoxically permits, and even encourages, a higher degree of substantive rationality in Japanese bureaucracies. Because the formally rational system runs so smoothly and effectively, the Japanese can allow greater flexibility in a variety of realms. For example, there are fewer status distinctions between managers and subordinates, white-collar and blue-collar workers, and so on. Responsibilities of one position are less clearly distinguished from those of other positions; there is more blending of roles and positions. Japanese workers are dominated by fewer rules and required to process far less paperwork. Workers are more likely to be viewed as people rather than as interchangeable bureaucratic parts. Managers and employees are far more flexible in terms of what they do and how they do it. This flexibility tends to lead to greater experimentation and openness to the generation and testing of new ideas. While in the West formal rationality tends to submerge substantive rationality, in Japan formal rationality is more likely to encourage and work hand-in-hand with substantive rationality. Given this convergence, let us turn more directly to some examples of substantive rationality within Japanese industry.

Substantive Rationality

Japan has been able to retain a consistent set of human values, which includes groupism; interdependence; *wa* (harmony); *on* (debt), and *giri* (obligation). In contrast, Western nations have tended to lose, or see a deterioration of, such a value system (Vogel 1979, 98). This system in Japan tends *to work in concert with* formal rationality while in the West it has tended *to lose out* to formal rationality.

Japanese groupism contrasts sharply with the individualism of the West. While in individualism the individual is opposed to the group, in groupism the goal is for the individual and the group to become one. A view is encouraged in which individual interests equal group interests and group interests equal individual interests (Iwata 1982, 39). Americans try to position themselves in society as individuals, and they attempt to restrict mutual relations both functionally and in terms of duration of encounters. In contrast, the Japanese are inclined to position themselves in society in terms of the group(s) with which they are affiliated. The word *individualism* in Japanese denotes selfishness, isolation from others, and persons concerned only with their own advantage rather than being willing to work for the welfare of others. The person weakens the group by being individualistic, while everyone gains when all seek to make the group more efficient (Alston 1986, 34).

There are a number of manifestations of Japanese groupism. For example, individual failure is minimized; failure is shared among the members of the work group. On the other hand, the group receives credit for any successes. There is intense group pressure to produce and to produce high-quality goods and services. It is not unusual for workers to stay late until everyone has finished their work. Japanese companies develop an ideology (Rohlen 1975, 208) that is similar to that of the traditional Japanese family (Alston 1986, 27). As in their families, the Japanese are devoted to their companies and in return they receive the kind of *amae* (caring) that they receive in the family setting. For the Japanese work and play are tightly intertwined; work groups and play groups tend to be one in the same.

As a result of groupism, corporate success in Japan is seen as resulting from group effort rather than from the activities of exceptional individuals (in the United States the opposite is true). Work groups, teams, and departments are seen as the reason why the company improves productivity or exceeds quotas.

Derived from groupism, with roots in Confucianism, is the concept of *wa*, the quest for harmony, unity, and cooperation. *Wa* exists at both the cultural level and more specifically in the family, schools, clubs, and the workplace (Pegels 1984, 67). Like groupism, *wa* operates against individualism since it demands considerable conformity. At the level of the industrial organization, it is manifested in consensus-type decision making and strong respect by each individual for all others. *Wa* is maintained through a strong team spirit; members must identify with the group and be loyal to it and its goals. Because *wa* is so important, Japanese leaders often feel that they can only lead when they know where their followers want to go. The act of reaching a consensus can be more important than what has been agreed to (Taylor 1983, 115). One by-product of *wa* is that superordinates and subordinates feel responsible for one another; *wa* helps bind them together (Pegels 1984, 73). Subordinates care about matters that in the United States are considered the sole responsibility of the supervisor. In turn, supervisors feel responsible for subordinates and their behavior both in and out of the work place.

At one level, the substantive rationality of *wa* helps to counter the excesses of formal rationality. For example, unlike in the West, the employee is not depersonalized or treated like a machine or an appendage to one (De Vos 1975, 218). For another, the Japanese will not use formally rational techniques if they threaten the *wa* (Alston 1986, 124).

Groupism and *wa* (as well as the other components of this value system) have permitted the Japanese to develop their distinctive system of permanent employment,[6] a system that can be seen as being composed of both formally and substantively rational elements. It is made possible because workers feel it necessary to be loyal to the group and the members would feel they were being disloyal if they left for another employer. For their part, it would be morally reprehensible for an employer to discard a worker because he or she was no longer needed. Permanent employment reinforces, and is reinforced by, groupism and *wa*. The Japanese tend to view themselves as workers for Toyota, who happen to have a set of skills (e.g., as welders). In contrast, Americans see themselves as welders, who happen to work for Ford. The Japanese system obviously helps to engender a far greater commitment to the employing organization. The Japanese view learning a skill and then moving on to another company, a common American practice, as selfish behavior.

While it is in many ways substantively rational, permanent employ-

ment also has many formally rational attributes. For example, standardized entrance exams are used to find those employees who are most likely
to contribute to the organization over the course of many years. For another, a hierarchy is employed to allow permanent employees to move up
in the organization over time. For still another, periodic wage increases
are based on a clearly defined seniority system so that those in whom the
company has invested heavily are motivated to remain in the company.
Furthermore, because pay is heavily tied to seniority, pay differences are
comparatively insignificant and this reduces conflict within work groups
and cohorts. All workers tend to do well together when the company is
prospering and to suffer together in bad times.

Permanent employment is not only formally rational in a number of
ways, but it also encourages the development of a series of formally rational by-products. For example, because the company is sure that its
employees will remain, it can engage in long-range planning of personnel
allocation and development. For another, because it is assured of a stable
pool of competent workers, the company is better able to make long-
range predictions about other aspects of its operation (e.g., long-term
production levels). More generally, long-term employment encourages a
longer-term perspective throughout the organization. In contrast, in the
United States employees and managers rarely are enthusiastic about anything but projects that get short-term results. In the United States, the
likelihood that one is going to change companies operates against a long-
term perspective.

Other aspects of permanent employment encourage heightened substantive rationality. For example, because they feel secure, managers are
willing to take risks, to experiment, and to test out new ideas. Managers
also tend to be more flexible than their American counterparts because
of their greater security. For another, because they are safe from layoffs,
Japanese workers will do their best even in the worst economic times. In
contrast, American workers may be paralyzed by a fear of an imminent
layoff and their anger may directly result in poor performance if they are
told they are to be laid off. Thus, here, as elsewhere, substantive rationality and formal rationality work together in Japan to produce a higher
level of overall rationality.

Theoretical Rationality

Japanese society in general, and industry in particular, have also been able
to maintain and develop theoretical rationality. From the national government to the individual firm, few things take precedence over the acquisition and development of knowledge and information (Vogel 1979,
27). At the societal level this is manifested in widely circulated newspapers

imparting highly technical information, a well-supported system of educational television, and a very active book publishing and book translation business.

For the Japanese, study and education continue well beyond the end of formal education. After they have been employed, workers are encouraged to participate in work-related study. Off the job, workers often look for opportunities to learn things that one day *may* be of use to them on the job (Vogel 1979, 28–9). This commitment to continuing education is made possible by the existence of the formally and substantively rational system of permanent employment which makes (some) employees willing to invest the time needed to learn and employers willing to pay the costs involved. This educational commitment is also supported by the substantively rational groupism and *wa* because employees are willing to do what is necessary for the welfare of the collectivity. Conversely, the collectivity, the employing organization in this case, wants to help the members improve themselves through education.

However, the major examples of the Japanese industrial emphasis on theoretical rationality are their commitment to engineering and research and development. This commitment may be linked to Japan's high literacy rate, as well as to its peoples' general knowledge of mathematics, economics, and basic engineering. In terms of engineering, Japan has substantially more engineers in senior management positions than the United States and graduates more engineers each year than any other Western country. In the workplace, Japanese industries employ many more engineers and rely on them far more heavily than do their Western counterparts.

The focus on research and development (R&D) is reflected in the fact that in the 1960s Japan's exports were heavily concentrated in industries (e.g., textiles, iron, steel, automobiles) with low investments in R&D, but in the 1980s the concentration shifted to those sectors (e.g., electronics, production processes, and biotechnology) that require large investments in R&D. Japanese industry has long passed the stage of being reliant on Western technology. Reflecting this reality, Japan currently registers two and a half times the number of patents as the United States, and eight times the rate of Great Britain.

At the national level, Japan spends 2.01 percent of its GNP on R&D. Although this figure appears to compare unfavorably to that spent by such Western nations as the United States (2.47 percent) and West Germany (2.24 percent), comparatively little of the Japanese investment goes into research related to national defense. Most of it (about three-fourths) is spent in the private sector, especially on commercial product development. In contrast, the U.S. spends much of its research and development money on national defense and space projects that tend to produce often spectacular developments with little commercial application (McMillan

1984, 117). Another difference between Japan and the West is that Japan's scientists are not as academically oriented as their Western counterparts. Many scientists in the West are in university settings where their focus is on publication and success in the scientific community. Many Western scientists employed in the commercial sector share these objectives. In contrast, in Japan the main rewards and career incentives for scientists lie in the corporation. Even university-based scientists work in close association with corporations, which often provide access, consultation, research support, and may even publish research findings provided by university researchers (McMillan 1984, 102).

The strong emphasis on theoretical rationality is linked to, and reinforces, the other types of rationality discussed above. For example, the substantively rational groupism and *wa* contribute to the commitment of scientists and engineers to their employers and to their eagerness to contribute their knowledge and expertise to the latter's success and well-being. The provision of this information, in turn, strengthens the collectivity and its *wa*. Permanent employment is also involved since engineers and scientists see that they will spend their entire worklives with an employer and are willing to contribute knowledge and information to the organization that will be their occupational home for life. Permanent employment also encourages engineers and scientists (and their employers) to invest the time and money in continual reeducation so that they stay abreast of the most recent developments. The long-range perspective produced by permanent employment allows engineers and scientists to work on projects that may not see tangible results, let alone profitable undertakings, for many years to come. Turning to formal rationality, MITI serves to encourage emphasis on science and engineering by its efforts to encourage technological developments within designated industrial sectors.

Practical Rationality

While in the United States practical rationality, like substantive and theoretical rationality, has been allowed to languish, the Japanese have encouraged it to coexist with, and contribute to, the other types of rationality. One manifestation of the Japanese commitment to retain practical rationality is their "bottom-up" management philosophy (including the *ringi* system of having documents originate with lower-level managers) which contrasts greatly with the "top-down" approach characteristic of the United States. While American managers focus on imposing decisions on lower echelons in the organization, the Japanese are interested in allowing lower-level supervisors to define problems and then work to solve them (Pegels 1984, 4). In many Japanese companies the key figures are lower-level department heads and division chiefs, rather than high-level executives. It is the lower-level managers who tend to work out the details of day-to-day planning. When top-down decisions do occur, Japanese executives go out of their way to disguise them and make them appear as if they resulted from bottom-up decision making (Gibney 1982, 61). As a result of this management approach, Japanese organizations get greater contributions from managers throughout the organizational hierarchy. In other words, the organization is able to give free reign to the practical rationality of its lower-level managers and to enjoy the gains from that rationality.

This bottom-up, practical rationality is reinforced by the substantive rationality of groupism and *wa*. That is, Japanese executives can feel secure in giving lower-level managers considerable leeway because they are assured that such managers will work for the good of the company rather than slacking off or working for their own interests. Furthermore, it can safely be assumed that subordinate managers will not attack top management policies or undermine an executive's authority. Bottom-up management also contributes to the formal rationality of the organization. That is, the ideas that flow from lower-level managers help in various ways to improve the functioning of such formally rational structures as the assembly-lines and bureaucracies. This is nowhere clearer than in another aspect of practical rationality in Japan, quality circles. While the bottom-up and *ringi* systems elicit the practical rationality of lower-level managers, quality circles are designed to extract and utilize the practical rationality of lower-level workers.

The concern for quality at the level of the worker has been institutionalized in "quality control circles" (QCs). The Japanese commitment to quality has been institutionalized in the QC which is nothing more than a group of workers (usually led by the immediate supervisor) who meet on a regular basis to identify, analyze, and find solutions to quality problems (as well as other issues). Because of the substantive rationality of groupism and *wa*, workers are willing to voluntarily meet, often during their off-hours. The idea behind this system is simple: because everyone possesses and practices practical rationality, workers often have ideas on how to improve their work process. The brainstorming sessions that occur in QCs allow people to express these ideas. Members of the QCs are encouraged not to be encumbered by the way things are currently done on the job, so that they will be more inclined to generate new, creative ideas. The Japanese have thus been able to exploit the practical rationality of those in the organization, particularly at the bottom of the organization, while in the West formally rational systems have ignored this and even tried to actively suppress it so that those at the bottom blindly conform to the demands of the formally rational system.

Like all of the other types of rationality in Japan, practical rationality reinforces, and is reinforced by, the other types of rationality. For example, the theoretically rational emphasis on knowledge and information supports the effort to utilize the skills and abilities of the lowest ranking members of the organization. Because of the substantively rational emphasis on groupism and *wa,* it can be assumed that workers will utilize initiative without fear that they will exploit these opportunities for their own benefit. The substantively and formally rational system of permanent employment encourages participation in QC circles because such involvement assumes, and reinforces, dedication among workers to the employing organization. Further, the high-speed operations of the formally rational JIT system requires that all workers be vigilant on the issue of quality.

Synergy

In the preceding discussion we have sought to demonstrate that Japanese industry is hyperrational in the sense that the four types of rationality exist simultaneously. This situation stands in contrast to the American case where the triumph of formal rationality led to the decline, or even disappearance, of the other three types of rationality. The coexistence of the four types of rationality may be seen as hyperrationality in the weak sense of the term. In a stronger sense, hyperrationality means that the four types of rationality interact with one another and out of this interaction emerges a heightened, historically unprecedented level of rationality, hyperrationality. In other words, there is a synergism among the four types of rationality so that their simultaneous interaction with one another produces a more rational system that would occur if we simply summed the effect of the four types of rationality, taken separately. Throughout the preceding discussion, a number of the synergistic aspects of hyperrationality have been underscored.

The goal in this discussion of Japanese industry has been to show how the concept of hyperrationality, derived previously from the Weberian theory of rationality, has also been derived from the case of the recent history of Japanese history. Thus, rather than being simply an abstract conceptual creation, hyperrationality is a historically saturated ideal type. Having discussed hyperrationality as it is manifest in the specific case of Japanese industry, we turn now to the creation of hyperrationality as an ideal type. The ideal type to be constructed below is a product of *both* the analysis of Japanese industry in this section and, more importantly, the conceptual analysis presented in the preceding section.

Hyperrationality: An Ideal-Typical Characterization

Consistent with its Weberian roots and its Weberian orientation, the concept of hyperrationality is discussed here in ideal-typical terms. In developing this ideal type we are following various guidelines laid down by Weber. The ideal type is to be rigorously rational and internally consistent. It involves the analytical accentuation of certain elements of reality. It resembles a utopian vision, although *not* in the sense that the social world "ought" to operate in this manner. Thus, the ideal type is unlikely to correspond exactly with any empirical reality (even Japanese industry). It is conceptually and historically derived. It is adequate both empirically and on the level of meaning (Weber 1921/1968, 1:20). It is a methodological tool that is abstracted from reality and that can be used to help us to better understand social reality. It is both transhistorical and transcultural, which means that it can be used to analyze a variety of historical periods and a variety of different societies. And, of course, the construction of an ideal type is not an end in itself, but rather a tool for empirical research.

The ideal type of hyperrationality has four elements:

First, hyperrationality involves the simultaneous existence of practical, theoretical, substantive, and formal rationality. All of the subtypes of rationality are used here in the way they are conventionally used by Weber and neo-Weberians.

Second, each of these subtypes exists to a high degree. That is, in a hyperrational system it is not just important that all four types exist, but that each of them flourishes. There is a high degree of practical, theoretical, substantive, and formal rationality in a hyperrational system.

Third, each of the subtypes of rationality is interrelated with all of the others.

Finally, out of this interaction a new level and type of rationality emerges; hyperrationality is an emergent phenomenon. This means that there is a synergism among the four types of rationality allowing for the emergence of an extraordinarily high level of rationality.

Implications

Various issues emerge from this analysis of hyperrationality that are worth at least mentioning in this closing section. For example, there is the issue of the utilization of the ideal type of hyperrationality. While it is derived in part from Japanese industry, it can be used as a tool to analyze particular Japanese industries, compare industries, and to analyze Japanese society as a whole. The ideal type of hyperrationality can also be used to analyze the industries of other societies, most importantly, American industry. The use of this tool can allow us to pinpoint the factors that are lacking in American industry from the point of view of ideal-typical hyperrationality. This, in effect, becomes a *sociological* way of helping one understand the recent failures of American industry in comparison to

Japanese industry. To a similar end, one could compare ideal-typical hyperrationality to the ideal-typical formal rationality which, following Weber, is associated with American industry as well as the West in general. The isolation of differences, as well as similarities, between these two forms of rationality would be a prelude to a causal analysis of why America moved in the direction of formal rationality while Japan moved toward hyperrationality.

Another line of analysis would be to trace out the implication of a hyperrational economy for other social institutions. Following Weber, Japan's hyperrational economy would need, among other things, a compatible political system as well as an educational system that produces the kind of people needed by such an economy.

As an ideal type, hyperrationality is a methodological utopia, but it is not an ideal in the sense that society, all societies, should move toward hyperrationality. Nor does it lead us to ignore the problems associated with hyperrationality. Just as Weber was ambivalent about formal rationality, seeing it both as liberating and enslaving, we have a similar ambivalence about hyperrationality. For example, while as we have seen hyperrationality as practiced in Japan has produced unparalleled growth, it has done so by enslaving people in a system that can be seen as unprecedented in its ability to exploit workers. A systematic study of Japanese-style hyperrationality would need to tease out both its liberating and enslaving dimensions.

Then there is the question of the future of Japanese and American society and industry. Given the relative success of Japanese industrial hyperrationality vis-à-vis American industry's formal rationality, can we assume that America will seek to emulate Japanese success by importing elements of Japanese hyperrationality just as after World War II Japan imported American formal rationality? While there is some evidence that this has occurred to some degree (e.g., American use of quality circles), will a wholesale adoption of Japanese techniques work in the United States? More generally, as a result of Japanese successes, does the world confront an iron cage of hyperrationality that dwarfs in terms of its problematic dimensions Weber's iron cage of formal rationality? Or, since Weber was wrong about an iron cage of formal rationality, is it just as unlikely that we will see an iron cage of hyperrationality? Just as Weber did not foresee hyperrationality, are we now unable to foresee the next stage in the march of rationality? Or, will the future bring with it a reversal in the direction of a less rational society? Are there viable alternatives in the modern world to rationality, be it formal, or hyper, rationality?

As we saw in chapter 4, Weber had deep reservations about the triumph of formal rationality. It is unlikely that the emergence and seeming supremacy of hyperrationality would ease Weber's fears. In fact, it seems likely that he would view the "polar night of icy darkness and hardness" of hyperrationality as even darker and harder.

Conclusions

One of the things the preceding section, as well as the chapter as a whole, demonstrates is the relevance of metatheorizing, in this case the use of M_P, to the social world. However, the main objective of this chapter has been to offer an example of M_P. Specifically, a metatheoretical analysis of the Weberian theory of rationality, in concert with an empirical examination of Japanese industry, has generated a new theoretical concept: hyperrationality.

Notes

1. This concept, as it is used here, was suggested by Ritzer and Walczak (1988). It is used in a very different way by Berger and Berger (1984, 118–20).

2. In this chapter we focus on Weber's substantive work, while in the last chapter the focus was on the underlying structure of his work.

3. In this case the task of the neo-Weberian is much like that of the neo-Marxian. Both Marx and Weber offered vast, complex, sometimes vague, sometimes internally contradictory theories of the modern world. The result is that multiple interpretations of these theories are possible and they can be defended by recourse to the work of the master as well as to that of the significant interpreters who have followed in his footsteps.

4. See Ritzer and LeMoyne (1990) for the details of the Japanese case.

5. Because the focus in this book is on metatheorizing, this section on the empirical sources of the concept of hyperrationality will be presented in a greatly abbreviated fashion. For much more on this, see Ritzer and LeMoyne (1990). In addition to leaving out much detail, this discussion also omits many of the problems associated with Japanese hyperrationality. The reader should not come away from a reading of this section with the view that Japanese hyperrationality is an unmitigated success. Indeed, it can be seen as permitting an unprecedented level of exploitation.

6. It should be noted that this system covers only a small percentage of Japanese workers.

6
The 1960s: Sociology, a Multiple Paradigm Science

A variety of tools have proven attractive to metatheorists interested in gaining a deeper understanding of theory (M_U) and more generally to metasociologists seeking to better understand the nature of sociology as a whole. While the architectonic I utilized in chapter 4 is a somewhat unusual tool, the *paradigm* concept has been widely employed and is extremely useful; that concept provides the basis for the analysis undertaken in this chapter. While the focus in this chapter is on American sociology as a whole, most of the chapter is devoted to attaining a more specific comprehension of American sociological theory.

The period of concern here is primarily the 1960s, although the multiparadigmatic status of sociology certainly predated that decade and did not disappear with the arrival of the 1970s. But the decade of the 1960s alone is best defined by the coexistence of multiple paradigms. A complete history of sociological theory will not be offered in this book, since one of my main objectives is to illustrate what metatheorizing has to offer to an understanding of that history (Ritzer 1991a). And what metatheory does provide, at least as it is used here, is a series of highly informative glimpses into that history. In the absence of such a history, it should be noted that in the decades prior to the 1960s sociology was dominated by structural functionalism. And, as we will see in later chapters, the decades after the 1960s were defined by a range of other theoretical developments.

The Ideas of Thomas Kuhn

The work of Thomas Kuhn (1962, 1970b) has provided an attractive metasystem to sociologists interested in analyzing the status of their field. One of the best known of these efforts is Robert Friedrich's *A Sociology of Sociology* (1970), but there are others, including works by Effrat (1972), Lodahl and Gordon (1972), Phillips (1973), Eisenstadt and Curelaru (1976), Strasser (1976), Colclough and Horan (1983), Falk and Zhao (1989), Falk and Zhao (1990) and Rosenberg (1989), as well as my own (Ritzer 1975c, 1975d, 1981b), on which this chapter is based. My goal here is to apply Kuhn's ideas, especially the paradigm concept, to sociology in general, and to sociological theory in particular, as they existed largely in the 1960s.

Kuhn sees a science at any given point in time as dominated by a specific paradigm (defined for the moment as a fundamental image of a science's subject matter). *Normal science* is a period of accumulation of knowledge in which scientists work on, and expand, the reigning paradigm. Inevitably, however, such work spawns *anomalies,* or things that cannot be explained within the existing paradigm. If these anomalies mount, a *crisis* stage is reached, which ultimately may end in a *revolution* during which the reigning paradigm is overthrown and a new one takes its place at the center of the science. Thus *a new reigning paradigm* is born and the stage is set for the cycle to repeat itself. It is during the period of revolution that great changes in scientific status take place. This view clearly places Kuhn at odds with the lay and textbook conceptions of scientific development, which suggest that scientific "progress" is cumulative.

The key term in Kuhn's model, and the one that is the backbone of this chapter, is his concept of a *paradigm.* Unfortunately, the concept of a paradigm is elusive; according to Masterman (1970), Kuhn uses the term in at least 21 different ways. In response to those who criticized his vagueness about the concept in his first edition, Kuhn offers a very narrow definition of a paradigm in the epilogue to the second edition. There he equates paradigms with exemplars, or "the concrete puzzle solutions which when employed as models or examples, can replace explicit rules as a basis for the solution of the remaining puzzles of normal science" (Kuhn 1970b, 175).

There is another reason for this narrow definition of a paradigm. As Kuhn (1970b, 191) himself notes, his original work was criticized for its "subjectivity and irrationality." The thrust of the first edition pointed in the direction of a very broad definition of a paradigm (as a "disciplinary matrix") encompassing "the entire constellation of beliefs, values, techniques, and so on shared by the members of a given community" (Kuhn 1970b, 175). (By 1970, Kuhn views this as an "inappropriate" use of the term *paradigm,* primarily because it makes science appear to be irrational.) The paradigm defines what scientists should and should not study; the paradigm tells scientists where, and where not, to look for the entities of concern to them; the paradigm tells scientists what they can expect when they find, and examine, the entities of concern to them. Thus the entire scientific craft is determined by the nature of the dominant paradigm. Furthermore, that craft will be radically altered when one paradigm is superseded by another paradigm. Kuhn sees the emergence of a new paradigm, at least in the first edition of his work, as a distinctly political phenomenon. One paradigm wins out over another because its supporters have more *power* than those who support competing paradigms and *not* necessarily because their paradigm is "better" than its competitors. For example, the paradigm whose supporters control the most important journals in a field and thereby determine what will be published is more likely to gain preeminence than paradigms whose adherents lack access to prestigious outlets for their work. Similarly, positions of leadership in a field are likely to be given to supporters of the dominant paradigm, and these leadership positions give them a platform to enunciate their position with a significant amount of legitimacy. Supporters of paradigms that are seeking to gain hegemony within a field are obviously at a disadvantage since they lack the kinds of power outlined above. Nevertheless, they can, by waging a political battle of their own, overthrow a dominant paradigm and gain that position for their own orientation.

In general, supporters of one paradigm make little effort to understand the basic tenets of its competitors. Instead, they are likely to launch attacks aimed at discrediting the validity of competing paradigms. The goal is not to understand the other paradigms, but to annihilate supporters of competing paradigms with verbal assaults.

In these, and many other ways, the emergence of a new paradigm, or the failure of one to emerge, may be attributed to political factors rather than to the relative "scientific" merits of the paradigms. This is not to deny that the relative "scientific" merits of a paradigm are important to its success. The point is that a meritorious paradigm cannot gain hegemony without first engaging in, and ultimately winning, the political conflict. Moreover, a less meritorious paradigm can first gain and then maintain hegemony through political means despite its lack of "scientific" assets.

In a later article, and in response to his critics, Kuhn argues that one paradigm wins out over another for "good" reasons, including "accuracy, scope, simplicity, fruitfulness and the like" (1970a, 261). Thus Kuhn seems to be retreating to a more "scientific" conception of scientific revolutions. "Good reasons" have replaced irrationality and political factors. This equivocation, like others in his later work, has, in my opinion, worked to the detriment of Kuhn's perspective. Phillips argues that Kuhn's later work has left open the question that Kuhn began with: "Are there good objective reasons for scientists proceeding as they do, or do we merely term them good because they are endorsed by the members of a certain scientific community?" (1973, 19). In Phillips's view, and mine too, the weight of the evidence points in the direction of the latter interpretation. That is, notions like "accuracy, scope, simplicity, and fruitfulness would be regarded as paradigm dependent" (Phillips 1973, 18). Put another way, paradigms rise and fall as a result of political factors.

As a result of my rejection of some of Kuhn's later ideas, I offer the following definition of a paradigm which I feel is truer to the thrust of Kuhn's earlier work and one which is highly relevant to attaining a deeper understanding of sociology (and other fields): *A paradigm is a fundamental image of the subject matter within a science. It serves to define what should be studied, what questions should be asked, how they should be asked, and what rules should be followed in interpreting the answer obtained. A paradigm is the broadest unit of consensus within a science and serves to differentiate one scientific community (or subcommunity) from another. It subsumes, defines, and interrelates the exemplars, theories, and methods and instruments that exist within it.*

It is important to underscore the point that in my view a paradigm has four basic components: (1) an exemplar,[1] or body of work that stands as a model for those who work within the paradigm; (2) an image of the subject matter; (3) theories; and (4) methods and instruments. Although a number of other components could conceivably be added (e.g., values), these additions would not increase significantly our ability to analyze the basic sociological paradigms.

The paradigm concept, as it is defined here in cognitive terms, can be used to analyze either scientific communities or subcommunities. At a given point in the history of some sciences, when consensus exists on a single paradigm, a paradigm can be seen as coterminous with the scientific community. These are what Masterman (1970) calls paradigmatic sciences; physics, during the era when the Newtonian perspective was preeminent, is a good example. However, most sciences, including contemporary sociology, lack a single overarching paradigm. They are, according to Masterman, multiple-paradigm sciences. In such sciences paradigms are related to the major subcommunities. It is this characteristic that allows us to apply the concept with equal facility to Newtonian physics and contemporary sociology.

American sociology, especially in the 1960s, was a multiple-paradigm science: each of its paradigms was competing for hegemony within the discipline as a whole as well as within virtually every subarea within sociology. Before identifying and delineating what I view as the three competing paradigms of sociology in the 1960s, I must first examine critically some early efforts to apply the paradigm concept to sociology.

Working with Kuhn's inadequate definition of a paradigm, Friedrichs (1970) examines the subject matter of sociology and proceeds to label almost every theory a paradigm, or at least a would-be paradigm. Thus system theory and conflict theory emerge as dominant sociological paradigms, with such a diverse lot as Marxism, dialectics, action theory, exchange theory, and phenomenology described as pretenders to that lofty status. However, as the definition used in this chapter makes clear, theories are *not* paradigms. Rather, theories are components of far broader paradigms. Because he lacks an adequate definition of a paradigm, Friedrichs mistakes theories for paradigms and thereby arrives at an overly splintered conception of the state of sociology.

Later in his analysis, Friedrichs seems to become concerned with his excessively fragmented conception of sociology and decides to differentiate between first- and second-order paradigms. He recognizes that the theories he has been calling paradigms may not be the "most controlling" fundamental images in sociology. So he relegates these theories to the status of second-order paradigms. The first order, or most controlling, paradigms in sociology relate to the image the sociologist has of "himself as a scientific agent," rather than to the scientist's basic image of the subject matter. There are only two such self-images in Friedrichs's view, the priestly and the prophetic, and they are the most controlling. This idea of first-order paradigms allows Friedrichs to make a much more parsimonious analysis of the paradigmatic status of sociology.

I have no quarrel with the differentiation between priestly and prophetic self-images, but I do not accept the necessity of resorting to this type of analysis. Friedrichs was forced to look for paradigms based on self-images because he was working with an inadequate definition of a paradigm as it relates to the subject matter of sociology. In my view, different images of the subject matter *are* the key paradigmatic splits in sociology.

Like Friedrichs, Effrat (1972) is faced with the problem of parsimony in his effort to analyze the paradigmatic status of sociology. Although he uses a reasonably good definition of a paradigm, Effrat also makes the error of mistaking theories for paradigms. This flaw leads him to create a cumbersome list of "paradigms" including Marxism, exchange theory, Freudian theory, Durkheimian theory, Weberian theory, Parsonsian theory, phenomenology, ethnomethodology, and symbolic interactionism. In addition, he enumerates a number of other theoretical perspectives that he is willing to call paradigms, and he implies that there are even more that he has not had time to discuss. If there really were so many paradigms in sociology, then the concept would be a useless tool for analyzing the status of the discipline. In fact, the paradigm concept *is* a useful instrument for analyzing sociology; its utility can be demonstrated by identifying and analyzing what I consider to be the three basic paradigms that characterized sociology in the United States in the 1960s: the *social facts, social definition,* and *social behavior* paradigms.

The Social Facts Paradigm

Exemplar. The exemplar for the social factist is clearly the work of Emile Durkheim, in particular *The Rules of Sociological Method* (1895/1964) and *Suicide* (1897/1951). In these works Durkheim developed and applied his concept of a social fact. Durkheim argued that social facts were to be *treated* as things external to individuals and coercive on them. He did *not* argue that they *were* things. They were only to be treated as things for purposes of sociological analysis. Social factists have tended to ignore this crucial equivocation in Durkheim's work and have proceeded to argue that social facts *are* things, real material entities. In addition, social factists have neglected the reality that a major type of social fact for Durkheim was the "social current," which is best seen as an intersubjective phenomenon rather than as a material entity. Paradox arises because, although Durkheim coined the term "social fact," some of the basic tenets of the social facts paradigm would be unacceptable to him. He would, I think, be comfortable with some aspects of the social definition paradigm. At numerous points in his work Durkheim makes it clear that he is concerned with the kinds of issues of concern to the social definitionist.[2] Just to give one example, Durkheim (cited in Lukes 1973, 498) contends "that sociology has not completely achieved its task so long as it has not penetrated into the mind of the individual in order to relate the institutions it seeks to explain to their psychological conditions."[3]

A more proximate piece of work can be seen as a clearer exemplar for the social facts paradigm: Charles K. Warriner's "Groups Are Real: A Reaffirmation" (1956). Although Warriner focuses on only one social fact, the group, the case that he makes could be made for any other social fact. Basically, Warriner upholds what he calls the realist position "that (1) the group is just as real as the person, but that (2) both are abstract, analytical units, and that (3) the group is understandable and explicable solely in terms of distinctly social processes and factors, not by reference to individual psychology" (1956, 550–51). This position, which best expresses the social facts paradigm, is the one Warriner defends: "The purpose here is calling attention to and defending the legitimacy and validity of the realist position, and to propose that this is the most valid and potentially fruitful sociological approach to the study of group and society" (1956, 551).

Following Warriner, social factists accept the reality of such social facts as groups, norms, institutions, or social systems. They focus on the study of these social facts and their coercive effect on the individual and they argue that a given social fact can only be explained by other social facts.

Image of the Subject Matter. The basic subject matter of sociology to those who adopt this paradigm is the social fact. A large number of phenomena could be labeled social facts, including roles, values, groups, society, the world-system, etc. Peter Blau (1960) performed a useful service by differentiating between two basic types of social facts: social structures and institutions.[4] Social factists are those sociologists who contend that the subject matter of sociology is social institutions and social structures. They argue further that an institution or structure can be explained only by other social facts. They view individuals, their social behavior, and their social activities as largely determined by social structures and social institutions.

Theories. A number of theories could be included within the social facts paradigm, but the two most important are structural-functionalism and conflict theory.

In perhaps the most important essay on structural-functionalism, Robert Merton (1968) makes it clear that it is oriented to the study of social facts when he says that the objects that can be subjected to structural-functional analysis must "represent a standardized (i.e., patterned and repetitive) item" (1968, 104). He offers the following examples of these items, all of which are clearly social facts: "Social roles, institutional patterns, social processes, cultural patterns, culturally patterned emotions, social norms, group organization, social structure, devices for social control, etc." (1968, 104).

Structural-functionalism is oriented to the analysis of social structures and institutions. The structural-functionalist is concerned with the (functional) relationship between structures, between institutions, and between structures and institutions. While not oblivious to the individual, the structural-functionalist, following Durkheim, sees the individual as primarily controlled by social facts that are external and coercive.

Conflict theory, especially the variant represented by the work of Ralf Dahrendorf (1959), while remaining firmly within the social facts paradigm, tends to take a series of positions directly antithetical to the ideas of structural-functionalism. While functionalists see society as static, or in a state of moving equilibrium, Dahrendorf and the conflict theorists see every society at every point subject to change. Where functionalists emphasize the fact that society is orderly, conflict theorists see dissension and conflict wherever they look. Functionalists (at least early functionalists) tend to argue that every element in society contributes to stability, while exponents of conflict theory see each societal element contributing to disintegration and change. Functionalists tend to see society as being held together informally by norms, values, and common morality, while conflict theorists see whatever order exists in society as stemming from the coercion of some members by others who rank higher in the system.

In spite of these differences, Dahrendorf, as well as conflict theorists in general, focus on social facts.[5] Central to Dahrendorf's thesis is the idea that differential *authority* is an attribute of various *positions* within society. The central concepts here are *authority* and *positions,* both of which are social facts. Authority resides not in individuals, but in positions. Thus societal positions and the differential distribution of power among them should be the concern of sociologists: "The structural origin of such conflicts must be sought in the arrangement of social roles endowed with expectations of domination or subjection" (Dahrendorf 1959, 165). The first task of conflict analysis to Dahrendorf is identification of various authority roles within society.

I should point out that I do *not* include the work of Karl Marx and a number of his followers under the heading of conflict theory. Marx is, as I point out later in this chapter, a "paradigm bridger."[6] Although Marx is certainly interested in analyzing social facts, in particular those in capitalist society, he is also interested in social action ("praxis") and mental processes, both cornerstones, as we will see, of the social definition paradigm. In fact, Marx's architectonic, as it was delineated in chapter 4, precludes the possibility of considering him a social factist. Marx was interested in reified social facts, but he was also interested in the microprocesses by which those facts come into existence (and through which they can be changed). Dahrendorf and other conflict theorists, although they contend that they are working in the Marxian tradition, have focused on social facts and have either ignored actors or have seen them as determined by external social facts. Although Marx saw social facts as coercive on the individual, much of his analysis was specific to capitalism. His hope was the creation of a society in which social facts would not determine social action. In any case, his theoretical system, unlike Dahrendorf's and other conflict theorists, does take significant account of social definitions. It is this that will lead me, in chapter 8, to view Marx's work as the exemplar for another, integrated, paradigm.

Methods. Those who accept the social facts paradigm should *tend* to use historical/comparative methods when they do empirical research (Snizek 1976). This methodology fits best with the social facts paradigm. It allows the social factist to focus on macro-level phenomena (social facts) in historical and cross-cultural contexts. While there are some fine examples of historical/comparative research (e.g., Mann 1986; Wallerstein, 1974; 1980; 1989), this method is not utilized as often as might be expected because it is so demanding and time-consuming and because it appears to be inconsistent with the positivism that dominates most research in contemporary sociology.

Snizek finds that, in fact, social factists rely heavily on the interview/ questionnaire[7] *and* that this was also the dominant methodology in the other two paradigms. This widespread acceptance of questionnaires and interviews is traceable to the ease with which data derived from them can be compiled and analyzed utilizing advanced statistical techniques. The use of the questionnaire and interview by the social factist points to a basic paradox in contemporary sociology. These methods elicit replies from individuals, but a basic tenet of the social factist is that the whole is more than the sum of its parts. Social factists accept the idea of emergence, that is, the idea that out of the interaction of individuals a social reality *emerges* that is more than the sum of the individuals. Thus, the sum of individual replies does not equal a social fact. In addition, individual replies yield *their* definition of a social fact, not what that social fact *really* is. No less a social theorist and student of the interview and questionnaire techniques than James Coleman recognizes that these methods do not tap social facts: "Survey research methods have led to the neglect of social structure and of the relations among individuals. . . . The *individual* remained the unit of analysis. . . . As a result, the kinds of substantive problems on which research focused tended to be problems of 'aggregate psychology' " (1970, 115). More recently, Marini (1988, 45) criticized the specific area of gender research for studying macro-level phenomena with micro-level data.

In spite of these liabilities, many of those who study social facts use questionnaire and interview methods. Social factists prefer these methods because they make data collection and analysis easier, and because the other major methods available to them do not lend themselves as well to the study of social facts. Social factists tend to reject the observation technique because they view it as unscientific and crude. They are equally likely to reject the experimental method because it is not easily applied to the study of the kind of macroscopic questions of interest to the social factist.

The Social Definition Paradigm

Exemplar. The exemplar for the social definitionist is a highly prominent, albeit very specific, aspect of Max Weber's work: his analysis of social action. Weber defines sociology as the study of social action: "Sociology . . . is a science which attempts the interpretative understanding of social action in order thereby to arrive at a causal explanation of its course and effects" (1947, 88). He defines social action as "all human behavior when and insofar as the acting individual attaches a subjective meaning to it. . . . Action is social insofar as by virtue of the subjective meaning attached to it by the acting individual (or individuals), it takes account of the behavior of others and is thereby oriented in its course" (1947, 88). This definition constitutes the basis of the social definition paradigm.

The paradox here is that while Weber's work is viewed as the ex-

emplar for the social definition paradigm, he spent most of his life analyzing social structures (and doing historical/comparative research).[8] Gerth
and Mills echo this view:

> Were one to accept Weber's methodological reflections on his own work
> at their face value, one would not find a systematic justification for his
> analysis of such phenomena as stratification or capitalism. Taken liter-
> ally, the "method of understanding" would hardly allow for Weber's use
> of structural explanations: for this type of explanation attempts to ac-
> count for the motivation of systems of action by their function as going
> concerns rather than by the subjective intentions of the individuals who
> act them out. According to Weber's method of understanding, we should
> expect him to adhere to a subjective theory of stratification, but he does
> not do so. (1958, 57)

In short, Weber, although the exemplar for the social definitionist, was
at least in part a social factist. Similarly, as we saw above, Durkheim is
considered the exemplar of the social factists, even though he is, at least
partly, a social definitionist.

Image of the Subject Matter. Four theories will be discussed under the
heading of social definitionism: action theory, symbolic interactionism,
ethnomethodology, and phenomenology. There are clearly many differences among them, but they share several overarching commonalities in
their image of the subject matter of sociology. Perhaps the major theme
consistent for all four theories is that people are active creators of their
own social reality. The converse is another consistent theme in the social
definition paradigm: social structures and institutions are not a static set
of coercive social facts. Social definitionists stand in stark contrast to
social factists who view people as controlled by such things as norms,
values, and social control agencies. They are also, as we will see, at vari-
ance with the social behaviorists, who see people as controlled by "contingencies of reinforcement." In fact, the high priest of behaviorism, B. F.
Skinner (1971) takes the extreme position and denies completely the view
of people as active and creative (what he calls "autonomous man").

Social definitionists tend to be interested in the mental process[9] as
well as the resulting action and interaction. Although they cannot examine
it directly, those who accept the social definition paradigm are generally
interested in what takes place in the minds of people. Something occurs
in a person's mind between the time a stimulus is applied and the time a
response is emitted—the creative activity that is at the base of the interests of the social definitionist. This interest in the mental process is manifested in Mead's "I" and "Me," Cooley's "looking glass self," Parsons's
voluntarism, Berger and Luckmann's "social construction of reality,"

Garfinkel's criticism of social factists for treating actors as "judgmental dopes," and most importantly, given the label applied to this paradigm, Thomas's "definition of the situation." In addition to a concern for such mental processes, social definitionists are interested in the resultant action and interaction.

Theories. Action theory, symbolic interactionism,[10] phenomenology, and ethnomethodology are all concerned with people as active creators of social reality. Conversely, they deny that social structure is merely a static set of coercive social facts.

Action theory has often been linked with symbolic interactionism. In fact, Hinkle (1963) views action theory as an intellectual antecedent of symbolic interactionism and he argues that the two theories share a number of common assumptions. It is somewhat less usual to link phenomenology with action theory and symbolic interactionism. Although the three theories share a common basis, the relationship between phenomenology and the other two theories has been obscured by the fact that phenomenology is believed by many to be more philosophical than sociological. Alfred Schutz (1932/1967, 1962, 1964, 1966), one of the major figures in phenomenology, has made it abundantly clear that his orientation is intimately related to both action theory and symbolic interactionism. Schutz points out that he is in accord with Weber's action theory, and in particular with the study of action that is meaningful to the actors involved. Subjective meaning is crucial to interaction both for the actor intending the behavior and for the others who must interpret it and act accordingly. Schutz is also in accord with Weber's method of *verstehen* which suggests that social scientists must involve themselves with interactants using a form of sympathetic introspection in order to understand the meaning contexts that serve as the impetus to action. Schutz also makes clear his admiration for the work of several symbolic interactionists (e.g., Mead and Thomas) and approves of their interest in how actors are socialized to internalize and share socially differentiated contexts of meaning that are experienced subjectively and serve as the basis for social action. Thus, it appears that Schutz would accept the association of phenomenology with action theory and symbolic interactionism and the inclusion of all three in the social definition paradigm.

Heritage offers a definition of ethnomethodology (one that fits well with the other theoretical varieties of social definitionism) as the study of "the body of commonsense knowledge and the range of procedures and considerations by means of which the ordinary members of society make sense of, find their way about in, and act on the circumstances in which they find themselves" (1984, 4). There is a micro-level focus on actors dealing with their social situations and acting on the basis of their decisions. The actors, following Garfinkel, are endowed with the ability to make judgments that decisively affect their actions. However, there is a stronger emphasis on the social situation than in the other forms of social definitionism. That is, the ethnomethodologists are concerned with "the body of commonsense knowledge" and the social practices and procedures through which actors deal with their social worlds. This is particularly true of a branch of ethnomethodology, conversational analysis, in which the focus is on "the procedures by which conversationalists produce their own behavior and understand and deal with the behavior of others" (Heritage and Atkinson 1984, 1). While there is focal concern with extant "procedures," there is also a concern, in line with other social definitionists, with people "producing" their actions.

Although action theory has a clear link to symbolic interactionism, phenomenology, and ethnomethodology, it also has a number of basic differences. In fact, I believe that action theory, more than the others,[11] combines an interest in social definitions with an interest in social facts. Social definitionists have often failed to see the interest in social facts in action theory, just as they have often failed to recognize Max Weber's interest in social facts. A major reason for both oversights lies in a misrepresentation of the concept of *verstehen*. The symbolic interactionists tend to see *verstehen* as a method for gaining insight into actors' mental processes, to understand the way they come to define a given situation. However, Weber, following the German intellectual tradition (e.g., Dilthey), saw *verstehen* not as a method for understanding the mental process, but rather as a method for gathering data on social institutions and social structures ("the meaning context"). Researchers put themselves in the place of the actor, not in order to understand the actor, but rather to understand the cultural and societal milieu in which the actor exists. Despite these and many other misinterpretations, action theory can still be seen as a theoretical component of social definitionism, even though in many ways it fits better into the social facts paradigm. After all, at its base, action theory sees the actor as possessing a dynamic, creative, voluntaristic mind. In contrast, social factists tend to see the actor as virtually totally determined by the broader social structure.

Although there are problems with assigning action theory to a single paradigm, I have no problem seeing symbolic interactionism, phenomenology, and ethnomethodology as theoretical components of the social definition paradigm. These theories share an interest in intrasubjectivity, intersubjectivity, action, and interaction, although each maintains a difference in emphasis. The symbolic interactionists tend to focus on action and interaction, the phenomenologists concentrate on intra- and intersubjectively, and the ethnomethodologists target the way actors use the body of commonsense knowledge (action theorists combine these interests with a concern for the social context).

Methods. Those who accept the social definition paradigm, like those who employ the social facts paradigm, most often use questionnaire and interview techniques. However, despite their obvious allure for all sociologists, these methods are generally ill-fitted to social definitionism (as they are to social factism) because they tend to gather information on static variables rather than the processual information on action and interaction of interest to the social definitionist. (The laboratory experiment is also ill-suited to this paradigm because of its comparative lack of ability to study spontaneous and natural action.)

The observation technique is best suited to the demands of social definitionist research because it allows the researcher to examine process over time in a natural setting. This accounts, among other things, for the attraction of symbolic interactionists to participant observation and the ethnomethodologists' focus on such things as telephone conversations. Social definitionists *should* be more likely to use observational techniques than the supporters of the other major paradigms.[12]

However, I must also ask whether observation is really well suited to the study of the topics of concern to the social definitionist. In fact, we cannot actually observe intra- and intersubjectivity, action and interaction. The best we can do is deduce information about these processes from the bits and pieces that we can observe. There is a very real question whether observation fulfills all of the demands of the social definition paradigm. Whatever its liabilities, observation comes closer to fitting the needs of social definitionists than any other methodology.

The Social Behavior Paradigm

Exemplar. Behaviorism has a long and honorable history in the social sciences, in particular in psychology. However, its modern resurgence in all of the social sciences, and in particular in sociology, can be traced to B. F. Skinner, whose work is the exemplar for the sociologists who have endeavored to adapt behaviorism to their discipline.

Image of the Subject Matter. Social behaviorists are interested in the relationship between individuals and their environment. Bushell and Burgess define the nature of the subject matter of sociology to the behaviorist as "the behavior of individuals that operates on the environment in such a way as to produce some consequences or change in it which, in turn, modifies subsequent performances of that behavior" (1969, 27). Thus the focus is on the functional relationship between behavior and changes in the environment of the actor.

Social behaviorists claim that they are focusing on an interaction process, but this process is conceptualized very differently from that of the social definitionists. Actors, to the social definitionist, are dynamic, creative forces in the interaction process. They are not simply responding to stimuli, but interpreting these inputs and acting on the basis of the way they define them. But the social behaviorist allows individuals far less freedom. Believing that peoples' responses are determined by the nature of the external stimuli, the behaviorist's image of people is much more mechanical than that of the social definitionist.

The social factist's image of people is almost as mechanistic as the social behaviorist's. The social factist sees the individual as determined by norms, values, structures, and the like. The difference between the social factist and the social behaviorist lies in the source of control over the individual. To the social factist, macroscopic structures and institutions exert control, while to the social behaviorist the contingencies of reinforcement are the source of control.

Theories. Behavioral sociology (Burgess and Bushell 1969) constitutes a theoretical effort to apply the principles of behaviorism to sociological questions. Take, for example, their effort to define socialization as "an interactional process whereby an individual's behavior is modified to conform to the rules and standards of the groups to which he belongs" (Burgess and Bushell 1969, 275). In the hands of the behavioral sociologist, socialization becomes a process of behavior modification. A similar tendency to reduce social processes to behavior is found in the way behaviorists treat a variety of other traditional sociological topics and concepts (e.g., self, social structure, and so on).

The major sociological theory encompassed by the social behavior paradigm is exchange theory. Although exchange theory can be traced to the work of Chavannes (Knox 1963) and Mauss (1954), it enjoyed a boom in interest in the 1960s as a result of the work of George Homans (1961/1974). Deeply indebted to Skinner's work on pigeons, Homans developed five basic propositions concerning elementary social behavior. Those propositions form the basis of Homans's exchange theory. Others participated in the development of exchange theory in the 1960s, the most notable being Peter Blau (1964).[13] Exchange theory is differentiated from behavioral sociology by its more traditional sociological orientation.

Methods. As was true for the other two paradigms, the most often used method in social behaviorism is the interview/questionnaire. However, once again, there is a poor fit between social behaviorism and the most often used method. Coming from psychology, social behaviorists prefer much more controlled scientific research than is possible in interviews or questionnaires. (An even greater lack of control leads social behaviorism to a rejection of the "soft" observation techniques.) Because of their linkage to psychology, their preference for studying behavior in a controlled setting, and their microscopic orientation, behaviorists are more likely to feel comfortable with the experimental method in their research. Behaviorists are also more likely to use laboratory experiments than those who accept the other paradigms (Snizek 1976).

Conclusions and Implications

There is some support in the literature for the tripartite differentiation of sociology in the 1960s into social factist, definitionist, and behaviorist paradigms. Brown and Gilmartin (1969), in a study of articles published in the *American Journal of Sociology,* found that articles focused on three variables: individual, individual-group, and group. Those three variables tend to parallel the three paradigms discussed in this chapter. The weakest correspondence is between the individual variable and the social behavior paradigm. Many of those researchers who focused on the individual did not support the social behavior paradigm. Nevertheless, the Brown and Gilmartin study is generally supportive. So is Theodore Abel's (1970) analysis of the way sociologists theoretically analyzed social collectivities. Abel argues that there are three theoretical conceptions of collectivities, and his conceptions parallel precisely the three paradigms discussed here. Again, this support is far from definitive since Abel only examined theories and focused on only one issue, collectivities.

The support offered above for the position outlined in this chapter is far from conclusive. The only true test is whether it enables the reader to better understand the status of American sociology, in particular sociological theory, in the 1960s. There are, of course, other classification schemes to which the one offered here can be compared. However, most such schemes—such as the work of Friedrichs and Effrat discussed above—list theories rather than true paradigms. Thus, the analyses of Friedrichs and Effrat are of a lower level of generality than the one offered here.

There are also a number of efforts at classifying the components of sociology (especially in the 1960s) that focus explicitly on theory. Some of these come to conclusions very different from the one offered here, for example, Martindale (1960), Timasheff (1967), Wallace (1969), and Mullins (1973), while others, for example, Abel (1970) are much closer. However, all of these classification systems are far more narrow than the one developed here. I have not tried to develop a classification system for sociological theory, rather I have attempted to classify the basic approaches in sociology. Since paradigms are far broader than theories, the paradigm approach allows us to do much more than simply understand our theoretical differences. It allows us to see our methodological differences and to see how methodological differences are intimately related to theoretical differences. It also enables us to see how theoretical and methodological differences are tied to our discipline's history in the work of the exemplars. Finally, it allows us to see how theories, methods, and exemplars are related to our fundamental images of the subject matter of sociology.

There are a number of important implications of this analysis of the paradigmatic status of sociology in the 1960s:

1. Spokespeople for each paradigm tend to claim to be able to explain all of the phenomena of concern to sociology.[14] Thus they are competing to gain hegemony within the discipline as a whole. In addition, they are competing within virtually every subarea within sociology. In my view, this competition and conflict has negative consequences for the discipline. Each of the paradigms, standing alone, is inadequate. Each needs insights from the other paradigms in order to fully explain any social phenomena. Therefore, we need less competition and conflict and more effort at paradigmatic integration (see chapters 7 and 8). The discipline is rife with political conflict. Much of it is interparadigmatic, although some of it is also intraparadigmatic (e.g., structural functionalism vs. conflict theory). This political conflict has more negative than positive consequences and often serves to divide the discipline unnecessarily.[15]

2. In the 1960s, and to some extent to this day, sociologists were often deceived into believing that the basic split in sociology was between structural-functionalism and conflict theory. I have sought to show that these two theories share the same paradigm and have far more commonalities than differences. The truly fundamental differences in sociology are among the three paradigms discussed in this chapter.

3. Theory and method are often practiced in virtual isolation from each other. A paradigmatic approach emphasizes the general link between the methods and theories.

4. Behaviorism is not often accorded the central place in sociology that it receives in my paradigmatic approach. Its elevation to paradigmatic status in sociology in this discussion is based more on its anticipated significance than on its position in the 1960s. In my view, social behaviorism is likely to become a powerful force in sociology.[16] This view is not idiosyncratic and is reflected in a variety of examinations of the status of sociology in the 1960s (Tarter 1973; Friedrichs 1974).

5. There is a considerable amount of irrationality in sociology. Sociologists often use methods that are not well-suited to the paradigm from which they operate. The works of Weber and Durkheim are viewed as the exemplars for paradigms with which these two men would be highly uncomfortable. Action theory has been erroneously viewed as being akin to symbolic interactionism. The erroneous view that the basic split in sociology is between structural-functionalism and conflict theory has already been discussed, as has the ubiquity of destructive political conflict. Finally, and perhaps most importantly, sociologists in the 1960s (and to this day) never truly understood their most basic differences.

Sociologists need to overcome their political differences and begin to create an integrated sociological paradigm. Although I doubt that sociology is likely to become a single-paradigm science in the near future, I do think that there are a number of points of reconciliation among the paradigms that have been obscured by the political allegiances and political efforts to destroy competitors on the part of the adherents of each of the paradigms. Sociologists need to spend less time destroying their political opponents and more time deriving useful insights from their perspectives. No single paradigm is adequate for explaining all social phenomena. There is a need for a halt to *destructive* interparadigmatic debates. Some of these debates are useful (e.g., the ideas of one paradigm can be sharpened as a result of attacks from adherents of other paradigms), but most have had far more negative consequences than positive effects. A more common base in sociology exists than paradigmatic differences have allowed sociologists to realize. Nevertheless, Kuhn's insights into the political character of paradigmatic differences in all sciences make it clear that we are unlikely to overcome completely our narrow political interests.

While I favor reducing, or eliminating, destructive interparadigmatic debates, the point needs to be underscored that constructive paradigmatic debates should, and will, continue. Destructive debates are preventing sociologists not only from seeing their common base, but also from doing the normal science within their paradigm through which anomalies can be uncovered and which, in turn, could lead to scientific revolutions. Sociologists are too busy defending their basic assumptions to themselves and others to concentrate on normal science. Kuhn (1970b, 160) supports this position when he argues that fields like sociology can make progress when they "achieve consensus about their past and present accomplishments." The multiple paradigms in sociology will continue to exist even after we find our common core, but the debates among them will be more likely to have positive consequences.

Although paradigmatic reconciliation will not come tomorrow, a number of efforts offer hope to those interested in bridging at least some of these differences. Historically, theorists like Weber, Durkheim, Marx, and Parsons have been able to bridge paradigms. Their work can serve as a starting point for those who seek an integrated sociological paradigm (see chapters 7 and 8).

Durkheim bridged the social facts and social definition paradigms, in particular in his analysis of material social facts and nonmaterial, intersubjective social currents. Weber bridged the same paradigms, most notably in his studies of religion. Marx devoted most of his attention to the social structure of capitalism, but his dialectical approach led him to recognize the significance of the actor's social definitions (Bender 1970). Parsons was the only one to deal with all three paradigms. His early action orientation, the influence Tolman's behaviorism had on him in the 1940s, and his later preoccupation with social structure and culture reflect Parsons's propensity to "leap" from paradigm to paradigm.

In the 1960s and early 1970s several pieces of work appeared that sought to integrate paradigms, or aspects of paradigms. For example, Blau (1964) sought to integrate social behaviorism and social factism. Singelmann (1972) attempted to integrate social behaviorism and social definitionism, although his effort was met by a political attack from the behaviorists (Abbott, Brown, and Crosbie 1973). Warriner (1970) combined social definitionism and social factism. Although all of these works were hopeful signs, paradigmatic integration did *not* immediately follow. The political goals and allegiances of sociologists continued to stand in the way of paradigmatic reconciliation, at least until the 1980s and 1990s (see chapters 10, 11).

Postscript

The paradigm analysis presented above elicited a great deal of reaction, both pro and con. (For a summary and analysis of the debate, see Abrams, Reitman, and Sylvester 1980). In this postscript I want to deal with the most important of the critiques.

Eckberg and Hill's (1979) essay is one of a spate of research studies (e.g., Snizek 1976; Picou et al., 1978; Friedheim 1979; Platt 1986; Falk and Zhao 1989; Falk and Zhao 1990) and conceptual essays (e.g., Martindale 1979; Snizek 1979; Wilke and Mohan 1979; Rosenberg, 1989) dealing at least in part with my application of Kuhn's paradigm concept to sociology in the 1960s. My objective in this postscript is to point to some basic differences between myself and Eckberg and Hill and in the process to help clarify the paradigm concept and its applicability to sociology.

There are three basic differences between Eckberg and Hill's (1979) work and my own. First, their main focus is the sociology of science, specifically Kuhnian theory. My major interest, and the interest of many others in this field, is metasociology: specifically, the paradigmatic status of sociology. Although these two interests are related, there is a significant difference in emphasis. Second, Eckberg and Hill are greatly concerned with being true to Kuhnian theory. My prime interest is in gaining as deep an understanding as possible of sociology and its future prospects. While these objectives are not necessarily incompatible, Eckberg and Hill's Kuhnian purism is not the best way of enhancing our understanding of sociology. Unlike Eckberg and Hill, I am willing to deviate from a strict interpretation of Kuhnian theory if it will help achieve a greater understanding of the discipline. Third, Eckberg and Hill and I disagree on which of Kuhn's definitions of a paradigm is best suited to the analysis of sociology. They prefer his later definition of a paradigm as an exemplar. In spite of the fact that he later rejected it, I prefer Kuhn's earlier definition of a paradigm as a disciplinary matrix, or the shared intellectual commitments of an intellectual community.

Operating from their three basic assumptions, Eckberg and Hill are virtually unassailable in their contention that the paradigm concept has been misused by those who have attempted to apply it to sociology. They are correct in recognizing the ambiguities of Kuhn's initial formulation. They understand that it is possible on the basis of his early work to equate paradigms with disciplinary matrices. They also recognize Kuhn's later equation of paradigms with exemplars, concrete solutions to problems. Eckberg and Hill argue that most sociologists are either unaware of the differences in, and subtleties of, Kuhn's conceptualization, or that they ignore them. Although they recognize that I understand the complexities of Kuhn's work, they criticize my work for disregarding those complexities in the study of the paradigmatic status of sociology.

While Eckberg and Hill are correct in both their formulation of Kuhn's perspective *and* in their accusation that I ignore some of his distinctions, their strict adherence to Kuhnian theory leads them to some questionable assertions about sociology. Because they are tied to a strict usage of Kuhnian theory, they define paradigms as exemplars and thus focus on specific areas of research that are "guided by concrete examples of scholarship, which serve to generate and to solve puzzles" (Eckberg and Hill 1979, 935). They argue that potential exemplars (paradigms) in sociology can be found in such areas as "political socialization, status attainment, ethnic relations" (Eckberg and Hill 1979, 933).

If we were to take both Kuhn and Eckberg and Hill literally, we would end up with hundreds, or maybe even thousands, of paradigms. Because paradigms (exemplars) are, in their view, found within substantive areas, and because numerous such areas exist in sociology, presumably it would be possible to have an enormous array of paradigms. For example, within one substantive area in sociology—occupational sociology—we could identify such paradigms, (following the model of status attainment) as job satisfaction, alienation, commitment, role conflict, professionalization, and innumerable others. Even if we had and were able to identify numerous exemplars, they would be useless tools for making sense out of the broad structure of the field. In fact, if we had so many exemplars, we would probably need another concept to help us divide them into reasonable groupings so that we could discern the basic structure of sociology. That basic structure would best be delineated then, as it is now, by paradigms as disciplinary matrices rather than exemplars.

Because I continue to believe that the disciplinary matrix is the more useful definition of a paradigm insofar as sociology is concerned, my sense of not only the present but also the future of sociology is not the same as that of Eckberg and Hill. While they believe that sociology needs more exemplars, my view is that what sociology needs is a new disciplinary matrix, one that deals in a more integrated fashion with the social world than extant paradigms. The next two chapters are devoted to the issue of an integrated sociological paradigm.

Notes

1. *Exemplar* is used here very differently from Kuhn's conception of it as a concrete solution to a scientific puzzle. In sociology, we have few such solutions and our exemplars tend to be more general bodies of work that stand as models for others.

2. See chapter 8 for a further discussion of this aspect of Durkheim's work.

3. Durkheim's tendency to accept at least some elements of social definitionism has been underscored by Robert Nisbet (1974) who argues that there is not "one iota of difference" between Durkheim's approach and that of such preeminent social definitionists as Mead and Cooley. Of course, not all analysts of any sociological theorist offer the same interpretation. In contrast to Nisbet (and earlier, Talcott Parsons), Pope (1973, 414) argues that "Durkheim never embraced a theory of action." Since action theory is a component of the social definition paradigm, Pope is taking a position in opposition to Nisbet's. Nevertheless, it is my view that a careful reading of Durkheim's work, in particular *Suicide,* reveals a deep interest in the mental process and social action.

4. Durkheim offers a similar distinction between material and nonmaterial social facts.

5. Collins (1990) clearly acknowledges this point by arguing that his own contribution to conflict theory (Collins 1975) was designed to add a micro level to the traditional macro-level concerns of conflict theory.

6. In chapter 8 we will see that this characteristic makes Marx the exemplar for an integrated sociological paradigm.

7. Platt (1986), however, has failed to find support for this association.

8. This wider set of concerns is also clear in the discussion in chapter 4 of

Weber's architectonic, which demonstrates considerable interest in reified social structures.

9. Ethnomethodologists are less interested in this than the other theorists associated with this paradigm. However, the former's focus on everyday practices assumes such mental abilities.

10. I am basically discussing here the Chicago brand of symbolic interactionism. Iowa symbolic interactionism (e.g., Manfred Kuhn) fits less well, but it still can be subsumed by the social definition paradigm.

11. See chapter 11 for a discussion of Fine's (1990) effort to deal with social facts from a symbolic interactionist base.

12. Although Snizek (1976) found social factists more likely to use the observation method than social definitionists.

13. More recently, the work of Richard Emerson (1981) and his colleagues (especially Karen Cook [1987b]) has become centrally important to exchange theory.

14. I will discuss these issues in the present tense since while they were particularly true in the 1960s, they remain true to at least some extent to this day.

15. There are innumerable examples of political attacks including, among others, Talcott Parsons's (1964) attack on George Homans's behaviorism, and Homans's (1971) response, which was an attack on Parsons's sometime-social factism; Kurt Back's (1970) social definitionist attack on behaviorism; James Coleman's (1968) acid critique of ethnomethodology; and Becker and Geer's (1957) praise of participant observation and assault on all other methods.

16. This assertion, made in 1975, has I think been borne out by the substantial interest in the late 1980s in the work of people like Emerson and Cook.

7
Levels of Social Analysis and an Integrated Sociological Paradigm

The metatheoretical (M_U) tool of levels of social analysis is implicit in chapters 4 and 6. The architectonic described in chapter 4 begins at the micro level of philosophical anthropology and moves progressively to the macro level of reified social structures. The paradigms outlined in chapter 6 descend from the social facts paradigm focally concerned with macro-level phenomena to the social definition and social behavior paradigms whose concerns are with more micro-level phenomena.

In the remainder of part II of this book, I will employ levels of analysis much more explicitly to form the basis of an integrated sociological paradigm, to analyze theoretical developments in the 1970s and 1980s and projections for the 1990s, and to review developments in the sociology of work and socioeconomics. Hence, we need to deal with the idea of levels of analysis in some depth before moving on. As we progress in this chapter, we will see that levels of analysis is often too general for our needs. Thus, we will need to develop two additional M_U tools that come under the broad heading of levels of analysis. These are the microscopic-macroscopic and objective-subjective continua. Beyond their independent utility, we will find that their interrelationship and the resulting formation of four major levels of social analysis (micro-objective, macro-objective, micro-subjective, macro-subjective) will prove particularly useful in the delineation of an integrated sociological paradigm as well as in later analyses.

Although the idea of levels of analysis is implicit in much of sociology, it has received relatively little explicit attention (at least until recently; see Wiley 1988, 1989; Ritzer 1989c). In fact, the idea of levels is so foreign to most sociologists, at least at a conscious level, that on the rare occasions when it is discussed it often encounters stiff opposition. The term *levels* is frequently attacked for distorting the nature of social reality and also for offering a static image of the social world. Although the idea of levels can be defended against these charges (as we will soon see), my guess is that it will still prove controversial. The irony of this situation is that sociology has long been dominated by a conception of levels of social analysis even though it has rarely been made explicit. In concentrating on levels here, I believe that I am doing little more than making explicit what has been implicit in sociology since its inception.

To underscore this point, I want to further clarify the fact that the three paradigms discussed in chapter 6 differ most basically in their views on what is the most important "level" of analysis in the social world. The social facts paradigm focuses on large-scale social structures and social institutions; the social definition paradigm focuses on the more microscopic aspects of action, interaction, and the social construction of reality; and the social behavior paradigm focuses on the similarly microscopic patterns of behavior. Levels of social analysis inform each paradigm's image of the subject matter of sociology. Furthermore, the adherents of each paradigm tend to believe that their paradigm focuses on the level(s) of social analysis that adequately explains all of the others. This reality lies at the root of all political conflicts among the adherents of the three major paradigms. Yet, despite their focal concern with levels, the adherents of each of these paradigms rarely address the issue directly, or in these terms. However, some work on the issue of levels of social analysis has been published and can be used to help us orient our thinking on this matter.

Before getting to that work, I want to make it clear that we are dealing with levels of social *analysis, not* levels of social *reality.* That is, levels are either theoretical or metatheoretical (M_U) tools; they are *not* ontological realities. The idea of levels of analysis does not imply that the social world is divided into levels. This crucial distinction constitutes one response to critics who feel that a levels approach distorts the social world. Levels are simply one way of thinking about the social world (and sociological theory); their use as tools does not imply that there are levels in that world. All such tools are distorting, but analysts are free to use a wide array of tools in their study of the social world. In spite of the distortions they cause, we must use such tools either explicitly or implicitly, for we have no other way of approaching the social world.

Most of the work to be discussed here uses the idea of levels of social analysis to analyze the social world; that is, it is used theoretically to analyze that world. My interest, however, is metatheoretical in that I wish to use this tool to analyze sociological theory. Thus, most of the work to be discussed below will need to be translated to fit my particular needs and interests.

Levels of Social Analysis: A Review of the Literature

One of the most sophisticated treatments of levels of social analysis available in the literature was written by the philosopher Abraham Edel (1959). Edel immediately and directly addresses one of the most crucial issues in using the idea of levels to analyze social reality: he confronts the question of whether it is inevitably a structural orientation that gives social reality a static and unchangeable character. While he admits that in the hands of some analysts the use of levels might yield a static conception of society, Edel is unwilling to reduce it to such a conception, arguing that the levels concept is "not merely a concern with the relations of qualitatively distinct bands of coexistent phenomena in a static field" (1959, 168). Instead, what Edel does is to embed the whole issue of levels within a very dynamic conception of social life, a conception that goes to the very heart of the field of sociology as a distinctive endeavor. That is, Edel views levels within the context of the emergence of the sociological aspects of the world. The essence of this perspective is that more macroscopic social phenomena emerge out of the interaction that takes place at the more microscopic levels. To put it another way, people create a macroscopic social reality that is more than the sum of the individuals who create, and compose, it.

By placing the idea of levels within the process of emergence, Edel gives it an inherently historical and dynamic quality rather than the static structure that it could easily degenerate into. Edel sensitizes us to the fact that people in the course of history have produced today's macrostructures. His idea of emergence also attunes us to the fact that larger structures are produced and reproduced on a daily basis by actors in the process of action and interaction. Both historicity and dynamism are built into Edel's conception of the levels of social analysis, and they are also inherent in the way levels of social analysis are dealt with throughout this book.

Within the context of this developmental and dynamic perspective, Edel offers a conception of levels of social analysis that begins at the microscopic level and moves to more macroscopic levels:

1. States of consciousness, actors' attitudes, and so on
2. Individuals
3. Interpersonal relations
4. Groups
5. Culture

Although this is a useful first approximation of some of the major levels of social analysis, it has a number of omissions and failings that will become clear as I move toward my own conception of these levels.

Not only does Edel identify the nature and the dynamics of the levels of the social world, but he also identifies the political problems associated with the traditional sociological perspectives that focus on one, or a few, levels. In identifying these problems, Edel differentiates between the reality claims and the ultimacy claims of those who support a specific perspective. *Reality claims* simply involve a preference for dealing with one level rather than another. *Ultimacy claims* involve the tendency to claim that one level is the ultimate subject matter of sociology. It is the ultimacy claims of the adherents of each of the paradigms discussed in chapter 6 that leads to much of the political conflict in sociology.

Finally, I would like to underscore an aspect of Edel's work that will become progressively more important as I proceed in this chapter. Although he has an obvious interest in the range from microscopic to macroscopic levels of social analysis, he has a less obvious but equally important interest in the continuum ranging from objective to subjective levels of social analysis. On the one end, he is very much aware of the objective level: "Ongoing human activity is seen as crystallizing into structured forms on various historical levels" (1959, 183). Edel complements this awareness with an equally vivid sense of the subjective level of the social world: "mind or intellectual reflection is to be viewed as an event in nature" (1959, 184). Edel also manifests his interest in the objective-subjective continuum by embedding himself in Marx's distinction between base and superstructure and by talking of the "underlying distinction between the material and the expression of spirit" (1959, 188). Despite the fact that he has a sense of an objective-subjective continuum, however, Edel does little with it and leaves it largely unrelated to the macroscopic-microscopic continuum.

Although Edel's work attracted relatively little attention in sociology (perhaps because he was a philosopher, not a sociologist), a similar, although somewhat less sophisticated, work on levels of social analysis by Helmut Wagner (1964) did attract some attention. Wagner is more specifically concerned with the macroscopic-microscopic continuum in terms of large-scale to small-scale sociological theories, or what he calls differences in "scope" in sociological thinking. Wagner clearly sees sociological interest in the macroscopic-microscopic issue as lying along a continuum: "Empirically, sociological interests range all the way from the study of interactional encounters between two persons to the analysis of whole societies. . . . most sociologists operate, at least in particular phases of their work, either within small-scale, or intermediate, or large-scale ranges" (1964, 572). In other words, the scope of sociological phenomena is one way sociologists divide up the work of studying social reality. Although Wagner is to be applauded for this insight, one of the problems with his work is that he fails to be either microscopic or macroscopic enough. The microscopic end of the continuum should be extended to include the concerns of ethnomethodologists and phenomenologists, and the macro level should be extended beyond the "society" to such suprasocietal units as the "world system" (Wallerstein 1974, 1989).[1]

Wagner chooses to focus on the poles of his micro-macro continuum in order to highlight some basic differences, and some inherent problems, in traditional sociological theories. Here, then, Wagner is using levels of analysis metatheoretically rather than theoretically. In his view, sociology emerged in the nineteenth century with a macroscopic focus in order to be able to carve out a clear niche for itself in academia. Durkheim with his focus on social facts is accorded key significance in this development. Microsociology developed slightly later, in the early twentieth century, through the works of such people as Mead and Cooley, but can be traced as well to the ideas of Simmel and Weber. In Wagner's view, a basic dualism was introduced into sociology, a dualism that went largely unrecognized at the time.[2] Furthermore, this dualism has yet to be reconciled adequately.[3]

I have great sympathy for Wagner's characterization of the dualism within sociology, although there is a considerable difference between the way he classifies thinkers like Simmel, Weber (chapter 4), and Durkheim (chapter 8) and the way I think about them. To put it briefly, they are much more integrative thinkers than Wagner leads us to believe. The theoretical ideas of people as sophisticated as Weber, Durkheim, and Simmel are done a great disservice by simply being compressed into micro or macro camps. In fact, Wagner himself recognizes this flaw as he proceeds further in his analysis. For example, despite his classification of Simmel as a micro sociologist, Wagner later says: "Simmel defies classification. It is often forgotten that he, with ease and elegance, transferred his statements about the relations between two and three persons to the relations between religious sects, political parties, economic groupings, power constellations of nations, and others" (1964, 573). As was typical of theoretical works of that epoch, Marx is pointedly ignored by Wagner. As we have seen in chapter 4, and will see again in chapter 8, Marx's work offers a highly integrated sense of social reality.

Wagner is also to be praised for his metatheoretical recognition of the relationship between theoretical orientation and level of social analysis. For example, he argues that structural-functionalism, a theoretical component of social factism, "starts with the conception of social system and sees smaller units, down to the individual, as structural subparts whose functions are essentially defined and confined by the whole system" (1964, 575). In the same way, Wagner is also very good on recognizing the politicality of paradigmatic claims: "In fact, most of them claim that their theory is applicable to the whole range of the micro-macro sociological continuum" (1964, 576). In a clever turn of a phrase, Wagner labels this the "fallacy of displaced scope."

Although he focuses almost exclusively on the micro-macro continuum, Wagner hints in his analysis about the objective-subjective continuum. In addition to a variety of indirect comments, Wagner addresses this issue directly in a footnote. He argues that structural-functionalism tends to be an objective theory while interpretative sociology tends to be a subjective theory. While I do not agree with the specific associations— that is, I think that structural functionalism and interpretative sociology have *both* subjective *and* objective orientations—I find it promising that Wagner at least recognizes subjectivity and objectivity. However, Wagner does almost nothing with this recognition. Furthermore, Wagner, like Edel, fails to relate the objective-subjective continuum to the micro-macro continuum.

Blalock and Wilken (1979) explicitly adopt a micro-macro orientation in their analysis of intergroup relations. At the micro end of the continuum, Blalock and Wilken (1979, 6) focus on the subjective states of the actors, "subjective probabilities," and utilities or subjective values attached to the importance of goals. At the other pole, they define the macro level as group phenomena. Although they have a very limited conception of the macro level, the authors do include a great deal under the group category including country clubs, colleges, and social categories (such as blacks and whites). Their goal is to operate between these two poles, at what they call the macro-micro level. They are basically interested in the impact of "contextual effects" on actors.

Blalock and Wilken's sense of the micro-macro continuum is limited in two ways. First, since they do not make explicit theoretical provision for individual behavior and action, they are not microscopic enough. By ignoring units larger than the group (such as society and the world system), they are also not macroscopic enough. Second, they have no clear sense of the difference between the micro-macro and objective-subjective continua. In fact, the two are hopelessly confused in their theoretical scheme. Nevertheless, Blalock and Wilken are to be applauded for their interest in integrating levels and for their criticisms of traditional sociology for its failures in this domain: "Ideally at least, the two perspectives (macro-micro) should be mutually reinforcing. Yet there has been surprisingly little systematic attention given to specifying the exact linkages between levels or to exploring the methodological difficulties one encounters when one attempts to move back and forth between them" (Blalock and Wilken 1979, 8). Their view, one that is in accord with the emerging thrust of this chapter, is that "micro and macro-level theories each need to make some provision for variables located at the other level" (1979, 27).

There seems to be little controversy involved in the use of the microscopic-macroscopic continuum of levels of social analysis. In fact, in chapter 10 I will deal with the explosion of interest during the 1980s in this specific aspect of the levels issue. Few would argue against the point that we can think in terms of large-scale and small-scale phenomena in social life, with most sociological entities falling somewhere in between. And most would have no difficulty thinking metatheoretically about sociological theories in these terms. What is far more difficult to explain, and to defend, is the objective-subjective continuum. However, my view is that this continuum is as important and as defensible as the micro-macro range. It is nothing more than another major theoretical and metatheoretical (M_U) tool that can be used to help us deal with the infinite complexity of the social world and of sociological theory. There are, of course, many other metatheoretical tools, including various other sociological continua, that could be developed; but these two, as well as their interrelationships with one another, are the underpinnings of this chapter as well as of several of the ensuing chapters.

Since it is less intuitively obvious, I need to devote some attention to explaining and defending the objective-subjective continuum.[4] I could go back to the philosophical roots of sociology and recast the continuum in terms of the split between Idealism and Materialism. But, given the vagaries of that philosophical debate, such an excursion might cause more harm than good. Instead of addressing this issue at a general philosophical level, I think it would be more relevant to the concerns of this book to discuss the objective-subjective continuum in terms of its influence on the work of Karl Marx.

It is well known that one of the early and important influences on Marx was German Idealism, particularly the work of Hegel. The Hegelian dialectic is a subjective process taking place within the realm of ideas. Although affected by this view, Marx and before him the "Young Hegelians" were dissatisfied with the fact that the dialectic is not rooted in the real, material world. Building on the work of Feuerbach and others, Marx sought to take the dialectic and extend it to the material world. On the one hand, this means that he is concerned with real, sentient actors rather than with idea systems. On the other hand, he focuses on the material structures of capitalist society, primarily the economic structure. What came to interest Marx increasingly were the real material (reified) structures of capitalism and the contradictions that exist among and within them. This is not to say that Marx lost sight of subjective ideas; in fact, notions of false consciousness and class consciousness played a key role in his work. It is the Materialism-Idealism split, as manifested in the work of Marx and others, that is one key philosophical root of the objective-subjective continuum in modern sociology.

We can also find this continuum, although in a different guise, in the work of Emile Durkheim (1895/1964). In his classic work on methodology, Durkheim differentiates between material (objective) and nonmaterial (subjective) social facts. In *Suicide,* Durkheim says: "The social fact is sometimes materialized as to become an element of the external world"

(1897/1951, 313). He discusses architecture and law as two examples of material (objective) social facts. However, most of Durkheim's work emphasizes nonmaterial (subjective) social facts:

> Of course it is true that not all social consciousness achieves such externalization and materialization. Not all aesthetic spirit of a nation is embodied in the works it inspires; not all of morality is formulated in clear precepts. The greater part is diffused. There is a large collective life which is at liberty; all sorts of currents come, go, circulate everywhere, cross and mingle in a thousand different ways, and just because they are constantly mobile are never crystallized in an objective form. Today a breath of sadness and discouragement descends on society; tomorrow, one of joyous confidence will uplift all hearts. (1897/1951, 315)

These social currents do not have material existence; they can only exist within and between consciousness. In *Suicide,* Durkheim concentrates on examples of this kind of social fact. He relates differences in suicide rates to differences in social currents. Thus, for example, where there are strong currents of anomie, we will find high rates of anomic suicide. Social currents, such as anomie, egoism, and altruism, clearly do not have a material existence, although they may have a material effect by causing differences in suicide rates. Rather, they are intersubjective phenomena that can only exist in the consciousness of people.

More contemporaneously, Peter Blau (1960) differentiates between institutions (subjective entities) and social structures (objective entities). He defines subjective institutions as "the common values and norms embodied in a culture or subculture" (1960, 178). He defines objective social structures as "the networks of social relations in which processes of social interaction become organized and through which social positions of individuals and subgroups become differentiated" (1960, 178).

While Marx, Durkheim, and Blau all demonstrate a concern for the objective-subjective continuum, their work is dominated by an interest in macro-level objective (e.g., the economy) and subjective (e.g., social currents) phenomena. We must turn to the work of Georges Gurvitch to find a more balanced use of both the micro-macro and objective-subjective continua.

The Work of Georges Gurvitch

Although all of the works discussed thus far are at least in some part related to the conception of levels of social analysis being developed in this chapter, the most directly relevant work on this issue is that of the French sociologist Georges Gurvitch. He is focally concerned with the four major interests of this chapter: levels of analysis, the macroscopic-microscopic and objective-subjective continua, and the dialectical relationship of one to the other. These foci are quite explicit in Gurvitch's definition of sociology (which is characteristically complex and jargonistic): "Sociology is the qualitative and discontinuous typology based on the dialectic of the total social phenomena in all their astructural, structurable and structured manifestations. It studies all their depth *levels,* scales and the sectors directly with the aim of following their movements of structuration, destructuration and restructuration and rupture" (1964, 11; my italics).

The key point is the fact that Gurvitch operates with a sense of levels of social analysis; in fact, he is the only thinker discussed to this point who has a strong sense of *both* the micro-macro and objective-subjective continua and their dialectical relationship to each other.

> The social reality to the practiced eye of the sociologist is arranged in levels, strata, planes, or in layers. These strata, or levels, interpenetrate and mutually impregnate each other. Moreover, they do not cease to enter into conflict: their rapport is tenuous, paradoxical, and dialectical. This has to do with the inextricable tensions inherent in all social reality, which one can qualify on a vertical scale. To these relative polarizations are added, at each depth level, the horizontal conflicts and tensions; the antagonism of classes is a good example. (Gurvitch, cited in Bosserman 1968, 79)

Let us examine the two different levels of continua that interest Gurvitch.

Depths (or Vertical) Levels. Although I will discuss each of Gurvitch's ten depth levels (Bosserman 1968) in this section, I should make clear from the outset that Gurvitch (like this author) is well aware that these levels are clearly differentiated from one another *only* for purposes of analysis; that is, levels (and a clear differentiation among them) do not exist in the social world. In addition, I also want to indicate that there is no magic associated with the number ten; the number of levels can be extended or contracted depending on the immediate needs and interests of the sociologist.

Gurvitch arranges his ten depth levels on the basis of the degree of difficulty of direct external observation. The first depth level is most easily observed, the last is least easily observed. Although Gurvitch does not use the same terms, this conception of depth levels is very close to the objective-subjective continuum that is being evolved in this chapter. That is, the initial depth levels are the most objective, the later ones more subjective. The following are the ten depth levels:

1. Morphology and Ecology. This surface level is the most superficial and the easiest to observe. Included here would be such phenomena as population density, mobility rates, kinds of churches, means of communication, and so on.

2. Social Organization. Organizations in Gurvitch's view involve "preestablished collective behaviors." They are centralized, possess a hierarchy, and are managed by those at or near the top. They serve to fix the behavior of participants in a more or less rigid manner.

3. Social Patterns. Here too Gurvitch is interested in social forces that guide and direct human beings. However, while social organizations primarily guide behavior, social patterns guide not only behavior but also individual and collective mental life. Included in the stratum of social patterns are customs, signs, signals, and rules, as well as the more temporary fads, modes, and fancies. They are influential not only within social organizations, but also in the collective behavior that takes place outside of organizations.

4. Unorganized Collective Behavior. These are irregular, nonconformist, and insubordinate forms of behavior.

5. Web of Social Roles. Unlike most sociologists, Gurvitch does not look at individual social roles, but rather at the webs, or "skeins," of social roles. There is a tendency to look at these roles in process, and in tension with each other, rather than in harmony. In Gurvitch's system, roles represent the bridge between the more organized, more objective forms discussed before and the less organized, more subjective forms to be discussed next.

6. Collective Attitudes. It is here that Gurvitch moves to the realm of what he thinks of as the more unorganized, spontaneous, immediate, and subjective aspects of social life.

7. Social Symbols. These are more spontaneous than the social patterns discussed in level 3. "Some examples of social symbols . . . are the statues of Joan of Arc calling forth certain collective values evoking national loyalty, the totem which symbolizes the god of the clan, the cross which reveals a whole gamut of values and ideas . . . and the national flag which brings forth the responses of patriotism" (Bosserman 1968, 124).

8. Creative Collective Behavior. This is group behavior oriented toward innovation and invention.

9. Collective Ideas and Values. The broad values and fundamental ideas of a collectivity.

10. The Collective Mind. This concept is deeply related to Durkheim's notion of the collective conscience. It overarches and interpenetrates all of the other depth levels. Although heavily indebted to Durkheim here and elsewhere, Gurvitch is also aware of Durkheim's theoretical shortcomings. For example, he argues, unlike Durkheim, that the collec-

tive mind is not totally transcendent. He also rejects the idea that there is just one collective mind; to him there are several collective minds.

Gurvitch's depth levels are extremely useful from the perspective of this chapter, especially to the degree that they parallel the objective-subjective continuum. But there are a number of problems with his system. For example, he postulates so many depth levels that using them is cumbersome. We need a much more parsimonious system. Second, it is sometimes hard to differentiate between some of the levels. This is especially true of levels 6 through 10. In fact, in her analysis, Korenbaum (1964) omits levels 8 and 9 (as well as 4). Finally, the overarching role played by the collective mind in Gurvitch's system, even with his criticisms of Durkheim, is difficult to defend.

The Horizontal Continuum. In addition to the ten depth levels that he offers as a vertical continuum, Gurvitch also has a sense of another hierarchy, one he things of as a horizontal continuum. However, what he is really interested in here, and he is quite explicit on the point, is the micro-macro continuum. In fact, the two key elements of Gurvitch's conceptualization of the horizontal continuum are microsociology and macrosociology.

At one pole of Gurvitch's horizontal continuum is microsociology, which, as he sees it, deals with the most basic and elementary forms of social life. They are the forms of sociality, the patterns of action and interaction. These represent the more spontaneous aspects of the social world. Gurvitch's macrosociology deals with progressively more organized forms of social life and progressively more large-scale phenomena. Within his macrosociology, Gurvitch differentiates among four levels:

1. Groupings. Following Durkheim, Gurvitch sees the group as a real collective entity that is more than the sum of its individual parts. Groups are created by people and those who belong to a group have a sense of identity with it. Groups are capable of acquiring a structure, although they are not necessarily structured.

2. Social Class. Here Gurvitch supplements his Durkheimian influence with a Marxian influence. Social classes are seen as important enough to deserve a separate category.

3. Social Structure. Gurvitch does not see these as hardened structures, but rather as composed of multitudes of hierarchies that are in constant tension. There is a precarious equilibrium that must be maintained by constant work. Structures are held together, but precariously, by "cultural cement." The various parts of the structure are in a constant dialectical process of structuration-destructuration-restructuration.

4. Global Structures. Finally, at the most macroscopic level, Gurvitch deals with such global structures as city-states, nations, empires, and so on.

Gurvitch's thinking on the micro-macro (horizontal) continuum is not as sophisticated as his work on the depth levels, the objective-subjective (vertical) continuum. Perhaps this weakness reflects his roots in phenomenology and Durkheimian notions of collective conscience, both of which tend to be preoccupied with subjectivity.

Gurvitch's work is useful not only for developing these two continua, but also for dealing with their interrelationship. He argues that each of the components of the horizontal continuum can be analyzed using each of the depth levels: "All those social microcosms and macrocosms represent totalities with depth levels of their own" (1964, 5). Bosserman has attempted to depict this interrelationship, but his image does not reflect the complexities of Gurvitch's thought. Figure 7–1 represents the way I depict the relationship between the two continua.

Despite a number of problems, Gurvitch comes closer than anyone discussed in this chapter to developing the conception of levels of social analysis that I am attempting to evolve here. He has a clear sense of both the micro-macro and objective-subjective continua; but the complexity of

Vertical "Depth" Levels	Horizontal, Micro-Macro Levels				
	Forms of Sociality	Groupings	Social Class	Social Structure	Global Structures
1) Ecological					
2) Organizations					
3) Social Patterns					
4) Unorganized Collective Behavior					
5) Social Roles					
6) Collective Attitudes					
7) Social Symbols					
8) Creative Collective Behavior					
9) Collective Ideas and Values					
10) The Collective Mind					

Figure 7–1. **Intersection of Gurvitch's Horizontal and Vertical Levels of Social Reality**

his model makes it cumbersome and ineffective. There are far too many permutations and combinations to make this a usable model for analyzing the social world (theoretically) and sociological theory (metatheoretically). While it is true that the world is infinitely complex, its complexity does not mean that we need similarly complicated models. In fact, a good case can be made that what is needed to analyze the complexities of the social world is a relatively simple model. I now turn to the creation of such a model.

An Integrated Sociological Paradigm

The model of an integrated sociological paradigm (actually, its image of the subject matter of sociology) to be presented here is informed not only by the preceding discussion of levels of analysis in general, and the microscopic-macroscopic and objective-subjective continua in particular, but also by the discussion in chapter 6 of sociology's multiple paradigms. That chapter ended with a discussion of paradigm bridgers and of the need to develop a more integrated paradigm. Since, as I noted above, each of the extant paradigms is linked to a specific level or levels of analysis, it should come as no surprise that an integrated paradigm must cut across levels of analysis. (The integrated paradigm seeks to integrate levels and *not* the extant social facts, social definition, and social behavior paradigms.) Furthermore, given my more specific focus on the microscopic-macroscopic and objective-subjective continua in this chapter, it should come as no surprise that an integrated paradigm must deal with the interrelationship of these continua.

Following the four dimensions of a paradigm laid out in chapter 6, an integrated paradigm would include a unique set of those components: image of the subject matter of sociology, exemplar, theories, and methods. The delineation of all of the elements of an integrated paradigm is beyond the scope of this chapter. However, in this section I will give a brief, schematic representation of the image of the subject matter of sociology for such a paradigm. In chapter 8 I will examine the ideas of two potential exemplars for an integrated paradigm. When, and if, such a paradigm develops—that is, attracts a group of adherents and supporters—I presume that distinctive theories[5] and methods[6] will evolve.

My intention is to try to cope with some of the problems in extant paradigms by trying to "create" an exemplar for a new integrated paradigm.[7] That is, I want to outline a model that I hope will prove attractive to a number of sociologists who are dissatisfied with available sociological paradigms. I hasten to add, and shall show in the next chapter, that this paradigm has existed in sociology since its inception as a distinctive discipline. I simply wish to call attention to an alternative that has always existed, albeit implicitly, in sociology.

The key here, of course, is the notion of "levels" of social analysis. As I have made clear above, for my purposes the major levels of social analysis can be derived from two basic social continua—the microscopic-macroscopic and objective-subjective continua—and their interrelationship. The microscopic-macroscopic dimension relates to the magnitude of social phenomena ranging from whole societies (or even more macroscopic world systems) to the social acts of individuals, whereas the objective-subjective dimension refers to whether the phenomenon has a real, material existence (e.g., bureaucracy, patterns of interaction) or exists only in the realm of ideas and knowledge (e.g., norms and values). Figure 7–2 is a schematic representation of the intersection of these two continua and the four major levels of social analysis that are derived from it.

It is my contention that an integrated sociological paradigm must deal in an integrated fashion with the four basic levels of social analysis identified in figure 7–2. An integrated sociological paradigm must deal with the interrelationship of macroscopic-objective entities like bureaucracy, macroscopic-subjective structures like culture, microscopic-objective phenomena like patterns of interaction, and microscopic-subjective facts like the process of reality construction. Remember: in the real world all of these gradually blend into the others as part of the larger social continuum, but I have made some artificial and rather arbitrary differentiations in order to be able to deal with social reality. These four levels of social analysis are posited for heuristic purposes and are not meant to be a depiction of the social world.

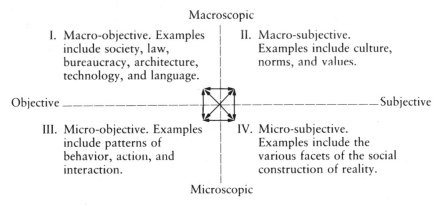

Macroscopic

I. Macro-objective. Examples include society, law, bureaucracy, architecture, technology, and language.

II. Macro-subjective. Examples include culture, norms, and values.

Objective ——————————————————— Subjective

III. Micro-objective. Examples include patterns of behavior, action, and interaction.

IV. Micro-subjective. Examples include the various facets of the social construction of reality.

Microscopic

*Note that this is a "snapshot" in time. It is embedded in an ongoing historical process.

Figure 7–2. Major Levels of Social Analysis*

Not only is an integrated paradigm concerned with these four major levels of social analysis, but also with the dialectical relationship among and between them. Thus, there is a dynamic sense of this interrelationship.

An obvious question is how the four levels depicted above relate to the three paradigms outlined in chapter 6 as well as the integrated paradigm being developed here. Figure 7–3 relates the four levels to the four paradigms.

The social facts paradigm focuses primarily on the macro-objective and macro-subjective levels; the social definition paradigm is largely concerned with the micro-subjective as well as that part of the micro-objective world that depends on mental processes (action); and the social behavior paradigm deals with that part of the micro-objective world that does not involve conscious processes (behavior). Whereas the three extant paradigms cut across the levels of social analysis horizontally, the integrated paradigm cuts across the levels vertically. This depiction makes it clear why the integrated paradigm does not supersede the others. Although

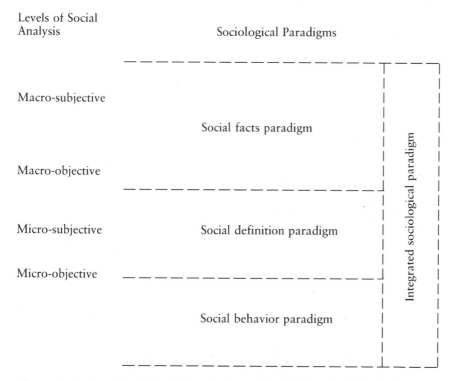

Figure 7–3. Levels of Social Analysis and the Major Sociological Paradigms

each of the three existing paradigms deals with a given level or levels in great detail, the integrated paradigm deals with all levels, but does not examine any given level in anything like the degree of intensity of the other paradigms. Thus the choice of a paradigm depends on the kind of question being asked. Not all sociological issues require an integrated approach, but it is certain that at least some do.

What is discussed above is a brief sketch of the image of the subject matter of sociology of the integrated paradigm, as well as those of the three other paradigms. Those images are all sketched in terms of the major concerns of this chapter: levels of social analysis, microscopic-macroscopic continua, and objective-subjective continua. I will have much more to say about the integrated paradigm in the next chapter, but before I can get to that I need to return to the issue of levels of analysis and use it as well as the integrated paradigm[8] as M_U tools in an analysis and a critical evaluation of a recent addition to the literature on levels.

Wiley on Levels: A Critical Analysis

Recently, Norbert Wiley (1988) dealt with the "levels" problem and related it to the boom in interest in the 1980s in the more specific issue of the micro-macro relationship. There is much merit in Wiley's approach: the sense that the levels issue is more inclusive than the micro-macro problem, the idea that levels represent "paradigm spaces," the four specific levels identified in his essay, the concern for connections among levels through the processes of emergence and feedback, and so on. However, there are some glaring weaknesses in Wiley's work that are largely traceable, I believe, to an acute case of "intellectual amnesia" (Sorokin 1956). Many of the ideas developed by Wiley bear a striking resemblance to earlier work on levels discussed above.[9] What is surprising is that rather than taking this body of work as his starting point, Wiley has roamed far afield (to linguistics, philosophy, anthropology) for intellectual roots. While I think casting such a wide intellectual net is laudable, it should be cast so far only after the most proximate sources of an idea are examined.

Unfortunately, Wiley chooses to deal with this proximate body of work with a general and offhand dismissal of it for using the levels idea too loosely. In fact, Wiley does not even choose to directly address this body of work, but rather dispatches it by critiquing a brief textbook (Ritzer 1988c) summary of it. In addition, Wiley is, in fact, implicitly dismissing his own work. His four major levels of social analysis bear a striking resemblance to the four levels discussed above (as well as in chapter 8) and developed in my work published almost a decade before Wiley's essay, a work that is part of the body of theory ignored by Wiley. In addition, my work and his reveal strong similarities in the analysis of the relationship among levels, in the sense that levels represent paradigm spaces, and in the idea that levels subsume the idea of the micro-macro relationship. One of my objectives here is to demonstrate that Wiley's work suffers from his intellectual amnesia, but I also want to take the occasion to point out various weaknesses in his analysis of levels that exist largely because he has not built carefully on the work of those who have earlier worked on this issue (Merton 1965).

Let me start by pointing out two strengths of Wiley's essay that make it superior to earlier attempts to deal with the levels issue. First, he offers a useful review of four different conceptions of levels (generalization-abstraction, meta or reflexive, historicist, and emergent), which are all potentially relevant to sociology, before settling on the one (emergent) of interest to him. Second, he clearly and explicitly recognizes his starting point for the delineation of the levels: their "relation to the subject."

While Wiley's point of origin is clear, this leaves Wiley with a totally subjective approach to levels of social analysis. In fact, he associates each of his four levels with a subjective orientation: individual-intra-subjective, interaction-inter-subjective, social structure-generically subjective, and culture-extra-subjective. While such an approach has some utility, it ignores the important and longstanding concern of sociologists with material (objective) structures.

As discussed above, in my own work a concern for subjective phenomena is complemented by an interest in objective structures since the micro-macro continuum (also of importance to Wiley) is cross-classified with the subjective-objective continuum to create the four major levels of social analysis detailed in figure 7–2. While these bear a striking resemblance to Wiley's four levels—self or individual (micro-subjective), interaction (micro-objective), social structure (macro-objective), and culture (macro-subjective)—it is clear that objective reality is neglected by Wiley. Let me briefly compare the ways in which the four levels are treated in the two approaches.

I certainly have no trouble with Wiley beginning with the micro-level self, or individual. However, he offers a much more limited conception of this level than I prefer. Most importantly, he gives undue importance to the self at this level and ignores a number of other components of this micro-subjective level (e.g., "mind," "consciousness," "the social construction of reality," etc.). To put it another way, the self, as any social psychologist would recognize, far from exhausts the micro-subjective level.

Similarly, his concern for interaction, or my micro-objective level, is also too limited. Much more goes on at this level than mere interaction. At the minimum, we must include action (including a conscious antecedent) and behavior (lacking such an antecedent) at this level. These clearly belong here because they are micro-level phenomena that cannot be included, at least totally, in Wiley's other, intra-subjective micro-level category. While action, interaction, and behavior may have a subjective component, they also have an objective existence; all three of them may come to be institutionalized in repetitive patterns. I prefer to deal with the subjective aspects of all of these at the micro-subjective level and the objective aspects under the heading of micro-objectivity. In any case, I think we must deal with *both* their subjective and objective moments.

Wiley's conception of social structure and my sense of macro-objectivity are closer, even though he continues the pattern of approaching this level from a subjective point of view. He writes of the "generic self" at this level, but he clearly implies the existence of macro-objective structures when he sees the generic self "as filler of roles and follower of rules" (Wiley 1988, 258). While Wiley emphasizes the subjective generic self here, I would place greatest importance on the objective structures (society, the world-system) that create the rules and roles filled by it.

Wiley's analysis at the level of social structure has an additional shortcoming. He has a difficult time knowing what to do with the organizations that intervene between interaction (and I would add micro-subjectivity) and larger social structures. He ultimately, and reluctantly, includes them as part of social structure. He sees a need for a "distinct level of organizations," but feels that "it has not been fully conceptualized yet." While it may not be "fully" conceptualized, the fact is that some attention has been devoted to this "meso" level of analysis. Hage (1980) has explicitly discussed organizations in terms of a meso level of analysis; Maines (1982) has discussed the negotiated order as a meso level of social analysis; and Ritzer (1981b, 223–27) has discussed the general problem of how to deal with the meso level.

There are few important differences between Wiley's cultural level and my macro-subjectivity. This is because both are discussed in large-scale, subjective terms. My only quarrel here is that Wiley's thoughts on "pure meaning" are too general and could profit from greater specificity and some discussion of such well-known sociological concepts as norms and values.

Not only are Wiley and I similar in terms of our conceptualizations of the four major levels of social analysis, but also in terms of our senses of the relationships among levels. He talks of a continuing process of "emergence" linking lower to higher levels, and of a (also presumably continuous) process of "feedback" flowing from higher to lower levels. I am concerned with the dialectical (i.e., the ongoing, multidirectional) relationship among all levels of social analysis. While my sense of the dialectical relationship among levels of social analysis may be seen as vaguer and more general than Wiley's emergence-feedback specification, it seems to me that there are many more kinds of relationships among and between levels of social analysis than Wiley suggests. A wide array of familiar sociological concepts (e.g., externalization, objectification, socialization, internalization, social control) concern themselves with various aspects of the dialectical relationship between macro and micro levels.

Another similarity between Wiley's work and my own is a shared sense that there is a relationship between levels and what he calls "paradigm spaces." In an earlier work, Wiley (1986, 20) made it clear that theories or paradigms enter the paradigm spaces created by levels. However, Wiley makes no effort to link theories or paradigms to the levels that he generates in the more recent essay. In my work, while I did not use the term "paradigm space," that phenomenon is clearly depicted in Figure 7–3. The *social facts paradigm* is shown occupying the "paradigm space" created by the macro-subjective and macro-objective levels; the *social definition paradigm* fills the space created by the micro-subjective level and part of the micro-objective level; and the *social behavior paradigm* occupies the remaining space created by the micro-objective level. In addition, an integrated sociological paradigm is proposed that occupies the paradigm space created by the dialectical interrelationship among all the levels of social analysis. Thus, while Wiley's work is useful in underscoring the importance of the idea of paradigm spaces, it fails to identify or describe the relevant paradigms or theories that fill these spaces.

It is in his work on paradigm space that Wiley's need to deal with the work of other predecessors is clearest. For example, he would have found Edel's distinction between "reality claims" and "ultimacy claims" of great utility. This differentiation serves to give greater specificity to the relationship between levels as paradigm spaces and sociological paradigms. In fact, Wiley (1988, 260) comes close to Edel's ideas on reality and ultimacy claims with a brief discussion of what he terms "levels imperialism," or "the subordination of one level to another." Unfortunately, it is unclear whether Wiley is describing reality, or ultimacy, claims in his discussion of levels imperialism. In addition, in his discussion of levels imperialism Wiley also ignores my discussion of the politics of interparadigmatic relations (Ritzer 1975c; also see chapter 6) in which supporters of each paradigm are seen as exaggerating its explanatory powers in order to carve out a larger role for it within sociology. This discussion is directly relevant to Wiley's levels imperialism, since paradigm-adherents are clearly depicted as being imperialistic and paradigms are explicitly related to levels.

Similarly, Wiley would have profited from an examination of Gurvitch's work on depth, or vertical, levels and their relationship to the horizontal continuum. There seems to be a strong relationship between Gurvitch's vertical and horizontal continua and Wiley's distinction between levels and sectors, which he, like Gurvitch, sees as involving, in turn, vertical and horizontal dimensions. This is not to say that the two conceptualizations are identical, but Wiley's approach would have been enriched had he dealt with Gurvitch's work and built upon it.

Finally, Wiley and I are in complete agreement that the levels issue is broader than the micro-macro issue. This is clearly implied by my use of the micro-macro continuum in combination with the objective-subjective continuum to identify the basic levels of social analysis. Furthermore, in chapter 1 (see also Ritzer 1988b) I discuss "efforts to deal with 'levels' of analysis within sociological theory . . . and more specific attempts to analyze 'micro-macro' linkages in sociology." However, since Wiley's discussion of levels is couched solely in micro-macro terms, it is difficult to see how his conceptualization actually shows the levels idea to be broader than the micro-macro concept.

In sum, Wiley's contribution to the body of work on levels is welcome, but his work is limited by its failure to be adequately grounded in the relevant literature. Wiley's effort would have been greatly improved had he taken previous work into account and built upon it. However, his ability to come up with a conceptualization of levels that is strikingly similar to the one developed in this chapter, on the basis of the work of a different set of predecessors, gives added credence to the importance of levels in general, as well as to the four specific levels, as metatheoretical conceptualizations.

Having discussed the general issue of levels of analysis in this chapter, and having derived an image of the subject matter of an integrated sociological paradigm from that discussion, I turn in the next chapter to a discussion of the work of two potential exemplars for such a paradigm: Emile Durkheim and Karl Marx.

Notes

1. To be fair to Wagner, the perspectives (ethnomethodology, phenomenology, world systems theory) that point to these additional levels of analysis either did not exist, or were much less significant, when he wrote his essay.

2. Kemeny (1976) said the same thing in the 1970s. However, it certainly is recognized now (see chapters 10–12).

3. Giddens (1984) is critical of the use of dualisms in social theory, while Archer (1988) defends their utility.

4. Actually, of course, objective-subjective is far less defensible as a continuum than the micro-macro relationship; it is more of dichotomy. However, we can think in terms of objective and subjective poles with mixed types in the middle.

5. It may be that integrative theoretical efforts of the 1980s (see chapter 10)

and the even more synthetic efforts of the 1990s (see chapter 11) will form the bases of these theories.

6. These methods may also now be developing in array of works that seek to integrate methods (see chapter 14).

7. Thomas Kuhn, especially in his later work, would clearly be uncomfortable with the idea of "creating" an exemplar. Moreover, Kuhn, at least in his later work, thinks of exemplars as concrete puzzle solutions. There are few, if any, of these in sociology. Our major exemplars are program statements like Durkheim's case for social facts as the subject matter of sociology (chapter 6). This is an attempt to create an exemplar in the Durkheimian tradition.

8. The integrated paradigm is an overarching theoretical perspective M_O (see chapter 3), but it can also be used, as it is below, as a metatheoretical tool.

9. Wiley does cite Edel in an earlier paper (Wiley 1986) in which he offers a preliminary and very different sense of levels of social reality. However, he does little with Edel's ideas in that essay and nothing with them in the essay being discussed here.

8
Potential Exemplars for an Integrated Sociological Paradigm

G iven the image of the subject of an integrated sociological paradigm outlined in the preceding chapter, the objective here is the search for an exemplar for such a paradigm.[1] In this chapter I will review the bodies of work of Emile Durkheim and Karl Marx to ascertain whether one or the other could be that exemplar.[2]

In the case of Durkheim, however, this review is merely academic; his work is not really a serious candidate for such exemplary status (see below). I undertake a review of Durkheim's work from the point of view of being an exemplar for an integrated paradigm because it points up some surprising things about it, especially Durkheim's level of interest in micro-level concerns. Thus, in the case of Durkheim, looking at his work as an exemplar merely serves to cast some new metatheoretical (M_U) light on it. But Marx's work, as we will see, proves to be a strong and obvious candidate for the exemplary role within an integrated paradigm.

Emile Durkheim*

Emile Durkheim is an unlikely choice as a possible exemplar for an integrated sociological paradigm. After all, Durkheim is already an exemplar for the social facts paradigm (see chapter 6), and that would seem to eliminate him as a possible exemplar for an integrated paradigm. It was Durkheim (1895/1964) who argued that sociology should focus on social facts, or what I have termed the macro-objective and macro-subjective levels of social reality. This implies, and Durkheim at times rather baldly took the position, that the micro-objective and micro-subjective levels are not part of sociological explanations. As Durkheim said, "The determining cause of a social fact should be sought among the social facts preceding it" (1895/1964, 110). It is this kind of orientation, as well as Durkheim's effort to carry it through by using social facts to study such individual acts as suicide,[3] that led Tiryakian to see Durkheim as the prototype of sociologism, "the viewpoint of those sociologists who, mak-

---

*This section is co-authored with Richard Bell.

ing sociology a science completely irreducible to psychology, consider it as necessary and sufficient for the total explanation of social reality" (1962, 11). If Durkheim in fact consistently took such an extreme position, then there would be little point in analyzing his work from the viewpoint of an integrated paradigm. But Durkheim does take a softer position on this issue, a position that is highlighted when we analyze his work from such a viewpoint.

Despite this enunciation of a general integrative interest, there remains the issue of whether Durkheim tells us enough about the microscopic levels to warrant further investigation. In fact, there is sufficient evidence of his interest in the microscopic level to at least begin such an exploration. Nisbet (1974), for example, argues that there is little difference between the approaches of Durkheim and George Herbert Mead. If this were only partially true, it would lend considerable weight to the idea, that Durkheim has something to offer on the microscopic levels since these were Mead's primary foci. Alpert (1939) argues forcefully that Durkheim not only understood the micro levels of social reality, but gave them a significant role in his system. He says that Durkheim "was keenly aware of the recalcitrant nature of human beings, of the give and take element in the process of acculturation, and of the fundamental tendency of individuals to be refractory to social discipline. It is erroneous to attribute to Durkheim, as Malinowski does, the theory of unswerving, automatic, 'slavish, fascinated, passive' obedience to social codes" (Alpert 1939, 208). This theme of individual freedom is repeated by Wallwork: "Durkheim was quite willing to accept Kant's claim that the self is free, in some sense to choose . . . 'it is not necessary to believe that the human personality is totally absorbed in the bosom of the collective being' " (1972, 36). Finally, Pope also stresses the microscopic level in Durkheim's work, but in a slightly different way by focusing on the conflict between the unsocialized individual and society: "The force opposing society is the nonsocial (unsocialized) individual . . . , an opposition that constitutes the central dynamic of his theory" (1975, 363). Thus, there seem to be enough claims (although there are certainly many counterclaims) to lead one to believe that Durkheim has some insights into the microscopic levels and these, in concert with his elaborate analyses of the macroscopic levels, might well make it useful to analyze his perspective from the vantage point of an integrated paradigm.

Levels of Social Analysis

Also leading one to look to Durkheim from this viewpoint is the fact that he had a sense of "levels" of social analysis, although he did not spell them out in precise detail. However, Lukes (1973, 9–10) made Durkheim's interest in levels of social analysis very explicit. Translating Durkheim's (and Lukes's) terms into those used in this book, it is clear that he was aware of a continuum of social reality encompassing the macro-objective (anatomical or morphological social facts), macro-subjective (norms, beliefs and practices, and stable social currents), and micro-subjective and micro-objective (the transitory outbreaks in an assembly of people) dimensions. Durkheim had a far clearer conception of the microscopic levels, particularly the micro-subjective, than he is usually given credit for; they will be dealt with later in this chapter along with an analysis of the weaknesses of Durkheim's work in this realm.

The fact that Durkheim views social reality as a continuum rather than as a discrete set of levels is an essential insight, and one that is accepted here wholeheartedly, even though it is often necessary for heuristic purposes to divide social reality into levels. Durkheim's conception of a continuum leads him (and me) to be imprecise on where one level ends and another begins. They all meld imperceptibly into each other.

For example, Durkheim is not precise on where macro-subjective phenomena like norms end and macro-objective phenomena like morphological factors begin. Norms and social currents are certainly macro-subjective, but we begin to move to the micro-subjective level in talking about currents of opinion and transitory outbreaks. The lack of a clear dividing line between the macro-subjective and the micro-subjective is highlighted by Durkheim's use of the French word "conscience" in his early and crucial concept of the collective conscience. According to Lukes, "the beliefs and sentiments comprising the *conscience collective* are, on the one hand, moral and religious and, on the other, cognitive" (1973, 4). The collective conscience encompasses *both* macro-subjective ("moral and religious") and micro-subjective ("cognitive") phenomena, although Durkheim almost always used the term to refer to macroscopic phenomena (see also Wallwork 1972, 37).

The fact that Durkheim did not in general clearly separate the macro-subjective from the micro-subjective is also found in his work on primitive classification where Durkheim (and Mauss) try to show the roots in the social world of the classification system used in the mind. Needham, in his introduction to *Primitive Classification,* points out how it is impossible to clearly separate the two levels in their work: "They aptly call their essay a 'contribution to the study of collective representations,' but their real concern throughout is to study a faculty of the human mind. They make no explicit distinction between the two topics . . . so that conclusions derived from a study of collective representations are taken to apply directly to cognitive operations" (Needham 1963, xxvi). Thus, the following discussion of Durkheim's work begins at the macro-subjective level with the clear sense that he systematically refused to clearly differentiate this level from at least some of the others; indeed, his commitment to the idea of levels of social analysis as part of a social continuum made such clear-cut differentiation impossible.

Macro-Subjectivity

Collective Conscience. As I have already pointed out, Durkheim's richest insights lie at the macro-subjective level. In fact, when Durkheim talked of social facts, he most often had in mind moral facts, or macro-subjective phenomena. In his early efforts at dealing with morality, Durkheim developed the idea of the collective conscience. Durkheim defined this basic concept in the *Division of Labor in Society:* "The totality of beliefs and sentiments common to average citizens of the society forms a determinate system which has its own life. . . . It is, thus, an entirely different thing from particular consciences, although it can only be realized through them" (1893/1964, 79–80). Several points are worth underscoring about this definition in terms of our interest in macro-subjectivity. First, it is clear that Durkheim conceives the collective conscience as being societal-wide when he speaks of the "totality" of people's beliefs and sentiments. Second, Durkheim clearly views the collective conscience as being an independent, determinate, macro-subjective system. But, third, he is also aware of its ties to the micro-subjective level when he speaks of it being "realized" through individual consciousness.

That the collective conscience is also related to the macro-objective form of society is made clear by the fact that Durkheim relates the collective conscience to the type of society in which it is found. Societies are dichotomized into those characterized by mechanical and organic solidarity. In societies characterized by mechanical solidarity the collective conscience covers virtually the entire society and its members, is believed in with great intensity (as reflected, for one thing, by the use of repressive sanctions when it is violated), is extremely rigid, and has a content that is highly religious in character. In societies with organic solidarity the collective conscience is much more limited in its domain and in the number of people enveloped by it, is adhered to with much less intensity (as reflected by the substitution of restitutive for repressive laws), is not very rigid, and has a content marked by "moral individualism," or the elevation of the importance of the individual, the human being, to a moral precept.

Collective Representations. As we have seen, the collective conscience is very general. Durkheim's dissatisfaction with its amorphous character led him to progressively abandon it in favor of the much more specific, but still macro-subjective, notion of collective representation. Collective representations may be viewed as specific states, or substrata, of the collective conscience (Lukes 1973). Although they are more specific than the collective conscience, collective representations are not reducible to the micro-subjective realm: "they have sui generis characteristics" (Lukes 1973, 7). It is the sui generis character of collective representations (as well as the collective conscience) that places them generally within the macro-subjective realm. They transcend the individual because they do not depend on any particular individual for their reality. In addition, they have independent existence because their temporal span is greater than the lifetime of any individual.[4]

Social Currents. Durkheim became even more specific (and more dynamic) in his analysis of macro-subjectivity in his discussion of "social currents":

> But there are other facts without such crystallized form which have the same objectivity and the same ascendancy over the individual. These are called "social currents." Thus the great movements of enthusiasm, indignation, and pity in a crowd do not originate in any of the particular individual consciousness. They come to us from without and can carry us away in spite of ourselves. (Durkheim 1895/1964, 8)

While Durkheim explicated the idea of social currents in *The Rules of Sociological Method* (1895/1964), he used it as a major explanatory variable in *Suicide* (1897/1951). In brief, his argument there was that suicide rates change as a result of changes in social currents. At the most basic level this means that a greater or lesser number of people commit suicide as a result of what happens at the macro-subjective level of social currents. Here is the way Durkheim describes his thinking on the relationship between social currents and suicide:

> Every social group has a collective inclination for the act, quite its own, and the source of all individual inclination, rather than their result. It is made up of currents of egoism, altruism or anomy[5] running through the society under consideration with the tendencies to languorous melancholy, active renunciation or exasperated weariness derivative from these currents. These tendencies of the whole social body, by affecting individuals, cause them to commit suicide. (1897/1951, 299–300)

It is difficult to think of a clearer or more explicit statement of Durkheim's conception of social currents and their impact on the thoughts (e.g., "languorous melancholy") and actions (suicide) of individuals.

Religion. Durkheim devoted an increasing amount of attention over the course of his work to religion as a macro-subjective phenomenon. This increasing concern is best seen in *The Elementary Forms of Religious Life* (1912/1965), which can be interpreted as focusing almost exclusively on macro-subjectivity. Religion, itself, may be seen as a macro-subjective phenomenon, and Durkheim defines this aspect of macro-subjectivity very broadly as "systems of ideas which tend to embrace the universality of things and to give us a complete representation of the world" (1912/1965, 165).

One of Durkheim's concerns in *The Elementary Forms of Religious Life* was the source of religion in earlier forms of macro-subjectivity. Durkheim argued that the roots of modern religion lay in primitive totemism and he made it clear that totemism too was part of the macro-subjective domain:

> Totemism is the religion, not of such and such animals or men or images, but of an anonymous and impersonal force, found in each of these beings but not to be confounded with any of them. No one possesses it entirely and all participate in it. It is so completely independent of the particular subjects in whom it incarnated itself, that it precedes them and survives them. Individuals die, generations pass and are replaced by others; but this force always remains actual, living and the same. It animates the generations of today as it animated those of yesterday and as it will animate those of tomorrow. (1912/1965, 217)

Not only does Durkheim make clear the macro-subjective character of totemism, and the roots of religion in totemism, but he also underscores an essential focus of an integrated paradigm: the *historical analysis* of social forms. On the issue of history, Durkheim is not only making clear the historic roots of religion, but also the fact the people in the past, present, and future are, and will be, faced with macro-subjective forms that shape their lives.

But there is even more to Durkheim's analysis of religion that is of significance for understanding macro-subjectivity. For one thing, Durkheim also demonstrates the degree to which primitive religion is at the root of other forms of macro-subjectivity, including morality and systems of scientific thought. Beyond linking religion to other macro-subjective forms, Durkheim also links it to the micro-subjective level: "we have established the fact that the fundamental categories of thought . . . are of religious origin" (1912/1965, 466).

By way of summarizing this discussion it can be said that Durkheim made the macro-subjective level the focus of his analysis and offered a number of insights including his unwillingness to completely and arbitrarily separate this level from the others, his sense of the multidimensionality of macro-subjectivity as a level of social reality composed of a number of sublevels, and his sense of the historicity of the macro-subjective level as well as of its historical impact on the other levels of social reality. Furthermore, and perhaps most importantly, there are the ways in which the various levels of social reality interpenetrate in Durkheim's work. Although the focus in this section was on macro-subjectivity, there has been much discussion of the other levels as they relate to macro-subjectivity. More of Durkheim's insights into macro-subjectivity will be encountered as we proceed, for Durkheim was ever aware of the way it affects, and is affected by, the other levels.

Macro-objectivity

The macro-objective level in conjunction with the macro-subjective level are what Durkheim (1895/1964, 13) means when he talks about social facts, or "every way of acting, fixed or not, capable of exercising on the individual an external constraint." All of the elements of macro-subjectivity discussed above fit this definition, as do the macro-objective phenomena that are about to be discussed. Macro-objective phenomena occupy a curious role in Durkheim's thinking. They often occupy a position of causal priority, but in spite of this priority they seem to interest Durkheim far less than macro-subjectivite entities. At other times macro-objective phenomena are treated as dependent variables determined by macro-subjective forces.

At the most general level, Durkheim discusses society as a macro-objective phenomenon, but he is not always consistent in the way he deals with society. As Lukes (1973, 12) points out, society was sometimes "real, concrete society, e.g., France or the State." At other times Durkheim tended to talk about more microscopic phenomena, such as the family or an occupation, as society. This tendency to identify disparate phenomena as society is underscored by Pope: "Durkheim's conception exhibits great 'displacement of scope.' . . . He treated France as a society; he also referred to a married couple as a society" (1976, 192). Although this is a problem, the situation is made even worse by the fact that Durkheim sometimes wrote about society as if it was the same as common morality. In this case, his refusal to differentiate the macro-objective and macro-subjective levels becomes a serious problem.[6] A society is best thought of as a structural reality that encompasses a common morality, but for heuristic purposes it is useful to think of society as a macro-objective (structural) phenomenon. More generally, while it is desirable to view the real world as a series of interpenetrating levels, it is best to keep them conceptually distinct for analytic purposes.

Durkheim's overwhelming interest in macro-subjectivity often led him to think of macro-objective phenomena as of secondary significance. For example, Durkheim clearly identifies the church as a macro-objective phenomenon.[7] A church is seen as a structure whose major function is to translate the common ideas of a religion into common practices (Durkheim 1912/1965, 59). But Durkheim is not interested in the church per se, but more in its functions for the macro-subjective religion. Thus, Durkheim defined the church as the structure that serves to differentiate one form of macro-subjectivity (religion) from another (magic). In politics Durkheim saw the state performing a variety of macro-subjective functions including the maintenance of the common morality and, more specifically in modern society, the cult of the individual (Giddens 1972, 18; Lukes 1973, 272). A similar argument can be made about occupational associations. Durkheim conceived of these associations as a means of coping with the pathological moral (macro-subjective) problems that he saw as part of the transition from mechanical to organic solidarity. Anomie is seen as the most important of these moral pathologies and the occupational association and its system of rules was to be designed to help resolve it (Durkheim 1893/1964, 5).

In addition to structural phenomena like society and occupational associations, Durkheim also makes much of what he calls morphological factors. Durkheim sometimes uses these morphological factors as the causes of important social changes; on other occasions he treats them as outcomes of these changes, or even as indexes to these outcomes. Perhaps the best known of the former type of morphological factor in Durkheim's work is "dynamic density." It is the main causal factor in the increasing division of labor. Key factors in dynamic density are the increasing number of people, and their increasing interaction, which, in turn, lead to the transition from mechanical to organic solidarity, or more generally from a society characterized by one form of macro-subjectivity to a society characterized by another form. Thus, somewhat ironically, given Durkheim's focus on macro-subjectivity, the central causal factor in his theory of social change is a macro-objective force (Tiryakian 1962, 17).[8] He is not focally interested in these morphological factors per se, but rather in their impact on macro-subjectivity.

Micro-subjectivity

It was Durkheim's overly zealous position for sociology and against psychology that led many (e.g., Lukes 1973, 228; Nisbet 1974, 32; Pope 1975, 368, 374) to assume that Durkheim's work was weak on consciousness (the micro-subjective level). As Pope (see also Nisbet 1974, 52) points out, a major reason that Durkheim is supposed to have ruled out concern for the micro-subjective is his concern for science. Pope makes this point in discussing why Durkheim did not deal with intent in his study of suicide: "Insofar as intent is employed, though, it will, in Durkheim's estimation, lack the objectivity that is the sine qua non for scientific definitions" (1976, 10–11).

Although there is some truth to these claims, they grossly exaggerate the reality to be found in Durkheim's work. While Durkheim may have made statements against the study of micro-subjectivity, the fact remains that he did deal with this level in many places and in a variety of ways. However, it is also true that he treats micro-subjectivity as a secondary, or residual, factor, or more commonly as a dependent variable to be explained by social facts.

Although one can cite many places where Durkheim was critical of dealing with the micro-subjective level, one can also cite a number of locations in which he demonstrated his awareness of the significance of micro-subjectivity and he even integrated it directly into his work. Although he makes a similar point in several places (e.g., *Suicide* [1897/1951], 315), the following is Durkheim's clearest statement on his ultimate interest in micro-subjectivity: "In general, we hold that sociology has not completely achieved its task so long as it has not penetrated into the mind . . . of the individual in order to relate the institutions it seeks to explain to their psychological conditions. . . . man is for us less a point of departure than a point of arrival" (Durkheim, cited in Lukes 1973, 498–99). It appears that Durkheim focused on "external" facts (e.g., suicide rates, laws, etc.) because they were amenable to scientific analysis, but he did not integrate an understanding of micro-subjectivity into his theoretical system. Even though he never quite achieved an adequate integration, he did address the issue of micro-subjectivity in several different ways.

Assumptions about Human Nature. One of his assumptions about human nature may be viewed as the basis of his entire sociology. That assumption is that people are endowed with a variety of egoistic drives[9] which, if unbridled, constitute a threat to people as well as to the larger society. To Durkheim, people were characterized by an array of passions. If these passions were unconstrained, they would grow and multiply to the point where the individual would be enslaved by them. This leads Durkheim to his curious (on the surface) definition of freedom as external control over passions. People are free when their passions are constrained by external forces and the most general and most important of these forces is the collective conscience. It can be argued that Durkheim's entire theoretical edifice, especially his emphasis on macro-subjectivity, is erected on this basic assumption about people's passions. As Durkheim puts it, "Passion individualizes, yet it also enslaves. Our sensations are essentially individual; yet we are more personal the more we are freed from our senses and able to think and act with concepts" (1912/1965, 307-8).

To return to an issue raised earlier, freedom for Durkheim comes from without rather than from within and this requires a morality to constrain the passions. But freedom, or autonomy, has another sense in Durkheim's work. That is, that freedom does not come from within, but rather is a characteristic of the common morality that is internalized in the actor. Individual autonomy is derived from the internalization of a common morality that emphasizes the significance and independence of the individual (Lukes 1973, 115, 131). Thus freedom is a characteristic of society, not of individuals. Here, as elsewhere, we see the degree to which Durkheim emphasizes the macro-subjective (in this case "moral individualism") over the micro-subjective.

Socialization. Given his views on innate human passions and the need to constrain them by common morality, it should come as no surprise that Durkheim was very much interested in the internalization of social morals through education and more generally through socialization. Social morality is simultaneously both inside and outside of us; common morality "penetrates us" and "forms part of us" (Durkheim, cited in Lukes 1973, 131). Although he based much of his work on it, Durkheim, in Pope's (1976, 195) view of *Suicide,* had "a primitive notion of internalization," one that lacked an adequate "social psychology of internalization." Thus, despite the fact that it is basic to his sociology, Durkheim did not explore the process of internalization in any detail.

Durkheim is not focally interested in the issue of internalization, but rather in how it bears on his interest in the macroscopic problems of his day. The essence of the problem for Durkheim is the decline in the degree to which macro-subjectivity exercises constraint over consciousness (Nisbet 1974, 192). Durkheim's interest in anomie in both *Suicide* and *The Division of Labor in Society* can be seen as manifestations of this concern.

Not only was Durkheim interested in this problem, he was also interested in suggesting reforms aimed at coping with the problem of inadequate socialization. Much of Durkheim's work on education, and socialization in general, can be seen in this context. Education and socialization were defined by Durkheim as the process by which the individual learns the ways of a given group or society. Learned in the process are necessary physical, intellectual, and, most importantly to Durkheim (1922/1956, 71), moral tools to function in society. Moral education has three important aspects (Wallwork 1972). First, its goal is to provide individuals with the discipline they need to restrain the passions that threaten to engulf them. Second, individuals are instilled with a sense of autonomy, but it is a characteristically atypical kind of autonomy in which children understand that they must freely accept constraint (Wallwork 1972, 127). Finally, the process of socialization is aimed at developing a sense of devotion to society as well as to its moral system. All of these aspects of moral education can be seen as efforts to combat the pathological loosening of the grip of macro-subjectivity on micro-subjectivity in modern society.

At the most general level, Durkheim is concerned with the way in which collective morality constrains micro-subjectivity, the way it stands "outside" people and shapes their thoughts (and actions). Of course, macro-subjectivity cannot act on its own, but only through agents. Of greater importance, however, is the degree to which the individual constrains himself by internalizing social morality: "For the collective force is not entirely outside us; it does not act upon us wholly from without; but rather, since society cannot exist except in and through individual consciousness, this force must also penetrate us and organize itself within us" (Durkheim 1912/1965, 240). Wallwork does an excellent job of clarifying the importance of the internalization of morality in Durkheim's system:

> A normal mind, Durkheim observes, cannot consider moral maxims without considering them as obligatory. Moral rules have an 'imperative character'; they exercise a sort of ascendancy over the will which feels constrained to conform to them. . . . Moral "constraint does not consist in an exterior and mechanical pressure; it has a more intimate and psychological character." . . . this . . . is . . . none other than the authority of public opinion which penetrates, like the air we breathe, into the deepest recesses of our being. (1972, 38)

Durkheim offers a specific example of this process of internal constraint in his study on religion: "if he acts in a certain way towards the totemic beings, it is not only because the forces resident in them are physically redoubtable, but because he feels himself morally obligated to act thus; he has the feeling that he is obeying an imperative, that he is fulfilling a duty" (1912/1965, 218).

These concerns with internalization, socialization, and education can all be seen in the context of the constraining effect of macro-subjectivity on micro-subjectivity. Whether the constraint is external, or internalized, it still comes down to external morality controlling the thoughts and actions of people.

Durkheim's limited thoughts on the micro-subjective level led many to assume that his ideal actor was one who was almost wholly controlled from without. His ideal actor would seem to be a total conformist. Although there is much to recommend this view, and some modern sociologists in following Durkheim seem to have adopted this position, Durkheim (cited in Giddens 1972, 113) himself did not subscribe to a view of the actor as a total conformist: "conformity must not be pushed to the point where it completely subjugates the intellect." Although Durkheim left open the possibility of individual freedom, the thrust of his work was in the direction of outlining external constraints on actors and furthermore the desirability of such constraint.[10]

Dependent Variables. Micro-subjectivity most often occupies the position of dependent variable in Durkheim's works determined by various macro-objective and especially macro-subjective phenomena (Pope, Cohen, and Hazelrigg 1975, 419). Although several examples of micro-subjective dependent variables will be discussed, it should be made clear that although Durkheim deals with them, it is often only in a vague and cursory sense. In *Suicide,* for example, Durkheim is quite uncertain how social currents affect individual consciousness and how changed consciousness in turn leads to a heightened likelihood of suicide (Pope 1976).

In *The Division of Labor* micro-subjectivity is dealt with in a most indirect sense, but it is clear that it is a dependent variable. That is, the sense of the argument there is that changes at the macroscopic level lead to changes in micro-subjective processes. In mechanical solidarity, individual consciousness is limited and highly constrained by a powerful collective conscience. In organic solidarity, individual potentialities expand as does individual freedom. But again, although this sense of micro-subjectivity as a dependent variable is certainly there, it is largely unexplored by Durkheim and is left largely implicit. In *Suicide,* however, the status of micro-subjectivity as a dependent variable is much clearer. Schematically, the main independent variables are collective morality and the ultimate dependent variable is suicide rates, but intervening is another set of dependent variables that can only be micro-subjective states. Lukes's point about "weak points" in the individual implies the micro-subjective level: "The currents impinge from the outside on suicide-prone individuals at their 'weak points' " (Lukes 1973, 214).

Lukes (1973, 216-17) goes further on this issue and argues that there is a social psychological theory hidden beneath the aggressively sociologistic language found in *Suicide.* One part of that theory is the belief that individuals need to be attached to social goals. Another aspect is that individuals cannot become so committed to such goals that they lose all personal autonomy. Finally, as has been discussed before, Durkheim believed that individuals possess passions and people can only be contented and free if these passions are constrained from without.

One can find in *Suicide* specific micro-subjective states associated with each of the three main types of suicide.

These subjective states, themselves effects of given social conditions, impel the individual to suicide. . . . "the egoistic suicide is characterized by a general depression in the form either of melancholic languor or Epicurean indifference." . . . Anomic suicide is accompanied by anger, disappointment, irritation, and exasperated weariness . . . , while the altruistic suicide may experience a calm feeling of duty, the mystic's enthusiasm, or peaceful courage. (Durkheim 1897/1951, 277–94; cited in Pope 1976, 197)

Thus Durkheim saw well-defined micro-subjective states accompanying each form of suicide. Just as clear is the fact that these are peripheral interests to Durkheim who maintained a steady focus on the macroscopic level (Lukes 1973, 35; Nisbet 1974, 115).

We can find a specific example of this in Durkheim and Mauss's work on the impact of the structure of society on the form of individual thought. Basically, Durkheim and Mauss argued that the form that society took affected the form of thought patterns. They were contesting those who believed that mental categories shape the social world. Their view is that it is the social world that shapes mental categories (Durkheim and Mauss 1903/1963, 82). While specific components of macro-objectivity (e.g., family structure, economic or political systems) played a role in shaping logical categories, Durkheim and Mauss devoted most of their attention to the effect of society as a whole:

Society was not simply a model which classificatory thought followed; it was its own divisions which served as divisions for the system of classification. The first logical categories were social categories; the first classes of things were classes of men. . . . It was because men were grouped, and thought of themselves in the form of groups, that in their ideas they grouped other things. (Durkheim and Mauss 1903/1963, 82–83)

Durkheim's emphasis on the macroscopic level is well illustrated by this discussion of the impact of society on logical categories. An essential problem is that Durkheim does not analyze the corresponding process— the way in which the operation of mental categories in turn shapes the structure of society.

To do a more adequate sociology, Durkheim had to do more with the micro-subjective level than treat it as an unexplored dependent variable. An almost total focus on the macroscopic level leaves out important elements of an adequate sociological model. Lukes makes some telling points here in his discussion of *Suicide*. He argues, quite rightly, that an adequate explanation of suicide cannot stop with an examination of social currents. In his view, "explaining suicide—and explaining suicide rates—*must* involve explaining why people commit it" (Lukes 1973, 221; emphasis added). Second, Durkheim was wrong in assuming that micro-subjectivity was not amenable to scientific inquiry and explanation. It can be done and furthermore must be done if we are to go beyond partial theories of social life. Nothing is solved by simply acknowledging the existence of the micro-subjective, but then refusing to examine it. Durkheim's commitment to a narrow view of science led him awry as did his tendency to make radically sociologistic statements that ruled out recourse to the micro-subjective:

> He need only have claimed that "social" facts cannot be wholly explained in terms of "individual" facts; instead he claimed that they can only be explained in terms of social facts. . . . it would have been enough to have claimed that no social phenomenon, indeed few human activities, can be either identified or satisfactorily explained without reference, explicit or implicit, to social factors. (Lukes 1973, 20)

In addition to not dealing with micro-subjectivity in any detail, Durkheim also failed to give it an active role in the social process. Despite his disclaimer mentioned above, people are in general controlled by social forces in his system; they do not actively control those systems. This leads Wallwork (1972, 65; emphasis added) to contend that "the principal weakness . . . is Durkheim's failure to consider *active* moral judgment." Durkheim gave too little independence to actors (Pope and Cohen 1978, 1364). When Durkheim did talk of autonomy, it was in terms of the acceptance of moral norms of autonomy. Individuals only seemed capable of accepting these norms and of controlling themselves through their internalization. But as Wallwork (1972, 148) points out, autonomy has a much more active component, "Autonomy also involves willful exploration, spontaneous initiative, competent mastery, and creative self-actualization." Indeed, research into cognitive processes, in part done by Piaget who was working in the Durkheimian tradition, indicates that this micro-subjective creativity is an important component of social life (Wallwork 1972, 67). In other words, a more complete sociology requires a more creative actor and insight into the creative processes.

In summary we have seen that contrary to the view of many, Durkheim *does* have a variety of things to say about micro-subjectivity. However, its residual character in his theoretical system makes his insights vague and amorphous. More damning is the fact that the thrust of this work leads to a passive image of the actor while an active actor is an essential component of an integrated sociological paradigm.

Micro-objectivity

Given his primary orientations to macroscopic and subjective factors in general, Durkheim is weakest on the micro-objective level. He has little or nothing to say directly on individual action and interaction. Implied in his system are various changes at this level as a result of changes at the macroscopic level, but they are not detailed. For example, it seems clear that the nature of action and interaction is quite different in mechanical and organic solidarity. The individual in mechanical solidarity is likely to be enraged at a violation of the collective conscience and to act quickly and aggressively toward the violator. In contrast, an individual in organic solidarity is likely to take a more measured approach such as calling a police officer or suing in the courts. Similarly, in *Suicide* the assumption behind changes in suicide rates is that the nature of individual action and interaction changes as a result of changes in social currents. People may be more or less likely to interact with peers; they would be more or less likely to kill themselves. Suicide rates are used as cumulative measures of changes at the individual level, but the nature of these changes is not explored, at least in any detail. Similar points could be made about Durkheim's other works, but the critical point is that micro-objectivity is left unanalyzed in Durkheim's work.

Conclusion

Does Durkheim offer us an integrated theory of social reality? The answer, given the preceding discussion, must be yes, but it is an integrated theory with a number of serious liabilities. These liabilities would tend to indicate that Durkheim would *not* be an adequate exemplar for an integrated paradigm, but he does offer insights that would be useful in the development of that paradigm. We can close this discussion with an enumeration of the strengths of Durkheim's work and then turn to the problems that prevent his work from being an adequate exemplar.

On the positive side, Durkheim has a number of things to offer to an integrated paradigm:

1. A sense of the multiple levels of social analysis.
2. Some insight into the interrelationships among these levels; indeed of the fact that in the real world they meld imperceptibly into each other.
3. A schema that makes it clear that not only are there major levels of social analysis, but also a number of sublevels within each. For example, there is his identification of collective conscience, collective representations, and social currents within the macro-subjective level.

4. A powerful theory of the macro-subjective level and its significance in the social world.

5. A sense of the importance of historicity and the need to study the multiple levels of social analysis historically.

However, a number of problems point to the fact that Durkheim would not be an adequate exemplar for an integrated paradigm:

1. His overemphasis on the macro-subjective level.

2. His corresponding tendency to downplay the significance of the other levels.

   a. Macro-objective forces tend to be comparatively unexplored causes or results in his theoretical system.[11]

   b. Micro-subjectivity, although there, tends to be underdeveloped. More importantly, it is viewed as a passive force, a dependent variable, that cannot play a dynamic role in his system.

   c. Micro-objectivity is almost entirely unexplored.

3. Although his lack of clear dividing lines is laudable, it sometimes led him to confuse phenomena that need to be kept distinct, at least heuristically (e.g., using collective conscience to refer to both macro- and micro-subjective phenomena simultaneously).

4. Although he has clear assumptions about human nature, they are comparatively unexplored in his work.

5. Durkheim's narrow sense of the nature of science and the scientific method led him to downplay the significance of factors, especially the micro-subjective, which need to be examined more fully in a more integrated paradigm.

6. His conservative politics led him to focus too much attention on the macroscopic level and on reforms that needed to be made at that level.[12]

7. Finally, and most importantly, Durkheim had a tendency to think in one-way causal terms. Although he often addressed feedbacks among various levels, he did not have an overall model that allowed the microscopic levels a dynamic role in shaping the macroscopic levels.

In sum, it should come as little surprise that Durkheim is *not* a suitable exemplar for an integrated paradigm, but his work is not without fruitful insights for those who are interested in developing such a paradigm. More importantly, from an M_U point of view, an analysis of his work as a potential exemplar for an integrated paradigm offers new insight into Durkheimian theory.

Karl Marx

The situation, of course, is quite different in the case of the work of Karl Marx. Given the dialectical image of the subject matter of the integrated paradigm, it is clear that Marx's work would be a likely candidate for exemplary status. Here I am not simply using the integrated paradigm as an M_U tool, but also seriously looking for an exemplar.

As was true of Durkheim, the dominant interpretations of Marx's work would lead one to doubt that his work could serve as an exemplar for an integrated paradigm. Marx has often been seen as a determinist, and not as someone who gives relatively equal weight to all aspects of the social world. An early (Kautsky 1927/1978) and to some degree continuing interpretation of Marx was as an economic determinist. More recently, Marx has been seen as a structural determinist (Althusser and Balibar 1970; Althusser 1977). While evidence to make such cases can be drawn from Marx's diverse and complicated body of work, it is also possible to see his work in such a way that it would be consistent with the integrated sociological paradigm. For example, Meszaros argues that "The Marxian system . . . is organized in terms of an inherently historical—'open'—teleology which cannot admit 'fixity' at any stage whatsoever" (1970, 118). More importantly, Gramsci explicitly rejects deterministic views of Marx's theory and argues that based on Marx's theory we must deal with the relationship between the structure of society and the actor, "the consciousness of the individual who knows, wishes, admires, creates" (1971, 353–54). As was the case with Durkheim, there is at least enough opposition to the macro-determinist position to encourage us to look further in Marx's work for the elements of an integrated paradigm. While with Durkheim we began at the macro levels and worked "down," with Marx we will begin at the micro levels and move "up" to the macro levels.[13]

Micro-subjectivity

Species Being. I begin here (as I did in chapter 4) with Marx's work on the (largely) micro-subjective level because it is, in my view, the basis of his entire theoretical system. The key concept in Marx's work on micro-subjectivity is species being. Marx's thoughts on species being essentially involve a set of ideas about human nature (his philosophical anthropology), although his concepts posit a human nature that is radically altered by the character of the environment. Furthermore, species being is not something that people have had in the past, or have now, but it is something that they have the potential to attain. People always have some level, some elements, of species being, but the full expression of species being can only be attained in communism.

The basis of Marx's conception of species being is his ideas on powers and needs (Ollman 1976). Powers are faculties, abilities, functions, and capacities. Needs are the desires people feel for things that are not immediately available. Both powers and needs are greatly affected by the nature of the social setting. People have natural powers and needs that they share with lower animals, but what interests Marx most are species powers and needs, those that set people apart from lower animals.

The heart of the notion of species-being lies in Marx's view that people differ from animals in their possession of self-consciousness as well as in their ability to link thought to action. Marx borrowed these ideas from Hegel, but Marx is critical of Hegel for discussing self-consciousness as if it exists independently of people rather than focusing on the consciousness of real, sentient human beings: "Hegel makes man *the man of self-consciousness* instead of making self-consciousness the *self-consciousness of man*, of real man, man living in a real objective world and determined by that world" (Marx and Engels 1845/1956, 254).

Marx does much more than simply assert that the consciousness of people is different than that of lower animals: he pinpoints some of the key differences. First, people unlike animals do not simply act mindlessly, but separate themselves mentally from what they are doing. Second, people choose to act or not to act; if they opt to act, they can choose which course of action to follow. Third, people can plan beforehand what they intend to do. Fourth, people are flexible mentally (and physically). Fifth, people can give close attention to what they are doing over long periods of time. Finally, people's mental capacities lead them to be highly social (Ollman 1976).

These mental capacities allow people to engage in activity of a distinctive kind, quality, and pace. People, unlike lower animals, can control their activities through consciousness.

> The animal is immediately one with its life activity. It does not distinguish itself from it. It is *its life activity*. Man makes his life activity the object of his will and of his consciousness. . . . Conscious life activity distinguishes man immediately from animal life activity. It is just because of this that he is a species-being. (Marx 1932/1964, 113)

Marx's abstract sense of human consciousness and activity had to be linked to the real world of other people and nature. Ollman (1976) details three aspects of that linkage. First, people perceive, in a rather unorganized way, nature and other people. Second, by a process of orientation people organize this array of perceptions. Finally, through appropriation people, often in concert with other people, use their creative powers on nature in order to satisfy their needs. People thus shape their settings, but the nature of perception, orientation, and appropriation is also affected by those settings.

We can generally distinguish among three broad, historically situated types of social settings. Primitive society provides people with a "narrow satisfaction" (Marx 1857–58/1964, 85). Life is so difficult that people are only able to use a small portion of their creative potential in the act of appropriation. Capitalism "leaves us unsatisfied, or, where it appears to be satisfied with itself, is *vulgar* and *mean*" (Marx 1857–58/1964, 85). Although in many ways life is not as hard as it was in primitive society because of organizational and technological advances, the nature of capitalism prevents people from expressing their species being. Instead of expressing their creative capacities in the act of appropriation, they are reduced to focusing on earning enough money so that they can afford the commodities that result from the collective acts of appropriation. However, in communism the structural forces leading to the distortion of human nature in capitalism are overthrown, useful organizational and technological advances are retained, and people are for the first time able to fully express their species being. As Marx puts it, communism is an epoch in which man "brings his species powers out of himself" (1932/1964, 151). Or, with slightly different emphasis, Ollman contends that "Communism is the time of full, personal appropriation" (1976, 93).

It is important to note that in discussing Marx's thoughts on species being, and especially consciousness, we are focusing on micro-subjectivity, but it is in the nature of Marx's dialectical thinking that we also must deal with micro-objectivity (the activity involved in appropriation) and macro-objectivity (the structures of the various social settings). Marx's characteristic of often engaging multiple levels simultaneously is one of the factors that makes Marx's work an attractive possibility for an exemplar for the integrated paradigm.

Marx's notion of work also links micro-subjectivity and micro-objectivity. Work may be defined as "conscious, purposive activity in the production process" (Ollman 1976, 98). Work therefore involves *both* consciousness (micro-subjectivity) and activity (micro-objectivity). Most generally for Marx, work involves creativity, but in capitalism people are prevented from expressing their creativity in their work.

In the activity involved in appropriating the natural world, people always objectify—that is, they engage in the process of *objectification*,[14] they produce objects. This process of objectification is normal and expresses species being, if it involves several characteristics (Israel 1971, 39). First, the activity must involve the consciousness of the actors. Second, the actors must be able to fully express their capabilities. Third, the actors must be able to express their sociality in the process of objectification. Fourth, the process of objectification must not merely be a means to some other end (e.g., earning money). In its most general sense, objectification must involve the creative capacities of individuals.

The process of objectification in capitalism clearly does not engage those creative capacities. In producing objects in capitalism, the consciousness of people is minimally involved, only a small proportion of their capabilities are required by their work, people often work in an isolated manner or even in competition with fellow workers, and objectification is often reduced to simply a means to an end. As Marx put it in terms of the last point: "Indeed, labor, *life-activity, productive life* itself, appears . . . merely as a *means* of satisfying a need—the need to maintain physical existence" (1932/1964, 113).

Implied in the discussion of objectification is still another aspect of species being, the fact that people are inherently social. At a micro-subjective level this means that people are oriented to relate to other people, but of course, this also manifests itself at the micro-objective level in terms of peoples' actual relationships with one another. People need to relate to other people both because they need human relationships and in order to be able to appropriate nature adequately. Meszaros underscores the significance of sociality to Marx: "the 'essence of human nature' is . . . *sociality.* . . . 'Sociality' as the defining character of human nature . . . can only exist in the relations of individuals to each other" (1970, 149).

Alienation. If species being expresses Marx's ideal of what people ought to be like, and what they ultimately will be like in communism, alienation deals with what happens to species being in capitalism. One could say that alienation is the state of species being in capitalism and that species being, from Marx's viewpoint, is in an abysmal state. In ideal species being everything is in harmony, everything is interconnected: people, thoughts, actions, other people, products, nature, etc. However, in capitalism that natural interconnectedness is broken by the basic macro-structures of capitalistic society. Thus, alienation is not itself a micro-level concept, but it does imply a breakdown in the most important aspect of micro-subjectivity in Marx's work, species being. As a result of alienation, the individual at work in capitalism does not affirm himself but denies himself, "does not feel content but unhappy, does not develop freely his physical and mental energy but mortifies his body and ruins his mind" (Marx 1932/1964, 110).

The distortions of species being caused by capitalism are numerous. While living in species being, people can be no more or less than they actually are; but in capitalism money has the power to bestow on people powers and abilities that they do not possess (Marx 1932/1964, 167). The structure of manufacturing turns the worker into a "crippled monstrosity" by forcing him/her to work on minute details rather than utilizing the whole of his or her capacities (Marx 1867/1967, 360). The worker also suffers the monotony of doing the same thing over and over again.

Engels (cited in Venable 1945, 137) underscores this problem: "Nothing is more terrible than being constrained to do alone one thing every day from morning to night against one's will . . . in such unbroken monotony, that this alone must make his work a torture . . . if he has the least human feeling left." Capitalism makes people so "stupid and one-sided" that they feel an object is only theirs when they possess it, that is, when it is "eaten, drunk, worn, inhabited." For all of these reasons (and many more) work in capitalism is not an expression of species being. In fact, in many ways it is the opposite of species being. With their human functions so highly alienated, people are no longer able to express their species powers and needs and are forced to concentrate on natural powers and needs. "As a result, therefore, man (the worker) only feels himself freely active in his animal functions—eating, drinking, procreating . . . and in his human functions he no longer feels himself to be anything but an animal. What is animal becomes human and what is human becomes animal" (Marx 1932/1964, 111).

Of course, Marx not only describes and critiques capitalism, he wants to see it overthrown. Species being needs to be emancipated from capitalism. "Human emancipation will only be complete when the real, individual man . . . has become a *species-being*" (Marx, quoted in Bender 1970, 66). Thus, Marx's work on species being, largely on the micro-subjective level, leads him to a critique of capitalist society and to a political program oriented to overcoming the structures of capitalism so that people will be able to fully express their species being for the first time.

Micro-objectivity

Production. The micro-objective level is probably the least developed in Marx's work. However, much of his work is premised on its existence and significance. That is, Marx's materialism, and his rejection of Hegelian Idealism, led him to focus on material, in our terms, objective (micro and macro) phenomena. As Marx and Engels put it: "The premises from which we begin . . . are the real individuals, their activity and the material conditions under which they live" (1845–46/1970, 42). While a focus on "real individuals" provided the basis of Marx's interest in micro-objectivity, activity, especially productive activity, lay at the heart of this interest.

While the form of their consciousness may abstractly differentiate people from animals, it is only when the creativity inherent in human consciousness is transformed into productive activity that people are actually distinguished from lower animals. People "begin to distinguish themselves from animals as soon as they *produce* their means of subsistence, a step which is conditioned by their physical organization. By producing their means of subsistence men are indirectly producing their actual material life" (Marx and Engels 1845–46/1970, 42). What they are is not what they think, but rather what they actually do. "As individuals express their life so they are. What they are, therefore, coincides with their production, both of *what* they produce and with *how* they produce" (Marx and Engels 1845–46/1970, 42).

Thus, a central focus for Marx at the micro-objective level is the act of production. But it is important to remember that Marx is a materialist and not an economic determinist. Thus, he is not restricting himself to economic production, but would also include artistic, religious, and political production, among other kinds of production.

Social Relationships. A second component of Marx's interest in micro-objectivity is the social relationships between people. Marx talks of "the need, the necessity, of intercourse with other men" (Marx and Engels 1845–46/1970, 51). Or, "Man is in the most literal sense of the word a *zoon politikon,* not only a social animal, but an animal which can develop into an individual only in society" (Marx 1857–58/1973, 84). These patterns of social relationships, as well as the pattern of productive activity (which, of course, cannot be done without relating to other people), are the core of a sociological interest in micro-objectivity. Marx does not offer us a great deal on micro-objectivity, but to his credit he is aware of it and the degree to which it (along with the micro-subjective level) provides the basis for the analysis of the macroscopic levels. It is these linkages that are far more insightful than Marx's work on the micro-objective level per se.

Macro-subjectivity

Class and False Consciousness. Marx's discussion of class and false consciousness leads to insight into his thinking at the macro-subjective level. Marx's thoughts on macro-subjectivity in general were affected by his efforts to distance himself from Hegel and the Hegelians who focused on macro-subjective phenomena such as the Spirit, the Geist. The idealism of such an orientation led Marx in the direction of materialism. At some points (e.g., Marx 1859/1970, 20–21) it seems as if Marx goes too far and argues that macro-subjectivity is determined by macro-objective structures. However, this *does* go too far because, as I have already discussed, Marx does *not* offer a deterministic perspective. Thus, while Marx is led at the macro level to focus on objective phenomenon, he does not lose sight of macro-subjectivity or reduce it to the status of an epiphenomenon.

The ideas of class consciousness and false consciousness are intimately related in Marx's work. What is characteristic of capitalism, for both the proletariat and the capitalist, is *false* consciousness. The idea systems of both contain erroneous conceptions of how the capitalist system works and their role and interest in it. We are not surprised to learn that the proletariat has false consciousness, but the capitalist is another matter. But the fact is that the capitalists have a number of elements of false consciousness. For example, they believe that profits come from their expertise rather than from the exploitation of the proletariat. Moreover, capitalists are unaware of the contradictions that exist within capitalism and the fact that their actions are contributing to the contradictions that will ultimately lead to their downfall as well as to the collapse of the capitalist system.

But there is a crucial difference between the two classes. The capitalists can never transform their false consciousness into true class consciousness; this transformation is *only* possible for the proletariat. Proletarians can gain a true sense of capitalism because they are at the bottom of the system, a propertyless class, basically excluded from the system. Capitalists, on the other hand, are so deeply enmeshed in the system that they can never attain the distance needed to see the system for what it really is.

But what exactly are class and false consciousness? Are they micro-subjective characteristics of individual consciousness? Or macro-subjective characteristics of social classes? Lukacs (1922/1968, 51) makes it clear that class consciousness is not reducible to micro-subjectivity; there is a separable macro-subjective realm in Marx's thinking and it has a coercive effect on individual thought and action:

> Now class consciousness consists . . . of the appropriate and rational reactions "imputed" . . . to a *particular typical position* in the process of production. This consciousness is, therefore, *neither the sum nor the average* of what is thought or felt by the single individuals who make up the class. And yet the historically significant actions of the class as a whole are determined in the last resort *not* by the thought of the *individual* and those actions can be understood only by reference to this consciousness. (1922/1968, 51)

Thus, in talking about class (and false) consciousness, Marx is not talking about individual consciousness, but the consciousness of the class as a whole. In other words, he is operating on the macro-subjective level.

Ideology. The other major dimension of Marx's analysis at the macro-subjective level is ideology. An ideology can be defined as an integrated system of ideas that is external to, and coercive over, the individual. Ideologies clearly take on an independent, macro-subjective existence in Marx's theoretical system.

At least two basic, interrelated ideas are involved in Marx's conception of ideology. First, ideologies represent the material interests of the ruling class, but they in turn have an impact on those interests. Second, and relatedly, these ideas constitute an "inverted, truncated reflection of reality" (Lefebvre 1968, 64). However, what is centrally important to our interest in an integrated paradigm is that these ideologies have an existence independent of individual actors. Lefebvre catches the essential point for us here in discussing the effect of ideologies on members of oppressed classes: "It is the role of ideologies to secure the assent of the oppressed and exploited. Ideologies represent the latter to themselves in such a way as to wrest from them, in addition to material wealth, their spiritual acceptance of this situation, even their support" (1968, 76).

An ideological system functions to alter the thoughts and actions of members of the oppressed class. Of course, ideologies do not function in a vacuum; they operate through agents who carry out their dictates. Thus, ideologies affect the actions of agents of the ruling class who, in turn, affect the thoughts and actions of the proletariat. In this way, macro-subjective ideologies are linked to the macro-objective structure of society. And they, in turn, are linked to the thoughts and actions of individual capitalists and members of the proletariat. Thus, as usual in Marx's work, each level is tied into every other level.

Macro-objectivity

Although Marx certainly dealt with all major levels of social reality, his richest ideas deal with the macro-objective structures of capitalist society. While Marx recognizes the independent and coercive existence of macro-objective structures (particularly economic structures), he is also aware that these structures are created by actors both historically and by their daily thoughts and actions. It is also important to note that Marx focused on macro-objective structures not because they are always centrally important, but because they had become centrally important in capitalism. The structures of capitalism had become reified and were exerting control over people's thoughts and actions; they were the cause of alienation. These structures needed to be understood both because of their central importance and because such an understanding would aid in their eventual overthrow.

Commodities. The basis of all of Marx's work on the macro-objective level, as well as the place that it is most clearly tied to the microscopic realms, is his analysis of commodities. As Lukacs puts it: "the problem of commodities is . . . the central *structural* problem of capitalist society"

(1922/1968, 83). While a commodity is not itself a macro-objective structure, it lies, as we will see, at the base of the development of such structures.

Production of commodities is related to the natural process of objectification. As long as people produce for themselves, or for those immediately around them, they are able to control the objects; the objects cannot achieve an independent existence. However, in capitalism this process of objectification takes on a new and dangerous form. Instead of producing for one's self, or for one's immediate associates, the actor produces for someone else (the capitalist) and the products, instead of being used immediately, are exchanged in the open market for money. While people produce objects, in capitalism their role in, and control over, commodities becomes mystified. The commodities, and the market for them, come to be separated from the individuals. As Marx puts it, "a commodity is . . . an object outside us" (1867/1967, 35).

Once we have commodities and a market for them, we have the development of the *fetishism of commodities*. This involves the process by which people lose sight of the fact that it is their labor that gives commodities their value. They come to believe that value arises from the natural properties of things, or that value is conferred through the impersonal operation of the market. Thus, the market takes a place in the eyes of the actors that in Marx's view only actors could perform: production of value. In Marx's terms, "a definite social relation between men . . . assume[s], in their eyes the fantastic form of a relation between things" (1867/1967, 72). According reality to commodities and the market for them, people in capitalism progressively lose control over them.

The beauty of Marx's discussion of commodities and their fetishism is that it takes us integratively from the micro-subjective and micro-objective levels to the macro-objective level. That is, people endowed with creative minds interact with other people and nature to produce objects, but this natural process is subverted and leads to the creation of a macro-objective level of commodities and the market that is external and coercive.

As pointed out earlier, this economic process can be extended to a variety of other realms because Marx conceives of production as something much broader than simply economic production. It is this ability to think of this process that brings us to the concept of reification which (as we saw in chapter 4) can be seen as similar to the fetishism of commodities, but applicable to a number of social institutions and not just the economy. That is, when people believe that a range of social structures are beyond their control and unchangeable, this belief often comes to be a self-fulfilling prophecy: the structures actually *do* acquire a life their own.

Economic Structures. The most general economic, macro-objective structure in Marx's work is *capital*. As an independent, macro-objective structure, capital (through the actors who work in its behalf, the capitalists) became coercive on, and exploitative of, the actors who were responsible for its creation. Thus, Marx talks of the power of capital as appearing "As a power endowed by Nature—a productive power that is immanent in Capital" (1867/1967, 333). Workers are exploited by a system that they have forgotten that they produced and continue to produce through their labor *and* that they have the capacity to change. "By means of its conversion into an automaton, the instrument of labour confronts the labourer, during the labour-process, in the shape of capital, of dead labour, that dominates, and pumps away, living labour-power" (Marx 1867/1967, 423).

Marx also analyzes the process by which private property becomes fetishized in capitalism. In his view, of course, private property, like the other macro-objective components of capitalism, is derived from the labor of workers. "*Private property* is thus the product, the result, the necessary consequence of *alienated labor,* of the external relation of the worker to nature and to himself" (Marx 1867/1967, 117). But people lose sight of this fact and ultimately control over it. Private property, like all reified structures, will need to be destroyed in order for communism to arise. In fact, Marx sees communism "as the *positive* transcendence of *private property*" (Marx 1932/1964, 135).

Division of Labor. The division of labor is another macro-objective component of capitalism that comes under Marx's scrutiny. As usual, Marx links his critique of this macro-structure to his sense of micro-subjectivity: "The examination of *division of labor* and *exchange* is of extreme interest, because these are *perceptively alienated* expressions of human *activity* and of *essential human power* as a *species* activity and power" (Marx 1932/1964, 163). Ollman goes even further in linking the division of labor not only to Marx's early interest in species being, but also to his later work on the structure of capitalism:

> the division of labor occurs and . . . it brings alienation in its wake. The further it develops, that is the smaller the task assigned to each individual, the more alienation approximates the full-blown form it assumes in capitalism. Even at its origins, however, Marx could speak of the division of labor affording us the first example in history of how man's own deed becomes an alien power opposed to him, which enslaves him instead of being controlled by him. (Ollman 1976, 159)

In its most general sense, the division of labor in capitalism refers to the division between the owners of the means of production and those who must sell their labor time to the owners in order to survive. But in a more specific sense, Marx is interested in the tendency to structure work so that people are forced to specialize in ever more minute areas. Such specialization prevents people from expressing all but a few of the aspects of their species being. The specialization of labor develops "at the expense of the whole of man's working capacity" (Marx 1867/1967, 350). For example, narrow specialization has the effect of "stunting him, dehumanizing him, reducing him to a mere fragment of a man, a crippled monstrosity, an appendage to a machine" (Venable 1945, 124).

Social Class. Marx did not devote a lot of explicit attention to social classes, but his isolated statements make it clear that social classes are macro-objective structures that are external to, and coercive on, people. For example, he says: "The social character of activity appears here as an alien object in relation to the individuals. . . . Their mutual relationship appears to the individuals themselves as something alien and autonomous, as an object" (Marx, cited in Ollman 1976, 204). Ollman (1976, 204–5) is explicit that social classes are "reified social relations" or "the relations between men have taken on an independent existence." Ollman also links classes to the prototypical macro-objective phenomena in Marx's work, commodities: *"Class and commodity are brothers under the skin"* (Ollman 1976, 205; my italics). Social classes arise out of the acts of production, people come to fetishize these classes, and as a result they come to have an independent life of their own which is coercive over people.

Conclusion

The preceding discussion makes Marx's multileveled theory much too static. Marx, of course, offered a very dynamic theory of the social world. At one level this is manifested in his general law of capitalist accumulation. But more generally, the dynamism in Marxian theory is provided by his dialectical orientation. It is the *dialectic* that is the key to understanding the interrelationship among the levels discussed above.

Thus, Marx's work, unlike Durkheim's, does provide a viable exemplar for those who wish to work within an integrated sociological paradigm. This is not to say that Marx's work offers anything close to all of the answers required by an integrated paradigm, but it is the place to begin in the development of such a paradigm.

Notes

1. To repeat once again, the exemplar concept is used here differently from Kuhn (from whom it is being borrowed). Kuhn sees an exemplar as a concrete

piece or research that serves as a model for groups of scientists. In my view, there are no such exemplars in sociology. Instead, our exemplars tend to be bodies of work done by particular sociologists that serve as models for groups of sociologists.

2. In *Toward an Integrated Sociological Paradigm* (Ritzer 1981b) I review the work of a number of potential exemplars. To make the discussion manageable, in this chapter I focus on Durkheim and Marx.

3. Although Durkheim is careful to point out that he is dealing with suicide rates, and not individual suicides, it seems clear that the basis of suicide rates is the individual suicide. Furthermore, a suicide rate is no more than the sum of individual suicides.

4. Although collective representations exist outside actors, it is also true that they may extend into the individual and be manifest in cognitive and affective states. This is similar to the contemporary view on norms and values and the degree to which they become internalized.

5. As well as fatalism.

6. Among those who also make this point are Gouldner (1958, xxi), Tiryakian (1962, 17), and Wallwork (1972, 75, 19).

7. Of course, a church also has a macro-subjective component.

8. One possible exception to his tendency to accord causal priority to morphological factors in Durkheim's macro-subjective notion of collective effervescence. The idea appears in several places in Durkheim's work, but is never spelled out in great detail. These are the great moments in history when a collectivity is able to achieve a new level of collective mental exaltation which in turn can lead to great changes in the structure of society such as happened during the Reformation and Renaissance. Although potentially very important, Durkheim never spells out collective effervescence with the effect that it plays a negligible role in his sociology.

9. Which were no doubt stimulated by society.

10. In an interesting paper, Mulligan and Lederman (1977, 539) argue that Durkheim could have conceived of a more creative actor had he adequately differentiated between rules that regulate social life (his focus) and rules "which bring into being *novel* forms of behavior." They argue, in effect, that had Durkheim analyzed these "rules of practice" he would have been able to account for creativity macroscopically. While this may be true, it does not negate the fact that Durkheim also needed a more creative conception of the actor.

11. His work in *The Division of Labor* is something of an exception to this.

12. While he is conservative in terms of our present political views, Durkheim was in the French politics of his day more of a liberal and he thought of himself as such.

13. This is no accident since in a very real sense Durkheim operates with a "top-down" model and Marx with a "bottom-up" model. Furthermore, as we saw in chapter 4, Marx utilizes an architectonic that begins at the "bottom" with a micro-level philosophical anthropology.

14. We have already seen (chapter 4) the importance of this idea not only in Marx's work, but also in that of Weber, Simmel, and Berger.

9
The 1970s:
The Rise of Micro
Sociological Theory

Although the idea of an integrated sociological paradigm will continue to be employed in this chapter, I will return more directly to the issue of levels of analysis, especially the micro-macro continuum (which, itself, is implicated in the integrated paradigm). While the previous two chapters have been more informed by the M_U tool of a paradigm, in this and the next three chapters the micro-macro tool is employed more focally.

As we saw in chapter 6, American sociology in the 1960s was best described as multiparadigmatic. This meant that sociology in general, and sociological theory in particular, was highly pluralistic. However, the social facts paradigm was the strongest of the three paradigms and the most important theories were macro-level theories, structural functionalism and to a lesser extent conflict theory. This first among equals status was probably traceable to the fact that prior to sociology's multiparadigmatic stage (particularly in the 1950s), it was dominated by the macro-level social facts paradigm and its similarly oriented theories, structural functionalism and conflict theory. However, in the 1970s power tended to shift away from macro paradigms and theories and toward the micro-oriented social definition and social behavior paradigms and their associated micro-level theories. This chapter focuses on the rise of those micro theories in the 1970s.[1]

Another general M_U domain of this chapter is politics, the struggles for power within sociology in general and within sociological theory in particular.[2] Such struggles are ubiquitous, existing between individuals, groups, departments, geographic regions, methodological orientations, theoretical perspectives, paradigms, and even national identities. Within this general context, the more specific arena of interest is the politics involved in the rise of micro sociological theories,[3] especially exchange theory, phenomenological sociology, and ethnomethodology. These micro theories waged a surprisingly successful effort to gain hegemony within sociology in the 1970s (Knorr-Cetina 1981a, 1). In fact, they were doing so well that the macro theories that once dominated the field (structural-functionalism and conflict theory) seemed in danger of dropping to secondary status. While a generally welcome development in the 1970s, the ascendancy of micro theories also posed a serious threat to the full range of sociological concerns.

In addition to a general discussion of the development of micro theories, this chapter focuses considerable attention on one example of such theorizing: Randall Collins's (1981b, 1981c) "radical micro sociology." In some senses, Collins's work can be seen as the culmination of the decade-long rise of micro sociology and as an extreme example of its development. Hence it is singled out for detailed metatheoretical critique utilizing the micro-macro and integrated paradigm (M_U) tools.

As we will see, Collins defines radical micro sociology in an extraordinarily narrow way as theoretically committed to the study of interaction patterns and as methodologically oriented to the use of such modern techniques as video tapes of five-second snatches of interaction processes. There is nothing inherently wrong with such a theoretical (and methodological) orientation; the problem lies in the fact that Collins wishes his theory (and method) to become the dominant approach throughout sociology. The predominance of such an orientation, should it ever come to pass, would pose a number of serious problems for sociology. First, its image of the subject matter of sociology (interaction patterns) is shaped primarily by what can be studied using Collins's limited sense of empirical research. Second, Collins's singleminded focus on interaction patterns foretells, should it become the dominant focus in sociology, the loss to the field of its long-standing interest in what can be variously called consciousness, cognitive processes, the social construction of reality, or micro-subjectivity. Concern for such phenomena are deemed out of bounds by radical micro sociology because they are not amenable to empirical-scientific research. Third, radical micro sociology also eschews an interest in large-scale social structures and social institutions, and for much the same reason that it ignores conscious processes: they do not seem capable of being studied empirically. In sum, in pursuit of a narrow scientific ideal, Collins seems fully prepared to eliminate, or downplay, most of sociology's traditional concerns. Were Collins to be successful, the radical micro sociologist would come to dominate a field so denuded that if the discipline's great thinkers, no matter what their particular orientation, were to return from the dead, they would probably choose to continue their work by joining other disciplines.

Collins writes as if he is doing little more than simply describing an ongoing social movement within sociology, but the fact is that Collins himself emerged as a leading figure in that movement. He is, as will be shown, taking a far more extreme position than most of the theorists whose work he applauds and purports to describe. His radical position is exemplified by his 1981 essays on the issue of the relationship between the macroscopic and microscopic levels of social reality in which he argues, in effect, that the macro levels should be reduced to micro-level phenomena.[4] Indeed, he took a far more radical position than that taken by people like Aaron Cicourel and Erving Goffman, sociologists whom Collins would think of as being in the forefront of the movement toward radical micro sociology.

Beyond being analyzed as a theory from the micro-macro point of view, radical micro sociology can also be seen and criticized as a potential sociological paradigm. In that way, Collins's work can be compared to, and critically evaluated from the point of view of, the integrated sociological paradigm (chapters 7 and 8). Such an analysis will underscore the narrowness of, and dangers inherent in, radical micro sociology.

The Emergence of Modern Micro Theories

It is convenient to begin a discussion of the rise of micro theories in the 1970s with the developments in exchange theory in the late 1950s and early 1960s, especially the work of Homans and Blau. It is significant that the first major development in the rise in micro theories occurred in the more scientifically and behavioristically oriented exchange theory than in the micro theories perceived to be more subjective and philosophical, which would gain popularity a decade or two later. It was as if in the 1950s and early 1960s sociologists could at least begin to accept a shift in theoretical focus from macro to micro levels as long as they did not have to endure a simultaneous assault on the field's basic commitment to science.

Homans was casting about for a theoretical alternative to Parsons's structural-functionalism, one that coped with its limitations, especially its macro orientation. Applying principles from psychological behaviorism to sociological questions, Homans (1961/1974) set in motion the development of a behavioral sociology that attracted, and retains, a small, but highly committed, group of followers. While Homans was self-consciously trying to develop a behavioristic and scientific micro theoretical alternative to macro theory, Blau (1964) developed a brand of exchange theory that extended its micro principles to the macro levels. Blau apparently believed that micro theory had to be made applicable to the macro levels in order to be acceptable to sociologists. This belief made sense given the history of sociology to that date, but Blau was misreading the emerging mood of sociologists in the 1960s. Many sociologists, unhappy with both structural functionalism and conflict theory, were open to micro theoretical alternatives and Homans's unabashed behaviorism proved more attractive than Blau's more integrative effort.[5] Sociological theorists, or at least a number of them, no longed needed micro theories subordinated to, or integrated into, macro theories. Some were quite willing to take their micro theory straight and they were even willing to accept Homans's radical, in terms of level of analysis if not orientation to science, departure.

While the work of Homans and Blau shaped the exchange theory that emerged in the 1970s, as the decade progressed the work of Richard Emerson (1972a; 1972b; 1976; Cook and Emerson, 1978) took on an increasingly central role. It moved off in a variety of new directions and attracted a whole new population of supporters.

Already underway while Homans and Blau were formulating their perspectives were developments in phenomenological sociology and ethnomethodology (and, a bit later, existential sociology). While these theories blossomed in the 1970s, the base was laid especially in 1967 with the publication of important works by Schutz (1932/1967), Berger and Luckmann (1967), and Garfinkel (1967). These pioneering works were perceived as representing not only a shift in level of analysis, but also as an assault on the scientific principles of mainstream sociology. I underscore *perceived* since, as I (Ritzer 1988c) have pointed out elsewhere, these theories were more macro oriented and more committed to science than is generally assumed. Whatever the reality, the work of individual theorists like Schutz (Bierstedt 1963; Mehan and Wood 1975; Morris 1977), as well as phenomenology and ethnomethodology in general (Ritzer 1975c; Morris 1977; Douglas 1980), were interpreted as non- (or even anti-) scientific micro sociologies.

Phenomenologists and ethnomethodologists were partially responsible for the misperceptions of them by mainstream sociologists. The political exigencies of their minority position led them to attack traditional macro theories and these attacks tended to exaggerate their position as well as their differences with extant macro theories. Examples include the work of Zimmerman and Pollner (1970), Mackay (1974), and most notably Garfinkel's (1967) attack on mainstream sociology for viewing actors as "judgmental dopes" rather than as people who play an active role in creating social reality.

As a result of such strong statements, as well as systematic misinterpretation by mainstream sociologists, phenomenologists and ethnomethodologists faced a great deal of hostility from conventional sociologists (e.g., Coleman 1968), especially for their concern with "trivial" micro sociological issues and for losing sight of the importance of social structures and social institutions. Their apparent focus on creative consciousness led to the view that theorists with such an orientation were not, indeed could not be, scientific. This led to political outbursts like Coser's (1975), in which he complained that ethnomethodology represented an "orgy of subjectivism." Much of this turmoil can be seen as efforts by macro theorists to fend off threats from phenomenology and ethnomethodology. In fact, Coser's tirade, coming as it did in mid-decade, was a clear manifestation of an emerging awareness on the part of macro theorists of the growing threat being posed by phenomenology, ethnomethodology, and exchange theory. It is in this political atmosphere, with the rise of micro theories[6] and the decline of macro theories, that we need to examine Randall Collins's radical micro sociology.

The Creation of Radical Micro Sociology

It is in Collins's 1981 work, coming just after the close of the decade marked by the rise of micro theories, that we witness a shift in the orientation, and a dramatic change in the ambitions, of the "sociologies of everyday life" (especially phenomenology and ethnomethodology). Sensing a shift in the political winds near the end of the 1970s, Collins appears to have believed that such micro theories not only had a chance of gaining wide-scale acceptance, but even predominance, within the field. This seemed especially likely to occur, in his view, if the traditional concerns of these sociologies were molded—it might even be claimed radically transformed—into a highly positivistic orientation. Collins, like Homans and others before, seemed to recognize that sociologists were more willing to accept a micro approach when it was linked to a conventional (positivistic) notion of science. In other words, in order to make phenomenology and ethnomethodology more attractive to larger numbers of sociologists, phenomenology-ethnomethodology had to be made more scientific. However, in shaping his perspective to fit these political exigencies, Collins created a seriously flawed micro theory that had little to offer in terms of many of the concerns of both micro and macro sociological theories. In the name of science, Collins offered sociology theoretical impoverishment. Collins's orientation posed a major threat not because of its narrow focus, but because it was a narrow perspective with grand ambitions.

Many of Collins's theoretical problems can be traced to his strong belief in a very narrow conception of scientific sociology. In the preface to an early book, *Conflict Sociology*, he predicts that when historians look back on this era they "will see a great intellectual revolution in the twentieth century—establishment of a true social science" (Collins 1975, x). On the very first page of the text he voices his optimism: "My contention is that sociology can be a successful science and that it is well on the way to becoming so" (Collins 1975, 1). He closes the book in a similar fashion: "Sociology is on its way. In the diffuse fashion characteristic of large twentieth-century fields, we are passing slowly into becoming a science" (Collins 1975, 541).

The problem arises not so much from Collins's acceptance of a narrow definition of science, but from the difficulties involved in reconciling his restricted view of science with the importance accorded to individual consciousness in theories that stand at the root of his theorizing. In order, apparently, to resolve this contradiction, Collins attempts to free himself from the nonpositivistic, romantic, idealistic, and aesthetic elements of phenomenology and ethnomethodology without totally rejecting the theories themselves. So, for example, in order to avoid the phenomenologist's idealistic concern with consciousness, Collins (1981c, 991) locates "people's cognitions in their concrete lived experience." More specifically, Collins (1981c, 1010) argues that phenomena like "personality" and "attitudes," ordinarily situated within individual consciousness, should instead be seen as part of social situations, especially conversational interactions. From Collins's positivistic perspective, things like cognitions, personality, and attitudes are not amenable to empirical research, while concrete lived experiences, especially conversations, are open to research conducted in this manner. Much of this interest in focusing on interaction, and in not being concerned with consciousness, is derived from Collins's sense of positivistic, empirical sociology.

Over the years Collins refined his sense of the nature of empirical sociology. In his earlier work he had only a general sense of the need for "immediate observational methods focusing on everyday life" (Collins 1975, 8). In other words, all sociological methods that do not involve direct observation of everyday life, including interviews, questionnaires, and historical research, are invalid approaches. Collins's extremely strong, but uncrystallized, views on methodology were clarified and specified in his work in the early 1980s. He argued that his colleagues in micro sociology had developed methods that were "epistemologically and empirically much more thorough than any previous sociological method" (Collins 1981b, 82). Reliance on this methodology is deemed as being crucial to Collins's aspirations (apparently still unfulfilled in 1981) to develop a truly successful science of sociology. The methodological advance that had Collins so excited is the relatively new and growing ability to study micro social processes in ultrafine detail through the use of such technologies as audio and especially video tapes. These technologies, according to Collins, provide us with an unprecedented ability to study directly the world of everyday life. Such research is beginning to allow us to uncover "pure micro-principles" of social life, and it is these principles that "should be at the core of all empirically causal explanations in sociology" (Collins 1981b, 101). As we will see, Collins's commitment to science, as well as to a specific set of empirical methods, plays a central role in shaping his own theorizing. Indeed, this emerges as a central criticism. His theoretical orientation is profoundly shaped, some might even say overwhelmed, by his methodological commitments.

Radical micro sociology takes as its image of the subject matter of sociology what Collins calls "interaction ritual chains," which he defines as bundles of "individual chains of interactional experience, crisscrossing each other in space as they flow along in time" (Collins 1981c, 998). In explicating this focus, Collins clarifies a great deal about his theoretical perspective as well as how it differs from other micro theoretical perspectives. First, Collins does not want his theory to be confused with exchange theory which he regards as (too) reductionistic. Thus, instead of focusing on the behavior of individuals, Collins raises the level of analysis to interaction, chains of interaction, and the "marketplace" for such interaction. He also rejects the exchange theorist's view of the actor as rationally deciding how to behave. This is just another unwarranted mentalistic assumption as far as Collins is concerned, one that is beyond the boundaries of scientific sociology.

Second, Collins takes pains to differentiate his position from that of ethnomethodologists and phenomenologists. Basically, he wants to avoid their concern with consciousness and focus instead on concrete lived experience. Although he is willing to admit that people do reflect on alternative actions, he comes to the truly startling conclusion that such deliberations do not make any difference. He says, "choices consciously made . . . would be the same as choices made without reflection" (Collins 1981c, 1005). In other words, it makes no sociologically meaningful difference whether people engage in conscious processes; consciousness is irrelevant to scientific sociology.

Having put distance between himself and the major micro theories, Collins turns his attention to macro-level phenomena and the macro theories that focus on them. While it is apparent that Collins is an ardent supporter of his own brand of micro theory, it is almost equally obvious that he is strongly opposed to macro theories. As early as *Conflict Sociology* (1975) Collins was critical of the foci of structural functionalism, including society, roles, and systems, for, among other things, not being amenable to observation. He seems particularly upset by the structural functionalist's long-standing and deeply rooted interest in norms as an explanation of social behavior. He goes so far as to say that "the terminology of norms ought to be dropped from sociological theory" (Collins 1981c, 991). Although norms are rejected, like most other structural-functional concepts, at least in part because they cannot be observed empirically, Collins has a number of other objections against this entire set of macro concepts including the fact that they are "empirically ungrounded," "inaccurate," "*glosses* on the underlying reality" and involve

"ideology or reification" (Collins 1981b, 85). Collins has a similarly negative attitude toward concepts associated with conflict theory. He argues,
for example, that there are no "inherent objective" entities like property
or authority; all there are are "varying senses that people feel at particular
places and times of how strong these enforcing coalitions are" (Collins
1981c, 997). Finally, Collins seems to be criticizing both structural functionalism and conflict theory on the issue of the sources of action in social
life. His point is that it is only people who do anything; structures, organizations, classes, and societies "never *do* anything. Any causal explanation must ultimately come down to the actions of real individuals"
(Collins 1975, 12).

Interestingly, in spite of his attacks on macro theories and macro-
level phenomena, Collins ends up bootlegging at least some of them into
his sociology. Since Collins's actors do not think creatively, and it would
not matter if they did, the issue is how they come to take the actions they
do? The answer is that in deciding what to do individuals rely "largely
on tacit assumptions and organization routines" (Collins 1981c, 994). It
seems to me that whether Collins cares to admit it, such assumptions
involve macro-, or at least meso-level, concepts. The use by Collins of the
concept of "generalized cultural resources" also indicates a concern with
macro-subjective constraints on actors. In spite of these apparent slips, it
is clear that programmatically Collins downplays the significance of macro-level concepts while focusing his attention on the interactional domain.

Although he rejects macro concepts and macro theories, Collins recognizes their (threatened) dominance in sociology. Given their centrality,
he attempts to undermine their position by showing that "all macrophe-
nomena" can be translated "into combinations of micro-events" (Collins
1981c, 985). More programmatically, Collins (1981b, 82) declares that
"the effort coherently to reconstitute macro-sociology upon radically empirical micro-foundations is the crucial step toward a more successful
sociological science." In terms of a specific example, this means that social
structures may be translated empirically into "patterns of repetitive microinteraction" (Collins 1981c, 985).

While making his case for micro sociology and against traditional
sociological conceptions of macro-phenomena, Collins does admit a number of (limited) uses of macro concepts. First, they can be used as sociological shorthand for a series of micro situations as long as we remember
that such concepts are based on micro situations and can *only* be validated
there. Second, Collins is prepared to use macro concepts to refer to the
times when people make reference to other situations, or to abstract or
reified entities. Third, macro concepts can be used to refer to the cumulative effect of repeated micro situations on the individual. Fourth, macro
sociology may refer to comparative analyses across a series of micro sit-

uations. Finally, and most curiously, Collins is willing to admit the existence of pure macro variables: "the dispersion of individuals in physical space," "the amount of *time* that social processes take," and "the *numbers* of individuals involved" (Collins 1981c, 989). Collins appears to mean that these are macro concepts because they apply to all social situations, but that is not the usual way in which "macroscopic" is used in sociology. Ordinarily, the term is used to denote large-scale social phenomena that have an impact on great numbers of individuals. Instead of being thought of as macro concepts, time, space, and dispersion should be used as Collins actually employs them, that is as useful tools for differentiating among phenomena all along the micro-macro continuum.

In sum, I believe that Collins offers an extreme form of micro sociology that involves politically motivated attacks on *all* existing sociological theories. Collins's ambitions for his radical micro sociology make it necessary to scrutinize his position very carefully. In the next two sections I critically analyze radical micro sociology, especially its position on the issue of the relationship between micro and macro levels, both from the points of view of the micro-macro continuum and the integrated sociological paradigm.

Radical Micro Sociology: A Critique Utilizing the Micro-Macro Continuum

In critiquing Collins in this section, my focus will be on one aspect of his work that goes, I think, to the heart of his perspective; that is, his thoughts on the relationship between the macroscopic and microscopic levels of analysis. As I made clear above, Collins's most basic position on this relationship is the elimination of the macro levels by reducing them to micro-level phenomena. Although Collins says that he does not want to completely discourage macro analyses, he makes it clear that these can at best be "merely plausible in a general way" and "theoretically incomplete" (Collins 1981b, 94). Among other things, this seems to imply that micro analyses are theoretically complete; they are all we need to do sociology. Whatever the merits of such an approach, it is hardly an adequate integration of micro- and macro-level concerns. In this section I will discuss the inadequacies of such an approach from the perspective of other micro sociologies. As we will see, more traditional phenomenologically and ethnomethodologically inclined sociologists take a far more balanced position on the relationship between the micro and the macro levels. This is another clear indication that Collins was not simply reporting on developments in radical micro sociology, but was in fact taking a leadership position in its development and was among the most radical of the radical micro sociologists.

We can start with the work of Knorr-Cetina (1981a) who was the coeditor of the volume in which one of Collins's essays on radical micro sociology appeared. Although she too accords great significance to the interactional domain, Knorr-Cetina is less enamored of empirical science than Collins with the result that both consciousness and macro-level phenomena are accorded a greater role in her work. Thus, she is not afraid to discuss things like "practical reasoning" or reluctant to give macro structures and macro institutions independent existence or significance. While Knorr-Cetina, like Collins, makes the case for a radical reconstruction of macro theory on a micro sociological base, she is also willing to consider the much less radical course of simply integrating micro sociological results into macro social theory. In addition, she seems to take the position that the ultimate goal of micro sociological research is a better understanding of the larger society, its structures and institutions:

> I . . . believe in the seeming paradox that it is through micro-social approaches that we will learn most about the macro-order, for it is these approaches which through their unashamed empiricism afford us a glimpse of the reality about which we speak. Certainly, we will not get a grasp of whatever is the whole of the matter by a microscopic recording of face-to-face interaction. However, it may be enough to begin with if we—for the first time—hear the macro-order tick. (Knorr-Cetina 1981a, 41–42)

Thus, it seems clear that Knorr-Cetina takes a far more balanced position on the relationship between the micro and macro levels than does Collins.

An even more integrative position on the micro-macro issue is taken by Knorr-Cetina's coeditor, Aaron Cicourel (1981). This is particularly surprising since Cicourel is clearly one of the people Collins would put in the forefront of the movement toward micro sociology. If Cicourel is leading a movement in sociology, it is not the same one that Collins is describing. The difference between the two is nowhere clearer than in the following statement by Cicourel: "Neither micro- nor macro-structures are self-contained levels of analysis, they *interact* with each other at all times despite the convenience and sometimes the dubious luxury of only examining one or the other level of analysis" (1981, 54). There is an implied criticism in this of Collins, but Cicourel takes another position which can be seen as a more direct critique of the kind of position adopted by Collins: "The issue is not simply one of dismissing one level of analysis or another, but showing how they must be integrated if we are not to be convinced about one level to the exclusion of the other by conveniently ignoring competing frameworks for research and theorizing" (1981, 76).

In many ways the most interesting contrast to Collins's position on the micro-macro issue is to be found in Erving Goffman's (1983) presidential address to the American Sociological Association. This comparison is particularly instructive because Collins is so high on Goffman's work and we would naturally expect to find a strong similarity between Goffman's thoughts on the "interaction order" and Collins's ideas on "interaction ritual chains." In the introduction to a book of his own essays, Collins (1981a, 6; see also Collins 1986c) discusses his "special effort to do justice to Erving Goffman. The more we look at his work . . . the more he emerges as the leading figure in the microsociology of our times." In Goffman, Collins *seems* to have found the exemplar for his radical micro sociology. Indeed, Goffman himself seems to define his life work in terms that are very close to those used by Collins: "My concern over the years has been to promote acceptance of this face-to-face domain as an analytically viable one—a domain which might be titled, for want of a happy name, the *interaction order*—a domain whose preferred method of study is microanalysis" (1983, 2). However, there are major differences between Goffman and Collins; what is especially important is the fact that while Collins has a singleminded focus on chains of interaction, Goffman is interested in the relationship between the interaction order and the larger society.

In addition to implying a broader, more integrative interest than Collins, Goffman also takes a series of positions that can be viewed as direct challenges to the kind of singlemindedness that characterizes Collins's work. For example, Goffman labels as personally uncongenial the reductionistic argument of some sociologists (including implicitly Collins) "that all macro-sociological features of society, along with society itself, are an intermittently existing composite of what can be traced back to the reality of encounters—a question of aggregating and extrapolating interactional effects" (Goffman 1983, 8). Goffman goes on to specify an array of macro social phenomena that he does not believe can be simply aggregated from the interactional domain. It seems quite clear from Goffman's point of view that Collins would be judged guilty of reductionism.

There is another basis on which Goffman would reject Collins's position and that is on the latter's view that the interactional level is the only truly empirical level of analysis. Goffman does not "subscribe to the notion that face-to-face behavior is any more real, any less of an arbitrary abstraction, than what we think of as the dealings between two corporations" (1983, 9).

In sum, it appears that leading figures in micro sociology like Cicourel and Goffman do not fit under the heading of "radical microsociologists" and, in fact, are in a number of places directly critical of the kind of sociology supported by Collins. I believe that there are good reasons to suspect that Collins was out of step with the mainstream of micro sociology. Among other things, other micro sociologists had a stronger sense of the macro levels and of the need to integrate macro and micro sociology. The views of the sociologists discussed in this section suggest the outlines of an internal, micro sociological critique of radical micro sociology. In the next, and final section, my objective is to offer an external critique of radical micro sociology from the point of view of the integrated sociological paradigm.

Radical Micro Sociology: A Critique Utilizing the Integrated Sociological Paradigm

This section is based on my work on the paradigmatic status of sociology (chapter 6) as well as the integrated sociological paradigm (chapters 7 and 8). With this as a base, I will first analyze what the growth in micro theories in the 1970s tells us about the status of the multiple paradigms that characterized sociology in the 1960s. Second, I will examine how radical micro sociology fits into the paradigmatic scheme of things. Third, I will compare Collins's radical micro sociology with the integrated sociological paradigm.

Given the multiparadigmatic image of sociology in the 1960s, the first issue is what does the rise in micro theories (and the decline in macro theories) in the 1970s tell us about the relative standing of these paradigms? First I believe it reflected the decline of the social facts paradigm which, at one time, had been far and away *the* most important paradigm in sociology. The decline in importance of both structural functionalism and conflict theory is indicative of the growing weakness of this paradigm. Second, there is a clear manifestation in this of the increasing strength of the other paradigms in the 1970s. Within the social definition paradigm, the boom in interest in phenomenology, ethnomethodology, and existentialism more than compensated for the comparative weakness, at least at the time, of symbolic interactionism. The attraction of exchange theory indicated the small, but if anything growing, following for the social behavior paradigm. Overall, I would say that a review of the history of sociological theory in the 1970s indicates that the robust character of phenomenology and ethnomethodology reflects the fact that the social definition paradigm might have been on the verge of replacing the social facts paradigm in the dominant position among sociological paradigms (with the social behavior paradigm retaining, and perhaps even improving on, its strong minority position). While the relative fortunes of the paradigms might have shifted in the 1970s, sociology remained a multiple paradigm science.

Given these general ideas on the relationship between theories and paradigms, the next issue is the place, more specifically, of Collins's radical micro sociology in all of this. By putting the issue in a paradigmatic context, we will be able to see more clearly the relationship between radical micro sociology and the other micro theories. While there is little difficulty involved in placing all of the other micro theories in either the social definition or social behavior paradigm, radical micro sociology cannot be pigeonholed[7] so easily. The only thing that is clear here is that radical micro sociology *cannot* be seen as part of the social facts paradigm. One would expect that Collins's work would fit comfortably within the social definition paradigm given, among other things, its roots in phenomenology and ethnomethodology. Although Collins's concern with interaction does fit within this paradigm, his desire to exclude consciousness from consideration ultimately sets him apart from social definitionism. It might seem that his exclusion of consciousness, as well as his commitment to study objective patterns of interaction, would put his work within the social behavior paradigm. However, there are problems involved in that association, in that Collins regards exchange theory as reductionistic and he cannot accept its assumptions about rational actors. While the supporters of behavioral sociology do not view actors as rational, they too would be rejected by Collins for being reductionistic.

Thus, radical micro sociology is in Collins's view incompatible with *every* extant sociological theory. This, in turn, leads to the thought that perhaps what Collins was trying to do, albeit not wholly consciously, was to carve out a domain somewhere between the social definition and social behavior paradigms for a *new sociological paradigm*.

If, indeed, it is the case that radical micro sociology might better be seen as an effort to lay the groundwork for a new sociological paradigm, then the politics of the endeavor are highlighted even further than they have been to this point in the analysis. The relationship between extant paradigms is characterized by an overheated political atmosphere dominated by efforts of supporters of each to make the case for their own paradigm and against competing paradigms. Given this kind of atmosphere, advocates like Collins of a new paradigm can anticipate a hostile reception. Their greatest chance of success lies in denigrating the significance of existing paradigms while making an exaggerated case for their own aspiring paradigm. The rhetoric of radical micro sociology's programmatic statements indicates that this may well have been what was going on here. In other words, steps were being taken to begin the difficult process of creating a "paradigm space" for a new sociological paradigm.

Looking at Collins's work as an effort to create a radical micro sociological paradigm brings us to the integrated sociological paradigm. In this final section of this chapter my objective is to try to cast still more light on the nature of radical micro sociology by comparing it to my effort to create the basis for an integrated sociological paradigm. Several things need to be kept in mind. First, while I sought consciously to develop a basis for a new sociological paradigm, Collins's intentions are much more ambiguous and such an objective is, at best, only implicit in his work. Second, the scope of my effort is very broad, while Collins is intentionally narrow in his delineation of radical micro sociology. Third, my personal bias is that what sociology needs is more integrative efforts rather than another narrowly defined paradigm.

It should be clear that the integrated sociological paradigm's image of the subject matter of sociology is very different from, if not diametrically opposed to, the image offered by radical micro sociology. While the integrated paradigm seeks to encompass all major levels of social reality, radical micro sociology defines for itself a very narrow domain, one that is clearly narrower than any existing paradigm. When we look at micro sociology as a potential paradigm, we can see that radical micro sociology defines interaction ritual chains as the subject matter of sociology. If they do nothing else, the ideas of sociology's multiple paradigms and the integrated sociological paradigm allow us to see the narrowness of radical micro sociology. Its sense of the scope of sociological concerns represents an infinitesimal portion of the parameters of sociology defined by the integrated sociological paradigm. By allowing us to see the narrowness of radical micro sociology (which is not inherently a problem), the integrated paradigm also highlights the danger associated with this approach. The danger lies not in the nature of the approach, but in the ultimacy claims of defining the entire field of sociology in such a limited manner. In other words, radical micro sociology might well be acceptable as *one* of several narrowly defined sociological paradigms, but it would be unacceptable as *the* sociological paradigm.

The integrated sociological paradigm not only allows us to better understand the scope and ambitions of radical micro sociology, it also allows us to pinpoint more precisely where its concerns fit within the broader scope of sociological interests. Of the four major levels of concern in the integrated paradigm, Collins is clearly *not* interested in three of them: macro-objective, macro-subjective, and micro-subjective. This leaves as Collins's major concern the micro-objective level of patterns of action and interaction, or what he calls interaction ritual chains. Although micro-objectivity is coterminous with a large part of interaction ritual chains, the latter does not exhaust the concerns at the micro-objective level. In order for the reader to more fully understand interaction ritual chains, I need to add a bit to my earlier conceptualization of the major levels of social reality.

In order to keep the original model simple, I had ruled out a number of complexities that threatened to muddle its orientation. One such complexity is the mesoscopic level (Hage 1980; Maines 1982) and it was with this (and other bits of unfinished business) in mind that I (Ritzer 1981b) concluded that there was "much more to be done" with the mesoscopic level. The addition of a mesoscopic level points to the existence, given the general perspective of the integrated paradigm, of the meso-objective and meso-subjective levels of social reality. The addition of these meso levels allows us to fully encompass Collins's interaction ritual chains. The notion of a "marketplace" for such interaction would seem to fall best within the meso-objective level, while the cultural rituals that play a key role in guiding interaction would fall within the meso-subjective realm. Bear in mind that Collins's interaction ritual chains exhaust only a small portion of the phenomena that could be categorized at the meso levels.

In sum, radical micro sociology defines as the subject matter of sociology a portion of the micro-objective, meso-objective, and meso-subjective levels of social reality. It not only does not exhaust these levels, but it ignores entirely the three other major levels of social reality: micro-subjective, macro-objective, and macro-subjective. To put this in more conventional sociological terms, virtually everything that is of importance to most sociologists—social structure, culture, and the processes of reality construction—is omitted from radical micro sociology. It is these omissions, coupled with its ambitions of being coterminous with sociology, that made radical micro sociology a profound threat to virtually all sociologists.

Conclusions

The excessive reach and intellectual problems of radical micro sociology aside, the fact remains that micro theories and the micro oriented paradigms with which they are associated were on the ascendancy in sociology in the 1970s. In spite of this trend toward micro theory, and its many desirable features, the thesis of this chapter is that we ought to be very wary of the excesses of radical microsociology.

The critical review of radical microsociology is useful in this context, not only in itself, but also because it points up several lessons that should be of utility to the supporters of all micro theories. First, although a micro theory may legitimately define its domain very narrowly, it should not seek to make that domain the focus of all of sociology. Second, no sociological theory should be subordinated to the demands of positivistic sociology and its rigorous methodologies. While a fit between theory and method is desirable, theory must not be reduced to the status of handmaiden to sociological method. The outcome of such a reduction can only be the further impoverishment of sociological theory, which is already badly hurt by the positivism of the field. Actually, the same point could be made about qualitative methodologies; no methodology should completely shape any theory. However, such a role for "soft" methodologies is hardly likely in contemporary, positivistic sociology. There should be a rough parity between theory and method, with each shaping, without dominating, the other. Third, while radical micro sociology focuses, for scientific reasons, on interaction, other micro sociologies could well push for a focus on other aspects of the micro domain, especially cognitive processes. While there is nothing wrong with studying cognition sociologically, problems would arise if cognition was defined as the entire domain of sociology. Fourth, I think that the best micro theories are those that leave room, if only for others to analyze, for a wide range of micro processes *as well as* the full spectrum of macro-level phenomena.

Beyond the specific lessons of the critical analysis of radical micro sociology, there is the more general issue of the implications of the rise in micro theories and micro paradigms in the 1970s. After years of macro-paradigmatic dominance, a shift toward micro perspectives had many things to recommend it. The danger lay in going too far and creating the possibility of losing sociology's long-standing interest in macro phenomena as well as their impact on actors and their thoughts and actions. It is true that many sociologists in the past had tended to overemphasize these factors and in the process had produced limited, macro-oriented perspectives, but that does not warrant or necessitate a reaction that involves a complete discarding of large-scale structures and institutions as sociologically meaningful dimensions. To my mind a truly useful micro perspective must not only leave room for an array of micro processes, but also for macro factors, even if they are little more than "black boxes" to be explored by other kinds of sociologists.

Notes

1. There were, of course, many other theoretical developments during this period, most notably the rise in interest in Marxian and neo-Marxian theories.

2. I have long been interested in the issue of politics in sociology (see chapter 6), although my focus has usually been on the issue of interparadigmatic politics. While this chapter focuses on politics among supporters of various theories, it

will eventually deal with the paradigmatic implications of political conflict among sociological theories.

3. There were, of course, micro theories in sociology prior to the 1970s (e.g., symbolic interactionism), but it was in this decade that these theories both proliferated and expanded their domain.

4. I will discuss a later and somewhat more balanced work by Collins in chapter 10. In effect, when the rise of micro sociological theory ran its course, Collins altered his position to be more in line with the trend toward micro-macro integration in the 1980s.

5. Blau's approach is more attuned to the synthetic efforts that have characterized the 1980s and the 1990s (see chapters 10 and 11). Ironically, Blau (1987b) has disowned his earlier integrative efforts in favor of a macro-structural orientation.

6. Other micro theories that enjoyed considerable popularity in the 1970s were existential sociology, the sociology of emotions, and sociobiology. More recently, in the 1980s there was a boom in interest in rational choice theory. Thus, this book is not contending that developments in micro-sociological theory ended with the close of the 1970s, but rather that the *defining* development in the 1980s shifted to the movement toward micro-macro integration.

7. As we saw earlier, Skocpol (1986) attacked metatheorizing for such pigeonholing, but it is obvious that this is but a minor part of metatheoretical work.

10

The 1980s: Micro-Macro (and Agency-Structure) Integration in Sociological Theory

I n chapter 9 I examined the rise of micro sociological theory in the 1970s with special attention to Collins's radical micro sociology. Much of my critique of Collins's approach concerned its micro-excesses and its failure to deal adequately with the micro-macro relationship. That critique sets the stage for this chapter in which the focus is on the major development in (largely) American sociological theory in the 1980s: the boom in interest in the micro-macro linkage. (In an epilogue to this chapter I will look at the parallel emergence in Europe of a concern for the relationship between agency and structure.) As in previous chapters, I will not merely describe this development, but will attempt to analyze it metatheoretically (M_U).

Micro-Macro Integration in (Largely) American Sociological Theory

The utilization of the micro-macro instrument will permit an examination of a wide range of theories in the 1980s and will reveal, among other things, that after decades of micro-macro theoretical extremism, there was a dramatic rebirth of concern with micro-macro linkages.[1] In some cases the theorists explicitly utilize micro-macro terminology, in other cases the theorists use very different terms, and in still other cases they vehemently oppose the use of such terms and of such an orientation. One of the things that I will demonstrate in this chapter is that whether they use micro-macro terminology, other terminology, or even appear to oppose the use of such terms (and apparently oppose such an orientation), a wide range of theorists *were* converging on the micro-macro linkage issue in the 1980s.[2]

However, my main interest in this chapter will not be to simply describe this situation, but rather to use the micro-macro instrument to analyze these developments and to show that there emerged almost simultaneously major new threats to theoretical progress on the linkage issue. The fundamental assumption behind this evaluative work is that an integrative theory must give reasonably equal weight to micro and macro phenomena. Theories will be criticized, even if their intent is integrative, if they overemphasize either end of the continuum. The chapter will also offer some ideas on what needs to be done in the future in theoretical work on the micro-macro linkage.

I am *not* implying that *all* theories must give rough equivalence to micro and macro phenomena. There is certainly a role for macro and micro theories; indeed, as I have shown in earlier chapters, sociology has been dominated by such theories (and paradigms). However, there must *also* be a place for theories that deal in a truly integrated manner with the two ends of the continuum. There is great lure in the micro and macro extremes; theories seeking integration must be wary of those poles lest they degenerate into being simply variants of micro or macro theories.

A review of the corpus of sociological theory reveals that the micro-macro tool can focus on two, only partially related, developments. On the one hand, one can examine efforts at integrating micro (e.g., symbolic interactionism) and macro (e.g., structural functionalism) *theories*. On the other hand, one can also look at a theory that deals in an integrated manner with micro (e.g., personality) and macro (e.g., society) *levels of social analysis* (see chapter 7). Both types of work will be encountered in this chapter as well as some that attempt to do both things simultaneously.

Those sociologists who focus on levels of social analysis[3] share a tendency to equate the micro level with the empirical reality of the individual in everyday life and the macro level with social reality or social structures and institutions. This is the *sociological conception* of the micro-macro continuum; even though we will see later that there are problems with its looseness, it will be used here to orient this chapter, at least at the beginning.

There is also a very attractive, *general conception*[4] that argues that micro and macro do not describe empirical realities, but are rather analytic concepts that can be used to analyze any empirical reality. Alexander (and neo-Parsonsians in general) is a strong advocate of this position: "There can be no empirical referents for micro or macro as such. They are analytical contrasts, suggesting emergent levels within empirical units themselves. . . . The terms 'micro' and 'macro' are completely relativistic. What is macro at one level will be micro at another" (1987, 290–91). While it is certainly useful to employ the terms *micro* and *macro* analytically, the fact is that most sociologists use these terms empirically.

This is not the first effort to use the micro-macro tool to analyze sociological theory. For example, as we saw in chapter 7, in the mid-1960s Helmut Wagner (1964) dealt with the relationship between small-scale and large-scale theories. At the end of the decade Walter Wallace (1969) utilized the micro-macro continuum, but it occupied a secondary role in his analysis and was included as merely one of the "complications" of his basic taxonomy of sociological theory. In the mid-1970s Kemeny (1976) called for greater attention to the micro-macro distinction as well as to the ways in which micro and macro relate to one another. Kemeny concluded at that time that so "little attention is given to this distinction that the terms 'micro' and 'macro' are not commonly even indexed in sociological works" (1976, 731).

However, in the 1980s we witnessed a growth in metatheoretical work on the micro-macro linkage issue. Collins (1986a, 1350), moving away from the micro-extremism of his 1981 essays, argued that work on this topic promised "to be a significant area of theoretical advance for some time to come."[5] In their introduction to a two-volume set of books, one devoted to macro theory (Eisenstadt and Helle 1985b) and the other to micro theory (Helle and Eisenstadt 1985), Eisenstadt and Helle (1985a, 3) concluded that "the confrontation between micro- and macro-theory belong[s] to the past."[6] Similarly, Munch and Smelser, in their conclusion to the anthology *The Micro-Macro Link* (Alexander et al. 1987), asserted that "those who have argued polemically that one level is more fundamental than the other . . . must be regarded as in error. Virtually every contributor to this volume has correctly insisted on the mutual interrelations between micro and macro levels" (1987, 385).

Things changed dramatically in the 1980s not only in metatheorizing about the micro-macro relationship, but also in theory where a great deal of attention was devoted, explicitly and implicitly, to the micro-macro issue. I will shortly turn to an interpretation of theoretical work in the 1980s from a micro-macro perspective, but first I need to provide a brief historical backdrop for these recent developments.

Although it is possible to interpret (and many have) the classic sociological theorists (e.g., Marx, Weber, Durkheim, Simmel, etc.) as either macro or micro extremists, the most defensible perspective, or at least the one that will orient this chapter, is that they were most generally concerned with the micro-macro linkage. In fact, I demonstrated Marx's, Weber's, and Simmel's concern for the micro-macro linkage in chapter 4 on the architectonic and Durkheim's and Marx's (again) concern in chapter 8 on exemplars for an integrated paradigm. If my readers accept my characterization of these classic thinkers as concerned with micro-macro linkage, then they are likely to agree with me in my belief that the half century of sociological theory ending about 1980 involved a loss of a concern for this linkage[7] and the dominance of macro and micro extremists. Among the most notable of the twentieth-century macro extremists were the later Parsons (1966), with his "cultural determinism,"[8] and the structural functionalism he helped to institutionalize; Dahrendorf, with his conflict theory (1959) which aligned itself with structural functionalism as a macro extremist position;[9] and Peter Blau, whose macrostructuralism is epitomized by his proud announcement, "I am a structural determinist" (1977a, x). Macro-structural extremism came from other sources as well (Rubinstein 1986), including network theorists like White, Boorman, and Breiger (1976), ecologists like Duncan and Schnore (1959), and structuralists like Mayhew (1980).[10] Few were more extreme than Mayhew, who said such things as: "In structural sociology the unit of analysis is always the social network, *never the individual*" (1980, 349).

On the micro extreme side one can point to a good portion of symbolic interactionism and the work of Blumer (1969) who often seemed to have structural functionalism in mind as he positioned symbolic interactionism as a sociological theory singlemindedly concerned with micro-level phenomena. An even clearer case of micro extremism was exchange theory and George Homans (1961/1974), who sought an alternative to structural functionalism and found it in the extreme micro orientation of Skinnerian behaviorism. Then there was ethnomethodology and its concern for the everyday practices of actors. Garfinkel (1967) was put off by the macro foci of structural functionalism and its tendency to turn actors into "judgmental dopes." Finally, of course, there was Collins's radical micro sociology, discussed in detail in chapter 9.

Micro-macro extremism characterized much of twentieth-century sociological theory. In earlier chapters I have already discussed the dominance of structural functionalism in the 1940s and 1950s, its continued strength in the multiparadigmatic days of the 1960s, and the rise of micro theories in the 1970s. However, in the 1980s it was possible to discern a movement away from micro-macro extremism and toward a broad consensus that *the* focus, instead, should be on *the integration (or linkage) of micro and macro theories and/or levels of social reality.*[11] It could be argued that at least in this sense sociological theorists rediscovered the theoretical project of the early masters (see chapters 4 and 8).

The efforts at micro-macro integration had a broad base of support and stemmed from a wide variety of theoretical directions.[12] This wide and deep base of support is important because it, like the relative youthfulness of most of its advocates, seemed to bode well for the future of such theoretical efforts. Had they been derived from a single source, or a limited number of sources, one would have been much less sanguine about their ultimate chances of success.

On the other hand, even though they were seeking to overcome it, these efforts at integration were shaped and distorted by the history of twentieth-century micro-macro extremism. Most sociologists working toward integration came at it from bases in either extreme micro or extreme macro theories and these bases often served as straitjackets that limited integrative efforts. Although this was a serious problem, there were some signs in the 1980s that it was being overcome.

While many of the works in the body of micro-macro theoretical work do not explicitly address this linkage, the use of the micro-macro tool demonstrates the commonality in their work. From the micro theoretical end there is Hechter's (1983a, 1983b, 1987; Friedman and Hechter 1988, 1990 [see also Wippler and Lindenberg 1987]) effort based on rational choice theory, Collins's (1987a, 1987b, 1988) attempts, while still focusing on "interactional ritual chains," to move to a more macro level, the largely social psychological efforts of the participants at the 1979 Symposium on Consciousness, Human Action, and Social Structure (Secord 1982), the micro side of the 1983 Symposia on Macro and Micro Sociological Analysis (Helle and Eisenstadt 1985), Coleman's (1986b, 1987) effort to move toward the system level from an action base, Boudon's (1979–81, see also Wippler and Lindenberg 1987) "methodological individualism" which, in spite of its name, does try to integrate actors and systems,[13] efforts (e.g., by Kurzweil [1987] and by Smelser [1987]) to build toward the macro level from a Freudian base, Schegloff's (1987) work building on an ethnomethodological/conversational analysis base as well as similar work by Knorr-Cetina (1981a) and Cicourel (1981), and Emerson's (1981) integrative work stemming from an exchange theory orientation.[14] Coming more from the macro theoretical end are Habermas's (1984, 1987) attempt, strongly influenced, at least originally, by Marxian dialectical theory, Alexander's (1982, 1987) multidimensional work stemming from a structural functional base, Munch's (1987) neo-Parsonsian effort, the macro side of the 1983 Symposia on Macro and Micro Sociological Analysis (Eisenstadt and Helle 1985b), Luhmann's (1987) systems theory approach, and Burt's (1982) integrative effort rooted in macro oriented network theory. There were also overtly integrative works without an apparent prior commitment to the macro or micro end of the continuum. Included in this latter category were Giddens's (1984) "structuration" theory, Bourdieu's (1977) work on "habitus," my (see chapters 7 and 8) "integrated sociological paradigm," Hindess's (1986) effort to deal with actors and social relations and, in the process, to avoid the extremes of "theoretical humanism" and "structuralism," and Fararo and Skvoretz's (1986) attempt to integrate network theory and the social-psychological expectation states theory. Thus, efforts came from both macro and micro directions and from a variety of theoretical positions within and between each. In general, whether they started with a macro or a micro base, or with an integrative orientation, many sociological theorists seemed to be converging in their efforts to develop an integrated theory. There is now enough work on the micro-macro linkage to begin to take stock of this body of work and to suggest where it ought to be headed in the near future.

Taking Stock of Work on Micro-Macro Integration

One of the major difficulties in micro-macro integration in the 1980s was a fundamental (and dimly understood) split among those working on the issue. Some focused on integrating macro and micro *theories*,[15] while others saw integration as a problem of developing a theory that dealt with the linkage between micro and macro existential *levels* of social reality. Earlier in this chapter, for example, I quoted from Eisenstadt and Helle (1985a, 3), who had concluded that the confrontation between micro and macro *theories* was behind them, while in contrast Munch and Smelser (1987, 385) came to a similar conclusion about the need to choose between emphasizing either micro or macro *levels*. There are important differences between trying to integrate macro (e.g., structural functionalism) and micro (e.g., symbolic interactionism) theories and attempting to develop a theory that can deal with the relationship between macro (e.g., social structure) and micro (e.g., personality) levels of social analysis. There was a tendency to slip back and forth between these two types of work and to encompass them under the broad heading of micro-macro integration. At the minimum theorists should have been more aware that these involve different kinds of work and that the relationship between them had to be specified.

Among those who defined it, at least in part, as a problem of integrating theories were Burt (1982), Fararo and Skvoretz (1986), Hechter (1983b), Hindess (1986), and Smelser (1987). On the other side were those who defined the task primarily in terms of developing a theory that focused on integrating micro and macro levels of existential reality, including Alexander (1982–83), Boudon (1979–81), Coleman (1986b), Giddens (1984), Munch (1987), Ritzer (1981b), and Wiley (1988). Gerstein (1987, 86) offered a good example of the latter approach when he distinguished between the two basic levels of analysis and then argued for the need "to create theoretical concepts that translate or map variables at the individual level into variables characterizing social systems, and vice versa." What was needed in the 1980s (and still has not been produced) was a delineation of the relationship between these two literatures.

In addition, there were substantial differences within the groups working toward theoretical integration and integration of levels of social reality. Among those who sought to integrate micro and macro theories important differences arose depending on which specific theories were being integrated. For example, Hindess (1986) sought to avoid the extremes of "theoretical humanism" and "structuralism," Hechter (1983b) pitted rational choice theory against normative and structural theories, Burt (1982) tried to bridge the schism between atomistic and normative orientations, Fararo and Skvoretz (1986) endeavored to integrate structural theory and expectation states theory, and Smelser (1987) sought to synthesize psychoanalytic and sociological perspectives. This work left two unanswered questions. First, how do efforts at integrating very different pairs of theories relate to one another? Second, how does each of these theoretical efforts contribute to our understanding of the linkages between levels of social analysis?

There were similar differences among the theorists who sought to deal with the relationship between micro and macro levels of social analysis. For example, were they seeking to integrate micro and macro structures, micro and macro processes, or more specific aspects of the micro and macro levels of social analysis? More specifically, differences in levels were reflected in Giddens's structuration theory which focused on "the structural properties of social systems [as] both medium and outcome of the practices they recursively organize" (1984, 25), Alexander's multidimensional sociology which involved an "alternation of freedom and constraint" in both action and order (1982, 65), Ritzer's (1981b) integrated paradigm which focused on the dialectical interrelationship of macro objectivity and subjectivity and micro objectivity and subjectivity, Wiley's (1988) effort to deal with the relationship between self, interaction, social structure, and culture, Coleman's (1986b) interest in the relationship between action and system, Boudon's (1979–81) *homo sociologicus* which integrated intentional agent and structural context, and Munch's work on the "interrelation between microinteraction and macrostructures" (1987, 320). How do these efforts at dealing with very different elements of the social world relate to one another and contribute to our broader understanding of micro-macro integration in the social world? In addition, what is the relationship between this kind of work and the previously discussed attempts at theoretical integration?

While there was a tendency for theorists to focus on either integrating theories *or* existential levels, a major exception (and a potential model for those who sought to do both) was Jurgen Habermas, who had devoted at least some of his attention to the theoretical problem of "integrating action theory and systems theory" (1984, 343). In the process of working on theoretical integration he had differentiated existentially between the lifeworld (a more micro-level world where "participants in communication come to an understanding with one another about something" [Habermas 1984, 337]) and the social system and its subsystems.[16] This distinction between lifeworld and social system had to be made, and the two examined independently, otherwise theoretical integration "can lead, as it did with Parsons, to a systems-theoretic absorption of action theory"

(Habermas 1984, 343). Obviously, Habermas did not want macro-level systems theory to overwhelm action theory and, as a result, he developed an approach that sought to integrate the two. Habermas did even more theoretical integration in his later examination of the work of "Mead with his communication-theoretic foundation of sociology" and "Durkheim with a theory of social solidarity connecting social integration and system integration" (1987, 1).

The task of empirical integration was made even more difficult because there were great differences among sociologists in terms of what they defined as the micro and macro levels (Munch and Smelser 1987). Depending on who was offering the definition, the micro level could range from psychological phenomena, to individuals, to interaction patterns among individuals. The macro level ranged from positions, to populations, to society and its structures, to world systems. Thus, seemingly similar views about integrating micro and macro levels were, in fact, quite dissimilar because they were integrating very different social phenomena. As a basic requisite, theorists working with the terms *micro* and *macro* needed to clearly define what they meant by each.

Furthermore, even though like-sounding terms may have been used by sociologists at the micro level (psychological characteristics, action, behavior, practices, intentional agent, micro objectivity and subjectivity, interaction, lifeworld, etc.), and at the macro level (structural context, system, population, positions, macro objectivity and subjectivity, structural properties of social systems, society, culture), there were in fact often substantial differences among these phenomena. For example, at the micro level, those who saw behavior as produced by rewards and costs (social behaviorists) tended to have a very different sense of the social world than those who were concerned with action produced by intentional agents (social definitionists). Similarly, there were substantial differences between those who worked at the macro level with population structures (macro-objectivity) and those who focused on culture (macro-subjectivity). Thus, more needed to be done than simply carefully defining terms; there was also a need to spell out the theoretical implications of the kinds of terms used at both levels.

Perhaps the major problem in the body of work devoted to the micro-macro issue stemmed from the fact that given the history of micro-macro extremism, most theorists working on the linkage question started at either the micro or the macro end and worked toward integration. Starting at one end or the other, the theorist often did not do full justice to the entire micro-macro continuum.

Kemeny (1976) labeled one stance on the micro-macro issue the cumulative position in which one begins at the micro end and builds up from there. Hechter (1983b) took this position theoretically by arguing *for* (micro) rational choice theory and *against* macro theories. Coleman's (1986b) work, given its action theory roots, seemed much stronger on the micro levels. Furthermore, Coleman (1987) expressed a highly limited interest in the "micro-to-macro" problem, but did not express a parallel interest in the "macro-to-micro" problem. Emerson (1981) sought to move to the macro levels, but he was hampered by the micro concerns of his base in exchange theory. Boudon's "methodological individualism" seemed aptly named since it did emphasize the importance of the actor. As he put it, "explaining any phenomenon . . . amounts to showing that it is the outcome of actions" (Boudon 1987, 55). Wippler and Lindenberg (1987) adopted a similar point of view in according theoretical primacy to the individual. Haferkamp (1987) began with complex meaningful action and built toward the intentional and unintentional creation of macro structures.

Many integrationists who began their efforts at the micro level tended to overemphasize that domain rather than giving equal weight to the macro levels, even though they claimed to be seeking integration. A notable example of this, as we saw in chapter 9, was Collins (1981b, 1981c) who, although he claimed to be dealing with the micro-macro connection, saw macro-structures as nothing more than repeated micro encounters. Even in one of his essays toward the end of the decade, Collins argued: "Macrostructure consists of nothing more than large numbers of microencounters, repeated (or sometimes changing) over time and across space" (1987b, 195). He concluded, unashamedly: "This may sound as if I am giving a great deal of prominence to the micro. That is true" (Collins 1987b, 195). However, in still later work on the issue, Collins (1988) seemed to be moving toward a conception that gave the macro-level greater significance. I will return to this work later in the chapter.

Another micro extremist is Schegloff (1987). Writing from an ethnomethodological, and specifically conversational analysis (CA), perspective, Schegloff (1987, 229) implied that sociology took "the understanding of human action as its goal." He seemed dubious about the macro level and micro-macro linkage: "It is not clear how the kind of microanalysis CA does (if it *is* microanalysis) is to be related to macro-level theorizing or whether it should be" (1987, 209).

The other major integrative approach was to start at the macro levels and build down. The best example was Alexander (1982–83, 1987). (See also many of the essays in Eisenstadt and Helle 1985b.) Alexander believed that according privilege to the micro level is "a theoretical mistake" (1987, 295). He was highly critical of all theories (e.g., symbolic interactionism) that begin at the micro levels with nonrational voluntary agency and build toward the macro levels. From his point of view, the problem with these theories was that while retaining notions of individual freedom and voluntarism, they were unable to deal with the unique *(sui generis)* character of collective phenomena. He was also critical of theories (e.g., exchange theory) that begin with rational action and link it to material structures like the economy. On the macro side, Alexander criticized "collectivist, rationalist," materialist theories (e.g., economic and structural determinism) that emphasize coercive order and eliminate individual freedom.

While he expressed an interest in focusing on the relationships between all four levels (individualist-nonrational; individualist-rational; collectivist-rationalist; collectivist-nonrationalist [normative]) Alexander's sympathies (not surprisingly, given his Parsonsian and structural-functional orientations) lay with the "collectivist, normative" position. As he put it, "the hope for combining collective order and individual voluntarism lies within the normative, rather than the rationalist tradition" (Alexander 1982, 108). Central to this belief is his view (his faith?) that because the sources of order are internal rather than external, voluntarism is maintained along with order. In addition, Alexander argued that an individualist perspective ends up with "randomness and complete unpredictability," rather than with order (1985a, 27). Again, Alexander was quite explicit about this: "the general framework for social theory can be derived *only* from a collectivist perspective" (1985a, 28; my italics). To him, social theorists must choose either a collectivist or an individualist perspective. If they choose a collectivist theory, they can incorporate a "relatively small" element of individual negotiation. If, however, they choose an individualist theory, they are doomed to the "individualist dilemma" of trying to sneak into their theory supraindividual phenomena to deal with the randomness inherent in their theory. This dilemma can only be resolved "if the formal adherence to individualism is abandoned" (Alexander 1985a, 27).

In spite of a number of promising leads, Alexander ended up giving inordinate significance to macro (subjective) phenomena and, as a result, his contribution to the development of a theory of micro-macro integration was highly limited. (However, it should be said that in his later work Alexander [1987; Alexander and Colomy 1990], like Collins, expressed a more balanced integrative perspective, which I will have more to say about shortly. The movement toward greater balance by prominent macro and micro extremists seemed to auger well for the future of micro-macro integration.)

While not directly addressing Alexander's work, Giddens (1984) came to the conclusion that *all* work derived from the Parsonsian distinction between action and order inevitably ends up weak at the micro level, especially on "the knowledgeability of social actors, as constitutive in part of social practices. I [Giddens] do not think that *any* standpoint which is heavily indebted to Parsons can cope satisfactorily with this issue at the very core of social theory" (Giddens 1984, xxxvii).

While efforts emanating from one end of the micro-macro continuum or the other (and most efforts discussed in this chapter have done just that) were useful beginnings and not to be rejected out of hand, a commitment to start theorizing at either end limited our understanding of integration and tended to lead toward a repetition of sociological extremism of one kind or the other. Alexander implied a similar criticism: "I believe theorists falsely generalize from a single variable to the immediate reconstruction of the whole" (1987, 314). While we might welcome all efforts at micro-macro integration, it would appear that a starting point different from either the micro or the macro end would likely be more successful. I will discuss this type of work later in this chapter.

Coping with the Strains toward the Macro or Micro Extremes

As we have seen, perhaps the most troubling issue in the work that sought to advance understanding of the micro-macro linkage was the fact that major tensions surfaced very quickly among those oriented to the development of an integrated approach. Given the fact that most people who worked on this issue were shaped by the history of micro-macro extremism in sociology, some integrationists tugged in a micro direction while others pulled the other way. Thus, they threatened to undermine the nascent effort at integration and to repeat *within* the integrative approach the largely unnecessary tension between micro and macro orientations that has dominated sociological theory in the twentieth century. In this section we will look at some ways of avoiding this problem.

One less than wholly satisfactory solution is for macro oriented theorists to focus on micro-level issues and micro oriented theorists to work at the macro levels. Three good examples of this were Alexander's (1987) focus (coming from macro-level neofunctionalism) on such micro-level processes as typification, strategization, and invention; Fine's (1990) effort to delineate (from a micro-level symbolic interactionist perspective) the "obdurate reality" of the built environment, institutional linkages, tradition, and beliefs in organizational primacy; and Collin's (1988) attempt to give greater weight to macro-level phenomena.[17] It is highly beneficial to the development of an integrated macro-micro approach for theorists to focus on the empirical realities that are on the opposite end of the continuum from their theoretical orientations. The major problem is the tendency for theorists to allow their theoretical biases to affect their work at the other end of the social continuum.

More promising are efforts at integrating macro and micro theories by those who are not apparently predisposed to one or the other (e.g., Fararo and Skvoretz; Hindess). But, while a lack of commitment (Mitroff 1974) may make such works more evenhanded, they may suffer from theorists' lack of intimate knowledge of, and devotion to, the theoretical perspectives they are working with.

Another possibility would involve starting at neither the micro nor the macro levels, but rather somewhere in the middle of the social continuum, at the "meso level." There are problems in meso-level perspectives. If one focuses at the meso level (formal organizations, negotiated order), can one adequately get at, and deal effectively with, macro-level phenomena? At the same time, it can also be asked whether such a meso-level focus allows one to be sufficiently microscopic? Meso-level analyses have yet to demonstrate the ability to be satisfactorily integrative.

A second promising direction involves focusing on ongoing relationships between the micro and macro levels. Munch and Smelser (1987) offered some useful beginnings here, but since their ideas were drawn from work influenced by micro-macro extremism, it shows again how easily we can move in either an extreme micro or an extreme macro direction. The useful part of their essay involved a discussion of the linkages between micro and macro; the focus is on relationships rather than the micro or macro extreme. Among these relationships they discussed aggregation; externalization; creating, sustaining, reproducing the macro; conformity; internalization; and limit setting. A focus on these relational processes helps us move away from micro-macro extremism and it is inherently integrative. However, Munch and Smelser divided these processes into micro-to-macro and macro-to-micro categories, thereby tending, once again, to reflect the strain toward micro-macro extremism.

A much more promising alternative is to reject a focus on *any* level (micro, meso, macro) of analysis and adopt instead an inherently integrative, a dialectical, approach. Despite my criticisms above of Alexander's collectivistic bias, his work exhibited signs toward the end of the 1980s of the development of such an inherently integrative position, one that defines macro and micro in terms of one another. Here is the way Alexander expressed this perspective: "The collective environments of action simultaneously inspire and confine it. If I have conceptualized action correctly, these environments will be seen as its products; if I can conceptualize the environments correctly, action will be seen as their result" (1987, 303). I think that Alexander was moving toward a much more complex, dialectical sense of the macro-micro nexus. Similarly, Collins, although he still gave inordinate significance to the micro level,[18] developed a more balanced approach in his later work: "The micro-macro translation shows that everything macro is composed out of micro. Conversely, anything micro is part of the composition of macro; it exists in a macro context. . . . it is possible to pursue the micro-macro connection fruitfully in either direction" (1988, 244).

However, the most promising efforts at developing a dialectical approach to micro-macro integration came from Europe and the related agency-structure literature (to be discussed shortly). They were Giddens's (1984) "structuration theory"[19] and Bourdieu's (1977) focus on "habitus."[20] Giddens defines structuration theory in inherently integrative terms: "The basic domain of the study of the social sciences, according to the theory of structuration, is neither the experience of the individual actor, nor the existence of any form of societal totality, but social practices ordered across time and space" (1984, 2). Structuration is premised on the idea that "the constitution of agents and structures are not two independently given sets of phenomena, a dualism, but represent a duality. . . . the structural properties of social systems are both medium and outcome of the practices they recursively organize"; or "the moment of the production of action is also one of reproduction in the contexts of the day-to-day enactment of social life" (1984, 25, 26). Structure is not external to the actor, it exists in both memory traces and social practices. Moving away from the Durkheimian sense of structure as constraining, Giddens makes the crucial point that structure "is *always* both constraining and enabling" (1984, 25; my italics). However, actors can lose control over the "structured properties of social systems" as they stretch away in time and space, but such a loss of control is not inevitable.

Similarly, Bourdieu sought to avoid the extremes of objectivism and subjectivism in his effort to develop "a science of the *dialectical* relations between the objective structures . . . and the structured dispositions within which those structures are actualized and which tend to reproduce them," or the *"dialectic of the internalization of externality and the externalization of internality"* (1977, 3). At the heart of this dialectic is "habitus," which is neither objectively determined nor the product of subjective intentionality. *Habitus* is defined as "systems of durable, transposable *dispositions"* (Bourdieu 1977, 72) that are produced by objective structures and conditions, but are capable of producing and reproducing those structures. "As an acquired system of generative schemes objectively adjusted to the particular conditions in which it is constituted, the habitus engenders all the thoughts, all the perceptions, and all the actions consistent with those conditions, and no others." Thus, Bourdieu's notion of habitus avoids the deterministic and free will extremes and offers us a dialectical sense of the relationship between micro and macro levels of social reality.

What Giddens and Bourdieu have done (and Alexander and Collins have begun to do), and what I think must be done if we are to avoid a repeat of micro-macro extremism, is to redefine the linkage issue and focus on it relationally, dialectically rather than dichotomously. The focus of integrationists should be on the relationship and not on the micro or macro ends of the social continuum. Given the macro or micro biases of extant theories, this means that we are going to need to create new theories (perhaps by combining parts of a number of existing theories); this is precisely what Giddens and Bourdieu appear to be doing.

Giddens's inclusion of the time factor in his analysis brings us to another continuing issue in the work on micro-macro integration: the effort to make it dynamic rather than static, interested in social change rather than in ahistorical structure. The key point here is that work on micro-macro integration can easily degenerate into static descriptions of unchanging, ahistorical realities. However, Giddens and Collins, among others, have explicitly sought to add a time dimension to the analysis of micro-macro linkages. Like Giddens, Collins is interested in time in addition to spatial issues. As Collins put it: "Micro and macro are relative terms in both time and space" (1981c, 987). Given the difficulties in defining macro, micro, and their interrelationship, it is clear that adding a time dimension complicates enormously what is already a daunting problem. Nevertheless, it seems clear that the future development of micro-macro theory depends on its ability to work with both temporal and spatial variables.

Micro-Macro Integration: Work to Be Done

While the various forms of micro and macro extremism are far from dead, and even highly likely to enjoy periodic resurgences, it is safe to say that integrative micro-macro work became well established in sociology in the 1980s and that it is likely to remain an attractive alternative into the foreseeable future. In fact, it is likely to attract more adherents in the 1990s because it is being advanced by some of the best young theorists in the field, because it is stemming from a wide variety of theoretical directions, because it represents a rediscovery of an orientation that lay at the base of the work of the discipline's classic theorists,[21] and because it is a vast and complex area that offers many challenges to sociological theorists.

More than a decade ago Kemeny argued that "[w]hat is first needed is increasing awareness of the problem of scope so that positions are not taken unwittingly and implicitly" (1976, 747). Given developments in the 1980s, it is doubtful that present and future sociologists will be able to operate without a sense of the issue of scope in their work. In other words, it is now unlikely that sociologists will ignore scale or unwittingly take a position on this issue.

In spite of the emerging consensus at the close of the 1980s, much work remained to be done. First, much of the work that is needed on the micro-macro linkage has to do with specifying in much greater detail the nature of what is at the moment only a very general orientation. Many of those working on this general issue are, in fact, focusing on very different things. They have different senses of what they mean by micro phenomena, macro phenomena, and the linkages between them. Careful definitions are needed and theorists must address conceptual differences between their work on this issue and that of others. In the same realm, much more work is needed of the type undertaken by Markovsky (1987) in specifying the conditions that affect the relative significance of micro-level and macro-level phenomena.

Second, while there is obviously great need to continue to extend work on the micro-macro linkage, additional work is also needed *within* the micro and macro domains. That is, there is a continuing need for sociologists to focus their attention on micro or macro issues, thereby extending knowledge of those domains. The emergence of a focal concern with the micro-macro linkage does not preclude work on a given level. Even the keenest advocates of a focus on micro-macro linkages do not see it as becoming the sole focus of sociology. In fact, advances in our knowledge of the micro and macro levels can serve to enrich work on micro-macro integration.

Third, while there is need for further work within the micro and macro domains, care must be taken that the still-immature effort at micro-macro integration is not overwhelmed by reinvigorated supporters of micro and/or macro extremism. While we are witnessing an increasing focus on micro-macro integration, some very powerful theoretical forces are pulling sociology away from this central problem and in the direction of micro or macro extremism. In other words, concomitant with the emergence of a theoretical consensus is the existence and emergence of theoretical perspectives that are threatening that consensus before it is even solidified. In this category are either extreme micro-oriented theories that deny or downplay the existence and significance of macro-level phenomena as well as extreme macro-level theories that deny or minimize the role of micro-level phenomena. There are also some very powerful sociologists overtly arguing *against* the possibility of micro-macro integration. One such voice is that of Peter Blau, who, by his own admission, has changed his mind on this issue since the publication of his (1964) integrative effort within exchange theory:

> An important issue in constructing macrosociological theory is the linkage with microsociological theory. One approach is to start with microsociological principles and use these as the foundation for building macrosociological theory. The alternative approach rests on the assump-

tion that different perspectives and conceptual frameworks are necessary
for micro and macro theories, primarily because the major terms of macrosociological theories refer to emergent properties of population structures that have no equivalent in microsociological analysis. *I have come
to the conclusion that the second approach is the only viable one, at
least at this stage of sociological development.* (Blau 1987b, 87; my
italics)

Thus, while I have made the case for a growing focus in sociology on
micro-macro integration, such an orientation is far from universal and
has some very powerful opponents.

Fourth, perhaps a greater danger lies in the extremists *within* the
group working on micro-macro integration. I have in mind here macro-
end extremists like Alexander (at least in his earlier work) and micro-end
extremists like Collins (although he, too, seems to be moving toward a
more balanced perspective). They threaten to tear apart this intellectual
movement before it has a chance to develop fully. We must be wary of
re-creating extremism within the micro-macro camp.

Fifth, there is a great need to clarify the relationship between efforts
at integrating micro and macro theories and those aimed at developing a
theory that deals with the integration of micro and macro levels of social
analysis. Our thinking on this relationship is most likely to be advanced
by more efforts that seek to bring together theoretical and empirical efforts.

Sixth, additional work is needed on the relationship between the micro-
macro continuum and the various other continua (e.g., methodological
individualism-holism) that have been used to analyze the social world.
Particularly promising are those efforts at integrating the micro-macro
and the objective-subjective continua and, as we will soon see, the agency-
structure literature.

Seventh, this highly abstract theoretical and metatheoretical work needs
to be translated into terms and approaches that are accessible to sociologists interested in concrete empirical and theoretical questions. In other
words, it needs to be transformed into ideas, concepts, tools, theories, and
methods that can be used by sociologists in their professional activities.
A welcome example of this is Calhoun's (1988) effort to use Habermas's
(1987) distinction between social system and lifeworld to analyze political
efforts at democratization.

Finally, there is a need for more methodologists and empirical researchers to address the micro-macro issue, which to this time has been
largely dominated by theorists. Some welcome signs in these areas are
Bailey's (1987) work on macro-micro methods, Markovsky's (1987) experimental efforts, and Marini's (1988, 45) criticism of gender research
for studying macro-level phenomena with micro-level data.

As we move into the 1990s it is likely that there will be a subtle, yet crucially important, shift in work on micro-macro integration. Up to this point, given the micro and macro extremism of much of twentieth-century sociology, those who have dealt with the issue have come at it from either the micro or the macro end of the continuum. As micro-macro integration becomes widely accepted as a central theoretical problem, the focus will shift to more inherently integrative orientations. Among the promising directions are the works that integrate micro and macro theories without being predisposed to either, the focus on the micro level from a macro theoretical orientation (and vice versa), work at the meso level, interest in the ongoing relationships between macro and micro, and most promising of all the work (e.g., Giddens's, Bourdieu's, Alexander's, and Collins's later statements, as well as my own integrated sociological paradigm) that defines micro and macro in terms of one another, thereby focusing on an ongoing dialectic. These types of work, especially the latter, promise to move work on micro-macro integration to a new level, a level in which the emphasis will be on *integration* or *synthesis,* rather than on the macro or micro poles of the social continuum. This is in line with the view expressed by Alexander and Giesen, who argue for the need for "establishing a radically different starting point" in order to make "a genuinely inclusive micro-macro link" (1987, 37). Since virtually all extant theories are primarily either macro or micro perspectives, such a shift in emphasis will lead to the need for the creation of new theories (or new combinations of several old theories) primarily attuned to such integrative concerns. Most generally, we are likely to move away from a concern for micro and macro levels and/or theories and in the direction of more synthetic existential interests and theoretical efforts.

While work on micro-macro integration will certainly continue to be important in the 1990s, signs already suggest that this work was merely a prelude to a broader body of synthetic work in sociological theory. In the next chapter we turn to some thoughts on the likelihood that it will be this broader move toward synthesis (which subsumes micro-macro integration) that will be what defines sociological theory in the 1990s. However, before we can get to that development, the following section deals with the European literature on agency-structure and how it relates to the (largely) American micro-macro literature discussed above.

Epilogue: Agency-Structure Integration in European Social Theory

While the issue of micro-macro linkage came to dominate theory in America during the 1980s, in Europe the focus was on the linkage between agency and structure. In many ways these are overlapping literatures and some of the key figures in the agency-structure literature (e.g., Giddens and Bourdieu) have already been discussed, at least in part, under the micro-macro heading. While there are some overlaps in these two literatures, there are also some significant differences; the objective of this epilogue is to sort out the similarities and differences.

Paralleling the American focus on micro-macro linkage, Archer contended that in Europe "The problem of structure and agency has rightly come to be seen as the basic issue in modern social theory" (1988, x). In fact, she argues that dealing with this linkage (as well as a series of other linkages implied by it) has become the "acid test" of a general social theory and the "central problem" in theory (1988, x). Earlier, Dawe went even further than Archer: *"Here, then, is the problematic around which the entire history of sociological analysis could be written: the problematic of human agency"* (1978, 379). Implied in Dawe's concern with agency is also an interest in social structure as well as the constant tension between them.[22]

Thus, many observers on both sides of the Atlantic have noted the emergence of what appears to be a new consensus. Not only are there apparent agreements within the United States and Europe, but the surface similarities between the micro-macro and agency-structure terminologies and orientations seem to imply the possibility of an international consensus in sociological theory.

Unfortunately, in spite of the use of like-sounding terms, the consensus that has emerged in the United States is somewhat different from the European consensus. Furthermore, there are substantial differences *within* the (largely) European literature just, as we have seen, there are important differences within the (largely) American work on micro-macro integration.

A concern for the agency-structure linkage lies at the core of the work of a number of theorists who write in the European tradition such as Giddens's (1979, 1982, 1984) structuration theory, Archer's (1982) interest in morphogenesis, as well as her (1988) later concern for the linkage between culture and agency, Burns's (1986; Burns and Flam 1986) social rule-system theory, Lukes's (1977; see also Layder 1985) power and structure, Abrams's (1982) historical structuring, Bourdieu's (1977) habitus, Touraine's (1977) self-production of society, Crozier and Friedberg's (1980) game theory approach, and so on.

However, there are significant differences among Europeans working on the agency-structure issue. For example, considerable disagreement exists concerning the nature of the agent. Most of those working within this realm tend to treat the agent as an individual actor (e.g., Giddens, Bourdieu), but Touraine's "actionalist sociology" treats collectivities such as social classes as agents. In fact, Touraine defines agency as "an organization directly implementing one or more elements of the system of historical action and therefore intervening directly in the relations of social domination" (1977, 459). A third, middle-ground position on this issue is taken by Burns and Flam (1986) (see also Crozier and Friedberg 1980) who regard either individuals or collectivities as agents. This lack of agreement on the nature of the agent is a source of substantial differences in the agency-structure literature.

There is much disagreement even among those who focus on the individual actor as agent. For example, Bourdieu's agent dominated by habitus seems far more mechanical than Giddens's agent. Bourdieu's habitus involves "systems of durable, transposable *dispositions,* structuring structures, that is, as principles of the generation and structuring of practices and representations" (1977, 72). The habitus is a source of strategies "without being the product of a genuine strategic intention" (1977, 73). It is neither subjectivistic nor objectivistic, but combines elements of both. It clearly rejects the idea of an actor with "the free and willful power to constitute" (1977, 73). Giddens's agents may not have intentionality and free will either, but they have much more willful power than Bourdieu's. Where Bourdieu's agents seem to be dominated by their habitus, by internal ("structuring") structures, the agents in Giddens's work are the perpetrators of action. They have at least some choice, at least the possibility of acting differently than they do. They have power and they make a difference in their worlds (see also Lukes 1977). Most importantly they constitute (and are constituted by) structures. In contrast, in Bourdieu's (1977) work, a sometimes seemingly disembodied habitus is involved in the dialectic of internalization and externalization.[23]

Similarly, there are marked disagreements among agency-structure[24] theorists on precisely what they mean by structure.[25] Some adopt a specific structure as central, such as the Crozier and Friedberg's organization and Touraine's relations of social domination as found in political institutions and organizations, while others (e.g., Burns [1986, 13])focus on an array of social structures such as bureaucracy, the polity, the economy, and religion. Giddens (1984, 25) offers a very idiosyncratic definition of structure ("recursively organized sets of rules and resources") that is at odds with virtually every other definition of structure in the literature (Layder 1985). However, his definition of systems as "[r]eproduced relations between actors or collectivities, organized as regular social practices" (Giddens 1984, 25) is very close to what many sociologists mean by structure. In addition to the differences among those working with structure, Archer excoriates Giddens (and implicitly all of the others) for focusing on structure to the exclusion of culture. I will have more to say about this issue shortly.

The attempts at agency-structure linkage flow from a variety of very different theoretical directions. For example, within sociological theory Giddens seems to be animated by functionalism and structuralism versus phenomenology, existentialism, and ethnomethodology, and more generally by new linguistic structuralism, semiotics, and hermeneutics (Archer 1982), while Archer is mainly influenced by systems theory, especially that of Walter Buckley (1967). One result of this is that Giddens's agents tend to be active and creative people ("corporeal beings" with selves) involved in a continual flow of conduct, while Archer's are often reduced to systems, particularly the sociocultural system. In France, Crozier develops his orientation primarily on the basis of organizational and game theory, while Bourdieu seeks to find a satisfactory alternative to subjectivism and objectivism within anthropological theory. One of the reasons for the substantial differences in work on agency-structure are basic differences in theoretical roots.

Another significant issue in the agency-structure literature concerns whether we should think in terms of dualisms or dualities.[26] "Dualisms" involve dealing separately with agency and structure while "dualities" involve treating them as inseparable and mutually constituting. Giddens, of course, has made this distinction, and is also a strong critic of dualisms and a powerful supporter of the use of dualities. The dispute here, and the source of diversity in the agency-structure literature, is between Giddens's case for dualities and Archer's critique of Giddens's devotion to dualities and her case for the utility of using (analytic) dualisms for analyzing the social world. In her view, structure (and culture) and agency are analytically distinct, although they are intertwined in social life. She clearly has Giddens in mind when she argues that "too many have concluded too quickly that the task is therefore how to look at both faces of the same medallion at once. . . . [This] foregoes the possibility of examining the interplay between them over time. . . . Any form of conceptualization which prevents examination of this interplay should therefore be resisted" (1988, xii). Archer's main fear is that thinking in terms of dualities of "parts" and "people" will mean that "their influences upon one another cannot be unravelled" (1988, xiv).

My own view is that both dualities and dualisms have a role to play in analyzing the social world. In some cases it may be useful to separate out structure and action, or micro and macro, in order to look at the way in which they relate to one another. In other cases, it may help to look at structure and action and micro and macro as dualities that are inseparable. In fact, it may well be that the degree to which the social world is characterized by dualities or dualisms is an empirical question. That is, in one case the social setting might better be analyzed using dualities, while in another instance it might be better to use dualisms. Similar points could also be made about different points in time. We should be able to study and measure the degree of dualities and dualisms in any social setting at any given point in time.

Furthermore, our rush to integrative concerns should not blind us to the fact that there is utility in focusing narrowly on micro or macro or agency or structural phenomena in social life. While there are many occasions when an integrative approach will be useful, on other occasions a narrower orientation may yield insight into the social world. To argue otherwise would be to contend that most of the theoretical approaches in the history of sociology—which, after all, tended to have a micro or a macro, an agency or a structure orientation—have contributed nothing to our understanding of the social world.

As with the strain in the micro or macro direction in micro-macro efforts in the United States, there is also a strain in either an agency or a structural direction in Europe. Certainly Bourdieu is strongly pulling in the direction of structure, while Giddens has a more powerful sense of agency than most other theorists of this genre (Layder 1985, 131). In spite of the existence of pulls in the direction of agency and structure, what is distinctive about the European work on agency-structure is a much stronger sense of the need to refuse to separate the two and to deal with them dialectically (e.g., Giddens, Bourdieu).

At a superficial level the micro-macro and agency-structure issues sound similar; indeed, they are often treated as if they closely resemble one another. I have tended to treat those works that deal with agency-structure as part of the concern for micro-macro linkage (see above). Similarly, Archer (1988) argues that the agency-structure issue connotes a concern for the micro-macro relationship (as well as voluntarism-determinism and subjectivism-objectivism). Such positions seem justified since there appears, after all, to be a fairly close association between the micro level and the agent and the macro level and structure. There is, *if* we are thinking of individual human actors (micro) and large-scale social structures (macro). However, there are other ways to think of both agency-structure and micro-macro that make the significant differences between these two conceptualizations quite clear.

While "agency" generally refers to micro-level individual human actors, it can, as we have seen, also refer to (macro) collectivities that act. For example, Burns sees human agents as including "individuals as well as organized groups, organizations and nations" (1986, 9). Touraine focuses on social classes as actors. If we accept such collectivities as agents, then we cannot equate agency and micro-level phenomena. In addition, while structure usually refers to large-scale social structures, it can also refer to micro structures such as those involved in human interaction. Giddens's definition of systems (which is closer to the usual meaning of structure than his own concept of structure) implies both types of structures since it involves "[r]eproduced relations between actors or collectivities" (1979, 66). Thus both agency and structure can refer to either or both micro- or macro-level phenomena.

Turning to the micro-macro distinction, "micro" often refers to the kind of conscious, creative actor of concern to many agency theorists, but it can also refer to a more mindless "behaver" of interest to behaviorists, exchange theorists, and rational choice theorists. Similarly, the term "macro" can refer not only to large-scale social structures, but also to the cultures of collectivities. Thus micro may or may not refer to "agents" and macro may or may not refer to "structures."

When we look closely at the micro-macro and agency-structure schema we find substantial differences between them. Since American theorists tend to focus on the micro-macro linkage and Europeans on the relationship between agency-structure, this means that there are substantial differences between the emerging consensuses in the United States and Europe.

One of the central differences between American and European theorists is their images of the actor. What is distinctive about American theory is the much greater influence of behaviorism as well as of exchange theory derived, in part, from a behavioristic perspective. The strength of these perspectives, even among theorists who do not accept or support them, has tended to give American theorists a more ambivalent attitude toward the actor. Yes, the actor is sometimes seen as actively involved in creating the social world, but there is also a recognition that actors sometimes behave in a mindless fashion in accord with histories of rewards and costs. Thus, American theorists share the interest of (some) Europeans in conscious, creative action, but this interest is limited by a recognition of the importance of mindless behavior. To put it simply, behavior (as opposed to action) has played a greater role in American social theory. This tendency to see the actor as behaving mindlessly is being enhanced today by the growing interest in rational choice theory in American sociology. The image here is of an actor more or less automatically choosing the most efficient means to ends.[27] The influence of rational choice theory in the United States promises to drive an even greater wedge between European and American conceptions of action and agency.

At the macro/structure level, Europeans have been inclined to focus on social structure. Or, where there has not been a singleminded focus on social structure, it has not been adequately differentiated from culture. Indeed, this is the motivation behind Archer's (1988) work in which the culture-agency issue is raised as a parallel to the structure-agency issue. Archer seeks to separate culture and structure and not have them "clamped together in a conceptual vice" (1988, ix). On the other hand, there has been a much greater tendency in the United States to deal with *both* structure and culture in efforts aimed at micro-macro integration. In my own work, I differentiated macro-objectivity (mainly social structure) and macro-subjectivity (mainly culture) and sought to deal with their dialectical interrelationship with micro-objectivity and micro-subjectivity. Similarly, Alexander (1985a) expresses an interest in focusing on the relationship among four basic levels: individualist-nonrational; individualist-rational; collectivist-rationalist (mainly structure); collectivist-nonrationalist (mainly culture). Wiley (1988) offers a similar four-level approach: self, interaction, social structure, and culture.

Another difference on the macro/structure issue stems from differences in theoretical influence in the United States and Europe. In the United States, the main influence on thinking on the macro/structure issue has been structural functionalism. The nature of that theory has led American theorists to focus on both large-scale social structures *and* culture. Structural functionalism clearly had an interest in social structures, but it ultimately accorded priority to the cultural system. In Europe, the main influence has been structuralism, which has a much more wide-ranging sense of structures extending all the way from micro-structures of the mind to macro structures of society. Culture has been far less important to structuralists than to structural functionalists.

If we ignore for the moment the far greater impact of behaviorism/exchange and rational choice theory in the United States, theoretical differences on the micro/agency issue seem to have been much less consequential than those on the macro/structural level. Existentialism and phenomenology (as well as Freudian theory) have had the greatest influence in Europe, while symbolic interactionism and exchange theory have been the key influences in the United States. However, differences in the impact of these theories on thoughts on micro/agency in the United States and Europe seem to have been negligible. Furthermore, the micro/agency theories seem to be more widely read and utilized on both sides of the Atlantic than macro/structural theories. For example, ethnomethodology seems to have had an almost equally strong impact on both sides of the Atlantic.

Another key difference between the two literatures is the fact that the micro-macro issue is subsumable under the broader issue of levels of analysis (see chapter 7) while the concern for agency-structure is not. We can clearly think of micro-macro in terms of some sort of vertical hierarchy with micro-level phenomena on the bottom, macro-level phenomena at the top, and meso-level entities in between. However, the micro-macro continuum is not coterminous with levels of analysis since other factors (e.g., objectivity, subjectivity) are involved in the levels issue than merely micro-macro concerns. On the other side, agency-structure seems to have no clear link to the levels of analysis issue since both agency and structure can be found at any level of social analysis.

The agency-structure issue is much more firmly embedded in a historical, dynamic framework than the micro-macro issue. This characteristic is clearest in the work of Giddens and Archer, but it is manifested throughout the literature on agency-structure. In contrast, those who deal with micro-macro issues are more likely to depict them in static, hierarchical, ahistorical terms. Nevertheless, those who choose to depict the micro-macro relationship rather statically make it clear that they understand the dynamic character of the relationship: "The study of levels of social reality and their interrelationship is inherently a *dynamic* rather than a static approach to the social world. . . . A dynamic and historical orientation to the study of levels of the social world can be seen as integral parts of a more general *dialectical* approach" (Ritzer 1981b, 208; see also Wiley 1988, 260).

Finally, I must mention that morality is a central issue to agency-structure theorists, but is largely ignored in the micro-macro literature. This situation may be traced, in part, to differences in theoretical roots and reference groups. Agency-structure theory has much more powerful sources in, and a stronger orientation to, philosophy, including the latter's great concern with moral issues. In contrast, micro-macro theory is largely indigenous to sociology and oriented to the hard sciences as a reference group where moral issues are of far less concern than they are in philosophy. The result is that a sense of moral concern, even moral outrage, is far more palpable in the agency-structure than in the micro-macro literature.

This leads to the point that the real issue is not agency-structure, but the relative weight of agency and structure. Contemporary European theorists are willing to give a rough equivalency to the power and significance of agency and structure, or are unwilling to disentangle them. Many Marxists and mainstream American theorists have tended to give structure primacy over action and praxis. Other American theorists (and some Marxists) have tended to give action primacy over structure. In this sense, virtually all theorists would seem to be concerned with the agency-structure linkage. This seems to be the position adopted by Dawe (1978) who differentiates between the sociology of social action and the sociology of social system, but sees both as sociologies of social action (and presumably social structure). However, to argue in this way is to lose sight of the significance of contemporary European work on agency and structure. What is distinctive about much of this work is its dedication to taking *both* agency and structure seriously. This is also one of its main contributions in comparison to the philosophy of agency which has little to offer to our understanding of social structure.

While I am sympathetic to the theoretical ideas being developed in Europe today, it seems to me that we cannot always assume that agency

and structure are of equivalent importance.[28] The degree of their equivalency is a historical question. In some epochs structure may gain the ascendancy over agency. (This was Marx's view of the situation in capitalist
society.) In other epochs the agent may play a greater role and the significance of structure is reduced. In still others, there may be a rough equivalence of the two. One cannot posit a single agency-structure relationship
for all of history. One of the pressing needs in the agency-structure literature is to begin to specify the relative weight of agency and structure in
different historical epochs. Furthermore, there are clearly contempora-
neous differences in the relative weight of agency and structure in various
societies around the world. It seems that all of these crucial differences
are lost if we only talk in very general terms about agency and structure.

In sum, metatheoretical analysis shows that parallel and partially
overlapping integrative efforts dominated sociological theory in the 1980s
in both the United States and Europe. However, in the United States at
least a still broader integrative movement has emerged as we move into
the 1990s. It is to that development that I now turn.

Notes

1. This growing interest in micro-macro linkage is clearly evidenced by the
fact that two sessions at the 1988 American Sociological Association meetings
were devoted to this theme and, most importantly, micro-macro integration was
the theme of the 1989 ASA meetings (Huber 1990).

2. While this chapter will consistently focus on the micro-macro linkage
issue in sociological theory, it should be made clear that there is much more to
all of these theories than a concern for this relationship. Thus, while it will be
shown later that a broad consensus emerged in the 1980s on the focus on the
micro-macro linkage, this similar concern far from exhausts the similarities (and
differences) of these theories. There are clearly many substantive differences (and
similarities) and the use of other metatheoretical tools (e.g., objective-subjective)
would show a wide array of additional similarities and differences.

3. An interesting metatheoretical concern, discussed in chapter 7, is the
relationship between the more broadly defined issue of "levels of analysis" and
the more specific micro-macro issue.

4. This conception is not only usable by sociologists, but also by those in
a wide range of other fields.

5. However, Collins devoted only a few lines to the issue in the context of
a broader discussion of current trends in sociology.

6. However, by creating separate macro and micro volumes, Eisenstadt and
Helle have done more to heighten the split than to develop an integrated approach.

7. Coleman (1986b, 1313) argues that a similar loss occurred in empirical
research with the shift toward micro-oriented survey research. This argument
raises the issue of the need for a study parallel to this one dealing with methods

and whether a similar trend in the 1980s toward micro-macro integration occurred there as well.

8. Even as sympathetic an observer as Alexander (1987, 296) admits Parsons's "own collectivist bias"; see also Coleman (1986b, 1310). However, while Parsons's greatest influence was in collectivistic theory, it is also possible to find within his work a strong micro-macro integrative theory.

9. Coleman also makes this point: "subsequent challenges to functionalism (the principal one being 'conflict theory') have acquiesced in remaining at the collective or systemic level, thus failing to provide a theory grounded in the purposive action of individuals" (1986b, 1312). I would, however, disagree with Coleman in his characterization of conflict theory as the principal challenge to structural functionalism. Conflict theory and structural functionalism are best seen as paradigmatic partners; the principal discipline-wide challenges to functionalism have long come from the micro theories (e.g., symbolic interactionism, ethnomethodology, exchange theory) associated with other paradigms (see chapter 6).

10. Interestingly, Rubenstein argues that even structural extremists end up with an integrated perspective because "elements of culture and consciousness are theoretically excluded and then smuggled back in through substantive concepts" (1986, 87).

11. My position is slightly stronger than the position taken by Alexander and Giesen who argue that the micro-macro problem "has emerged as *a* key issue in contemporary sociological theory" (1987, 1; my italics).

12. I will focus only on the major works on the micro-macro linkage in this discussion, but many other works can be subsumed under this heading including: Rossi's (1983) "dialectical conception of structure and subjectivity," Shalin's (1986) dialectical sense of symbolic interactionism, Thomason's (1982) effort within the context of an analysis of Schutzian theory to develop a conception of reification based on a "positive bridging of the constructionist/realist divide," Markovsky's (1985) multilevel justice theory and his effort to deal with the macro-micro link experimentally (Markovsky 1987), Swidler's (1986) analysis of culture as a "tool kit" of habits, etc., out of which actors construct strategies for dealing with social reality, Hilbert's (1986) effort to integrate Durkheim's macro-level theory of anomie with the "reality construction tradition, particularly ethnomethodology," Haines's (1985) effort to reorient ecology (inspired by the integrative work of Giddens, Collins, and Burt) away from a macro-level orientation and toward "a relational methodology which views social phenomena as both causes and consequences of individual phenomena," Hayes's (1985) attempt to integrate "causal and interpretive analyses," Hekman's (1983) analysis of Weber's ideal-type methodology in which she sees him as having "effected a synthesis between the analysis of subjective meaning and the analysis of structural forms," Podgorecki and Los's (1979) "multi-dimensional sociology," Kreps's (1985) effort to use the Alexander-inspired "dialectical relationship between social action and social order," and a similarly oriented paper by Bosworth and Kreps (1986).

13. Coleman (1986b) also sees himself as a methodological individualist endeavoring to build a more integrated theory.

14. Cook says of Emerson's approach: "it can provide one coherent, systematic basis for building a theory of social structure and structural change that is

not devoid of actors and the microprocesses that generate and modify these structures" (1987a, 218).

15. Yet to be dealt with adequately is the issue of whether at least some of these theories are incommensurable and therefore impossible to integrate. On the latter, there are some (Gergen and Gergen 1982; Bhaskar 1982, 285) who argue against the possibility of theoretical integration; their position needs to be considered by those who are working on such integration.

16. I do not want to go too far here in my praise for Habermas's two-pronged effort. On the existential side, it is clear that his micro (lifeworld) and macro (social system) levels are highly abstract and theoretical. In spite of his effort to be both theoretical and empirical, it could easily be argued that Habermas is not nearly empirical enough. Given his philosophical orientation, this would not be a difficult argument to defend.

17. Still another example was Friedman and Hechter's (1988, 1990) effort to deal with macro-level phenomena from a base in micro-level rational choice theory.

18. For example, he still saw the "big challenge" in showing "how micro affects macro" (Collins 1988, 244).

19. Giddens (1984) directly addresses the macro-micro issue and explains why he does not use those more familiar terms rather than ideas like "social and system integration." First, he feels that macro and micro are often pitted against one another and he does not believe "that there can be any question of either having priority over the other" (1984, 139). Second, even when there is no conflict, "an unhappy division of labour tends to come into being between them" (1984, 139). That is, theories like symbolic interactionism tend to focus on the activities of free actors while theories like structural functionalism devote their attention to structural constraint. In the end, Giddens (1984, 141; my italics) concludes that "the micro/macro *distinction* is not a particularly useful one." The key point here is that a rigid distinction between micro and macro is *not* useful, but their integration *is*, as Giddens himself demonstrates. The view in this chapter is that we need not jettison macro-micro terminology since rigid distinctions between them, and between theories that deal with them, are *not* inherent in the use of the terminology.

20. My own work (see chapters 7 and 8) on an integrated sociological paradigm is also of this genre; see also Wiley 1988.

21. It is also likely that we will witness a rethinking of the work of the master theorists in light of these developments. It is likely that there will be much more emphasis on the integrative character of their work.

22. In fact, agency is often used in such a way as to include a concern for structure (Abrams 1982, xiii).

23. While I am emphasizing the differences between Giddens and Bourdieu on agency, Giddens (1979, 217) sees at least some similarities between the two perspectives.

24. I am focusing here mainly of Europeans who deal with social structure and not those who see structure as hidden, underlying elements of culture.

25. In a useful paper, Porpora (1989) distinguishes among four concepts of social structure: patterns of aggregate behavior stable over time (e.g., Homans,

Collins), lawlike regularities governing the behavior of social facts (e.g., Blau, Mayhew), systems of human relationships among social positions (Marxian and network theory), and collective rules and resources structuring behavior (e.g., Giddens).

26. One can also think about micro-macro in terms of dualisms and dualities.

27. Deville (1989) sees such an actor as robotlike. There are, however, other, more complex views of such an actor (Elster 1985).

28. This discussion assumes that we are dealing with a dualism rather than a duality. Since a Giddens-like duality assumes that agency and structure cannot be separated, it would be hard to assess their relative significance.

11
The 1990s:
The New Syntheses
In Sociological Theory

s I have discussed in the last several chapters, the landscape of American sociological theory has changed many times in the twentieth century. However, in spite of the changes, sociological theory, at least until the 1980s, was characterized by theoretical (and paradigmatic) extremism of one kind or another and the destructive political conflicts that often went hand in hand with such extremism. The developments that took place during the 1980s were very different from those of any previous epoch,[1] as a wide range of theorists moved away from theoretical extremism and began to grapple with synthesis in the specific micro-macro domain. Micro-macro integration appears to have been the pioneering movement that paved the way for a wide array of synthetic efforts. It set the stage for the much broader and dramatic change to be discussed in this chapter: the emergence of a wide range of efforts at theoretical synthesis.[2] It is clear that sociological theory finally shows strong signs of moving away from decades of destructive political conflict among extremist theories of one stripe or another.

The Movement toward Theoretical Syntheses

Once theorists had a sense of the advantages of synthesis from the work on micro-macro integration, the floodgates seemed to open and integrative efforts began to flow from and in all directions. In some cases these attempts were direct results of efforts at micro-macro integration as sociologists sought to synthesize a wide range of micro and macro theories. In addition, once the movement toward theoretical synthesis began, a variety of other efforts at theoretical integration emerged. Thus, we now not only see micro-to-macro and macro-to-micro attempts at integration, but also more micro-to-micro (e.g., symbolic interactionism and ethnomethodology) and macro-to-macro efforts (e.g., conflict theory and structural functionalism) as well. And the movement toward synthesis does not stop with various micro-macro possibilities since there now also seems to be a new openness to ideas from an array of other disciplines and nations.

By the 1980s theorists had grown weary of the micro-macro split, both theoretically and in terms of levels of analysis, but as we move into the 1990s a more general dissatisfaction with the straitjacket of *any* theoretical label or level has emerged. The old, reified labels that have dominated sociological theory for many decades ("structural functionalism," "symbolic interactionism") seem increasingly less meaningful and important. As Alexander and Colomy put it, "The conventional debates have become stale and dry. We are in the midst of a sea change in sociological theory. Old alignments are dissolving; new configurations are being born" (1990, 56). As a younger generation of sociological theorists takes center stage, older theoretical (e.g., structural functionalism vs. symbolic interactionism) and conceptual (e.g., micro-macro) boundaries and divisions are breaking down and some younger theorists are even taking an active role in trying to shatter those borders. Contemporary supporters are much less interested in defending traditional interpretations of theories and far more interested in reaching out to other theoretical traditions in an effort to develop new, more synthetic theories. In addition, more recent theories are less likely to focus on a single level of social analysis and more apt to be interested in the interrelationship of multiple levels. Instead of viewing theories and theoretical domains solely as important bases of operation, many sociological theorists are now coming to see that theories and domains can be blinders that are greater hindrances than aids in dealing with the social world. In contrast, in the past there was a strong need on the part of sociologists to identify with and to defend a particular theoretical perspective (and/or domain). The only thing that varied much in the past was the theory with which sociologists identified.

It was this reality that led to a call on my part (Ritzer 1979, 1981b, chapters 7 and 8 here) for a more integrated paradigm. While such a paradigm did not emerge immediately, and in fact has not emerged to this day, I believe that developments in the 1980s and the beginning of the 1990s auger well for the possibility of the development of such a paradigm. The efforts at micro-macro linkage in the 1980s were just the beginning of this movement. The more general movement toward theoretical synthesis at virtually every theoretical juncture shows real promise as the base for the development of an integrated sociological paradigm. It may not occur immediately, it may not add up to a new paradigm, and it may not be called an integrated paradigm, but powerful developments are afoot that indicate a major transformation of sociological theory in particular and sociology more generally.[3]

The main type of synthesis to be discussed in this chapter is the integration of various theories. Along the way, I will also remark about the effort within theories or integrated sets of theories to deal with various levels of analysis. Rather than focusing on a given level of analysis, more and more theories are examining the interrelationships among multiple levels.

While there is great interest in syntheses of all types, there seems to be a recognition that earlier efforts to create a single, overarching synthetic theory were misguided. Thus, the new move toward syntheses is very different from past efforts at creating a massive, overarching synthetic perspective. Examples of the latter are the grand theories of Karl Marx and Talcott Parsons. In fact, a number of recent intellectual developments (e.g., neo-Marxian theory, postmodernism, poststructuralism) involve an attack on the very idea of such a grand synthesis (Antonio 1990; Kellner 1990; Lemert 1990).[4] For example, the postmodernist Lyotard argues: "Let us wage a war on totality" (1984, 82). Those now working toward theoretical syntheses see such overarching efforts as misguided and are working on much narrower attempts at integration. These may not be as dramatic as efforts like those of Marx or Parsons, but they are likely to be more fruitful and productive. These theorists are working at integrating the "nuts and bolts" of specific theories; their highly detailed efforts are likely to be very useful to sociologists. Thus, we can think of the "new synthes*es*" rather than a "new synthes*is.*" *This move toward theoretical syntheses is, in my view, the overriding theme of this chapter and of sociological theory as we move into the 1990s.*

This new movement might take its marching orders from the comments of Robert Merton at the Thomas and Znaniecki conference on sociological theory:

> Pessimism results from the growing pains of a rapidly differentiating discipline in which the differentiation has multiplied so fast that we haven't the human resources to develop each sphere of inquiry in sufficient degree. The sociological enterprise requires a sense of tolerance rather than of battle, consolidating a mutual awareness of various theoretical orientations with a reasonable confidence that their mutual theoretical connections will be progressively defined. (1986, 61)

I think that Merton's confidence in the fact that we will see more theoretical synthesis was borne out by developments in the 1980s and especially those occurring as we enter the 1990s.

Although I am emphasizing the emergence of the movement toward theoretical syntheses on the threshold of the 1990s, I do not want to suggest that synthetic efforts did not occur in the past. Indeed, every epoch in the history of sociological theory has had its share of such efforts. However, in previous eras they were much more likely to be isolated and aberrant cases swamped in a sea of theoretical extremism. Furthermore, they were likely to be met by hostile reactions from the supporters of one or the other of the theories that was the object of integration. What distinguishes the new set of synthetic developments is that they are widespread and are forming a coherent whole which appears to be coming to define the entire period. We can anticipate hostile reactions to these efforts, but they are likely to be met by more effective responses from the wide variety of theorists interested in integration.

This move toward theoretical syntheses in sociology can be linked to some broader intellectual developments.[5] One such development is the multidisciplinary interest in postmodernism (Kellner 1988, 1990), particularly as it is manifested in the contemporary works of Baudrillard (1983), Lyotard (1984), and Jameson (1984). One of the key aspects of postmodernism is its tendency to "subvert" and "explode" boundaries between disciplines and subdisciplines and to create a multidisciplinary, multidimensional perspective that synthesizes ideas from a range of fields (e.g., philosophy, political economy, cultural theory, history, anthropology, and sociology) and perspectives within a given discipline. Postmodernism proclaims the end of an era in social and intellectual life and the beginning of the search for "new paradigms, new politics, and new theories" (Kellner 1990, 276). In Kellner's view, such new theories will involve new concatenations of Marxism, critical theory, feminism, postmodern social theory, and other currents of critical social theory to solve the theoretical and political problems that confront us today. From the narrower perspective of sociology, it indicates efforts to develop new synthetic theories from ideas drawn from a wide range of theoretical sources.

Similar developments are occurring in neo-Marxian theory (Antonio 1990). For many years neo-Marxian theory was dominated by a "grand theory," one of Marx's totalistic perspectives, his materialist emancipatory modernism. In this, Marx offered a grand view of society moving toward its teleological end (communism) impelled by the collective subject, the proletariat. For a time, this view shaped (and distorted) Marxian theory, but later an array of neo-Marxian theorists sought in a variety of ways to distance themselves from this grand narrative. In some cases, however, they merely replaced Marx's materialist emancipatory modernism with other equally problematic grand narratives. More recently, an array of decentered neo-Marxian theories have emerged. While they have served to overcome the excesses of Marx's materialist emancipatory modernism, they threaten to offer an excessively pluralistic image of society. Efforts to deal with this excessive pluralism would involve syntheses of a variety of these neo-Marxian theories.

This development of an array of theoretical syntheses, while quite promising, threatens to cause us to lose sight of any possibility of holistic thinking. Such a development would be unfortunate because while it may be impossible to develop a grand theory, that does not mean that all forms of holistic thinking are useless and undesirable. Today there is a clear need for holistic thinking that does not suggest that it offers the ultimate answer to all theoretical issues. Thus, Antonio suggests that neo-Marxists build on Marx's "historical holism" rather than his emancipatory modernism. Historical holism is a global theory of capitalism without the excesses (e.g., claims to provide all answers to all questions, teleology) of materialist emancipatory modernism. Importantly, Antonio argues that this new holistic perspective would not only integrate ideas from an array of neo-Marxist perspectives, but should also involve "theoretical infusions from non-Marxist approaches" (e.g., Habermas's use of Weberian and pragmatist ideas) which will "presage a richer historical holism" (1990, 109). Similarly, while supporting the postmodernist attack on grand theory, in his own ideas on "technocapitalism" Kellner (1990) seeks to develop a holistic approach that rescues viable aspects of Marxian theory and synthesizes them with the ideas of the postmodernists. In this sense Kellner, like Antonio, comes down on the side of the need for a new holistic perspective while, at the same time, accepting the need for a wide range of synthetic efforts. Overall, in the rush toward an array of syntheses, it would be disastrous to lose all traces of holistic theory in sociology.

In spite of the promising synthetic developments, the same caution is in order here as was offered in the last chapter. The forces of theoretical extremism are alive and well in sociology (e.g., Blau 1987a; 1987b) and stand ready to snuff out the movement toward syntheses with a renewed burst of theoretical extremism. Given our long history of theoretical extremism, and our relatively brief fling with integration and syntheses, sociologists interested in the latter directions, in spite of their growing numbers and influence, cannot afford to grow complacent.

In looking at this latest development in theory I will continue to operate from a metatheoretical (M_U) perspective. While in the last chapter I used the micro-macro tool, especially micro-macro synthesis, in this chapter I will focus on theoretical synthesis more generally, or more accurately, on the multitude of syntheses occurring in sociological theory. In the rest of this chapter I will examine a wide range of theoretical works that come from virtually every major theoretical perspective and which are all striving in one way or another toward some sort of synthesis.

Specific Synthetic Efforts

The place to start is with structural functionalism since it, its macro extremism, its social factism, and its other excesses dominated sociological theory for such a long period of time. Contemporary followers of this perspective are well aware of structural functionalism's excesses and hence have jettisoned that label in favor of "neofunctionalism," a label which is clearly designed to show continuity with structural functionalism,[6] but also to indicate that the new perspective seeks to overcome some of the problems associated with structural functionalism as well as to extend that perspective. Alexander has enumerated the problems associated with structural functionalism that neofunctionalism will need to surmount including "anti-individualism," "antagonism to change," "conservatism," "idealism," and an "anti-empirical bias" (1985a, 10). By outlining these criticisms Alexander implies an openness to other kinds of theories: more microscopic, more dynamic, more liberal, more material, and more empirically oriented theories. Efforts are being made to overcome the above problems programmatically (Alexander 1985a) and at more specific theoretical levels—for example, Colomy's (1986) attempt to refine differentiation theory—but even Alexander was forced to admit in mid-decade that "neofunctionalism is a tendency rather than a developed theory" (1985a, 16).

More recently, Alexander and Colomy (1990) have tried to cope with some of these problems and in the process they have staked out a very ambitious claim for neofunctionalism. They do not see it as, in their terms, a mere modest "elaboration," or "revision," of structural functionalism, but rather as a much more dramatic "reconstruction" of it in which differences with the founder (Parsons) are clearly acknowledged and explicit openings are made to other theorists and theories.[7] Efforts are made to integrate into neofunctionalism insights from the masters such as Marx's work on material structures and Durkheim's on symbolism. In an attempt to overcome the idealist bias of Parsonian structural functionalism, especially its emphasis on macro-subjective phenomena like culture, openings are urged to more materialist approaches. The structural functional tendency to emphasize order is countered by a call for rapprochement with theories of social change. Most importantly, to compensate for the macro-level biases of traditional structural functionalism, efforts are made to integrate ideas from exchange theory, symbolic interactionism, pragmatism, phenomenology, etc. In other words, and consistent with the basic theme of this chapter, Alexander and Colomy are endeavoring to synthesize structural functionalism with a number of other theoretical traditions. Such reconstruction can both revive structural functionalism and provide the base for the development of a new theoretical tradition.

Alexander and Colomy recognize an important difference between neofunctionalism and structural functionalism:

> Earlier functionalist research was guided by . . . envisioning a single, all-embracing conceptual scheme that tied areas of specialized research into a tightly wrought package. What neofunctionalist empirical work

points to, by contrast, is a package loosely organized around a general logic and possessing a number of rather autonomous "proliferations" and "variations" at different levels and in different empirical domains. (1990, 52).

The thoughts of Alexander and Colomy are in line, here, with those of Kellner and Antonio discussed above. That is, I think they are moving away from the Parsonsian tendency to see structural functionalism as a grand overarching theory. Instead, they are offering a more limited, a more integrative, but still a holistic theory, of the type suggested by Kellner and Antonio.

It has been difficult on the surface to see much life of any kind in conflict theory. Conflict theory enjoyed a miniboom in the 1960s as the macro-level alternative to structural functionalism. However, except for Collins's *Conflict Sociology* (1975), there have been few notable explicit contributions to this theoretical perspective. From the point of view of this chapter, Collins's book was highly integrative because it moved in a much more micro-oriented direction than the conflict theory of Dahrendorf and others. Collins himself says, "My own main contribution to conflict theory . . . was to add a micro level to these macro-level theories. I especially tried to show that stratification and organization are grounded in the interactions of everyday life" (1990, 72). Later, "My own contributions to conflict theory came by way of building in the empirical[8] contributions of Goffman, Garfinkel, Sacks and Schegloff" (1990, 72–73). In fact, Collins sees conflict theory as preferable to most other theories because of its willingness to be integrative: "Conflict theory . . . engages freely in what may be called intellectual piracy: it is quite willing to incorporate . . . elements . . . of micro-sociologies" (1990, 72). However, neither a micro, nor a micro-macro, nor any other direction was taken up by conflict theorists during the late 1970s and the 1980s.

That situation has been rectified, at least in part, by Collins (1990) himself who, after devoting more than a decade to other concerns, especially interaction ritual chains (see chapter 9), has returned to his interest in conflict theory. In Collins's view, conflict theory, in spite of appearances, was not moribund for a decade and a half, but had been developing quietly under a variety of different guises in a number of areas within sociology. For one thing, Collins believes that conflict theory has become the dominant perspective within a number of subareas within sociology. Although he does not go into it in detail, one example of what he has in mind is the emergence of the "power approach" as the dominant orientation in the sociological study of the professions (Ritzer and Walczak 1986). An integrative effort worth doing, but only implied by Collins, would be a review of the array of specific conflict perspectives that have developed within various subareas in sociology, with the objective of putting this disparate body of work together, combining it with extant conflict theory, and thereby greatly enhancing the broader conflict theory of society.[9]

Collins, himself, seeks integration in two other directions. For one thing, he sees a conflict approach lying at the heart of much of historical/comparative research, especially the work of Michael Mann (1986). Thus, conflict theory stands to be enriched by an integration of a wide range of insights to be derived from historical/comparative research. Furthermore, Collins sees Mann as doing a kind of network theory; this insight leads to an interest in synthesizing Mann's approach with mainstream work in network theory. More generally, there is the possibility of integrating network and conflict theory. In fact, as we will see, network theory plays a prominent role in contemporary efforts at synthesis since there are those from other theoretical perspectives, especially exchange theory, who see possibilities of integration with it. Curiously, Collins does not address the possibility of integration with his own theory of interaction ritual chains. This is surprising since the latter's micro-level insights would mesh well with the traditional macro-level concerns of conflict theory. Perhaps Collins did not suggest such an integration because his own variety of conflict theory is itself highly microscopic and already encompasses interaction ritual chains.

More generally, Collins defines conflict theory in such a general way that it seems open to insights from all theories and seems capable of covering all levels of social reality. Specifically, Collins seeks to differentiate between narrow *theories of conflict* (e.g., Simmel, Coser) and *conflict theory* which he defines as "a theory about the organization of society, the behavior of people and groups; it explains why structures take the forms that they do . . . and how and what kinds of changes occur. . . . Conflict theory is a general approach to the entire field of sociology" (1990, 70). Thus, Collins is after more than a series of specific syntheses: he is interested in pushing conflict theory in the direction of a more holistic perspective. While such holistic perspectives are welcome as an antidote to excessive pluralism, one must be wary of the theoretical imperialism implied by this and the similar tone that pervades Collins's essay.

Perhaps out of self-defense, symbolic interactionism, as it evolved primarily under the stewardship of Herbert Blumer, moved in a decidedly micro direction. This stood in contrast to at least the implications of the more synthetic title of George Herbert Mead's *Mind, Self, and Society*.[10] However, symbolic interactionism has entered a new, "post-Blumerian" age (Fine 1990). On one front, efforts are underway to reconstruct Blumerian theory and to argue that it always had an interest in macro-level phenomena (see the special issue of *Symbolic Interaction* [1988] devoted to Herbert Blumer). The "new" symbolic interactionism has, in Fine's terms, "cobbled a new theory from the shards of other theoretical approaches" (1990, 136–7). The "new" symbolic interactionists "are almost promiscuous in their willingness to thrash in any theoretical bedding they can find: there are Durkheimian . . . Simmelian . . . Weberian . . . Marxist . . . postmodernist . . . phenomenological . . . radical feminist . . . semiotic . . . and behaviorist interactionists" (Fine 1990, 120). Symbolic interactionism now combines indigenous insights with those from other micro theories like exchange theory, ethnomethodology and conversation analysis, and phenomenology. More surprising is the integration of ideas from macro theories (e.g., structural functionalism) as well as ideas of macro theorists like Parsons, Durkheim, Simmel, Weber, and Marx. Symbolic interactionists are also endeavoring to integrate insights from poststructuralism, postmodernism, and radical feminism. Post-Blumerian symbolic interactionism is becoming a much more synthetic perspective than it was in Blumer's heyday.

Even action theory, long a weak component of the contemporary theoretical scene, is showing some faint signs of life by developing a more integrative orientation. Coleman (1986b, 1987) has sought to revive action theory by returning to its roots in Parsons's *The Structure of Social Action* (1937/1949). He is trying to undo Parsons's mistake of abandoning action theory in favor of structural functionalism. Thus Coleman is seeking to move action theory away from the system level and back toward the actor who for Coleman, as for Parsons, can be "either persons or corporate actors" (1986b, 1312). In other words, Coleman is seeking the development of a broader action theory that synthesizes interests in actors and systems.[11]

After years of micro-level, behavioristic excess, exchange theory too is moving in a more synthetic direction. This has been made possible mainly by the work of Richard Emerson (1981) and his disciples, especially Karen Cook (1987a, 1987b), who seem to have moved to the center of ongoing work in exchange theory. Starting with the traditional micro-level concerns of exchange theory, this group is seeking to build toward the macro level and to develop a more synthetic exchange theory.

For example, Cook, O'Brien, and Kollock (1990) define exchange theory in inherently integrative terms as being concerned with exchanges at various levels of analysis including among interconnected individuals, corporations, and nation states. They identify two strands of work in the history of exchange, one at the micro level focusing on social behavior as exchange and the other at the more macro level of social structure as exchange. They see the strength of exchange theory in micro-macro integration since "it includes within a single theoretical framework propositions that apply to individual actors as well as to the macro-level (or systemic level) and it attempts to formulate explicitly the consequences of changes at one level for other levels of analysis" (Cook et al. 1990, 175).

Cook et al. identify three contemporary trends, all of which point toward a more integrative exchange theory. The first is the increasing use of field research focusing on more macroscopic issues, which can complement the traditional use of the laboratory experiment to study microscopic issues. Second, they note a shift in substantive work away from a focus on dyads and toward larger networks of exchange. Third, and most important, is the ongoing effort to synthesize exchange theory and structural sociologies, especially network theory. (I will have more to say about this last issue shortly.)

Along the way, Cook et al. discuss the gains to be made from integrating insights from a variety of other micro theories. Decision theory offers "a better understanding of the way actors make choices relevant to transactions" (1990, 168). More generally, cognitive science (which includes cognitive anthropology and artificial intelligence) sheds "more light on the way in which actors perceive, process, and retrieve information" (1990, 168). Symbolic interactionism offers knowledge about how actors signal their intentions to one another and this is important in the development of trust and commitment in exchange relationships. Most generally, they see their synthetic version of exchange theory as being well-equipped to deal with the centrally important issue of the micro-macro relationship. In their view, "exchange theory is one of a limited number of theoretical orientations in the social sciences that explicitly conceptualize purposeful actors in relation to structures" (1990, 172).

Even ethnomethodology, one of the most determinedly micro-extremist perspectives in sociological theory, has shown some signs of openness to synthesis and integration. For example, ethnomethodology seems to be expanding into domains that appear more in line with mainstream sociology. A good example is Heritage and Greatbatch's (1986) analysis of British political speeches and the methods used to generate applause from audiences. The typology of devices developed by them seems little different from the kinds of typologies employed by various other types of sociological theorists.

However, ethnomethodology remains embattled and insecure and thus, in some ways, seems to run counter to the trend toward theoretical synthesis. Boden (1990), for example, finds it necessary to make a strong, albeit somewhat self-conscious, case *for* ethnomethodology and conversation analysis. It is certainly true, as Boden suggests, that ethnomethodology has widened and deepened its support in sociology. However, one wonders whether it, or any sociological theory for that matter, is, as Boden contends, "here to stay." In any case, such an argument contradicts the basic theme of this chapter, which is that theoretical boundaries are weakening and new synthetic perspectives are emerging. It may be that ethnomethodology is still too new and too insecure to consider an erosion of its boundaries.

Nevertheless, much of Boden's essay deals with synthetic efforts *within* ethnomethodology, especially in terms of dealing with such integrative issues as the relationship between agency and structure, the embeddedness of action, and fleeting events within the course of history. Boden also deals with the extent to which an array of European and American theorists have begun to integrate ethnomethodology and conversation analysis into their orientations. Unfortunately, what is lacking is a discussion of the degree to which ethnomethodologists are integrating the ideas of other sociological theories into their perspective. Ethnomethodologists seem quite willing for other theorists to integrate ethnomethodological perspectives, but they seem far less eager to reciprocate.

Rational choice theory is very interesting from the point of view of theoretical synthesis. On the one hand, this is one of the most micro-extremist theories in sociology. This work is unified in its methodological individualism and seeks to base sociological theory on a philosophical anthropology *(homo economicus)* of rational, maximizing, self-interested actors making correct, most efficient choices of means to ends on the basis of information available to them. It was just such a philosophical anthropology that was rejected by many of the early sociological theorists who sought to develop a more realistic (i.e., less rational) view of the actor as driven by such things as beliefs. Furthermore, the micro extremism of rational choice theory was rejected by many who moved in the direction of developing more macro-oriented theories. However, in recent years, the success of economics has lured some sociologists back to the micro model of the rational actor with the promise of clean, simple, and elegant theories.

Friedman and Hechter (1988, 1990) recognize some of the limitations of rational choice theory and, among other things, they urge extending the model on the micro level on such issues as the rationality of individual actors and its internal limits and the origin of preferences within actors. In other words, they are pushing more integration on the micro-levels and at least some movement toward such micro theories as symbolic interactionism and ethnomethodology. In addition, they are pressing for more integration with such macro-level concerns as how to aggregate from individual actions to macrosocial outcomes, and on how rational egoists produce institutions. Friedman and Hechter are urging a fuller sense of the actor and greater concern with various facets of the micro-macro linkage. In emphasizing this linkage, Friedman and Hechter are urging a more synthetic type of rational choice theory than is usually found in the literature: "Why, then, prefer rational choice? Perhaps the most compelling reason is that it is explicitly concerned with linking micro and macro levels of analysis rather than asserting the analytical supremacy of one or the other" (Friedman and Hechter 1988, 212). This is clearly a very different image of rational choice theory than the micro extremism that we usually associate with it.

As indicated above, network theory shows great promise from the point of view of theoretical synthesis. The focus of network theory is on social structure, the pattern of ties linking individual (Granovetter 1973, 1983, 1985) and collective (Clawson, Neustadt, and Bearden 1986; Mizruchi and Koening 1986) members of society. While these may be seen as deep structures, that is, as structures that lie below the surface (Wellman 1983), they are closer to sociology's traditional sense of social structure than to the structures of concern to, for example, French structuralists (see below). It is its closeness to traditional senses of social structure that makes network theory an attractive target for those interested in synthesis. Furthermore, since the networks can be either micro (among individual actors) or macro (among collective actors), both micro (e.g., exchange) and macro (e.g., conflict) theories can seek integration with it. Furthermore, this interest in both micro and macro networks makes network theory, at least in some senses, inherently integrative.

Of prime interest, as mentioned above, are the emerging ties between network theory and exchange theory (and, as I have noted, between network theory and conflict theory). Network theory appears to offer exchange theory a highly compatible macro theory that complements exchange theory's micro orientation. For example, network theorists, like exchange theorists, are little interested in individual motives. The network theorists' interest in objective ties meshes nicely with the exchange theorists' interest in objective patterns of behavior. To put it in negative terms, network theory would not fit as well with the sociological theories that are primarily interested in consciousness (symbolic interactionism, phenomenology, existentialism). On the other side, exchange theory would not tie in as well with the (macro) subjectivistic orientation of other macro theories such as structural functionalism and critical theory. Network theory also allows exchange theorists to see the dyads of traditional concern to them as being embedded in larger networks or relationships. This means that exchange theorists can examine the effects of interpersonal exchange transactions on larger networks and conversely the effect of those networks on exchange transactions. However, Cook et al., like others (e.g., McMahon 1984), are wary of the dangers associated with moving a traditionally micro-level theory in a macro direction:

> While exchange network theory has much promise, there are potential
> pitfalls in any attempt to extend a well-developed micro-level framework

to apply to more macro-levels. Exchange theory will need a more explicit specification of the processes at the macro-level it seeks to explain and some vision of the nature of these macro-level processes in relation to other existing structures and events (e.g., an explicit acknowledgement of the historical, political, and institutional context in which events of interest are likely to occur). (Cook et al. 1990, 174–175)

While much of the above deals with the integration of extant, usually American, sociological theories, another kind of synthesis is also taking place in sociological theory. This is the integration into American theory of ideas and theories drawn from other disciplines and/or nations.[12] A few examples are examined below.

While it has yet to occur on a large scale, Lemert (1990) makes a strong case for the integration of structuralism and poststructuralism into mainstream sociology. These perspectives have developed outside of sociology and in various European countries (especially France). In spite of the barriers to such integration, Lemert feels that structuralism has much to offer to sociological analysis. One hurdle has been the dense and elusive language of the French structuralists. More important is the threat posed by structuralism to mainstream sociology because of its focus on discourse and texts rather than the "real world." However, the latter problem may be mitigated by the fact that sociology is already showing evidence of a greater openness to the integration of linguistic tools and ideas (Brown 1987, 1990).

There is a boom in interest in cultural sociology in both Europe and the United States (Lamont and Wuthnow 1990). The theorists (and empiricists) who are producing this body of knowledge come from various nations and a wide array of traditional theoretical approaches, but their collective body of work is now coalescing into a new and distinctive approach to the social world. Theorists (and empiricists) in the United States and Europe have focused on the study of symbolic codes and culture-mediated power relations. Such concerns are found in the work of many of the most notable contemporary theorists in Europe (e.g., Levi-Strauss, Foucault, Bourdieu, Habermas, Douglas) and America (Goffman, Parsons, Berger, Alexander). While not all of their work falls under the heading of cultural sociology, enough of it does, and there is sufficient coherence in it as a set, to provide cultural sociology with a powerful theoretical base and to ensure its continued development. And it is a theoretical perspective that is inherently integrative across disciplinary and national boundaries.

An even more striking development with a similar integrative character is the rise of feminist sociological theory. As Lengermann and Brantley (1988) point out, feminist sociological theory is inherently synthetic since it has been formed out of the intersection of three broad inputs:

theories of gender differences, including biological, institutional, and social psychological theories of gender; theories of gender inequality, including liberal feminism and Marxian feminism; and theories of gender oppression, including psychoanalytic, radical feminist, and socialist feminist theories. Some of these idea systems are indigenous to sociology while others feed into sociology from a variety of external sources. The confluence of these internal and external forces is leading to the development of a distinctive feminist sociological theory. While that theory is in its early, formative stages, it seems clear that such a theory (or theories) will undergo expansion and consolidation in the coming years.

In addition to the integration of feminist theory into sociological theory in the next few years (Alexander and Colomy and the neofunctionalists, Fine and the symbolic interactionists, and others are welcoming it), Lengermann and Brantley (1990) point to other areas of future development. While they urge a focus on subjective and micro social situations, they are also conscious of the need to link these to macro-level phenomena. They describe the "dialectic tension between the need to respect the individual and the equally compelling need to generalize" (Lengermann and Brantley 1990, 330). In addition, they discuss the requirement that feminist sociologists continue to critically analyze sociology's penchant for dualistic rhetoric (e.g., male-female and, especially important given the focus of this chapter, micro-macro) and attempt to develop more integrated conceptions of the social world.

Conclusions

It is abundantly clear that many sociological theories are now borrowing heavily from one another and cutting across multiple levels of social analysis with the result that the traditionally clear borders between theories (and paradigms) are growing increasingly blurred and porous. How this will sort out is not yet clear. It may be that in the near term we will see a dramatically different, less differentiated, more synthetic theoretical landscape in sociology. Or it may be that old theoretical allegiances will be revived, thereby solidifying the separate and warring fiefdoms that have characterized sociological theory for the last several decades. Many observers (e.g., Cook, O'Brien, and Kollock 1990; Lamont and Wuthnow 1990) worry explicitly about a renewal of such fiefdoms, and the interminable political infighting that inevitably accompanies them. One indicator of this possibility is Boden's (1990) citation of a recent statement by Garfinkel that ethnomethodology is an "incommensurably alternate sociology." This coupled with the absence of much indication of a willingness on the part of ethnomethodology to adopt the ideas of other theories indicates a high probability of continued conflict between ethnomethodology and other theoretical perspectives. While we need to continue to be concerned about this problem, the diverse body of work pointing in a synthetic direction allows us to luxuriate for the moment in the glow of the new movement toward syntheses within sociological theory.

While it is tempting to end on such an uplifting note, instead let me turn the basic thrust of this chapter on its head and argue that what these syntheses are really succeeding in doing is turning strong theoretical perspectives, ones that have demonstrated their usefulness over long periods of time, into the equivalent of theoretical "pablum." If all sociological theories are seeking syntheses with one another, might we not end up with a series of flabby theories that are weak and useless? Take the example of Collins's definition of conflict theory discussed earlier as a theory of the organization of society and the behavior of people and groups in society. Defined in this way as a general approach to the entire domain of sociology, it is unclear precisely what conflict theory has to offer to sociology. It is certainly no longer a theory of conflict that Collins takes pains to differentiate from conflict theory. If all theories are intent in moving in this direction—and there is evidence that they are—then what are we left with?

One answer, I suppose, could be one grand integrative theory. Certainly, the neofunctionalists, symbolic interactionists, exchange theorists, and others discussed in this chapter would be quite comfortable with the umbrella definition offered by Collins. But this flies in the face of the movement away from the production of grand overarching theories. Instead, what may be evolving, perhaps for the first time, is a sense of sociology's common ground (perhaps, in paradigmatic terms, a common image of the subject matter of sociology). It has often been lamented that unlike many other established fields, sociology lacks an agreed-upon domain. The development of such a common base would be a most welcome outcome of theoretical syntheses.

However, I do not think that we are in the process of evolving one grand, commonly agreed-upon sociological theory. In order to achieve such agreement, the theory would need to be so general, vague, and amorphous that it could hardly be called a theory and would be virtually useless. Returning to my argument about an integrated sociological paradigm (which bears strong similarities with the movement toward theoretical syntheses described here), my view was that the integrated paradigm would not replace extant paradigms but rather supplement their extremist perspectives with a more integrative one. If we are in the process of developing an integrated sociological theory (or theories), it should supplement, *not* replace, extant theories. This means that extant theories will need to retain their distinctive "teeth" (while at the same time searching out the integrative core). Thus, for example, if I were a conflict theorist, I would be concerned about Collins's eagerness to surrender a theory of conflict. After all, whatever conflict theory has achieved has been based on its theory of conflict. Take that away, and what is left?

It is interesting to note in this context that an undercurrent of uneasiness runs through this body of work on theoretical syntheses. For example, Collins (1990) talks of intellectual "piracy" and Fine (1990) of symbolic interactionism's "promiscuity." In addition, Cook et al. (1990) explicitly address the "pitfalls" of integration within exchange theory. Although they are not explicit on this, it may be that all the authors are expressing an underlying concern about the costs of excessive integration.

A natural damper on this movement toward excessive integration may arise from the fact that even though theorists with many different perspectives are espousing integration, many of these same sociologists are likely to reject the specific efforts stemming from other theories. For example, Friedman and Hechter (1988) anticipate hostility to rational choice theory's integrative efforts from two sources. For one thing, they believe that what they call interpretive approaches (e.g., phenomenologists, hermeneuticists) will be hostile to these efforts because they are based on rational choice theory's positivistic orientation. They also believe that all structuralists (e.g., Durkheimians, Marxists, network theorists) will "object on principle to *any* approach that is based on methodological individualism" (Friedman and Hechter 1988, 212). If Friedman and Hechter are right about the synthetic efforts of rational choice theory, and this is extended to theoretical syntheses from all theoretical directions, then it is unlikely that the efforts toward theoretical syntheses will grow too excessive.

On the other hand, there is delicate balance here. While traditional theoretical allegiances can serve to prevent excessive integration, they can also, as was the case with the movement toward micro-macro integration in the 1980s, lead to a repetition of theoretical extremism within the movement toward syntheses. In other words, we will end up little better off than we were during the decades of theoretical extremism. Thus, a more realistic, albeit less inspiring, conclusion to this chapter is to suggest that we are moving into a particularly interesting and important era in the history of sociological theory. Great gains can be made, but there are great dangers as well. Theorists will need to walk a very fine line as they strive toward greater synthesis without gutting their theories or setting the stage for a renewed period of theoretical extremism.

Notes

1. This is not to say that there were no efforts at integration and synthesis during these periods. In fact, sociology has always had such attempts, but they were clearly in the minority and swamped by theoretical extremism.

2. I am certainly not the first to recognize this development. Among others, Smelser (1988) has described this trend and Alexander and Colomy (1990) deal with it as a backdrop to their focal concern with synthetic efforts in neofunctionalism; see also Fararo (1989).

3. Again, this may be as close as we come in sociology to a Kuhnian paradigm revolution.

4. While Antonio attacks the idea of Marx's grand narrative and Kellner is critical of the idea of a master narrative, both see a crucial role for some sort of holistic thought, without the liabilities of the above grand theories, in social theory.

5. In looking at this, we are doing an external-intellectual subtype of M_U analysis.

6. Turner and Maryanski (1988a) have challenged neofunctionalism by arguing that it is not really functional in its orientation; it has abandoned many of the basic tenets of structural functionalism.

7. This seems to be in accord, at least partially, with Turner and Maryanski's (1988a) claim that neofunctionalism has little in common with structural functionalism.

8. Collins also stresses the point that conflict theory, more than other sociological theories, has been open to the integration of the findings of empirical research.

9. More generally, an integration of all theoretical ideas specific to subareas in sociology with the broader theories of which they are part would be highly profitable.

10. Fine (1990) points out that symbolic interactionists are in the process of distancing themselves from Blumer's interpretation of Mead and are in the process of constructing a "new" Mead.

11. Another work of this genre is Sciulli's (1986) effort to clarify the meaning of voluntaristic action and to link it to work in legal theory.

12. Again, there is nothing new about this; sociological theory has always been open to such things. This synthetic work is notable here because it is now just a part of a much broader integrative movement.

12

The Sociology of Work and Socioeconomics: Metatheoretical Analyses

U p to this point in part II, I have analyzed metatheoretically a number of the broadest theoretical developments in the history (especially the recent history) of sociology. However, metatheory (M_U) can also be used to analyze more specific theoretical developments in each of sociology's many subareas. My objective in this chapter is to illustrate this in the cases of the sociology of work and socioeconomics. I will utilize metatheoretical ideas developed throughout this book, and especially in the last two chapters, to analyze these two subfields.

Sociology of Work

This section takes as its starting point Ida Simpson's essay "Sociology of Work: Where Have the Workers Gone?" (1989). In that essay, Simpson discusses three major,[1] but only partially overlapping, changes[2] in the sociology of work.[3] The first is the historical shift in dominant external disciplinary influence away from anthropology and toward economics.[4] In the process of discussing this historical change, Simpson critiques the failure of the sociology of work to take seriously relevant work in another external discipline: history. The second is a methodological shift over time away from descriptive, qualitative approaches (e.g., participant observation) and toward quantification, abstract variables, and multivariate statistical methods. Finally, she describes a change from a primarily micro-level concern in the early years of the sociology of work toward the direction of a more macro-level focus. Because I think this last is the most important change and because it fits well with the concerns of the last several chapters of this book, in this chapter I am going to concentrate on the micro-macro issue in the sociology of work and I will relate it to developments in sociological theory.

I should make it clear, if it is not already clear, that Simpson is working broadly in the domain of metasociology. That is, she is reflexively studying the field of the sociology of work. Simpson is doing metasociology in analyzing the relationship between the sociology of work and other disciplines. This is also the case when she discusses the role played by business schools in the changing concerns of the sociology of work. She is also doing a more specific metamethodological analysis when she relates changes in the sociology of work to the methodological changes mentioned above. As is my pattern, I am consciously and specifically undertaking still another type of metasociology in doing a metatheoretical (M_U) analysis of the relationship between changes in theoretical orientations in the sociology of work and changes in sociological theory in general. More specifically, I will use the internal-intellectual subtype of M_U to examine changes in what could be called the dominant paradigm within the sociology of work, especially its theoretical component, and how it relates to more general changes in sociological theory. Once again, I will rely heavily on the micro-macro metatheoretical tool to make sense of these changes. Simpson's analysis, when it relates to theoretical concerns, is also largely of the internal-intellectual type when she examines, for example, the micro-macro shift, although she also does some analysis of the external-intellectual type when she focuses on changing external disciplinary influences. Both Simpson and I focus on changes within the internal (and to a lesser extent external) intellectual domains. One of the main things omitted from both works,[5] of course, is any discussion of the relationship between changes in (theories of) the sociology of work and changes in the work world itself (the external-social type of M_U). It would be instructive to examine how such changes as the automation of the factory, the computerization of the office, the corporatization of medicine (Ritzer and Walczak 1988), and the decline of "smokestack industries" (to mention just a few) have affected theorizing about the sociology of the work world since the 1920s. An argument could probably be made linking such social changes to the kinds of shifts in the sociology of work discussed by Simpson. While such an analysis would be welcome, it is beyond the purview of this chapter.[6]

I believe that the kind of work being done by Simpson (and by me in this section) once again clearly demonstrates the utility of metasociology and metatheory. That is, periodic and serious reexaminations of the history and current status of sociology in general, and more specifically its subareas and its theories, are of great importance in helping us understand where we are and where we ought to be heading. Far from impeding our progress as a discipline, metasociological and metatheoretical analyses can help us take dramatic leaps forward. Specifically, the major goal of this section is to point sociologists of work who are beginning to develop an integrated micro-macro approach toward the already established body of theory utilizing such an approach (chapters 10 and 11). This should allow sociologists of work to refine their micro-macro approach much more quickly than if they did not have a body of theory on which to build.

I begin by generally accepting Simpson's characterization of the history of the sociology of work. While I think a more systematic history is needed, I am comfortable with her characterization of the broad outlines of the development of the field. I also think that the kinds of external influences she delineates (e.g., anthropology, economics, business schools) have played a key role in changes over time in the basic orientations of the sociology of work. However, what interests me most is the parallel between Simpson's historical sketch of the sociology of work and my sense of the history of sociological theory, especially in the United States. Thus, another way of looking at the history of the sociology of work is through understanding its relationship to the changing nature of sociological theory. Perhaps more importantly, I want to argue that the near-term development of the sociology of work can be enhanced by a rapid and explicit utilization of some of the most recent developments in sociological theory.

While it is certainly true that anthropology played a key external role in the early development of the sociology of work, internally there was at least an elective affinity between the sociology of work and symbolic interaction theory. Indeed, the subfield of the sociology of work and symbolic interactionist theory developed side-by-side, and sometimes in overlapping fashion, at the University of Chicago, primarily in the 1920s and 1930s. The people who ultimately came to dominate their respective fields, Everett Hughes in the sociology of work and Herbert Blumer in symbolic interactionism, developed and refined their perspectives in the same milieu and in close proximity to one another.[7] By 1937 Blumer had given symbolic interactionism its name and by 1938 or 1939 Hughes had given his course the title "Sociology of Work."[8] I am not arguing that symbolic interactionism was *the* theoretical approach of sociologists of work, but I am suggesting that there were strong ties and similarities between the two. The ethnographic work on occupational processes done by sociologists of work was compatible with the micro- and meso- (Maines 1982) level concerns of symbolic interactionism. Thus, the symbolic interactionists could be said to be interested in the way people negotiate order and the sociologists of work to be interested in the negotiated order of the occupational world. What strikes me about this correspondence is that both perspectives stress a view of people as the active creators of their social world; this, to Simpson, is the defining characteristic of research in the early period of the history of the sociology of work. I agree with Simpson, but the internal theoretical influence of symbolic interactionism was probably at least as great as the external influence of anthropology.[9]

Simpson's discussion of the middle period, as well as her description of at least part of the latest period of work since 1970, focuses on the loss of concern for the creative actor and the increasing emphasis on external constraints (e.g., technology, bureaucracy, labor markets, etc.) on the (passive) actor. This of course, parallels the shift in sociological theory from the dominance of micro-level symbolic interactionism in the 1920s and 1930s (and the social definition paradigm, more generally) to the hegemony of macro-level structural functionalism (and the social facts paradigm) from the 1940s to the beginning of the 1960s. Even through the multiparadigmatic days of the 1960s and into the 1970s, the social facts paradigm was first among equals. The major theoretical competitors during this period were other macro-level (social factist) theories, especially conflict theory. Many of these macro-theories remain strong to this day—this is even true of structural functionalism which, transformed into neofunctionalism, seems to be reversing two decades of decline.

The linkage between the orientations of the sociology of work and theory during this middle period is not nearly as neat, clean, and direct as it was in the early period when both symbolic interactionism and the sociology of work coexisted to a large degree in the Chicago department. However, a broad correspondence can be traced between the move to macro-level theories in sociology in general and to macro-level explanations in the sociology of work. One of the clearest manifestations of this correspondence is the rather startling growth of macro-level neo-Marxian theories (Agger 1978) and neo-Marxian studies of work (e.g., Braverman 1974) that stress the impact of larger structures on actors.

While Simpson does not discuss this subject, I think a flowering took place, especially during the 1970s, in micro-sociological theories (see chapter 9). This too was paralleled by a modest rebirth of interest in more micro-level studies of occupations. Such work can be found in journals like *Journal of Contemporary Ethnography* (formerly *Urban Life*), *Symbolic Interaction,* and, to a lesser extent, in *Work and Occupations*. In fact, *Work and Occupations* was founded in the early 1970s to serve as an outlet for these more micro-level, observational studies. However, over time that journal has published less and less of that type of work.

Turning to more contemporary research in the sociology of work (e.g., Burawoy 1979), Simpson sees more of an effort to link active, social actors and the larger structures in which they exist. In other words, she sees more of an integrated micro-macro (or agency-structure) approach to the study of work. Furthermore, she specifically calls for a bridging of the micro-level behavior of concern in the job search literature and the macro-structures of interest to those studying labor market segmentation. In fact, one of the overriding themes in her paper is a call for a more integrated, micro-macro approach to the study of work. (Ford [1988], in fact, uses such an approach in her recent text on industrial sociology.) The fascinating thing to me, of course, is that such an approach developed in sociological theory in the 1980s (chapter 10).

While sociological theory has clearly moved in the direction of a focus on micro-macro (and agency-structure) integration and, if Simpson is correct, so too have at least a few of those interested in the sociology of work, these two developments seem to parallel one another without showing much, if any, mutual impact. It is certainly true that the major theoretical works on micro-macro integration have not been affected by the sociology of work. Conversely, how much research in the sociology of work has been done utilizing Giddens's "structuration" theory, Habermas's "colonization of the life world," Bourdieu's "habitus," or my own "integrated sociological paradigm"? While I do not have systematic data on this issue, my guess is that few, if any, studies of work have been done utilizing any of these theoretical perspectives.

More generally, this means that there has been an increasing separation over time between the sociology of work and sociological theory. The early period was marked by a close linkage between Chicago-style studies of occupations and symbolic interactionism. The middle period was characterized by a more indirect linkage between the more macro-level concerns of occupational sociologists and the dominant macro theories in sociology. But in the 1980s, despite the fact that they seem to be evolving a common micro-macro focus, the sociology of work and sociological theory seemed to be practiced in virtual isolation from one another. This reality, of course, merely confirms in a specific domain the widespread belief that research and theory in contemporary sociology are largely isolated from each other.

To add further depth to this analysis, let us look briefly at the history and contemporary status of the major subfield within the sociology of work, the sociology of the professions, from the point of view of the theme of this chapter. The earliest approach to the study of the professions was the process approach (e.g., Hughes 1958; Bucher and Strauss 1961; Wilensky 1964). It had many things in common (e.g., dynamism, micro-meso level concerns, etc.) with symbolic interactionism. In fact, the process approach developed at the University of Chicago in the 1920s and 1930s and many of its practitioners were aligned with the Chicago school. Needless to say, symbolic interactionism also had its roots in the Chicago school during the same period. The middle period in the study of the professions was dominated by the structural-functional approach (Greenwood 1957) which obviously bore a strong resemblance to structural-functionalism in general. The emergence of the power approach (e.g., Freidson 1970; Johnson 1972; Kelgon 1978; Ritzer 1975a) followed the emergence of conflict theory as an alternative to structural functionalism and paralleled the emergence of neo-Marxian theories as viable approaches within mainstream sociological theory.[10] The general resurgence of interest in micro theories in the 1970s even had a parallel in the sociology of the professions in, among other places, Dingwall's (1976) "Accomplishing Professions." However, in the 1980s one is hard-pressed to find integrative micro-macro works on the professions that are explicitly drawing on the major theoretical works of the decade that adopt this orientation. Perhaps this represents nothing more significant than the inevitable time lag between the development of theories and their utilization in specific substantive areas, but if that is the case, metasociological works like this present monograph can draw attention to the gap and expose occupational sociologists much more quickly to what is as yet not a widely known development in sociological theory.

In this section I have argued that there are strong parallels between the histories of the sociology of work and sociological theory. Both fields have moved from a focus on creative actors, to a concern for the constraining effect of structure, to a concern for a more synthetic conception of the actor-structure relationship. I think that both fields would be enhanced by exposure to recent developments in the other. On the one hand, developments in sociological theory would be enriched by efforts trying to relate them to recent research on the reality of workers and work settings. This would be an important step in relating the abstractions of sociological theory to at least one aspect of the "real world." On the other hand, the sociology of work would be enhanced by explicit use of theoretical models that synthesize micro-macro and agency-structure relationships.[11] This would serve to put the specific findings of this subfield into a broader and more general context.

The reader is entitled to ask what a sociology of work drawing on these micro-macro theories might look like? Needless to say, this is an enormously complex question that simply cannot be handled within the confines of this discussion. Furthermore, since there are great differences among integrative micro-macro theories, much would depend on which specific theory (or theories) is being used. I will use my own integrated paradigm (informed by various micro-macro theories) to suggest a few ideas of relevance to the sociology of work with special attention to the study of the professions.

First, there should be a focus on micro-(meso)-macro *linkage*. This means that students of the professions should be concerned with the *relationship* among individual professionals, the meso structures in which they exist (e.g., employing organizations, professional associations), and their larger macro (e.g., societal, cultural) context. Second, this focus on linkage does not mean we should ignore the important details of what goes on at the micro, meso, and macro levels. Thus, even while we concentrate on linkage, we would want to be concerned with the strategies of individual professionals, the dynamics of professional associations and employing organizations, and the specific character of the larger social and cultural context. Third, if one level (or a part thereof) is lifted out for specific study or analysis, the sociologist of work should always bear in mind that any level is part of a broader relationship and that it should always be analyzed with that larger context in mind. Thus, a study of a given (meso-level) profession should not lose sight of either the actions of the micro-level professionals or the larger social context. Fourth, there should be a refusal to elevate a given level (or levels) of analysis to permanent primacy (as, for example, the structural functionalists who studied the professions did in focusing on meso- and macro-level phenomena). Fifth, actors should be seen as both partially constrained and partially capable of creating and changing the larger structures in which they exist. An individual professional—for example, a physician employed by a for-profit corporation—is both constrained by the new structural realities in medicine and is simultaneously creating, re-creating, and even changing those structures. Sixth, macro structures should be seen as both partially constraining and partially enabling. American culture, with its emphasis on economic success, may tend to force some physicians into working for for-profit medical organizations, but it also provides a fertile environment for the development of new and innovative ways of making one's way as a professional physician. Seventh, some effort should be made to examine meso-level phenomena as a prime arena in which micro- and macro-level (as well as indigenous meso-level) forces play themselves out. More specifically, we might want to look at the changing nature of a for-profit hospital to see the way in which micro-level professional physicians, meso-level organizational dynamics, and macro level economic forces interpenetrate. Finally, we must always be concerned with the possibility of actors losing control over the meso and macro structures they create, but such a loss is not inevitable. Thus, individual physicians *may* lose control over for-profit hospitals and the more general growth of a capitalistic structure and mentality within medicine, but such a loss is not inevitable; they are always capable of regaining control over those meso- and macro-level phenomena. The preceding is neither a very exhaustive nor a very detailed enumeration, but it is suggestive of the beginnings of what a micro-macro approach to the sociology of work (in this case, the professions) would look like.

This need to draw upon sociological theory is not an alternative to drawing on other disciplines, but rather a supplement to it. There are advantages (and disadvantages) to drawing on ideas, theories, and methods from other fields, but Simpson (1989) argues, at least in the case of the recent reliance of the sociology of work on economics, that we have lost sight of social factors. Drawing on sociological theory, especially the recent work on micro-macro (and agency-structure) linkage, offers a variety of potential rewards and, at the minimum, would not pose a threat to our focal interest in social issues. Contemporary empirical researchers in the sociology of work seem more open to ongoing developments in other disciplines (or in sociological methodology) than they are to those in sociological theory.

I want to close this section by reiterating the point that metasociological and metatheoretical analyses of the type undertaken here and in Simpson's paper can be important aids in the advancement of sociology.[12] Not only have we uncovered a surprising and striking parallel in the histories of two subareas in sociology, but we have shown that each has much in common with, and to gain from, the other. Now we need some sociologists of work to read contemporary theory seriously and for some theorists to immerse themselves in empirical research into the work world. As mutually enriching as this exchange might me, it will not be an easy task for either empiricists or theorists. But the potential gains are great and it is one of the responsibilities of metatheorists to keep nudging empirically and theoretically inclined sociologists toward one another. Overall, the theoretical literature on micro-macro (and agency-structure) integration can help meet Simpson's call for a sociology of work that deals with the relationship between creative actors and constraining structures without sacrificing a sociological approach upon the altar of economics.

Socioeconomics

A good portion of the current debate over socioeconomics and economic sociology has been framed in metatheoretical, particularly paradigmatic, terms. I would like to address the recent work in socioeconomics, especially Amitai Etzioni's *The Moral Dimension: Toward a New Economics* (1988), from those points of view. Such a metatheoretical (M_U) examination should allow us to better understand these works, their objectives, and their strengths and weaknesses.

Since the term *paradigm* is bandied about by many of the new socioeconomists, we are entitled to ask precisely what they mean when they use that term and whether socioeconomics can be seen as a new paradigm (or a theoretical component of a paradigm). Those who use the paradigm concept leave themselves open to a wide range of criticisms. As we saw in chapter 6, the basic source of the problem is ambiguities in Kuhn's (1962) original work on the paradigm concept. Stung by his critics, Kuhn (1970b) later tried to give the paradigm concept more specificity by defining it as an exemplar, or a concrete solution to a scientific puzzle. However, many observers felt that Kuhn had done a disservice to the basic thrust of his original work by limiting the paradigm concept in this way. Their view was that the truer meaning(s) of the paradigm concept was to be found in his earlier, more ambiguous work.

The latter view, of course, leaves considerable latitude in how one uses the paradigm concept. As someone who has been criticized for using the concept too loosely (see chapter 6), I am loathe to critique the new socioeconomists on this ground. However, even I am tested by the wide range of things that they call a paradigm. Take, for example, Swedberg's (1989) notion of *the* sociological paradigm (*homo sociologicus*). For one thing, this implies that there was, or is, a single, dominant sociological paradigm. *No* analyst of sociology from a paradigmatic perspective has *ever* come to such a conclusion; sociology is *always* seen as multiparadigmatic (Friedrichs 1970; Effrat 1972; Ritzer 1975c 1975d; Hirsch, Michaels, and Friedman 1987, 318). More specifically, Swedberg sees the sociological paradigm as, among other things, focusing on a collective actor and on the constraining effects of social structure. However, in my view, *no* sociological paradigm has ever focused on the collective actor. The social facts paradigm comes closest, but its main concern is with social structure and culture and their constraining effects on the individual actor. The social definition paradigm focuses not on structural and cultural constraints, but on the way individual actors create their own actions as well as the larger society. In the social behavior paradigm, the (individual) actor is constrained, but by contingencies of reinforcement not by social structure and culture. The paradigm described by Swedberg is not in accord with any of sociology's multiple paradigms, let alone with some imagined dominant sociological paradigm. Furthermore, it communicates the erroneous idea that sociology is, or has been, a single paradigm science.[13]

Etzioni does not define what he means by a paradigm, but it seems clear that a paradigm is, for him, characterized by the fact that its assumptions play a key role in a variety of fields. Thus, it appears that the neoclassical approach is a paradigm (in Etzioni's sense of the term) because its assumptions span theories in economics, political science, psychology, sociology, anthropology, and history. In contrast to the neoclassical paradigm, but with a similar sense of cross-disciplinary breadth, Etzioni offers his "deontological I&WE paradigm." Socioeconomics is portrayed as a theory within the deontological I&WE paradigm that is supposed to provide a way of dealing with economic behavior that stands in contrast to neoclassical economic theory derived from the neoclassical paradigm. Etzioni's very broad sense of a paradigm has little, if anything, to do with Kuhn's original sense of a paradigm, and it certainly is far removed from Kuhn's later sense of a paradigm as an exemplar. I do not want to take this argument too far. The neoclassical and deonto-logical approaches are perspectives worth thinking about and delineating. We need to call them something, but in labeling them "paradigms" we are stretching the meaning of the concept farther than even I can tolerate.

While Swedberg associates paradigms with disciplines[14] and Etzioni sees paradigms as multidisciplinary, Kyle (1989) goes in the other direction and describes a specific subfield, the sociology of development, as multiparadigmatic. Clearly, the paradigm concept cannot be meaningfully applied at all of these levels; it cannot apply across disciplines, to all of sociology, and to a small part of sociology. Some years ago there was a call for a moratorium on the use of the concept of *alienation* because it was being used so indiscriminately; perhaps a similar call needs to be made on behalf of the *paradigm* concept.[15]

While I do not agree with their use of the paradigm label, I do like several things that Swedberg and Etzioni do with their "paradigmatic" analyses. For example, Etzioni correctly subsumes narrower theories under broader "paradigms." I am especially attracted to Swedberg's focus on the imperialism of the neoclassical paradigm. Good paradigm analysis always leads us into the realm of politics, the battle for power between adherents of different paradigms. I think Swedberg is quite right in arguing that economists have been imperialistic in their efforts to export the neoclassical approach into other fields. By the same token, Etzioni's work can be seen as something of a counterattack into economics of a paradigm informed by different assumptions and based on research results from an array of social sciences. In fact, although he relies primarily on nonsociological sources to make his case, I believe that Etzioni is articulating an eminently sociological approach to economics that focuses on traditional sociological concerns with social, cultural, and personality factors. Needless to say, one can anticipate hostility from supporters of the neoclassical approach within economics.

It also may be that Etzioni harbors imperialistic ambitions of his own. On the one hand, he clearly intends that his approach would subsume neoclassicism within economics. On the other hand, we must ask whether he intends that his socioeconomics apply only to economic behavior or to all social behavior? The fact that he marshalls many noneconomic examples throughout his book would lead one to suspect that he has the latter, more ambitious objective. But Etzioni is even quite open about the breadth of his objective when he discusses the foundation "for a valid theory of behavior and society, including economic behavior, a theory referred to as socioeconomics" (1988, 63). Such imperialism fits with basic paradigm dynamics even if we have difficulty thinking of Etzioni's approach as a paradigm.

Whether what is occurring is labeled a new paradigm, several different things of great importance are happening in and between sociology (and other social sciences) and economics. First, within sociology a number of observers (Swedberg 1987; Swedberg, Himmelstrand, and Brulin 1987; Ritzer 1989d) have recently called for the resuscitation of economic sociology. In their view, recent sociological attention to economic issues has been divided among an array of subfields: sociology of work, industrial sociology, organizational sociology, sociology of development, etc. The problem with these subfields is that they offer only highly limited glimpses of the economy. What is needed is a revival of economic sociology that would adopt a more holistic view of the economy, its relationship to the subsystems of society, and its impact on actors. The revival of economic sociology is related to, but far narrower in scope than, socioeconomics. That is, what is being called for is merely the revival of a longstanding field in sociology, not the development of new theories, paradigms, or disciplines.

At another, even more specific, level, we are witnessing increasing interest in sociological theories with strong roots in the neoclassical paradigm, most notably rational choice theory (Friedman and Hechter 1988, 1990) and game-theoretic Marxism (Roemer 1982; Elster 1985). This is part of the economic imperialism described by Swedberg and others; the neoclassical paradigm is clearly making inroads in sociological theory. One metatheoretical issue concerns how much of this development is a result of imperialistic pressures from without and how much of it reflects legitimate theoretical needs within sociology. Another issue is whether rational choice theory is part of a new emerging paradigm in sociology, or whether it can be subsumed under extant paradigms. While it may grow into a full-fledged paradigm[16] of its own, my guess is that its limitations and the historic hostility of sociologists to it will prevent it from attaining paradigmatic status within sociology. However, in a more limited way, rational choice theory can be included rather easily as a new theoretical component of the extant social behavior paradigm. In fact, elements of the neoclassical approach were important in the formation of the roots of that paradigm in psychology and of its major theoretical component, exchange theory, in sociology.

But the most important metatheoretical issue is the relationship between socioeconomics and developments in sociological theory. I will argue two points here. First, that socioeconomics is in tune with major developments in sociological theory in the 1980s and as we enter the 1990s. Second, in spite of such general similarities, socioeconomics, especially as it is espoused by Etzioni, seems largely out of touch with these developments. I believe that socioeconomics (like the sociology of work) can be greatly enriched by drawing on the latest developments in sociological theory.

It is ironic that Etzioni, who is a sociologist, is being accused of being unaware of the latest developments in sociological theory. As I read his book, his major roots in sociological theory seem to lie in Parsonsian structural-functional theory[17] as well as in the theory of Parsons's critic, Dennis Wrong. Parsons's emphasis on culture (in fact he labeled himself a "cultural determinist" [Parsons 1966]), and on the relationships between the social, cultural, and personality systems, all play a prominent role in Etzioni's approach. Also important is the Parsonsian emphasis on socialization and internalization as well as Wrong's (1961) caution that we must be wary of producing an oversocialized conception of people. However, these are ideas that reached their height of influence in sociological theory several decades ago. One wonders why, if Etzioni wants to operate within a modified, Parsonsian approach, he does not draw upon the work of Alexander and his supporters who are endeavoring to overcome earlier weaknesses by constructing a neo-Parsonsian, neofunctionalist perspective.

How could Etzioni, who seems so up-to-date in economics, psychology, and political science, be so out of touch with sociological theory? I think the answer lies in the implicit politics of *The Moral Dimension*. Etzioni does not have to convince sociologists of the importance of moral, social, and personality factors. What sociologist is going to object to Etzioni's closing message that "[s]ocio-economics is . . . to view pleasure and self-interest within the broader context of human nature, society and ultimate values" (1988, 251)? However, he does have to convince others, especially economists, psychologists, and political scientists, with the result that the overwhelming majority of his references are drawn from those fields. Furthermore, Etzioni is also addressing a larger public policy audience, and evidence amassed from these other fields is far more influential with this particular group than evidence drawn from sociology. Etzioni has clearly done his homework in economics, psychology, and political science, but in the process he has slighted his own roots in sociology and sociological theory. Thus, paradoxically, Etzioni's work may be even more assailable from a sociological point of view than from an economic or psychological viewpoint. However, my main goal in this chapter is not to criticize Etzioni, but to point to some recent theoretical developments that would have greatly enhanced his socioeconomics.

The two developments I have in mind are, of course, the broad movement toward micro-macro (and agency-structure) integration in sociological theory in the 1980s (chapter 10) and the broader movement toward theoretical syntheses as we enter the 1990s (chapter 11).

Looking at it first from the point of view of the micro-macro literature, one of my theses is that Etzioni's work on socioeconomics is very much of this time (the 1980s) and genre even though there is no evidence that this vast body of work had any influence on Etzioni's thinking. Not willing to lose useful ideas from the neoclassical paradigm, Etzioni begins with and accepts its micro-level insights into individual behavior. However, he believes that there is more to the micro level than simply behavior: we must also be concerned with personality factors. More importantly, we cannot be content to operate exclusively on the micro level: we must include macro-level factors. Furthermore, these macro-level phenomena are more than aggregated, micro-level phenomena. Thus, Etzioni includes the basic sociological principle of emergence and focuses a good deal of his attention on emergent social and cultural phenomena. Most importantly, Etzioni is concerned with the interrelationships among these micro- and macro-level phenomena. Here is the way Etzioni expresses his integrative, micro-macro concerns:

> Radical individualism, which is imbued in the neoclassical paradigm, leads it to focus on one level of human activities in its study of human purpose and its instruments: on that of myriad individuals. The paradigm evolved here sees a great deal of the explanation of human achievements—and what holds them back—on the collective level of historical and societal forces. Individuals *do* play a role, but within the context of their collectivities. These are pivotal even for those individuals who challenge their collectivities and work together to change their We-ness. Moreover, the collective level is not an aggregation of myriad individual decisions, transactions or actions, but has a form, a structure, of its own, which affects all behavior significantly. Individuals must either act within the constraints imposed by the structure or learn to change it. (1988, 181)

Such a perspective is in accord with the body of theory (reviewed in chapter 10) dealing with micro-macro and agency-structure integration. Etzioni's perspective would have been enhanced had he built upon at least part of that work, but he appears to be unaware of it.

The second body of work that Etzioni would have found helpful is the wide range of efforts, as we move into the 1990s, at theoretical syntheses, including continuing work on micro-macro synthesis.[18] Once again, even though Etzioni ignores the body of work, his orientation is in accord with it. Specifically, Etzioni seeks to synthesize neoclassical theory and socioeconomics. He expresses this goal in this way:

> the approach followed here is one of *codetermination:* It encompasses factors that form society and personality, as well as neoclassical factors that form markets and rational decision-making. Moreover, we can go beyond suggesting that *both approaches need to be synthesized* [my italics]; we can identify to some extent how they are related to one another: The paradigm advanced here seeks to characterize the context within which the forces that the neoclassical approach focuses on are played

out, a context that sets limits and provides direction to those forces. (1988, 3–4)

However, Etzioni is far from alone in setting such a synthetic goal for himself. In fact, Etzioni is not even alone in seeking a more synthetic approach from a base in the neoclassical paradigm. As we saw in chapter 11, for example, operating within the neoclassical paradigm, Friedman and Hechter (1990; see also Friedman and Hechter 1988) not only offer a spirited defense of rational choice theory, but, like Etzioni, they also recognize some its limitations and point future theorists in the directions needed to overcome these limitations. To put it simply, Friedman and Hechter are using a fuller sense of the actor and greater concern with various facets of the micro-macro linkage. In emphasizing this linkage, Friedman and Hechter are urging a more synthetic type of rational choice theory than is usually found in the literature. There is a broad correspondence between Etzioni's socioeconomics and efforts by Hechter and Friedman to develop a more synthetic rational choice theory.

Thus, two major developments in sociological theory would have greatly enhanced socioeconomics. What might Etzioni have gained had he drawn more on the body of sociological theory concerned with micro-macro linkage? Many things suggest themselves, but one is a sense that there is a growing consensus in sociological theory that macro-structures are *both* constraining and enabling; that structures and actors mutually constitute one another. Operating with a more old-fashioned theoretical orientation, Etzioni (1988, 4) tends to see social structures primarily as limiting and constraining.

While Etzioni has a limited sense of macro-objective structures, his views on macro-subjective phenomena (e.g., values, norms) are closer to the newer, more integrative theories. For example, he argues that "values . . . render some decision-making more effective" (1988, 4). Or, later he argues that "normative values often play important positive functions, and . . . they are not merely hindrances to reason" (1988, 108). A similar viewpoint applied to macro-objective structures would have greatly enhanced Etzioni's effort.

Another type of work on micro-macro linkage that Etzioni might have found useful deals with the nature of the relationships between micro and macro. Munch and Smelser (1987) discuss such relationships as aggregation; externalization; creating, sustaining, reproducing the macro; conformity; internalization; and limit setting. Some of these, especially internalization, are found in Etzioni's work. He could have utilized these other relationships and enriched his analysis of the relationships he did deal with by drawing on works such as this.

Turning to the new synthetic work being produced as we move into the 1990s, Etzioni would have profited from, among others, the recent work of the neofunctionalists. For one thing, he might have avoided the tendency to exaggerate the significance of moral and cultural phenomena. As the title of his book makes clear, Etzioni errs in this direction and fails to give equivalent attention to macro-structural phenomena. Indeed, explicit and detailed attention to such phenomena is left to the last part of the book. And when he does deal with macro-structural phenomena, he tends to focus on their subjective aspects, the ways in which they are internalized in actors (1988, 189). The opening of neofunctionalism toward more structural theories and phenomena would have helped here. In addition, Etzioni fails to give adequate attention to micro-level sociological theories and their insights. Again, the efforts by the neofunctionalists to integrate ideas from various micro theories would have been helpful. Or, Etzioni could have turned more directly to micro theories such as symbolic interactionism and phenomenology for ideas and insights. For example, Etzioni stresses the idea that unlike in the neoclassical paradigm, rationality for him involves conscious deliberations and not automatic, unconscious responses. Micro theorists have had a lot to say about such conscious processes that Etzioni would have found useful.

The above has been largely a critique of socioeconomics in general, and Etzioni's work in particular, from a metatheoretical point of view. Clearly, there are important weaknesses in that work from a paradigmatic, and more generally metatheoretical, perspective. However, this emphasis on critique should not be taken to imply that there are not important strengths in this body of work. I do think that sociology needs a revival of economic sociology and that theories derived from the neoclassical approach (e.g., rational choice theory) have an important role to play in sociological theory. More specifically, I think Etzioni is to be praised for seeking to systematically delineate a socioeconomic alternative to neoclassicism. In doing so, he has mined the literature in fields such as economics and psychology to present a highly detailed picture of socioeconomics. While he continually reminds the reader that he is offering only a first approximation, the detail represents a real strength of this work in contrast to the theoretical literature within sociology discussed throughout this book. While Etzioni could certainly profit from exposure to that literature, those theorists could greatly enrich their theoretical perspectives by following Etzioni's model of utilizing detailed empirical evidence to support each position. While most sociological theorists present hollow theoretical shells, Etzioni has created a theoretical structure that is rich in detail. My main quarrel is not with the detail, but with the theoretical structure which could have been greatly enhanced by exposure to recent work in sociological theory.

Notes

1. Among the other (less important?) changes is the splintering of what was once a fairly homogenous field into several diverse subfields: industrial sociology, sociology of work, and formal organizations.

2. The exact relationship between these three changes is worthy of further metasociological analysis. For example, the shift in the direction of the influence of economics cannot be coterminous with the shift toward macro-level analysis since economics has both micro and macro orientations.

3. By the way, I wish to keep this discussion focused on the sociology of work (or occupations) rather than combining it with the somewhat different subfields of industrial sociology and formal organizations. For a clarification of the differences, compare Ritzer and Walczak's (1986) basic text in occupations, Ford's (1988) in industrial sociology, and Hall's (1982) in organizations.

4. On another metasociological issue, it is interesting, but not surprising (given the topical similarities between economics and the sociology of work and the fact that much of sociological theory developed in reaction against economistic [utilitarian] theories), to note that economics had a profound positive impact on the sociology of work long before it affected sociological theory. It is only in very recent years that theory has seen a major incursion from economics—primarily in rational choice theory. There are now critics of this theoretical development (e.g., Hirsch, Michaels, and Friedman 1987) who take a position similar to the one taken by Simpson on the negative influence of economics on the sociology of work.

5. The other major omission is an internal-social analysis of the sociology of work (e.g., the effect of "schools" on perspectives toward work).

6. I would like to thank my former colleague Tom Ktsanes for chastening me for losing sight of the "real world" in my pursuit of the "lofty" heights of metatheory.

7. Rock (1979) considers Hughes an interactionist and describes students like Howard Becker moving between courses taught by Hughes and Blumer.

8. Hughes described this to me in a personal communication written almost two decades ago.

9. Of course, Simpson has a broader focus that also encompasses industrial sociology; in that broader arena the influence of symbolic interactionism was negligible and that of anthropology great.

10. The sociology of the professions now, of course, has work (e.g., the various essays in Derber, 1982) from an explicitly neo-Marxian perspective.

11. This latter, by the way, is part of a broader need to do a more theoretically sophisticated sociology of work as I have attempted (Ritzer and Walczak 1988) in efforts to use Weberian rationalization theory to analyze the changing nature of the medical profession and Japanese industrial success (chapter 5; Ritzer and LeMoyne 1990).

12. It should be noted that there are a variety of metasociological issues that can be derived from this discussion and would be worthy of further study and discussion. For example, how do we account for the parallel histories of the

sociology of work and sociological theory? That is, is there some exogenous factor that accounts for the similarities in the histories of these subareas? And has a similar path been followed in other subareas in sociology?

13. Swedberg might be on firmer ground on his image of the neoclassical paradigm (*homo economicus*). However, it may not even be possible to think of economics as a single paradigm science. The work of critics such as Simon, Lindberg, the historical economists, etc., are so influential that we can conceive of economics as possessing competing paradigms. Etzioni offers an image of the neoclassical paradigm similar to that of Swedberg, although he is certainly cognizant (as is Swedberg) of, and even stresses, its critics and alternatives.

14. In another essay, Swedberg (along with Himmelstrand and Brulin) uses *paradigm* in still another way to describe the paradigm of economic sociology, but at least they acknowledge that its usage is closer to Merton's sense of a paradigm (in functional analysis) than Kuhn's (Swedberg, Himmelstrand, and Brulin 1987).

15. In spite of this call, as well as the previously discussed confusion over the term, I will, following the work of the authors being analyzed, use the (ambiguously defined) term *paradigm* throughout the rest of this chapter.

16. In my sense of the term (chapter 6).

17. Parsons and structural functionalism also play a central role in Etzioni's (1968) earlier major theoretical work, *The Active Society*. He writes of "the functional analysis employed here" and makes it clear that he is modifying it so that it is better able to deal with change (1968, 121; see also page 418).

18. Work on micro-macro integration and theoretical syntheses are not the only relevant bodies of work in sociology that Etzioni ignores. To take another example, Etzioni has a lot to say about emotions, but shows no familiarity with the growing body of literature on the sociology of emotions.

III
Current Status,
Future Directions
of Metatheorizing

This final part is concerned with analyzing both the current status and the future prospects of metatheorizing in sociology. Chapter 13 examines a range of more established fields and subfields both outside and within sociology that metatheorizing can draw upon for ideas, perspectives, and methods. Among the external disciplines are a variety of areas within intellectual history, including the history of ideas and its "contextualist" critics, the history of mentalities, *Begriffsgeschichte*, history of science, and biography in the history of science. I also examine a number of subfields within sociology, including the sociology of science, the sociology of the professions, and the sociology of knowledge. In chapter 14 I review the case for and against sociological metatheorizing. I discuss a number of the gains from sociological metatheorizing and rebut many of the criticisms of it. Some of the characteristics of sound metatheorizing are reviewed. The chapter, and the book, close with some thoughts on the coming of age of metatheorizing in sociology.

13
Sociological Metatheorizing: Lessons from Other Disciplines

To this point in the book I have dealt with metatheorizing in sociology as if it is, and has been, an intellectual endeavor that is independent of developments in neighboring disciplines. However, this is not true, at least not completely true. As we have already seen, external influence is particularly noticeable in the external-intellectual subtype of M_U. One major example of external influence on metatheorizing is the philosophy of science, especially the ideas of Thomas Kuhn. In addition, there have been a range of other influences from the philosophy of science (e.g., Lakatos), as well as a smattering of inputs from an array of other fields (e.g., linguistics). Several other external influences will also be encountered in this chapter (e.g., from the history of ideas), but the fact is that up to this point sociological metatheorizing has been practiced in relative isolation, even though an array of other fields have much to offer to metatheorizing. In fact, metatheorizing has been impoverished by the fact that it has not drawn nearly enough on neighboring fields. The goal of this chapter is to examine at least some of these fields and delineate some of the ideas that should prove useful to the metatheorist.

Intellectual History

The field of intellectual history is highly relevant to sociological metatheorizing, although not all of metatheorizing is entirely concerned with either historical or intellectual issues. M_U involves studies of either historical *or* contemporary realities in sociological theory. M_P is inherently historical since it involves the systematic study of one's theoretical predecessors as a prelude to developing a new theoretical orientation. M_O is also largely historical since the goal is the study of the work of theoretical predecessors in order to discover and/or create an overarching theoretical perspective. Thus, historical analysis is central to a very large portion of metatheorizing. In addition, most of metatheorizing involves an analysis of intellectual issues, and especially the analysis of the ideas of theoretical predecessors. Exceptions to this concern with intellectual issues are the works found in the internal-social and external-social subtypes of M_U. In spite of the fact that a substantial portion of metatheorizing is in accord with the interests of intellectual history, startlingly, little evidence indicates that metatheorists have been cognizant of work in intellectual history and its various subdisciplines. In this section, I examine some of this vast body of work in an effort to discover what it has to offer to metatheorizing in sociology.

The key historical figure in intellectual history is R. G. Collingwood (1956) who argued for the need to grasp the ideas of historical actors as they were conceptualized in their own act of thinking. Collingwood believed that all history is the history of thought. Historical events are really actions that express the thoughts of actors. Methodologically, historians should reenact in their own minds the thoughts of those whose history they are studying.[1]

A number of different approaches may be grouped under the broad heading of intellectual history (Burke 1986). First, there is the history of ideas, an approach that is distinctively American. Second, there is the movement, spearheaded by British thinkers, away from the "presentism" characteristic of the history of ideas to "contextualism." Third, there is the history of mentalities, which is strongly French in orientation. Fourth, there is the German field of conceptual analysis known as *Begriffsgechischte*. Fifth, there is the history of science. Sixth, even though not strictly a form of intellectual history, there is the study of biographies in the history of science.

History of Ideas

Schulin (1981) traces the development of the history of ideas to the rise of the "New History" in the United States after 1900.[2] This New History shifted "from a concern for political-diplomatic and descriptive history to explorations into collective developments, economic growth and social phenomena" (Schulin 1981, 200). This shift led, among other things, to an interest in intellectual history, which in turn helped to create the narrower field of history of ideas. While it has a number of earlier roots (for example, the work of Charles Beard), the modern history of ideas was created largely by Arthur O. Lovejoy. He played a key role in the development of this field not only in his writings, but also in his role as editor of the *Journal of the History of Ideas*, founded in 1940.

In his famous *The Great Chain of Being: A Study of the History of an Idea* (1936/1960) Lovejoy sought to distinguish his approach from the established history of philosophy. While the history of philosophy tended to focus on individual philosophical systems (e.g., Aristotelian), the history of ideas focused on "unit ideas" that cut across a number of such philosophical systems, as well as a range of other types of idea systems. Lovejoy defines the history of ideas as "the study of the (so far as possible) total life-history of individual ideas, in which the many parts that any one of them plays upon the historic scene, the different facets which it exhibits, its interplay, conflicts and alliances with other ideas, and the diverse human reactions to it, are traced out with adequate and critical documentation, with analytical discrimination, and, finally, with imagination" (1948, 9). The goal is to look behind surface dissimilarities in ideas across a range of idea systems in order to find the underlying and crosscutting unit idea. As Lovejoy puts it, "the same idea often appears, sometimes considerably disguised, in the most diverse regions of the intellectual world" (1936/1960, 15). Not only does the history of ideas examine ideas across ideational systems, but also over time. The goal is to trace unit ideas "through more than one—ultimately, indeed, through all—of the provinces of history in which it figures in any important degree, whether those provinces are called philosophy, science, literature, art, religion, or politics" (Lovejoy 1936/1960, 15). Unit ideas not only cut across disciplines and epochs, but also across nationalities and languages. This enormous sweep and diversity makes the history of ideas inherently interdisciplinary and highly demanding of the researcher.

The history of ideas includes an emphasis on the historical continuity of ideas, rather than on the development of new ideas. In Lovejoy's view, new ideas do arise, but such an occurrence is far rarer than is commonly assumed. Lovejoy is certainly interested in the process by which a new idea is introduced, but he is far more interested in tracing that idea over time and across disciplines. He is interested in how a new idea is diffused; how it joins with other ideas; how it comes to have an impact across diverse fields and over many time periods; how ideas go in and out of vogue and influence; how an idea influential in one generation gives way to another; how later generations interpret ideas in ways undreamed of by previous generations (unanticipated consequences); and how peoples' emotions are affected by these changing ideas. Lovejoy does not see the history of ideas as a neat evolutionary process. In his view, the history of ideas is characterized by repeated processes of trial and error and numerous confusions and misinterpretations. Terms may be used in confused and ambiguous ways over time, and there may well even be confusion within the work of a single thinker.

Lovejoy's unit ideas rarely correspond to familiar ideas such as "God." He suggests that there are many unit ideas, including "types of categories, thoughts concerning particular aspects of common experience, implicit or explicit presuppositions, sacred formulas and catchwords, specific philosophic theorems, or the larger hypotheses, generalizations or methodological assumptions of various sciences" (1948, 9). Lovejoy himself deals with a unit idea that he calls "the great chain of being." This unit idea envisions a hierarchy of ideas: it is better to live than to exist, preferable to feel than to live, and more desirable to think than to feel. Such unit ideas usually involve mixed collections of more specific ideas. Lovejoy also describes unit ideas as "effective working ideas" (1936/1960, 6). These ideas are not restricted to the work of the intellectual elite or to eminent thinkers, but are diffused widely throughout the collectivity.

The history of ideas has come under considerable criticism. I shall turn to the critics, their ideas, and the implications of those ideas for metatheorizing shortly, but first I need to pause and suggest some directions to be taken by metatheorists interested in building on Lovejoy's work.

I can begin by discussing one of the few exceptions in sociological metatheory to the ignorance of intellectual history, and more specifically the history of ideas, Robert Nisbet's *The Sociological Tradition* (1967).

While he is working in the tradition of the history of ideas, Nisbet's work is inherently metatheoretical, particularly M_U, since he is studying the history of sociology, especially sociological theory, with the goal of uncovering its core ideas. Nisbet begins by rejecting staples of those who do M_U: the focus on the thinkers themselves or on schools of thought (e.g., Marxism). Rather than dealing with people or schools of thought, Nisbet chooses to focus instead on "unit ideas." Lovejoy's work was a very natural place for Nisbet to look and he was rewarded with an approach that allowed him to do highly distinctive metatheorizing. Specifically, Nisbet's use of Lovejoy's perspective allowed him to identify five unit ideas in the history of sociology: community, authority, status, the sacred, and alienation.[3] Nisbet then goes on to link each of these concepts to their opposites (community-society, authority-power, status-class, sacred-secular, alienation-progress) and to argue that these "linked antitheses . . . form the very warp of the sociological tradition" (1967, 7). While Nisbet shows the utility of Lovejoy's work for metatheorists, much more could be done with Lovejoy's ideas, many more of which remain to be mined by metatheorists.

Despite efforts like Nisbet's, conceptual analysis is one of the least developed areas within metatheory. While I will discuss other approaches that should aid metatheorists in doing conceptual analyses, I begin with the relevance of the history of ideas. There are exceptions to the tendency to ignore conceptual analyses, such as Nisbet's work, as well as studies by Rubinstein (1986) and Porpora (1989) of the concept of structure, but they display no knowledge of the history of ideas. More conceptual studies are clearly needed: Lovejoy's work offers the metatheorist some powerful leads.

It should be recognized from the beginning that metatheorists are likely to use Lovejoy's approach in a more limited manner than he suggested. That is, the focal concern of metatheorists must be with unit ideas *within* sociology rather than with ideas that cut across a wide range of disciplines. That being said, there is no reason that a metatheorist interested in sociology's unit ideas cannot trace out the degree to which they are found in other disciplines as well as in the larger collectivity. In following the latter course, the metatheorist is becoming more of an historian of ideas than a sociologist, but there is nothing wrong with such intellectual reach. Nevertheless, the nature of sociological metatheorizing leads its practitioners to be focally concerned with sociology.

In order to clarify the following discussion let us, following Nisbet, take alienation as one of sociology's unit ideas.[4] The origins of this idea in sociology would need to be traced to the work of Karl Marx.[5] Taking Marx as our starting point, we would want to do a life history of that unit idea in sociology. We would be interested in the relative significance of the idea over the course of different epochs in the history of sociology (e.g., was alienation of greater interest to sociologists in the more radical atmosphere of the late 1960s than in the more conservative 1980s? was the nature of the interest in alienation different in the two periods?) It might be important to decompose the idea and outline its various subcomponents (e.g., the more philosophical ideas of Marx and the Marxists, the American empiricists' interest in such measurable dimensions as powerlessness, meaninglessness, isolation, and self-estrangement). Relatedly, it would be useful to see the degree to which these various elements cohere or come into conflict with one another. Another important step would be to systematically trace out the degree of similarity and difference between alienation and sometimes closely aligned concepts like anomie.

Alienation is an idea that we closely associate with Marxian theory in particular and conflict theory more generally. However, the idea is not absent from other theoretical systems where it may appear in a different guise and under different terms. Thus, we would need to ferret out the degree to which the alienation idea is found in structural functionalism, symbolic interactionism, phenomenology, ethnomethodology, exchange theory, and so on. Following Lovejoy, we would want to look beyond surface dissimilarities to find the underlying unit idea that may be shared by these theories. Similarly, we would want to trace the use of alienation across the wide range of subareas in sociology: sociology of the economy, political sociology, urban sociology, the sociology of education, etc. Furthermore, we might want to venture outside of sociology, being mindful of retaining sociology as our focus, and look at the use of alienation in neighboring fields such as political science and anthropology, as well as in more distant fields such as art or literature. We also might want to venture outside of American sociology and explore the use of the alienation concept in British, French, and German sociology, as well as in related fields in those national contexts and many others. And, of course, we would want to do all of this over time so that we could get a sense of the changing use of the concept within and between sociology and all of these other fields and national settings.

We would want to examine the way in which alienation diffused from its base in Marxian theory. We would want to examine how the idea migrated out of Marxian theory and fused over time with other ideas, thereby changing its basic meaning. A likely result of all this work would be the discovery that many sociologists have come to use the idea of alienation in ways that are far removed from, and were unanticipated by, Marx and the early Marxists. In looking at the historical development of the use of this concept we would find confirmation of Lovejoy's view that this is not a neat evolutionary process. Alienation's history is characterized by much trial and error, many confusions, substantial distortions, misinterpretations, and ambiguity.

Lovejoy's unit ideas are not restricted to academic disciplines; they are diffused throughout the larger collectivity. This is certainly the case with the alienation concept which is widely used in the general population. A metatheorist may want to trace this process of diffusion. A substantial concern would have to be the fact that the ways in which the concept is used in the general population bears only a faint resemblance, at best, to its more formal and systematic usage within sociological theory.

These are but a few of the things that a sociological metatheorist could do with Lovejoy's ideas. Moreover, there is much more to intellectual history than Lovejoy's work; a which wider body of work exists that should be of interest to the metatheorist.

Critics of the History of Ideas: From Presentism to Contextualism

Lovejoy's history of ideas is seen as an example of "presentism" in history, or the tendency to see a continuity between the past and the present and to affirm the legitimacy of interpreting and understanding the past from the point of view of the present intellectual context. This tendency has been criticized as "Whiggish" in that history is seen as progressive and evolutionary (Butterfield 1931). The main alternative is "historicism" in which the goal is to understand the past in its own terms.[6] Historicism leads to a focus on the context of past ideas, to "contextualism." A leading exponent of this latter point of view is the British political historian Quentin Skinner (Jones 1981).

Skinner has been a severe critic of Lovejoy's type of history of ideas as well as the creator of an alternative approach to this type of study. Skinner (1969) associates Lovejoy's approach with that which seeks to understand a text itself; that is, a text (or texts) is seen as autonomous and the key to its own meaning. Those (like Lovejoy) who subscribe to such an approach search within the text(s) for "timeless elements," "universal ideas," "dateless wisdom," and ideas with "universal application." They are disinclined to examine the context within which the text(s) is produced because to do so would be to vitiate the claim that the ideas being studied are timeless (see also Mandelbaum 1965). (In terms of sociological metatheorizing, this type of work involves a focus on the internal-intellectual subtype of M_U.)

Skinner sees many problems with works that focus on the texts themselves. In his view, our perspective on past texts is always distorted by our current paradigms. This distortion, in turn, leads to all sorts of specific errors such as mistaking incidental statements for the doctrine the researcher is looking for, converting isolated statements into a coherent doctrine, reading into a doctrine a perspective that the author had no intention of conveying, and according far more coherence to a set of ideas than the author(s) ever intended. Dunn sees these as "a history of fictions—of rationalist constructs out of the thought processes of individuals" (1972, 160). Not only are these ideas often fictions, but they are also often accorded by the analyst a degree of formal articulation of which there is no evidence the author had ever attained.

A very important criticism of the history of ideas is the tendency to hypostatize a doctrine into an entity, as Lovejoy does with the great chain of being. Diggins calls this the "parthenogenetic fallacy" that "ideas breed other ideas and somehow have a 'life' of their own" (1984, 153). Dunn argues that the history of ideas "is written as a stage in which all the great deeds are done by entities which could not, in principle, *do* anything . . . Its protagonists are never humans, but only reified abstractions—or, if humans by inadvertence, humans only as the loci of these abstractions" (1972, 158). Skinner concludes: "the history thus written becomes a history not of ideas at all, but of abstractions: a history of thoughts which no one ever actually succeeded in thinking, at a level of coherence which no one ever actually attained" (1969, 18). (Again, in metatheoretical terms, this means that the author is focusing on internal-intellectual [M_U], and ignoring internal-social, factors.)

In Skinner's view, even if all of the dangers outlined above could be avoided, the focus on the texts themselves "must necessarily remain a wholly inadequate methodology for the conduct of the history of ideas" (1969, 31). Among his reasons for this view are the facts that the literal meanings of terms change over time and even repeated readings of a text cannot reveal the author's oblique strategies used sometimes to obscure meaning. Skinner concludes that "there *is* no determinate idea to which various writers contributed, but only a variety of statements made with the words by a variety of different agents with a variety of intentions . . . there *is* no history of the idea to be written" (1969, 38).

While metatheorists who do a history of sociological ideas may wish to ignore the latter, extreme position taken by Skinner, they cannot afford to ignore the major criticisms of the history of ideas. Heeding those criticisms, they must strive to avoid mistaking incidental statements for the idea they are examining; they must be wary of converting isolated statements into a coherent idea system; they must be careful not to read into a body of work an idea that the author had no intention of conveying; and they must not see a coherent set of ideas where none exists. Above all, they must be wary of reifying these ideas and treating them in isolation from the human actors who created and refined them. It seems to me that such cautions, if heeded, can lead to a greatly improved history of ideas that metatheorists can make use of in their examinations of major ideas in the history of sociology.

The major alternative to focusing on the text itself is to study the social and cultural context in which the text(s) is produced. (In terms of metatheorizing in sociology, this involves a shift to the external-social and external-intellectual subtypes of M_U.) A look at the context can help solve many of the problems associated with the history of ideas and it can help in understanding a text. As a result, the contextual approach has gained increasing acceptance in intellectual history (Diggins 1984). However, in Skinner's view it is a mistake to see the context as the determinant of a text.[7] Rather, he suggests that we view the context as the "ultimate framework for helping to decide what conventionally recognizable meanings, in a society of *that* kind, it might in principle have been possible for someone to communicate" (1969, 49). Rather than focus on the context as a cause, Skinner (1975–76) seeks to examine the context of meaning within which a text appears. Such a context "serves to endow its constituent parts with meaning while attaining its own meaning from the combination of its constituent parts" (1975–76, 216). The analyst is to place the text to be interpreted within the context of basic assumptions and conventions from which it derives its meaning and to which it contributes. Particularly important is the linguistic context of a text. We can only understand the words and concepts used by an author by examining them within the context of the precise usages of a given time and place. This examination *in context* allows us to understand not only what the author meant, but also what the text would have meant to those reading it. As Jones puts it, this means attempting "to reconstruct the linguistic conventions governing the performance of *those* actions in a society of *that* kind— in short, to read virtually everything written by the author's contemporaries, and then to set the work of special concern firmly within that context" (1983a, 456).

However, Skinner does not simply want to look at the text, but also at the people who author the text, "on the various agents who used the idea, and on their varying situations and intentions in using it" (1969, 38). This approach takes him into the realm of linguistics and agreement with the view that the agent who creates a text is not merely saying something but also doing something. In order to understand this saying *and* doing, we must grasp both the sense of what is being said and the "illocutionary force" of the actor, or what he/she saw himself doing in creating a particular text. This concern for a creative actor does much to deal with the "bloodlessness" that Dunn (1972) associates with most of the history of ideas.

Skinner (1978) put many of these principles to work in his two-volume work on the foundations of modern political thought. His focus there is on the formation of the modern concept of the state. In contrast to the traditional method in studying the history of a political idea by focusing on classic texts, Skinner focuses on the "more general social and intellectual matrix out of which [those] works arose" (1978, x). Relatedly, Skinner moves away from an exclusive focus on classic texts and toward political thinking expressed in a wide array of forms. Consistent with his interest in context, he wants to examine the general political vocabulary of the age available to its actors. Consistent with his interest in agency, Skinner wants to be able to understand what agents were doing when they authored texts. However, in the end, Skinner, like Lovejoy, is interested in understanding texts.

Contextualism in its various forms is very compatible with a sociological perspective and has much to offer to the metatheorist. A look at the social, political, and economic conditions in which an idea is created or changed is very compatible with the well-established sociology of knowledge (see below), as well as with the external-intellectual and external-social subtypes of M_U. A focus on the extant linguistic conventions in which ideas were communicated is consistent with the general turn toward linguistics in sociology in general and metatheory in particular (Brown 1987, 1990). When we combine this concern with context with Skinner's emphasis on a creative, active agent, we have an orientation to the study of ideas that is in tune with recent developments in the study of agency and structure in Europe and micro-macro linkage in the United States (see chapter 10).

While contextualism is a promising approach, we cannot assume that is solves all of the problems associated with studying the history of sociological ideas. For example, the danger of reducing ideas to the context or giving the context too much power, remains. Moreover, ideas occur in many contexts: how do we know *which* context (or contexts) is having the most profound effect? Diggins asks: "Why cannot a text constitute its own context?" (1984, 153). He goes on to argue that "meaning may have as much to do with the internal demands of the mind as the external pressures of the cultural or political environment" (1984, 153). He concludes that "the act of knowing on the part of a thinker is not necessarily determined by the available means of knowing, the paradigms of language and discourse . . . there are thinkers whose depths of knowledge surpass the ordinary range of words, thinkers in whom we feel that some truths, especially the truths of moral insight, are introspectively discoverable" (1984, 169). In light of these criticisms Skinner (1974; see also Mandelbaum 1965) has acknowledged the fact that the author of a text can be innovative:

> I have obviously never intended to commit myself to the absurdity of denying that it is open to any writer to indicate that his aim is to extend, to subvert, or in some other way to alter a prevailing set of accepted conventions and attitudes. I am astonished to be told that my approach would make it impossible to map out this kind of innovation and change. It seems to me, on the contrary, that I am providing the means—the only sure means—of exhibiting the precise character of these changes, and of indicating the precise moment at which they actually took place. (1974, 287)

Also to be taken into consideration is the tension between the constraining effects of context and the creative intentionality of the actor. All of these concerns and criticisms carry with them a series of directions of great potential utility to sociologists interested in the history of sociological ideas. Clearly, the metatheorist must be wary of according the context too much power, must be careful to delineate the various contexts of an idea and to try to assess their different impacts, must focus on the agent as the active creator of ideas, and must reconcile the relative impact of a constraining culture and a creative agent. To put this in terms of metatheorizing in sociology, in seeking to fully understand texts, all four types of M_U should be employed.

On History, Systematics, and Metatheory. Skinner's ideas have already had an impact on sociology, especially in the history of sociology practiced, and lobbied for, by Jones (1977, 1978, 1981, 1983a, 1983b, 1985; see also Seidman 1983, 1985). In fact, Jones's best-known work (1977) involves a utilization of Skinner's ideas to better understand Durkheim's *Elementary Forms of Religious Life*. While Jones's effort is clearly an exercise in the history of sociology, it also fits my definition of metatheorizing, specifically the internal-intellectual subtype of M_U. What needs to be sorted out here is the relationship between the history of sociology and sociological metatheorizing.

While history in general, and intellectual history in particular, has much to offer to the metatheorist, the metatheorist must remain conscious of the fact that historical inquiry far from exhausts the concerns of metatheory. Even supporters of intellectual history like Jones recognize that there are other reasons to study the work of our predecessors: "This is not to say that sociologists ought not to read (and reread) the classics for . . . other heuristic, non-historical purposes; nor is it to say that the classics, in this setting, might not have a 'meaning' for *us* which is different from that intended by their authors. But it is to insist . . . that these activities be clearly distinguished from those which are genuinely *historical*" (1983b, 137). Similarly, Jones (1983a, 462) seeks to distinguish a genuine history of sociology from a "sociology of sociology" (what I would call metasociology, or metatheory) which utilizes Kuhnian theory. In fact, most of part II of this book is devoted to historical issues, but they are clearly metatheoretical examinations and not "genuine" histories.

From my point of view, the systematic study of the history of sociology can be seen as a form of metatheorizing. However, a detailed study of our own history far from exhausts our interest in past sociological works. In making this point I am touching on a debate over Robert Merton's (1967) differentiation between "history" and "systematics."

Merton's distinction is based on whether ideas have withstood the tests of empirical research. Those ideas that have are the concern of "systematics," while history is concerned with "the intelligent but mistaken conceptions which made good sense at the time of their formulation but were later shattered by compelling empirical tests or replaced by conceptions more adequate to the enlarged facts of the case. It includes also the false starts, the now archaic doctrines and both the fruitless and fruitful errors of the past" (1967, 3). The history of science is oriented to "understanding how things came to develop as they did in a certain science or in a complex of science" (1967, 5). The goal is distinct from that of systematics since it is "not designed to instruct today's scientist in the current operating theory, methodology or technique of his science" (1967, 5). Merton is animated in his distinction between history and systematics by Alfred North Whitehead's statement that "A science which hesitates to forget its founders is lost" (cited in Merton 1967, 1). Those who practice systematics should forget the founders of the discipline; study of their ideas should be left to the historian of sociology.

Jones rejects this distinction because "we would hardly say that such statements *would cease* being historical once the propositions to which they referred received empirical warrant; nor would we say that they *became* historical the moment they were falsified" (1983b, 128). Furthermore, many other aspects of a work are of interest to the historian other than propositions that can be falsified. While accepting the Jones's critique, I reject Merton's criteria for another reason. That is, it offers a strictly positivistic[8] basis for distinguishing between history and systematics (see also Seidman 1985).

Merton does suggest a series of other objectives in studying past theoretical ideas from a systematic rather than an historical perspective. First, theorists may discover, often deflatingly, that their "original" ideas have been anticipated by their predecessors, and perhaps even articulated better by them. Second, theorists can find elements of their own theories in the ideas of the masters, highlight those ideas which heretofore may have been hidden from others, and thereby carry on a kind of intellectual dialogue with the masters. Third, theorists may find that predecessors adopted orientations similar to their own, that study of these ideas reveals defects, and that the discovery of these defects leads the theorists to revise their own orientations. Fourth, past theorists can be used as models of intellectual work in terms of the formulation of problems and construction of solutions. Finally, each time theorists return to a text, they do it at a different point in their intellectual lives and/or the intellectual development of sociology, leading them to new understandings of a past work. While none of these may be legitimate "historical" undertakings, they are valid "systematic" approaches.

We need not accept the bases of Merton's distinction in order to accept the idea that there is a difference between history and systematics. It seems to me, following Skinner and Jones, that the history of sociology is interested in getting at the intentions of theorists within the contexts in which they lived. In contrast, the main objective of systematics is the construction and advancement of contemporary theory. It also involves the study of the ideas of earlier theorists, although not in the detailed manner suggested by historians. In my view, both Merton's systematics and the history of sociology are forms of metatheorizing, or the systematic study of sociological theory. In both cases, we are studying the ideas of our predecessors. The history of sociology, as articulated by Jones, might fit best under the heading of M_U, while systematics can be seen as related to both M_P and M_O, but *both* history and systematics clearly involve the process of metatheorizing. There are, however, as Jones acknowledges, many other ways to study the history of sociological theory. It is the totality of these various types of studies of sociological theory that constitutes a significant portion of metatheorizing in sociology.[9]

From the point of view of metatheorizing, the biggest problem with the work in intellectual history, not surprisingly, is that it remains narrowly focused on questions and issues of concern to historians. Metatheorists will probably want to utilize the findings, ideas, and methods of historians to reflect on a far broader range of issues than the historian is willing to contemplate. In other words, some metatheorists are in the position to take the ideas of the historians and to use them in ways unthought of by (and often unacceptable to) the historian.

History of Mentalities

While the history of ideas is primarily American in origin, the history of mentalities is mainly a product of French intellectual life.[10] Burke (1986) argues that the history of mentalities has three key features. First, it focuses on collective rather than individual attitudes (and is therefore very Durkeimian). That is, it is more likely to be concerned with differences in mentalities between groups than it is to be concerned with individual differences in attitudes. Second, it is concerned not only with conscious thoughts or well-elaborated theories, but also with "unspoken or unconscious assumptions, on perception, on the workings of 'practical reason', or everyday thought" (Burke 1986, 439). Third, the history of mentalities is concerned "with the structure of beliefs as well as their content, with categories, with metaphors and symbols, with how people think as well as what they think" (Burke 1986, 439). The French emphasize, perhaps overemphasize, subconscious mental structures. Burke sees the history of mentalities as broader than the history of ideas, but narrower than social history. In Burke's view, the history of ideas leaves society out, while social history omits thought. Thus, the history of mentalities combines an interest in thought with a concern for the social context. In this, it would seem to move close to the kind of contextualism espoused by Skinner.

One of the distinctive orientations of the history of mentalities is highlighted in Febvre's call for a study not of the ideas of past ages, but of their sensibilities and human feelings: "there is as yet no history of love, no history of death. There is none of compassion, none of cruelty, and none of joy. Let us begin with the all-embracing collective exploration of fundamental human feelings and their modes of expression" (cited in Schulin 1981, 206). More recently, Foucault (who held a Chair in Mental and Cognitive Systems) can be seen as having carried forth this program in his investigations of changes in attitudes and feelings toward the imprisoned, the sick, and the insane.

It seems to me that the main application of this approach to metatheorizing lies in trying to analyze the differences in mentalities (attitudes, values, modes of thought, etc.) over time among practitioners of different types of sociological theory. How does the mentality of contemporary ethnomethodologists compare to that of symbolic interactionists? Or, how does the mentality of today's neofunctionalists compare to that of the structural functionalists in the 1940s and 1950s? In doing the latter kind of historical analysis, we must be wary of assuming that the modern view is somehow better, more rational than the older theory. In both contemporary and historical analysis we must not assume, even if we are identifying mentalities, that there is no individual variation within a given mentality. While historians of mentalities treat them as fairly autonomous from social structure and various interest groups, there is no reason why a concern for the latter cannot be integrated into a history of mentalities in general and a history of sociological mentalities in particular. What, for example, were the structural sources of the hegemony of structural functionalism in the 1940s and 1950s? And what structural changes helped account for its decline? Another possibility for the metatheorist using a history of mentalities approach would be to look for the metaphors (machine, organism, etc.) that characterize different theoretical approaches (Burke 1986, 447). An examination of metaphors would be an example of the internal-intellectual subtype of M_U while a look at the impact of interests and social structure could be included under the heading of the external-social type of M_U.

We can look more specifically to the work of Michel Foucault for insights useful to metatheorizing. In his early work on methodology, Foucault (1966) is doing an "archaeology of knowledge." His objects of study are bodies of knowledge, ideas, modes of discourse; in other words, mentalities. He contrasts his archaeology of knowledge to intellectual history and the history of ideas, both of which he regards as too rational and as seeing too much continuity in the history of knowledge. Alan Sheridan contends that Foucault's approach involves a search for a "set of rules of formation that determine the conditions of possibility of all that can be said within the particular discourse at any given time" (1980, 48). He is particularly interested in early statements in the history of a field (like sociology). He wants to uncover the basic conditions that make (sociological) discourse possible. Foucault was interested in the discursive practices that formed the base of scientific discourse, particularly in human sciences like sociology.

While the archaeology of knowledge offers a general methodology to metatheorists, Foucault's more substantive studies provide more specific hints and guidelines. In *Madness and Civilization* (1965) Foucault is doing an archaeology of knowledge, specifically of psychiatry. For psychiatry to come into existence, madness had to be separated from sanity, a distinction in mentalities that did not exist prior to 1650. Once madness was distinguished, medicine was the first field to wrest control of its physical and moral treatment. Thus, psychiatry had to win control of the insane from medicine. In terms of sociology, this approach might lead metatheorists to look for changes in mentalities that made the birth of sociology possible. In addition, one would be led to look to the competition between sociology and other social sciences for control over knowledge of the social world.

Medicine was seen as an important precursor of the human sciences, and that was an even more central theme in *The Birth of the Clinic* (1975) in which Foucault says that "the science of man . . . was medically . . . based" (1975, 36). Medicine evolved from a classificatory science to one that focused on diseases, leading to a distinction between healthy and unhealthy people, and ultimately to the differentiation between normal and pathological states. Medicine is also an important precursor of the human sciences because it came to shift its focus from the disease to people (the patients). As Foucault puts it, "It is understandable, then, that medicine should have had such importance in the constitution of the sciences of man—an importance that is not only methodological, but ontological, in that it concerns man's becoming an object of positive knowledge" (1975, 197). Foucault, of course, does not trace out the linkages here between these changes in medicine and the development of sociology in particular. The task remains for metatheorists interested in using Foucault's ideas as a springboard for metatheoretical analysis.

In his later work, Foucault (1969) tended to shift from an archaeology of knowledge to a genealogy of power. In his earlier work Foucault was silent on the issue of power and the relationship between knowledge and power. But Foucault grew more concerned with how people govern themselves and others through the production of knowledge. Among other things, he sees knowledge generating power by constituting people as subjects and then governing the subjects with knowledge. He is critical of the hierarchization of knowledge. Because the highest-ranking forms of knowledge (the sciences) have the greatest power, they are singled out for the most severe critique. Foucault is interested in techniques, the technologies that are derived from knowledge (especially scientific knowledge), and how they are used by various institutions to exert power over people. (A metatheoretician here might be led to look at technologies developed in related, practical fields [e.g., social work, nursing, management, education] that can be traced, at least in part, to sociological knowledge.)

Substantively, the themes of knowledge and power appear in *Discipline and Punish* (1979), when Foucault focuses on prisons and prisoners. Foucault is concerned with the period between 1757 and the 1830s during which torture was replaced by a more rationalized system of control. Foucault identifies three instruments of the new, more rationalized system of control. The first is hierarchical observation, or the ability of officials to oversee all they control with a single gaze. The second is the ability to make normalizing judgments (being late, inattentive, impolite) and to punish those who violate the norms. The third is the use of the examination to observe subjects and make normalizing judgments about people. The third instrument of disciplinary power involves the other two. These ideas are also basic to sociologists who use observation techniques, make normalizing judgments (deviant, nondeviant), and employ a type of examination (questionnaires). A metatheorist might be concerned with tracing out the linkages between the development and use in sociology of these techniques and their relationship to how they were utilized in the prison system.

Foucault provides hints about the direction such an analysis might take. The transition from torture to a more rationalized system constitutes a switch from punishment of the body to punishment of the soul or the will. This change, in turn, brought with it considerations of normality and morality. Eventually, this ability, first restricted to prison officials, was extended to others such as psychiatrists and educators (and sociologists?). Out of this emerged new bodies of scientific penal knowledge, and this knowledge in turn served as the base of the modern "scientifico-legal complex." In the new mode of subjugation people were defined as the object of knowledge, of scientific discourse. The key point Foucault makes is that the modern human sciences have their roots in the penal system. Here is the way Foucault bitterly depicts the roots of the human sciences in the "disciplines" such as prisons: "These sciences, which have so delighted our 'humanity' for over a century, have their technical matrix in the petty, malicious minutiae of the disciplines and their investigations" (1979, 226).

In addition to the specific leads mentioned above, Foucault's perspective offers innumerable useful ideas to the metatheorist. The focus should be on the intellectual roots of sociology, its relationship to other disciplines, its relationship to its subjects, and its (often implicit) links to power and technologies of power. Of course, these are only the most direct implications of Foucault's work which is so dense and rich that the enterprising metatheorist will find many other fruitful ideas in a careful examination of it.

Begriffsgeschichte

The roots of *Begriffsgeschichte* lie in the German school of the history of ideas known as *Geistesgeschichte*. Schulin distinguishes *Geistesgeschichte* from the history of ideas in the following way: "[the history of ideas] can be said to refer generally rather more to clearly defined ideas and their progress, viewed as units in themselves and as only secondarily dependent on the surrounding historical field. Geistesgeschichte deals predominantly with streams of mentalities or consciousness, is more firmly tied to and interdependent with social climates or political change, and closer to cultural history" (1981, 196–97). This sounds very close to the French history of mentalities I have just discussed, and it is, but the German approach focuses more on political history while the French are more concerned with social history. It also has similarities with Quentin Skinner's contextualism, although it lacks his concern with the linguistic context. Another distinction between *Geistesgeschichte* and the French approach (as well as those of Lovejoy and Skinner) is a greater focus on the ideas of great personalities and creative thinkers. While *Geistesgeschichte* has a lively history, it is Schulin's view "that surprisingly little has been added here in the last two or three decades" (1981, 207). *Geistesgeschichte* need not detain us, but its relevance to sociological metatheory may lie in pushing the latter to focus more on the linkage of sociology to politics and political change.[11] In addition, it attunes the metatheorist to the importance of creative thinkers (see discussion of biography below).

Stemming in part from *Geistesgeschichte,* but demonstrating considerably more liveliness is *Begriffsgeschichte.* Carr differentiates *Begriffsgeschichte* from *Geistesgeschichte:* "Its focus is neither on the literary and philosophical products of high culture, as in *Geistesgeschichte,* nor political and social events, but *basic concepts that govern the discourse, action and attitudes of all levels of society"* (1987, 197; my italics). In contrast to the history of ideas, we might think of *Begriffsgeschichte* as a history of key concepts such as *Politik, Demokratie, Gesellschaft, Kritik,* and *Arbeiter.* Koselleck (1985) criticizes the history of ideas for treating ideas as fundamentally unchanging. *Begriffsgeschichte* looks at the changing nature of concepts in the context of a changing society. Tribe (1985) sees *Begriffsgeschichte* as having some resemblance to the French history of mentalities, although it has a series of distinctive German inputs (e.g., Kant, Heidegger). Koselleck differentiates *Begriffsgeschichte* from social history: "a *Begriffsgeschichte* concerns itself (primarily) with text and words, while a social history employs texts merely as a means of deducing circumstances and movements that are not, in themselves, contained within the texts" (1985, 73). In other words, *Begriffsgeschichte,* like the works of Skinner and Lovejoy, looks at texts while social history focuses on society.

The leading figure in contemporary *Begriffsgeschichte* is Reinhart Koselleck. Koselleck is the key organizer and editor of *Geschichliche Grundbegriffe,* a six-volume dictionary of historical concepts. The concepts included in these volumes must be those that are relevant to the genesis of modernity in the eighteenth century at the point of the dissolution of the old world and the emergence of the new world. Koselleck sees the eighteenth century as a watershed, a period of great conceptual changes. New concepts (e.g., class, socialism) emerged during this period and older concepts (e.g., democracy, revolution, republic) acquired new, often double, meanings. An effort is made to sort out the diversity of meanings and to understand conceptual changes. It is the task of *Begriffsgeschichte* to refer backward to this period as well as forward to our time and the contemporary usage of concepts in German political and social life. Concepts are to be placed in a hierarchy of meaning, "a complex network of semantic change in which particular concepts might play a varying role over time" (Tribe 1985, xii).

Koselleck does not see *Begriffsgeschichte* as an end in itself, but rather as "a methodologically independent part of sociohistorical research" (1985, 88). Tribe sees is as "more a procedure than a definite method. It is intended not as an end in itself but rather as a means of emphasizing the importance of linguistic and semantic analysis for the practice of social and economic history" (1985, xiii). Whether a developed method or merely a procedure, *Begriffsgeschichte* is oriented to the search for key concepts and how they are transformed over time. Koselleck sees *Begriffsgeschichte* as a methodology that should be of great use to the historical sciences because of its focus on terminology relevant to politics and society and on expressions that have social or political content. "Persistence, change, or novelty in the meaning of words must first be grasped before they can be used as indices of this extralinguistic content, as indicators of social structures or situations of political conflict" (Koselleck 1985, 81–82). Specifying concepts should help in formulating sociohistorical questions. However, in Koselleck's view, *Begriffsgeschichte* can also have some degree of autonomy and independence from social history. It can detach words from their historical situational context, order their meaning in a time sequence, and then order the concepts with respect to one another. "The individual historical analyses of concepts assemble themselves into a history of the concept. . . . *Begriffsgeschichte* . . . shed[s] its subordinate relations to social history" (Koselleck 1985, 80). In spite of this potential for autonomy, Koselleck argues that *"Begriffsgeschichte* must always keep in view the need for findings relevant to intellectual or material history" (1985, 85–86).

Koselleck's personal interest is in concepts that relate to temporality, especially the future. In his view the great conceptual shifts in the modern world are traceable to shifts in conceptions of historical time, especially the future. Carr says that "his project is *metahistorical:* his [Koselleck's] writing a history of conceptions of historical time, not just those of historians or philosophers but those of whole societies and periods" (1987, 199). One could similarly say that all of *Begriffsgeschichte* is metahistorical. It is for this reason that this body of work should be of such intrinsic interest to metatheorists in sociology.

More specifically, *Begriffsgeschichte,* in contrast to the history of ideas (which emphasized continuity), leads the sociological metatheorist in the direction of studying the changing nature of sociological concepts. Following Koselleck, the metatheorist (M_U—internal-intellectual subtype) would be concerned with the persistence, change, or novelty of sociological concepts. In contrast to the contextualism of Skinner and others, *Begriffsgeschichte* leads to a focus on concepts per se. Eventually, of course, this analysis must be linked to broader societal analyses. In sociology, the first conceptual watershed occurred in the late nineteenth century. Careful study of the concepts that preceded this period and the way in which they were transformed during it is required. One would also need to be concerned with tracing out conceptual changes in sociology since the late nineteenth century. One might even wonder whether we have had, or are we approaching, a new conceptual watershed?

History of Science

The history of science, in particular the history of scientific thought, is a subarea within the history of thought (Crombie 1986), although it has been influenced by the social sciences (for example, the sociology of knowledge [Shapin 1982] and, more specifically, the use of social anthropologist Mary Douglas's grid/group model [Oldroyd 1986]) and the philosophy of science (Whitaker 1984). The history of science is dependent on the differentiation between scientific thinking and other kinds of ideas and ideologies. Crombie accepts the view that science is a distinctive kind of problem solving with distinctive "modes of self-correction and criteria of acceptability" (1986, 23). Crombie sees the history of science as closely linked to the history of ideas and the history of mentalities:

> So we are dealing at once with a process of accumulation of objectively certifiable particular knowledge; with the development of general theories which may change; and always with people and their vision. In this way the history of scientific ideas becomes intimately connected, at a highly sophisticated level, with the history of mentalities. The history of ideas and of mentalities is after all the history of people thinking. (1986, 23)

While it is a history of people thinking, it is in Crombie's view the history of people doing a very distinctive kind of thinking.

The history of science can concern itself with an array of issues, but the focus is on scientific thinking. Crombie sees the history of scientific thinking as a history of argument: "Scientific argument forms the substance of the scientific movement, a discourse using experiment and observation, instruments and apparatus, but with significance always in relation to the argument" (1986, 23–24). It is as forms of argument that Crombie looks at six different types of scientific inquiry and demonstration: postulation, controlled experiment and observation and measurement, hypothetical modeling, taxonomy, statistical and probabilistic analysis, and historical derivation. Not only are these important in the history of science, but so too are the arguments more overtly aimed at persuading an audience of the scientific merits of a given position. Crombie sees the "use of such arguments to reinforce or create the power of ideas to convince, especially when the ideas were new and the audience uncertain or unsympathetic, [as] . . . a somewhat neglected phenomenon in history of science" (1986, 24). Crombie argues that "Galileo and Descartes were masters of the current rhetorical techniques of persuasion" (1986, 24).

Crombie also sees the history of science as sharing with the histories of ideas and mentalities a concern for the absorption of scientific ideas into society and the ways in which they interacted with accepted belief systems. Widely accepted belief systems at first are likely to oppose scientific ideas, then perhaps accommodate to them, and finally in at least some cases adopt and use those ideas.

Those who do histories of scientific thought must combine historical sensitivity and competence with technical scientific and linguistic competencies. Thus, metatheorists who seek to do a history of sociology as a science must supplement their familiarity with the technical aspects of sociology with knowledge about how to do historical analyses well.

The questions put to the history of scientific thought change with each passing generation. New developments lead us to look at the past in a different, and perhaps more illuminating, way. Crombie offers the following example: "The growing power of probabilistic thinking within contemporary science and logic for example has promoted a fresh look into the intellectual contexts in which it can be seen that concepts of probability have been in substantial use, notably in medicine, law and moral philosophy, from antiquity" (1986, 28). (This might lead the metamethodologist to examine, for example, the roots of changing tastes in statistical techniques in sociology as well as their impact on the overall practice of sociology.) While new conditions may lead us to raise new questions, we must retain a commitment to use rational methods: "If each generation in dismantling the history written by its predecessors in their image then rewrites it in its own, we are committed by the whole critical process of scholarship to distinguish evidence from interpretation" (Crombie 1986, 28).

Research over the last decade in the history of science shares a number of specific concerns with metatheorizing in sociology. Given its longer and more clear-cut history of accumulation of knowledge, the history of science should be a useful place for many metatheorists to turn. Those interested in the M_U issue of schools of sociological theory would find Geison's (1981) and Secord's (1986) work instructive. Another M_U concern, creativity in sociological theorizing, would be advanced by knowledge of the work of Holmes (1981) and Rothenberg (1987). Still another M_U interest, the professionalization of sociology, would find the work of Sutherland and Sharp (1980) on British psychology informative.

However, metatheoretical interest in the literature on the history of science is dependent on the degree to which a specific metatheorist regards sociology as a science. Those who do will find much of use in the history of science. Those who do not will probably wish to draw upon other fields discussed throughout this chapter.

Biography in the History of Science

Biography has a key but underestimated role to play in the history of science, and also in sociological metatheorizing. Biography can be at least a partial antidote to the tendency in the history of ideas and the history of science to write history as if it is an inevitable series of steps leading to a splendid climax. It can help prevent the tendency to see science "as a string of influences, each scientist carrying and shaping the ideas of his predecessors for transmission to the next link in the chain" (Hankins 1979, 4). In Hankins view, "Biography which is carefully researched can be the ruin of all kinds of historical generalities" (1979, 6).

Hankins details a series of characteristics of solid biographies of scientists. For example, the biography must deal with science. That is, the technical details must be there and the reader must be informed about "how the scientist went about his task, how his ideas developed, and how he tested them" (1979, 8). For another, the various aspects of the subject's life must be integrated into a coherent picture. Hankins does not recommend biography as a way to approach all issues in the history of science (for example, it is not a suitable way to get at the larger social structure of science), but he does see a "fully integrated biography of a scientist which includes not only his personality, but also his scientific work and the intellectual and social context of his times, [as] . . . still the best way to get at many of the problems that beset the writing of history of science . . . science is created by individuals, and however much it may be driven by forces from outside, these forces work through the scientist himself. Biography is the literary lens through which we can best view this process" (1979, 14).

While we have some biographies of sociological theorists available to us, there are comparatively few of them and they vary greatly in quality. It seems clear that the careful study of the lives of major (and not so major) theorists can cast considerable light on the nature of sociological theorizing. In that sense, biography is a kind of metatheorizing (M_U; especially the internal-intellectual and internal-social subtypes) and has a substantial role to play in the advancement of metatheorizing in sociology. Put in terms of the agency-structure issue, biographical studies permit us to examine in detail the role of the sociological theorist as agent.

Other Fields in Sociology

This chapter has focused on the lessons to be learned by sociological metatheorists from an array of fields outside of sociology. However, it is also true that a number of subfields within sociology should prove useful to the metatheorist. In this section I will briefly discuss the relevance of three other subfields within sociology—the sociology of science, the sociology of knowledge, and the sociology of the professions—to sociological metatheorizing.

In many ways, the most obvious place to turn for ideas that can be useful in metatheorizing is the sociology of science. As with the history of science, this can be done to the degree that one is willing to accept the idea that sociology is a science (or a would-be science), or can be analyzed as if it is a science. A good portion of the sociology of sociology, especially studies of such things as citation rates and patterns, can be seen as the sociology of science applied to sociology. If one focuses on sociological theory, and utilizes ideas drawn from the sociology of science, one will be doing metatheorizing and advancing the development of metatheorizing in sociology.

The sociology of science, like the other fields to be discussed in this section, is in itself a vast area, so I can do little more than suggest a few directions that might prove attractive to metatheorists. One such direction might stem from Karin Knorr-Cetina's (1981b) anthropological study of the social construction of scientific reality within scientific laboratories. The parallel in theory might be such a study within a school of sociological theory. One such school that suggests itself immediately is the ethnomethodologists. While such a study is made more difficult because there is no laboratory in which to do the study, there are enough ethnomethodologists in close contact with one another, perhaps even working on collaborative projects, that one could study the way they construct their distinctive theoretical reality.

Of course, there are many other leads to be derived from the sociology of science. It might be useful to simply enumerate some potential issues (some of which may have already received some attention within metatheory) in sociological metatheorizing suggested by recent work in the sociology of science: sociological paradigms in the history of sociological theory (Crane 1980; Turner 1987); citation patterns among sociological theorists (Cozzens 1985; Dolman and Bodewitz 1985; Lomnitz, Rees, and Cameo 1987); boundary disputes among sociological theories (Jasanoff 1987); why some sociological theorists become famous and others do not (Missner 1985); the relationship between marginality and the creation of innovative theoretical perspectives (Gieryn and Hirsch 1983); the relationship between the nature of funding and sociological theory (Cozzens 1986); the impact of different national cultures on the nature of sociological theorizing (Handberg 1986); the politics involved in producing consensus within theoretical traditions (Wright 1986); the impact of national political policies on sociological theory (Fries 1984); the cultures of various theory groups and their impact on the nature of theorizing (Mulkay and Gilbert 1982); and the relationship between professionalization and sociological theory (MacLeod and MacLeod 1979)

The issue of professionalization in science brings us to the sociology of the professions and the question of its applicability to metatheorizing in sociology. The applicability of this subfield hinges on our willingness to accept the idea that sociologists in general, and sociological theorists in particular, can be thought of as professionals, or at least as assessable on a scale of levels of professionalization. While not in the realm of established professions like medicine and law, it seems clear that sociologists have some professional standing and are therefore analyzable utilizing ideas derived from the sociology of the professions (Ritzer and Walczak 1986, chapter 3; Abbott 1988; Macdonald and Ritzer 1988).

The dominant orientation in the study of professions in recent years has been the power approach. It attunes one to the power of a profession or would-be profession as well as the power of forces that oppose its professionalization. Thus, medicine has been an occupation with sufficient power to win professional recognition and counter the power of opposing forces. However, in recent years social changes are serving to erode that power and are leading to some deprofessionalization of medicine (Ritzer and Walczak 1988). Nursing has been an occupation that has only been able to achieve marginal professional status, in part because of weaknesses in its own power base and in part because of the strength of the opposition (including the medical profession).

The professional status of sociological theorists is clearly tied to the professional status of sociology as a whole. The inability of sociology to move very far on the professionalization scale means that sociological theorists must be content with their marginal professional status. Of greater interest and importance is the professional status of theorists *within* the field of sociology. This brings us to the issue of "professional segments" (Bucher and Strauss 1961) and the fact that theorists clearly represent a segment within sociology. The study of professional segments leads to a concern for the relationships and struggles among and between the various segments that make up a (marginal) profession. The most obvious issue is the relationship between theorists and the empiricists that dominate contemporary sociology. Are theorists considered less professional than empiricists? Has there been change over time in the professional status of these segments? How does each relate to the (marginal) profession (of sociology) as a whole? How do both relate to other segments (e.g., clinicians, practitioners)?

Our understanding of sociological theory can clearly be aided by attaining a better understanding of the professional status of sociologists in general and sociological theorists in particular. For example, if we assume that the theoretical segment had greater professional status in the past than it does today, we might ask whether the weakness of theorists today compared to the grand theorists of the past can be traced, at least in part, to a decline in professional status? Were the theorists of the past able to produce such massive and ambitious theories because they were more secure in their professional status? Are today's theorists less able to produce such theories because of their increasingly marginal professional status vis-à-vis empiricists? Are contemporary European theorists better able to produce theory because of their higher professional status in comparison to their American counterparts?

The sociology of knowledge offers the metatheorist a particularly rich set of ideas that should prove useful in metatheoretical analyses. The sociology of knowledge when it is brought to bear on sociological theory as a body of knowledge is clearly metatheoretical (especially external-social, external-intellectual M_U). In fact, we have encountered elements of the sociology of knowledge throughout this chapter, especially in the discussion of contextualism in intellectual history. Traditionally, in the work of Marx (1859/1970, 20–21) and Mannheim (1936), or perspectives derived from them, the emphasis has been placed on the way the larger society determines, conditions, and/or distorts knowledge. While it is virtually impossible to argue that the larger society determines sociological theory, it is certainly the case that society conditions, and perhaps distorts, sociological theory. Metatheorists have studied the impact of society and societal changes on sociological theory (e.g., Huaco's [1986] analysis of the relationship between the rise and decline of structural functionalism and America's position in the world order), and that study could be enhanced by a more systematic application of ideas derived from the sociology of knowledge.

There are other strands in the sociology of knowledge that might prove useful to metatheorists. For example, instead of focusing on the impact of society on knowledge, Holzner and Marx (1979) are interested in the impact of knowledge on the larger social and cultural system. The metatheoretical concern, here, would be the effect of sociological knowledge on these larger systems. More particularly, the issue may be an effort to explain why sociological theory has so little impact on the larger society? Or why sociological theory has so much less impact than theories in other social and behavioral sciences (e.g., economics)? Then there is Berger and Luckman's *The Social Construction of Reality: A Treatise in the Sociology of Knowledge* (1967). Their variant of the sociology of knowledge moves away from the study of grand systems of ideas and toward the study of the everyday construction of knowledge. The application of this approach to metatheory would lead us to a concern for the ways in which sociological theorists construct their theories. The latter would be very much in line with the kind of sociology of science practiced by Knorr-Cetina.

There is much more of interest to metatheorizing in the sociology of science, sociology of the professions, and the sociology of knowledge than has been suggested above. Furthermore, there is much else within sociology that can be drawn upon by metatheorists. The goal of this last section, as well as the chapter as a whole, has been to simply suggest a few of the fields to which metatheorists can turn in a search for ideas that can be applied to the study of sociological theory.

One concluding note: all of the fields and subfields discussed in this chapter manifest the centrality of reflexivity; the reflexive study of a discipline is widely accepted outside of sociology. If such work is so widely accepted, then why would it not be an acceptable practice within sociology? This brings us back to critics of metatheorizing in sociology. Those critics need to understand that reflexivity is an established and essential part of intellectual life in a variety of disciplines and that there is every reason to believe that it can and should be at least a part of the sociological world.

Notes

1. In addition, Collingwood (cited in Salas 1987, 55) argued that "no historical problem should be studied without studying . . . its second-order history; that is, the history of historical thought about it." In the terms used in this book, the latter is a clear call for a metahistory that parallels the kind of metasociology, especially metatheory, discussed in these pages.

2. Although some see Dilthey as the founding father of the modern history of ideas.

3. It is questionable whether Lovejoy would regard these as unit ideas in the sense that he uses the term.

4. Again, Lovejoy might not see alienation as fitting his definition of a unit idea.

5. One could also delve farther back into the philosophical roots of the idea.

6. However, Jones (1985, 156), a supporter of historicism, argues that some presentism is "unavoidable" since our "observations are guided by our preconceptions about the things, people and/or events observed."

7. This is a position taken by some sociologists of knowledge. See a later section of this chapter for a discussion of the relevance of the sociology of knowledge to metatheorizing in sociology.

8. Although Merton himself rejects this characterization of his work, arguing that "I have rejected most of the tenets encompassed in that omnibus term [positivism]" (Merton 1985, 141). While the term is very broad, and much of positivism has been rejected by Merton, the fact remains that his criterion for distinguishing history from systematics (withstanding empirical test) *is* positivistic.

9. But not all, since such metatheorizing focuses on contemporary theoretical work.

10. Although Jones (1983a, 458) sees the Englishman Skinner doing a kind of history of mentalities. This points to the fact that the differences among the various types of intellectual history are not as clear-cut as is being suggested in this chapter.

11. See Smelser (1989) for an effort within sociological metatheorizing to adopt just such a focus.

14

Conclusion:
The Case for (and against)
Sociological Metatheorizing

T his book is devoted to two basic tasks. The first is the delineation of sociological metatheorizing in general as well as of its three basic types: metatheorizing as a means of attaining a deeper understanding of theory (M_U), metatheorizing as a prelude to theory development (M_P), and metatheorizing as a source of perspectives that overarch sociological theory (M_O). The second is the demonstration of what can be done with all three types of metatheorizing (especially M_U) through a series of case studies.

My task in this concluding chapter is to draw together the strands of many arguments expressed throughout this book and make the case *for* metatheorizing as a distinctive undertaking in sociology. In the process, I will also discuss some of the problems in the field, some potential resolutions of those problems, some of the future directions in metatheorizing, and the future of the subject matter of metatheorizing: sociological theory. I hope that this chapter, and this book as a whole, will help to legitimate what has been a widely practiced, but largely hidden, and often reviled, approach within sociology since its inception.

In many ways, the most visible aspects of metatheorizing, at least until very recently, have been the criticisms, often quite vicious, leveled at it. This must be something of a first in academic history: the appearance of highly visible and influential critiques *before* the overt emergence of the field being attacked. What this means, of course, is that the field, at least in an inchoate state, was there all the time. A great deal of metatheorizing has been done under a wide range of other headings: sociology of sociology, sociology of science, sociology of knowledge, history of sociology, and most notably as an integral part of sociological theory. As we saw in the introduction, most of the criticisms have been made by closet metatheoreticians (e.g., Collins, Skocpol, Turner) who have had only a very dim and limited sense of what they are criticizing. I hope that my clarification of the nature of sociological metatheorizing in this book will lead to the elevation of the level of such criticism and to the realization that most of the critics are, themselves, metatheoreticians. More importantly, I hope that sociological metatheorizing will become accepted as a legitimate and crucially important enterprise within sociology, one that should be practiced openly by at least some sociologists, especially those interested in sociological theory. Obviously, as the literature cited in this book makes abundantly clear, metatheorizing is already widely, if covertly, practiced.

In fact, the evidence suggests that we are currently witnessing a boom in interest in metatheorizing. A study by Fuhrman and Snizek (1990) of publications over the last decade indicates strong and growing interest in metatheorizing in sociology. A very large proportion of the references in this paper are to recently, or soon-to-be, published works. This growth is noticeable in the journal *Sociological Theory,* which has devoted increasing space to essays that are explicitly metatheoretical (for example, Ritzer 1988b; Fararo 1989; Levine, 1989). In addition, a number of recent books have also been overtly metatheoretical (Fiske and Shweder 1986; Osterberg 1988) and many, perhaps even most, other books in sociological theory are implicitly metatheoretical. In March 1990 *Sociological Forum* devoted a special mini-issue to metatheorizing in sociology (Ritzer 1990c) and in 1991 Sage Publications will publish an anthology devoted to a series of studies in metatheorizing (Ritzer 1991b). Metatheoretical works are moving off in new directions such as the effort to relate postmodernism to metatheory (Lemert 1990; Weinstein and Weinstein 1990) and the realization that there is much of relevance to metatheory in the work of Bourdieu (Swartz 1990), as well as a continuing and accelerating effort to bring linguistic tools to bear on sociological theory (Brown 1990).

Beyond this is a whole, and seemingly expanding, range of works that have dealt with more specific metatheoretical issues such as the micro-macro linkage (Collins 1981c, 1988; Alexander et al. 1987; Ritzer 1990b), the relationship between agency and structure (Bernstein 1971; Archer 1982, 1988; Giddens 1984), and levels of social analysis (Wiley 1988, 1989; Ritzer 1989c). There are also signs that work in substantive areas in sociology is coming to be affected by these more specific metatheoretical issues. Examples include Huber's (1990) work on gender stratification informed by the micro-macro issue and Gottdiener and Feagin's (1988) essay on urban sociology that deals with agency and structure.

Professional associations have been devoting more space and time to sessions devoted to metatheorizing in general as well as to more specific metatheoretical issues. Thus, for example, two sessions at the 1988 meetings of the Eastern Sociological Society, one session at the 1990 Pacific Sociological Association, and two sessions at the 1990 American Sociological Association (ASA) were devoted to metatheory. Turning to more specific metatheoretical concerns, the 1988 ASA meetings took as a theme the micro-macro link and the 1990 German-American theory conference focused on agency-structure. Although it is possible that all this activity represents a peak in metatheorizing in sociology, there are many reasons to believe that it more truly represents the take-off point for an increasing variety, and a growing number, of explicitly metatheoretical works in sociology.

Beyond the boom in metatheorizing, and yet to be related to it, are parallel expansions of work in metamethodology and meta-data-analysis. Recent works in metamethods include Kirk and Miller, *Reliability and Validity in Quantitative Research* (1986); Noblit and Hare, *Meta-Ethnography: Synthesizing Qualitative Studies* (1988); and Brewer and Hunter, *Multimethod Research: A Synthesis of Styles* (1989). In meta-data-analysis there are recent publications by Wolf *Meta-Analysis: Quantitative Methods for Research Synthesis* (1986), and by Hunter and Schmidt *Methods of Meta-Analysis* (1989). Clearly, there is a great need to relate these bodies of work to metatheory.

At one level, I am simply demonstrating that metatheorizing (and, more generally, metaanalyses of various types) occurs on a wide and increasing scale in sociology. At another level, and more strongly, I am arguing that sociological theory, and more generally sociology, desperately needs strong metatheorizing (as well as the other types of metaanalysis). Its practice would be greatly improved if there was greater understanding of, and sympathy for, it in the larger community of sociologists. Such understanding and sympathy would permit more sociologists to metatheorize even more overtly and self-consciously and this, in turn, would help metatheorizing become even more widely accepted as a legitimate form of sociology.

Metatheorizing makes three absolutely essential contributions to sociological theory. First, (M_U) offers a systematic method of understanding, evaluating, criticizing, and improving extant theories. Second, (M_P) is one of several important bases for creating new theory. Third, (M_O) provides a mechanism whereby sociologists can produce useful overarching theoretical perspectives. In combination, these three functions have contributed, and should continue to contribute, dramatically to the development of sociological theory. Let us look at each of the three contributions in turn.

The Contributions of Metatheorizing

Before getting to the contributions of M_U, we need to briefly review the parameters of this type of metatheorizing. M_U has been widely practiced in contemporary sociology, although practitioners have not always been aware of the broader domain within which their work fit. To return to the four subtypes of M_U discussed in chapter 1, the internal-intellectual subtype has included work on the paradigmatic status of sociology, non-Kuhnian efforts to map the cognitive structure of sociology, "schools of thought," the dynamic development of sociological theory, the development and use of various tools to analyze sociological theory, and the more direct study of sociological theory. The internal-social subtype involves the study of theoretical schools, networks, and the backgrounds of theorists themselves. The external-intellectual subtype includes the study of the impact of other academic fields on sociological theory and the extraction and use of metatheoretical tools derived from other disciplines. Finally, the external-social subtype involves a look at the impact of the larger society and a variety of its components on theory. This disparate body of work is unified in its concern for deepening our understanding of sociological theory, and as such has made important contributions to sociological theory and sociology in general.

While most theorists understand one theory (usually the one with which they identify) or a few theories very well, they generally lack a deep understanding of the full range of sociological theories. If theorists do not fully understand many theoretical perspectives, the vast majority of practicing sociologists are even more in the dark. Furthermore, even those theorists who identify with, and have a profound understanding of, a given theory, need the insights offered by metatheorists. Deep involvement with a particular theory can lead to an inability to look at it objectively and to fully recognize its nature, strengths, and limitations. Metatheorists, because they identify with no single theory and take all theories as subjects of study, are able to distance themselves from all of them and render more impartial analyses of them.

Thus, it is the task, indeed the distinctive responsibility, of metatheorizing (M_U) to deepen the level of understanding of all sociological theories. While many sociologists read theory, often very casually, metatheorists systematically *study* theory. Metatheorists have the interest and ability to do detailed comparative studies of an array of sociological theories. Further, metatheorists have at their disposal an arsenal of tools that allows them to uncover many things about sociological theory that would not be visible to the more casual student of theory. Beyond a deeper comprehension of theory, systematic metatheorizing allows us to more adequately evaluate and critically analyze extant theories. Finally, and perhaps most importantly, we are better able to uncover ways of improving specific theories as well as theory in general. Since a large portion of the second part of this book was devoted to case studies of M_U, let me give concrete examples of each of these functions.

In what ways have the M_U tools utilized in part II of this book deepened our understanding of sociological theory? For one thing, the use of these tools allows us to uncover some surprising things about theories and theorists. The architectonic employed in chapter 4, for example, allows us to see basic, underlying similarities in the work of three classic theorists, Marx, Weber, and Simmel (as well as the contemporary theorist, Peter Berger), who on the surface offer very different substantive theories. Most casual observers recognize the substantive differences, but few see the underlying similarities. While we should continue to recognize that Marx's theory of capitalism, Weber's theory of rationalization, and Simmel's theory of the growing gap between objective and subjective culture have substantial substantive differences, it is also the case that they operate with very similar architectonics. This truth serves to give us a whole new outlook on their work and their intellectual relationships to one another. In other words, we need to recognize the simultaneous existence of substantive differentiation and architectonical similarity.

Not only does the use of the architectonic give us a new and surprising understanding of these theorists, but it also leads to a set of interesting metatheoretical issues. For example, how can the use of the same architectonic lead to such substantively different theories? While it does not account for all of the differences, subtle distinctions in the way each theorist uses the same architectonic help account for major substantive differences. For example, Marx's philosophical anthropology takes into account not only the ability of people to think, but also to act creatively, while Weber's actors largely lack creative ability. As one consequence of this difference Marx's actors have the ability to get themselves out of the reified world they create, while Weber's cannot escape. Weber's reified world is the result of a series of unanticipated consequences; since people do not seem to create this world, they lack the ability to get themselves out of it. Hence, we end up substantively with Marx's communist revolution on the one hand and Weber's iron cage of rationality on the other.

On a more purely metatheoretical level, the outlining of this one architectonic leads to a recognition of the likelihood that there are other such sociological architectonics lurking below the surface of other sets of substantive theories and in need of similar discovery and delineation. Furthermore, it suggests the possibility of a limited number of architectonics that lie at the base of the bewildering array of substantive sociological theories. Were we able to uncover such a limited set of architectonics, we would have a much better handle on the field of sociological theory in general.

However, the major demonstration of the utility of M_U in this book is found in the several chapters (6, 9, 10, and 11) devoted to the recent history of sociological theory. M_U tools have enabled me to do a series of comparative analyses within and among decades that show that sociological theory has moved through four major periods over the last four decades (Ritzer 1991a).[1] The paradigm instrument permitted description of the 1960s as multiparadigmatic with theoretical divisions and conflicts among paradigms (e.g., structural functionalism [social facts paradigm] vs. symbolic interactionism [social definition paradigm] vs. exchange theory [social behavior paradigm]) and within paradigms (e.g., structural functionalism vs. conflict theory within the social facts paradigm). The micro-macro tool demonstrated both the rise of micro sociological theories in the 1970s and of theoretical efforts at micro-macro (and agency-structure) synthesis in the 1980s. The latter, in turn, led to the use of the concept of theoretical syntheses to demonstrate the emergence of a much wider array of synthetic theoretical efforts as we enter the 1990s.

These chapters, taken together, do *not* constitute a history of recent sociological theory, but they do represent a metatheoretical analysis of that history. It is doubtful that a historian would have come up with this picture of the recent history of theory. Such a view requires a metatheorist and a set of metatheoretical tools. I am not arguing that the theoretical history presented here is "right." I am arguing, however, that such a history helps us to better understand where we have been, where we are, and where we may be going in sociological theory. It is not offered as an alternative to a history of sociological theory. Indeed, the combination of metatheoretical and more straightforward historical analyses would greatly increase our level of understanding.

M_U tools can be utilized not only to analyze sociological theory in general, but also the state of theoretical development in any subarea within sociology. For example, in chapter 12 I discussed the recent history of theory in the sociology of work and demonstrated that that history is strikingly similar to the overall development of sociological theory. My analysis points to a time lag between developments in theory in general and theories in the sociology of work. Specifically, work on micro-macro integration in the sociology of work lags behind such work in general theory. A similar analysis of recent work in socioeconomics (chapter 12) shows that it is in tune, but out of touch, with recent integrative theoretical developments. Similar kinds of analyses could be done in all subareas in sociology.

The use of metatheoretical tools to systematically evaluate and critique theories can make an important contribution to sociology. For example, the micro-macro tool permitted my critical examination of Collins's (1981b, 1981c) work on interaction ritual chains and led to my conclusion that, among other things, it fails to give equivalent and adequate weight to the micro and macro poles of the social continuum; more specifically, it errs on the side of micro reductionism. While not overtly recognizing this weakness, Collins's (1988) later work tries to rectify this imbalance by giving greater importance to the macro end of the continuum. However, it remains true that Collins's perspective is still weighted in a micro direction.

M_U tools can also be used to evaluate and critique other metatheoretical works. For example, my use of both a micro-macro and an objective-subjective continuum for the creation of the four levels of analysis that define the image of the subject matter of the integrated sociological paradigm led to a critical evaluation of Wiley's (1988) metatheoretical work on levels of analysis (Chapter 7). While Wiley has a strong sense of the micro-macro continuum, he lacks a similar sense of the objective-subjective continuum. To put it more specifically, he operates purely in the subjective realm. The result in his work is four levels of *subjective* social analysis—two at the macro level and two at the micro level. The use of the four levels of analysis in the integrated paradigm formed by the intersection of the micro-macro and objective-subjective continua allows one to see the weaknesses in Wiley's system, especially its lack of objective levels. More specifically, Wiley's work is greatly weakened by his lack of micro-objective and macro-objective levels of analysis. Wiley can only offer us a subjective image of interaction (micro-objective) and social structure (macro-objective). While a case could be made that these levels have subjective elements, it would be extremely difficult to defend the argument that that is all they possess. Clearly, they possess objective components; indeed, it is the objective moments that best define these levels.

M_U analyses not only permit analysts to better understand, to evaluate, and to critique theories (and metatheories), but they also play the more constructive role of helping to enhance sociological theories. For example, the metatheoretical analysis in chapter 11 suggests that sociological theory would be enhanced if *some* supporters of virtually all sociological theories were to move away from narrow adherence to a specific theory and/or level of analysis and in the direction of more synthetic orientations. Most sociological theories have suffered from an overly narrow allegiance to a given approach and an equally narrow commitment to focus on a given level of social analysis. (However, as I will explain later in this chapter, I do not mean to imply that all theorists should move toward synthesis. Narrower theoretical perspectives have their own utility.) The model might be, for example, structural functionalism which is being enhanced by people like Jeffrey Alexander as they seek to integrate insights from a range of other theoretical perspectives (e.g., conflict theory, ethnomethodology). At the same time, the traditional focus of structural functionalism on macro-level phenomena (social structure, culture) is being extended to include greater interest in micro-level phenomena. This two-pronged extension is transforming structural functionalism into neofunctionalism and at the same time greatly enhancing its scope and power. Out of this development we may see either the triumph of the more integrative neofunctionalism or a bifurcation with structural functionalism remaining committed to a macro-level focus and neofunctionalism becoming a distinctive, integrative perspective. Similar kinds of things are occurring at the cutting edge of many other theoretical perspectives (e.g., symbolic interactionism).

However, certainly not all theories and theorists are moving in this direction. For example, Peter Blau seems to have moved in the opposite direction over the years, backing away from his integrative variety of exchange theory to a form of structuralism committed to working within the confines of that theory alone and exclusively at the macro-objective level. Given the thrust of chapter 11, I could argue that Blau's macro-structuralism would be strengthened by greater openness to other theories and other levels of analysis. On the other hand, it may be that Blau and his supporters ought to continue to work at the macro-structural level where they can make distinctive contributions and leave it to others to move toward integration and synthesis. Perhaps the optimum course would be for some macro-structuralists to singlemindedly focus on that theory and level of analysis while others moved toward a more synthetic orientation from a base in macro-structuralism.

Chapter 12 suggests a very different means of improving sociological theory. As discussed above, what is revealed, among other things, is signs of greater micro-macro integration in the 1980s in the sociology of work, but also evidence that this work has been carried out in virtual isolation from the explosion of interest in such integration in sociological theory in general. Research in the sociology of work would be greatly enhanced by a careful reading and internalization of this body of work in general theory. At the same time, the abstractions of general theoretical work on micro-macro integration would profit from the more specific insights being produced in such areas of sociology as the sociology of work (as well as socioeconomics). Needless to say, much the same sort of thing can be said for every other subarea within sociology.

In sum, then, M_U gives us a powerful array of tools that not only allow for an increase in the understanding of sociological theory, but also provide the mechanisms whereby metatheorists can evaluate, critique, and suggest improvements to extant theories.

The second major contribution of metatheorizing is the creation of new theory. While this is the distinctive goal of the second type of metatheorizing, M_P, it would be wrong to conclude that no theory creation results from M_U (or M_O for that matter). In fact, the reality that M_U leads to improvements in sociological theory brings it very close to being able to create new theory. The dividing line between an improved theory and a new theory is often quite indistinct. For example, I have argued that Alexander, in part through an M_U analysis of structural functionalism and Parsonsian theory, has embarked on an effort to enhance structural functionalism. However there are those who see so many differences between traditional structural functionalism and Alexander's new functionalism that the latter might be considered an entirely new theory.

More generally, while M_U works do not take new theory creation as an objective, they may well lay the groundwork for new theories. For example, critiques of Collins's work on interaction ritual chains for its micro extremism might have helped push him in a more balanced direction in his recent theorizing. However, the theory that may be in the process of being created may be very different from the original theory; a new theory may be emerging from M_U analyses of Collins's earlier work and perhaps his metatheoretical musings on his own theory. To take another example, were sociologists of work and socioeconomists to take my suggestions in chapter 12 seriously, dramatically different theories of work and the economy would emerge.

It is also the case that M_O works can lead to the creation of new theory. It is certainly true that overarching perspectives like positivism, antipositivism, and postpositivism have helped generate a wide range of theories over the years. Theories like structural functionalism and exchange theory have clear roots in positivism, while many varieties of neo-Marxian theory and phenomenology are more rooted in anti-positivistic overarching perspectives. Postpositivism may be seen at the base of postmodernism, poststructuralism, and perhaps even neofunctionalism.

More specifically, it may be that the recent outpouring of work in micro-macro, and theoretical, syntheses indicates the implicit existence of something that might be called an integrated sociological paradigm. In fact, I will be bold on this issue and argue that the blossoming of work on micro-macro integration in the 1980s and on theoretical syntheses as we move into the 1990s strongly indicates the emergence of an integrated paradigm, the need for which I wrote about first in the late 1970s and early 1980s. Now it cannot be argued that that specific paradigm was overtly in the minds of the diverse array of sociologists working on integration of one kind or another. Thus, in my view it was a broad and vague sense that a new (integrated) overarching perspective was needed that led to recent developments in theory (and, to a lesser extent, in methodology as well; see Bailey 1987; Coleman 1987; Marini 1988; Brewer and Hunter 1989; etc.). However, there was certainly a clear dissatisfaction with the extremism of extant theories and paradigms and a sense that something else was needed. If that is in fact the case, then the overarching perspective of an integrated paradigm will need to be fleshed out in much greater detail than I was able to postulate in the late 1970s and early 1980s. Today a much wider body of work relevant to it can aid in the clarification and extension of an integrated paradigm.

When, and if, such an overarching perspective is in place, we might be in a position to begin to make some sense out of this bewildering array of new theoretical work. My guess is that the clarification of such a paradigm would lead to the coalescence of a limited number of theories that fit under its umbrella. At the moment, it is impossible to ascertain any underlying structures in this new body of theory. The recognition and clarification of an integrated paradigm would make it possible to begin to identify a limited number of theoretical (and methodological) strands. Once the strands are identified, systematic work can commence in developing those theories. In this sense, we can see that an overarching perspective can lead to theory creation.

While new theory creation may be, perhaps even should be, the indirect result of work in M_U and M_O, it is *the* goal of M_P. In addition to the example of M_P offered in this book (the derivation of the concept of hyperrationality from an analysis of the work of Weber and the neo-Weberians), there are many examples in the historical and contemporary landscape of sociology. Metatheoretical reflections on the work of other theorists has been, continues to be, and should be an important source of new theory. The arguments of chapter 2 need not be repeated here. Suffice it to say that one of the most important functions of metatheorizing, especially M_P, for the discipline of sociology is the production of a steady and continuing supply of new theory. In my view, M_P is the lifeblood of sociological theory; the production of new theory would slow to a trickle were it not for this type of metatheorizing.

Sociologists need not be embarrassed by the fact that they generate new theories out of a systematic review and critique of the work of other theorists. In fact, they should exult in that fact. Virtually all of our greatest theorists (Marx, Weber, Durkheim, Parsons) spent a great deal of time metatheorizing; it was on this basis that they produced their own theories. Contemporary theorists could do far worse than emulate these masters. In fact, most of our leading contemporary theorists (Giddens, Habermas, Collins, Alexander) have done a considerable amount of metatheorizing as the basis of their own theories. Once again, however, one must offer the caution that metatheorizing is not, and should not be, the only basis of new theory development. New theory should also be derived from, among other sources, empirical research in the social world.

The third major positive consequence of metatheorizing is the production of overarching theoretical perspectives. While this is the distinctive role of M_O, it is not impossible for work in M_U and M_P to lead to new overarching perspectives. To take one example, my own M_U work on the paradigmatic structure of sociology led ultimately to the generation of an overarching perspective, the integrated sociological paradigm. Again, however, it is M_O work that specifically and directly leads to the generation of such transcendent perspectives. Of course, I deal with one example of M_O in this book, the delineation of major components of the integrated sociological paradigm in chapters 7 and 8. However, a number of examples of M_O, O_M, and mixed types were offered in chapter 3. In an era characterized by a focus on narrow syntheses of extant theories and levels (as desirable as such work is), it is important that at least some sociologists produce such overarching perspectives. In slightly different terms, both Antonio (1990) and Kellner (1990) have stressed the need for some holistic thinking in an era marked by a massive rebellion against the creation of grand perspectives. I think it is important that at least some sociologists continue to generate such overarching perspectives in order to help prevent the mass of sociologists oriented to narrower kinds of work from losing sight of the parameters of the field. More specifically, I think that an integrated paradigm allows us to see commonalities in the large and diverse body of work on micro-macro integration and theoretical syntheses (to say nothing of the recent synthetic metamethodological and meta-data-analytical work). Without that vantage point, such works might continue to be produced independently with little or no appreciation of their ties to other works of the genre.

However, as we have seen, efforts at M_O, as well as the related attempts to O_M and mixed types, often have far more negative than positive consequences. I will return to this issue later in a more general discussion of the problems associated with metatheorizing.

Of course, metatheorizing can do much more than merely contribute to the development of sociological theory (and research); it can also contribute to theoretical developments in other fields. What does this book have to offer in this regard? At one level, it is highly likely that all of the three types of metatheorizing described in part I of this book exist in many other fields. However, since the reflexive nature of the discipline leads sociologists to be particularly inclined toward metatheorizing, all three types are likely to be much further developed in sociology than other fields. In my view, those in many other fields have much to learn from M_U, M_P, and M_O in sociology. Furthermore, the specific tools discussed in part II of this book are also likely (if they have not already been) to prove useful in an array of fields. A tool like the paradigm, because it was created in the philosophy of science, has already been used in a wide array of fields. However, the paradigm idea has undoubtedly been used and applied most by sociologists who, in the process, have refined and developed it. More importantly, there are tools that have been created by sociologists (e.g., integrated paradigm, micro-macro, theoretical syntheses) that would certainly be useful in other disciplines. Thus, I think sociological metatheorizing can be the source of the generation of perspectives and tools that can be used in metaanalyses in many other fields (e.g., psychology, economics, political science, etc.).

What Makes for Good Metatheorizing?

One of the things that has frustrated me over the years has been the propensity of many sociologists, even sociological theorists, to denigrate metatheorizing. There is a strong tendency to dismiss this kind of work by saying that it is not theory. Critics complain that metatheorists do not deal with the social world, but rather take extant theories as their subject matter. Well, that is true, metatheorizing is *not* theorizing, but that is no reason to dismiss it as inconsequential. By that standard, much of Marx's work, and Parsons's *The Structure of Social Action,* and Gouldner's *Enter Plato,* to mention just three examples, would never have been published. Indeed, I would venture to guess that a vast amount of work in sociological theory would have never been published since it is so highly metatheoretical. We need to stop using the standard applied to works in sociological theory in assessing metatheoretical works. Material produced in the latter need to be evaluated, and some of it rejected, but by standards indigenous to metatheorizing. Not all metatheorizing is worth publishing, but it is equally true that not all of it ought to be rejected out of hand merely because it is not sociological theory.

This brings us to the issue of what constitutes good metatheorizing. To some extent that depends on the type of metatheorizing being discussed, but all three types of metatheorizing do involve in the main the same process of the serious study of texts. The exceptions are the internal-social and external-social subtypes of M_U. In most cases the standard sociological research methods can be used to do research into the social issues that bear on sociological theory. As a result, for those subtypes of M_U the same standards apply as in all types of sociological research. What is distinctive about the rest of metatheorizing is the serious and systematic study of texts. What standards can be applied to this process?

At one level, the same standards are used that apply to all types of documentary research. Since there are many good sources available on this issue (e.g., Stewart 1984), and the standards are well known, they need not detain us here.

In addition to such general guidelines, more specific standards need to be applied to metatheorizing. For example, I regard as virtually essential to successful metatheorizing a process that can be called *nesting.* By this I mean that each text needs to be studied carefully not only in its own right, but also for how it relates to a series of progressively larger bodies of work in which it "nests," or is embedded. Thus, no work can be fully understood on its own, but must be studied as part of an array of contexts.[2] For example, a specific piece of work needs to be examined in the intellectual context of the larger body of the author's work, the theoretical tradition or traditions of which it is part, competing theoretical traditions, ongoing debates between traditions that might have informed the work in question, the overall state of sociology at the time, the state of relevant other disciplines, etc. It is only by relating a given piece of work to some or all of these larger contexts that we will begin to fully understand and appreciate it. And such an understanding is not only important in M_U, but also to M_P and M_O as well.

Let us take, as an example, Collins's (1990) recent contribution to conflict theory. Relevant to an understanding of this work is Collins's (1975) earlier work on conflict theory as well as the fact that he had not grappled directly with this issue for fifteen years. Also important is the fact that Collins self-consciously took a micro sociological approach to conflict in 1975 and over the years has plunged more deeply into micro theory (Collins, 1981b, 1981c). In understanding Collins's contribution to conflict theory it is important to understand that that theory has been dominated by macro-level approaches and that Collins sought to complement that perspective with his own micro-level orientation. Thus, Collins was seeking to create a more integrated micro-macro theory of conflict. Collins has long been concerned with micro-macro linkage, although he frequently erred in the micro direction. Collins's interest in a more integrated conflict theory meshed well with the broad movement toward micro-macro integration in the 1980s. In addition, in understanding Collins's contribution to conflict theory, it is impossible to ignore its competition (within the social facts paradigm) with structural functionalism. More positively, in the specific case of Collins's conflict theory, other work in various micro sociological theories were especially important in shaping his orientation to that theory. In his more recent formulation of conflict theory, he was particularly influenced by macro historical research and network theory. Turning to the broader status of sociology, Collins's work on conflict theory has always been shaped by his generally proscience position (Collins 1989a) in the ongoing debate over the scientific status of sociology. Furthermore, his very broad definition of conflict theory, and his desire to distance it from theories of conflict, can be seen as part of an effort to stake out a broader domain for conflict theory within sociology in general. Thus, Collins's work needs to be seen in the context of theoretical politics within sociology. One could go on with this type of analysis, but my point is that it this kind of linkage, this nesting, that can lead to a fuller understanding of a theoretical work. Each piece of theory is cradled in a series of intellectual contexts; if we want to enhance our understanding of that work, we need to understand as many of those contexts as possible.

In the preceding discussion I have focused on the importance of the intellectual context of theoretical works. Of at least as great importance would be an examination of the social context of such work. This would be the focal concern of the internal- and external-social subtypes of M_U. The impacts on theoretical work of such social contexts as the university, invisible colleges of sociologists, professional associations, and the larger society would need to be examined. This, of course, brings us very close to the traditional concerns of the sociology of knowledge.

The preceding discussion is related to another important aspect of metatheorizing: its inherently comparative character. In a sense, nesting is a comparative technique, but there are other aspects of comparative analysis in metatheorizing. Much of part II of this book has been devoted to the comparative analysis, using M_U tools, of paradigms (chapter 6), theories (chapters 9, 10, 11), theorists (chapter 4), and subareas within sociology (chapter 12). M_U tools provide a solid basis on which to do various types of systematic comparative analysis.

M_U tools also serve as "searchlights" highlighting various aspects of the theoretical landscape and permitting us to see things that otherwise might remain hidden from us. A good portion of this book is taken up with the delineation and use of metatheoretical tools: architectonic, philosophical anthropology, paradigm, levels of social analysis, integrated sociological paradigm, image of the subject matter, exemplar, micro-macro, and theoretical syntheses. In my view the use of these tools allows us to uncover things about sociological theory that would have remained obscure without their use: the underlying similarity in the work of Marx, Weber, and Simmel, the multiparadigmatic 1960s (and, coincidentally, such things as the existence of the supposed opponents, structural functionalism and conflict theory, within the same paradigm), the need for an integrated paradigm, Marx as an exemplar for such a paradigm (and, along the way, the surprising interest of Durkheim in micro-level phenomena), the rise of micro theory in the 1970s, the emergence of interest in micro-macro integration in the 1980s, the move toward theoretical syntheses as we enter the 1990s, and the confluence of interests (or lack thereof) in the sociology of work, socioeconomics, and sociological theory. It is also certain to be the case that the use of these tools has led to many distortions. Thus, one can anticipate various debates over the use of such tools and the accuracy of the results; out of these debates will emerge new applications as well as new metatheoretical tools.

While there is clear utility in such tools, it would seem that one need not necessarily use them in order to metatheorize. In fact, much of the field appears to be dominated by quite direct studies of theories without any metatheoretical paraphernalia. There are those who argue that one should proceed in this way because the application of various tools can easily serve as blinders that bias perceptions and analyses of the work under scrutiny. It is certainly true that such tools can serve as blinders. Thus, the user of these tools must constantly be alert to the fact that they can serve to bias and misdirect analyses. Even in the hands of the most vigilant metatheoretician, tools will have some negative and limiting effects on research.

A good example of the mixed effects of the use of a metatheoretical tool is Parsons's *The Structure of Social Action* (1937/1949). In my view, one can interpret that work as a metatheoretical (M_U) analysis of the work of some of the major figures in the history of sociology. Of course, the work was more than that since it also involved M_P: Parsons used his metatheoretical analysis of the work of the masters to begin building toward his own action theory and structural functionalism. The bulk of the book, however, was an M_U analysis utilizing voluntarism as the main metatheoretical tool. On the plus side, this allowed Parsons to see coherence in a body of work that others had failed to recognize. Furthermore, it allowed him to put together a perspective that led to his own creative theorizing. On the negative side, of course, are the well-known distortions in Parson's analysis of the masters (Cohen, Hazelrigg, and Pope 1975; Pope, Cohen, and Hazelrigg 1975). In this sense Parsons, while a pioneer, had his weaknesses as a metatheorist. Furthermore, it is highly likely that his liabilities as a metatheorist helped contribute to some of the later problems in his theories. It is certainly true that those distortions had negative effects on the later development of sociological theory in the United States.

In spite of the distortions, in my view, the positive results from the use of metatheoretical tools far outweigh the problems. In any case, I suspect that one has little choice if one wants to engage in metatheorizing. That is, metatheorists *always* use such tools—the only difference is whether they are employed explicitly or find their way into the analysis implicitly. The implicit use of such a tool or tools is less desirable because the reader is less likely to be aware that one is being used and how it is contributing to the analysis in both negative and positive ways. In contrast, where the use of the metatheoretical tool is explicit, the reader knows exactly what the analyst is doing and why, and is much more readily able to assess the pros and cons of the use of the tool.

In addition to evaluating the general process involved in all metatheorizing, each major type of metatheorizing also needs to be evaluated independently by standards specific to it and that relate to the distinctive goals of each. Since the processes are essentially the same in the three types of metatheorizing, specific evaluations refer more to their end products. This comes down to three essential questions. First, have we in fact increased our understanding of sociological theory? Second, has new theory been produced? and is the theory produced useful and important? Third, have we produced an overarching perspective that has more positive than negative consequences for the discipline in general, or sociological theory in particular? It is certainly not the case that all works in the history of metatheorizing produced positive answers to some or all of these questions. However, enough of those works have produced a sufficient number of positive answers to each of the questions to enable us to consider metatheorizing to be a legitimate, even a mandatory, part of sociology.

However, the positive case for metatheorizing must not blind us to problems in the field as a whole as well as in each of its three main subtypes. I need to examine some of these problems and before closing with some thoughts on the future of metatheorizing.

Problems in Metatheorizing

What are the basic problems confronting metatheorizing? The major ones, and the ones this book is designed to address, are its lack of legitimation and institutionalization. As long as those basic problems persist, metatheorizing will be confronted with a series of specific difficulties arising from them. Cumulation of metatheoretical knowledge will continue to be difficult because there is no agreed-upon knowledge base to which researchers and thinkers are contributing. Critics will continue to be unclear about precisely what they are attacking with the result that their criticisms will often miss the mark. The dialogue, such as it is, between metatheorists and their critics will be of little utility until critics know what they are attacking and metatheorists have a better sense of what they are defending. Needed changes in the field will be slowed because of this lack of clarity among metatheorists and the critics. These and related problems will persist as long as metatheorizing remains diffuse, unfocused, uninstitutionalized, and not completely legitimized.

Beyond this general problem and its derivatives are a series of other problems that confront part or all of metatheorizing. Chapter 1 dealt with a series of criticisms aimed at M_U. To some degree many of these same criticisms can be aimed at all three forms of metatheorizing. Let us look at some of these criticisms, as well as a number of others, this time from the viewpoint of metatheorizing in general.

The charge of being ideological, especially pro-, anti-, or postpositivistic, applies best to M_O and O_M. Many of the overarching perspectives produced by either approach tend to take a strong stand on positivism (e.g., the strongly positivistic position of Furfey and the antipositivism of Gross). In fact, it is the ideological character of M_O (and O_M) that helps make it the most problematic form of metatheorizing. However, the charge of being ideological has no more relevance to the other two types of metatheorizing than it does to sociology in general. While there are certainly some ideological aspects to all work in sociology, M_U and M_P are not particularly noteworthy in this regard.

Metatheorizing is often dismissed as nothing more than a critique of the work of others. This charge has little relevance to most types of M_U, but it does relate to M_P and M_O. Much of M_P involves a critical review of the work of other theories as the base for the creation of new theory. And much of M_O involves a similar critique oriented to the production of overarching perspectives, or metatheories.[3] While the charge of being "merely a critique" is more true in the latter cases, I do not see it as a very damning accusation. For one thing, the critical review of the work of other scholars is, after all, a basic form of scholarship in virtually all disciplines (chapter 13). For another, much more than merely critique is involved in both M_P and M_O.

Overarching perspectives, in particular, are criticized for their vagueness. The objectives of the other two types of metatheorizing—a deeper understanding of theory (M_U) and the creation of new theory (M_P)—are inherently less general and vague than the creation of an overarching perspective. They might both be vulnerable to the charge that they are nebulous about the processes involved in gaining greater theoretical understanding or creating new theory, but this is an entirely different order of vagueness than that associated with overarching approaches. In any case, this charge applies in widely varying degrees to the other two types of metatheorizing. Some theorists associated with both types are quite clear and explicit about what they are doing (e.g., Mullins's network analysis of theory groups), while others are less so.

Where the charge of vagueness does fit M_U and M_P is that practitioners have been casual and less than clear about what they are doing and how it is metatheoretical. Too often, haphazard metatheorizing is used as a basis to attempt to gain a deeper understanding of theory or for theory development. Frequently, metatheorizing is only implicit (e.g., the way Weber deals with Marx) and the reader is unable to fully understand the deeper meaning of a theory or the metatheoretical roots of a new theory. I believe that these and other problems exist because metatheorizing has evolved in a half-hidden and unarticulated way. Most sociologists who have done metatheorizing have only been dimly aware that that is what they have been doing. For example, as mentioned above, I think many metatheorists have thought of themselves as doing theory when, in fact, their work is much better thought of as metatheorizing. That is, they have not been theorizing, but have rather been gaining a better understanding of theory, doing the necessary prelude to theory development, or developing perspectives that overarch theory. Indeed, most sociologists who think of themselves, and are thought of, as theorists are in fact metatheorists. I hope that works like this one will make metatheorizing in general, as well as the various specific types and subtypes of metatheorizing, more explicit, with the result that practitioners of each will be clearer and more specific about what they are doing. Metatheorizing cannot progress until its practitioners have a clear sense of what they are doing and then communicate to others the procedures involved.

Overarching orientations have also been criticized for being framed at such an abstract level that they are of little use to practicing theorists and empiricists. This charge does not apply to the other two types of metatheorizing, or at least it does not apply in the same way. Overarching approaches must, almost by definition, be remote from the interests of practitioners. But the end products of the other two types of metatheorizing are far less removed and far more likely to be used by sociologists in their everyday work. Furthermore, the methods used by all types of metatheorists are not remote from most sociologists; indeed I think many sociologists do this kind of work in their own endeavors. A review of the literature, especially when it is carefully done, is a kind of metasociology (metatheorizing if the focus is exclusively on theories). The methods used by some metatheorists (e.g., studies of citation rates, interpersonal ties, historical/comparative research) are no different than those used by many sociologists.

Overarching approaches have been attacked because they assume all or most of sociology can be subsumed by a single, "right," transcendent orientation. Such as assumption is *not* part of either M_U or M_P. All of the major types and subtypes of M_U take theory as the subject of study and seek a deeper understanding of it. This involves a far more modest and attainable objective than that of the overarching orientations. A bit more ambitious, but still far more humble than the goals of transcendent perspectives, is the objective of M_P. Here the purpose is to create new theory, but not to create a grand perspective that transcends all of theory, the entire discipline, or even an array of fields.

Another issue is the supposed lack of creativity in metatheorizing. Here M_U might be most vulnerable, although since I have devoted a good portion of my academic life to this kind of work (to say nothing of a significant portion of this book), I have a difficult time agreeing with this accusation. It does seem to me that most work in M_U is on the order of normal science with the best work leading to small increments to our knowledge and understanding of sociological theory. On the other hand, both M_P and M_O are clearly creative; in fact, I view them as among the most creative areas within all of sociology. Those who have done successful work in M_O and especially M_P have been among the most creative minds in the history of sociology and they have often made dramatic contributions to the discipline through their imaginative work. Contrary to the critics, I find metatheorizing, taken as a whole, to be among the most creative of sociological endeavors.

Then there is the pragmatic critique that metatheorizing prevents us from getting on with the business of doing sociology. For one thing, I think that all of the major objectives of metatheorizing—gaining a better understanding of theory, creating new theory, creating an overarching perspective—are crucial components of the business of doing sociology. If we mean the business of doing empirical research, then it strikes me that the best case can be made against M_O and O_M, although empirical researchers are certainly free, as they most often do, to ignore this work and get on with their research. M_u often involves empirical research and therefore represents no problem to empiricists. M_P should be welcomed by empiricists since it is creating the theories that researchers can take into the field and test. Furthermore, if they would incorporate more of this work (new theories created, old theories clarified), their work would be improved and perhaps even expedited. For example, if their work is muddied and hampered by older ideas that put structural functionalism and conflict theory at odds with one another, metatheoretical work showing their profound similarity may help practitioners get beyond false differences and use a new, more coherent perspective to push their work forward. Even M_O ought to be welcomed because in a discipline dominated by highly detailed research on minute problems, at least a few are surely welcome to grapple with the broadest possible issues.

Beyond these criticisms is the issue of whether any of this metatheoretical work is of any immediate utility to practitioners. Clearly M_P has produced a great deal of work (Marx's theory of capitalism, alienation; Parson's action theory, structural functionalism) that has been directly important to the work of a wide range of theorists and empiricists. The issue is harder in the case of M_U. Have these works that have sought to better understand theory been of much use to practicing sociologists? The answer, unfortunately, is no. However, I would hasten to add that this work could and should be relevant to practitioners. Practitioners often have a limited and distorted sense of the theories they are using in their work. This work would be greatly improved by the kinds of clarifications being offered by those who practice M_U. By the way, the same goes for metamethodologists who could help researchers better understand the methods they are using. Used in conjunction with one another, metatheoretical and metamethodological work can help the researcher gain a better understanding of the fit between the theories and methods being utilized. For example, such a combined metaanalysis would indicate the lack of fit between a macro theory like structural functionalism and a micro method like survey research.

Thus, the above criticisms, at best, apply to only parts of metatheorizing and then only to some degree. If the above are not the real problems confronting the field, then what are? Following up on the idea of the lack of institutionalization of metatheorizing, I would say that the major problems are derived from that failure. Because of it, what we have in metatheorizing are what appear to be a series of isolated works, isolated subareas within types of metatheorizing, and isolated types of metatheorizing. There are a few specific traditions within metatheorizing on which to build (e.g., paradigm analysis), but most of it involves seemingly isolated works. Practitioners often feel as if they are out there on their own, without a tradition in which to embed themselves, and very vulnerable to outside criticism. For this reason, specific metatheoretical works and the field in general have been easy targets for critics. Metatheorists often feel defensive about what they are doing, because they lack a sense of the field and an institutional base from which to respond to the critics. Thus, what stand out are the criticisms which, in fact, often go unanswered. What chance does a field have if its most visible characteristic is the criticisms directed at it? It is difficult to get on with the day-to-day business of metatheorizing when the leading journals are publishing critiques of metatheorizing by some of the leading sociologists of the day. In fact, it often seemed, at least in the past, far easier to publish a critique of metatheorizing than it was to publish a good example of metatheorizing. Progress in metatheorizing has been hampered by these criticisms and the lack of an institutionalized base to respond to the critics.

The Future of Metatheorizing

In spite of the problems I have outlined above, I obviously believe that metatheorizing has a bright future. A type of work that has existed covertly since the founding of sociology is now attaining its own identity and developing into a distinctive subfield in its own right. What is unusual here is that we are witnessing the institutionalization of a field that already possesses an enormous body of work. Thus, even though it is becoming newly institutionalized, it is not a new field. Many of our most important contemporary theorists can also be seen, at least in part, as major metatheoreticians, my list would include, Alexander, Collins, Giddens, Habermas, Tiryakian, and Turner. Furthermore, a significant portion of the work of our predecessors can now also be redefined as contributions to metatheorizing; Marx, Weber, Durkheim, Parsons, Schutz,

Gouldner, Sorokin, Merton, Foucault, Bourdieu, and many others produced metatheoretical work. I do not mean to imply that we need to redefine these people as metatheorists and alter their identity as theorists. However, we should recognize that they are also important contributors to metatheorizing and offer an enormous legacy to those seeking the institutionalization of metatheorizing.

What are the gains to be derived from the institutionalization of sociological metatheorizing?[4] There are many, but let me mention just three. First, recognition of a distinctive domain will facilitate the accumulation of knowledge within this subfield. To this point, because the subfield has been ill-defined and diffuse, the knowledge produced has existed in isolated bits and pieces that have yet to be put together into a coherent whole. I believe that the institutionalization of sociological metatheorizing will lead to a rapid and dramatic growth in the field. This will occur because an enormous body of metatheoretical knowledge is already in existence. With institutionalization, that knowledge base will rapidly crystallize and new work in the field will quickly have a solid base on which to build. Second, the critics will be able to define their positions better once they have a clear, well-defined field to attack. Today's ill-advised and ill-defined critiques will be replaced by much sharper critical analyses of metatheorizing in general, as well as of each of its major types and subtypes. In my view, sharpened critiques will also help the development of metatheorizing. The need to deal with valid criticisms will force metatheoreticians to bolster their subfield. Third, the institutionalization of metatheorizing will benefit sociological theory and research in an array of subareas within sociology because a more secure process of metatheorizing will yield greater insights to be used throughout sociology.

What of more specific work in the future of metatheorizing? Certainly, there is much to do within each of the types and subtypes of metatheorizing. But an area in need of great expansion is the obvious, but it seems to me totally unexplored, issue of the relationship among the three types of metatheorizing. It strikes me that there are a series of linkages that need to be explored. Works in M_U are obviously dependent on the fact that previous M_P efforts have given them theories that they are able to study and analyze. On the other side, ongoing works in M_U can be important aids to those engaged in M_P. That is, a better understanding of extant theory is clearly an important base for new theory creation. Furthermore, work in both M_U and M_P are important to those engaged in M_O. Creating a solid overarching theoretical perspective is dependent on a steady supply of works clarifying extant theory and creating new theory. Given the existence of theory (through prior works in M_P), there is a linear relationship among the three types of metatheorizing—solid M_U helps in M_P and both, in turn, provide the base for M_O. However, it is important to note that the causal arrows also point the other way with all types of metatheorizing contributing, at least potentially, to the development of the others.

At the risk of appearing ludicrous because of a seeming process of infinite regress, I would also argue for the need in the future for work in *meta-metatheorizing*. As a matter of fact, a good portion of this book, especially part I and this last chapter, are exercises in meta-metatheorizing. As is clear from the voluminous list of references at the end of this book, there is already a large body of work in metatheorizing. Hence it is perfectly appropriate to stand back and try to attain a deeper understanding of it. As work in metatheorizing progresses, there will be more and more need for periodic works in meta-metatheorizing in order to take stock of the field (and its components), where it is and where it might be headed.

I would like to close this book with some thoughts on the future of the subject matter of metatheorizing: sociological theory. What has all of the metatheorizing throughout this book led me to conclude about the future of sociological theory? In the short term, it seems clear that efforts at theoretical syntheses will dominate sociological theory.[5] The discipline seems sure to see more such efforts in the near term. Furthermore, attempts to integrate these diverse efforts at synthesis will probably become more common. For example, how can such works as Alexander's in neo-functionalism, Fine's in symbolic interactionism, and Cook's in exchange theory be brought together? Out of these kinds of efforts should emerge a more coherent sense of theoretical syntheses. We are likely to see emerging from this, for the first time, a consensus over the agreed-upon domain of sociological theory in particular and sociology in general. We also might see, and this is a far more difficult task, the emergence of an image of the subject matter of sociology in an integrated sociological paradigm. And out of that we may be able to discern, for the first time, a limited number of synthetic theories (and methods).

While all of the above might well occur, it would not, indeed should not, mean the disappearance of other, narrower paradigms and their attendant theories (and methods). While synthetic theories and an integrated paradigm would be welcome and important *additions* to sociology, they would not and should not mean the elimination of extant theories and paradigms. From my viewpoint, synthetic theories (and methods) and an integrated paradigm would be too general to deal with many of the specifics of social life. We will continue to need extant theories and paradigms to deal with these narrower domains.

Thus, these synthetic developments will and should bring us an even more complex and variegated theoretical landscape in the future. That is to be welcomed since the landscape of social reality is complex and varied and grows more so every day. But there is a very thin line to be walked here. Too many paradigms and too many theories will further complicate rather than aid in analyzing the social world. Practicing sociologists need a parsimonious set of paradigms and theories if they are to be able to handle them and deal with a complicated social world. Thus, one needs to be wary of an overexpansion of paradigms and theories.

At the same time, sociologists also need to worry that new paradigms and theories will not peacefully coexist with extant paradigms and theories, but will signal a reemergence of the political conflict among paradigms and theories that reached something of a crescendo in the 1960s and 1970s. There is a kind of natural tendency, at least in the current political climate in sociology, on the part of adherents of paradigms and theories to want to overwhelm the opposition. There is also a tendency to believe that one's own paradigm and theory explains everything, leaving no need for any other theories and paradigms. If this was true of the far narrower theories and paradigms of the multiparadigmatic 1960s (and it was), then it is certainly going to be a temptation for the supporters of the far more integrative theories and paradigm(s) that seem to be emerging as we enter the 1990s. However, supporters of such synthetic orientations need to bear in mind that while their sweep is wide, it is also very shallow. Depth will be supplied by the narrower paradigms and theories. Sociology needs both wide and deep paradigms and theories (and methods).

Thus, while there is a trend toward, and need for, more synthetic theoretical approaches, I will conclude this last chapter by somewhat paradoxically coming down on the side of the need for the continued existence of narrower theories and paradigms. It would be a disaster for all theorists to rush off in the direction of integrative nirvana. There is a strong need for many theorists to continue to work on narrower theories and paradigms. An integrated perspective can provide the kind of holistic approach called for by people like Kellner (1990) and Antonio (1990), but in the modern era we simultaneously need pluralism in theories, paradigms, and syntheses. Returning to the central theme of this book, an even more pluralistic sociological theory requires the institutionalization of metatheorizing in order to help sociologists deal with this increasingly complex theoretical world.

Notes

1. The actual dividing line between periods is not nearly as sharp as I am suggesting. None of these epochs began at the beginning of a decade and ended precisely at its close. Rather the decade markers are offered to give a rough ap-

proximation of the time frames in which particular types of theorizing were dominant.

2. One can see here the influence of several of the approaches discussed in chapter 13.

3. O_M, of course, lacks such a critical review—that is a major source of its extraordinary problems.

4. There is a downside to this, particularly in the further proliferation of subspecialties within sociology. However, in my view this subspecialty already exists, but simply has not been recognized overtly. In this sense, institutionalization will not contribute to a further splintering of the field. Furthermore, metatheoretical work should be related to, and inform, not only work in theory, but empirical research as well.

5. While these synthetic efforts are welcome, we should be wary of the fact that they are motivated by the need to shore up internal theoretical problems and not by the need to deal better with social issues. There is a danger that such efforts will grow increasingly less relevant to the social world.

References

Abbot, Andrew. 1988. *The system of professions: An essay on the division of labor*. Chicago: University of Chicago Press.

Abbot, Carroll, Charles R. Brown, and Paul V. Crosbie. 1973. Exchange as symbolic interaction: For what? *American Sociological Review* 38: 504–506.

Abegglen, James C., and George Stalk, Jr. 1985. *Kaisha, the Japanese corporation*. New York: Basic Books.

Abel, Theodore. 1970. *The foundations of sociological theory*. New York: Random House.

Abrams, Denise, Roger Reitman, and Joan Sylvester. 1980. The paradigmatic status of sociology: Current evaluations and future prospects. In *Sociology: A multiple paradigm science*, revised ed., edited by George Ritzer, 266–87. Boston: Allyn and Bacon.

Abrams, Philip. 1982. *Historical sociology*. Ithaca, N.Y.: Cornell University Press.

Agger, Ben, ed. 1978. *Western Marxism: An introduction*. Santa Monica, Calif.: Goodyear.

Albrow, Martin. 1974. Dialectical and categorical paradigms of a science of society. *Sociological Review* 22: 183–202.

Alexander, Jeffrey C. 1982. *Theoretical logic in sociology*. Vol. 1, *Positivism, presuppositions, and current controversies*. Berkeley and Los Angeles: University of California Press.

Alexander, Jeffrey C. 1982–83. *Theoretical logic in sociology*. 4 Vols. Berkeley and Los Angeles: University of California Press.

Alexander, Jeffrey C. 1985a. The "individualist dilemma" in phenomenology and interactionism. In *Macro-sociological theory*, edited by S.N. Eisenstadt and H.J. Helle, 25–57. London: Sage.

Alexander, Jeffrey C., ed. 1985b. *Neofunctionalism*. Beverly Hills, Calif.: Sage.

Alexander, Jeffrey C. 1987. Action and its environments. In *The micro-macro link*, edited by Jeffrey C. Alexander, Bernard Giesen, Richard Munch, and Neil Smelser, 289–318. Berkeley and Los Angeles: University of California Press.

Alexander, Jeffrey C., and Paul Colomy. 1990. Neofunctionalism: Reconstructing a theoretical tradition. In *Frontiers of social theory: The new syntheses*, edited by George Ritzer, 33–67. New York: Columbia University Press.

Alexander, Jeffrey C., and Bernhard Giesen. 1987. From reduction to linkage: The long view of the micro-macro link. In *The micro-macro link*, edited by

Jeffrey C. Alexander, Bernard Giesen, Richard Munch, and Neil Smelser, 1–42. Berkeley and Los Angeles: University of California Press.

Alexander, Jeffrey C., Bernard Giesen, Richard Munch, and Neil Smelser, eds. 1987. *The micro-macro link*. Berkeley and Los Angeles: University of California Press.

Alford, Robert R., and Roger Friedland. 1985. *Powers of theory: Capitalism, the state, and democracy*. Cambridge: Cambridge University Press.

Alpert, Harry. 1939. *Emile Durkheim and his sociology*. New York: Russell and Russell.

Alston, Jon P. 1986. *The American samurai: Blending American and Japanese managerial practices*. Berlin: Walter de Gruyter.

Althusser, Louis. 1969. *For Marx*. Harmondsworth, England: Penguin.

Althusser, Louis. 1977. *Politics and history*. London: NLB.

Althusser, Louis, and Etienne Balibar, eds. 1970. *Reading capital*. New York: Pantheon.

Antonio, Robert J. 1990. The decline of the grand narrative of emancipatory modernity: Crisis or renewal in neo-Marxian theory? In *Frontiers of social theory: The new syntheses*, edited by George Ritzer, 88–116. New York: Columbia University Press.

Archer, Margaret S. 1982. Morphogenesis versus structuration: On combining structure and action. *British Journal of Sociology* 33: 455–483.

Archer, Margaret S. 1988. *Culture and agency: The place of culture in social theory*. Cambridge: Cambridge University Press.

Aron, Raymond. 1965. *Main currents in sociological thought*. Vol. 1. New York: Basic Books.

Arthur, C. J. 1970. Editor's introduction to *The German ideology*, part 1, by Karl Marx and Freidrich Engels. New York: International Publishers.

Avineri, Shlomo. 1968. *The social and political thought of Karl Marx*. London: Cambridge University Press.

Back, Kurt. 1970. Review of Robert Burgess and Don Bushell, eds., *Behavioral sociology*. *American Sociological Review* 35: 1098–1100.

Bailey, Kenneth D. 1987. Globals, mutables, and immutables: An alternative approach to micro/macro analysis. Paper presented at the meetings of the American Sociological Association, Chicago, Illinois, 1987.

Barbalet, J. M. 1983. *Marx's construction of social theory*. London: Routledge and Kegan Paul.

Baudrillard, Jean. 1983. *Simulations*. New York: Semiotext.

Bealer, Robert C. 1979. Ontology in American sociology: Whence and whither? In *Contemporary Issues in theory and research*, edited by William E. Snizek, Ellsworth R. Fuhrman, and Michael K. Miller, 85–106. Westport, Conn.: Greenwood Press.

Bealer, Bob [Robert C.] 1990. Paradigms, theories, and methods in contemporary rural sociology: A critical reaction to critical questions. *Rural Sociology* 55: 91–100.

Becker, Howard, and Blanche Geer. 1957. Participant observation and interviewing: A comparison. *Human Organization* 16:29–32.

Bender, Frederick, ed. 1970. *Karl Marx: The essential writings*. New York: Harper.

Benton, Ted. 1984. *The rise and fall of structural Marxism: Althusser and his influence*. New York: St. Martin's.

Berger, Brigitte, and Peter Berger. 1984. *The war over the family: Capturing the middle ground.* Garden City, N.Y.: Anchor Press/Doubleday.

Berger, Charles R., and Steven H. Chaffee. 1988. *Handbook of communication science.* Newbury Park, Calif.: Sage.

Berger, Joseph, David G. Wagner, and Morris Zelditch. 1989. Theory growth, social processes, and metatheory. In *Theory building in sociology: Assessing theoretical cumulation,* edited by Jonathan Turner, 19–42. Newbury Park, Calif.: Sage.

Berger, Peter, and Thomas Luckmann. 1967. *The social construction of reality: A treatise in the sociology of knowledge.* Garden City, N.Y.: Anchor Books.

Berger, Peter, and Stanley Pullberg. 1965. Reification and the sociological critique of consciousness. *History and Theory* 4: 196–211.

Berki, R. N. 1983. *Insight and vision: The problem of communism in Marx's thought.* London: J. M. Dent and Sons.

Bernstein, Richard J. 1971. *Praxis and action: Contemporary philosophies of human activity.* Philadelphia: University of Pennsylvania Press.

Besnard, Philippe, ed. 1983a. *The sociological domain.* Cambridge: Cambridge University Press.

Besnard, Philippe. 1983b. The "Annee Sociologique" team. In *The sociological domain,* edited by Philippe Besnard, 11–39. Cambridge: Cambridge University Press.

Bhaskar, Roy. 1982. Emergence, explanation, and emancipation. In *Explaining human behavior,* edited by Paul F. Secord, 275–310. Beverly Hills, Calif.: Sage.

Bierstedt, Robert. 1963. The common sense world of Alfred Schutz. *Social Research* 30: 116–121.

Blalock, Hubert, and Paul Wilken. 1979. *Intergroup processes: A micro-macro perspective.* New York: Free Press.

Blau, Peter. 1960. Structural effects. *American Sociological Review* 25: 178–193.

Blau, Peter. 1964. *Exchange and power in social life.* New York: John Wiley.

Blau, Peter. 1977a. *Inequality and heterogeneity: A primitive theory of social structure.* New York: Free Press.

Blau, Peter. 1977b. A macrosociological theory of social structure. *American Sociological Review* 83:265–54.

Blau, Peter. 1979. Levels and types of structural effects: The impact of university structure on professional schools. In *Contemporary issues in theory and research: A metasociological perspective,* edited by William E. Snizek, Ellsworth R. Fuhrman, and Michael K. Miller, 141–160. Westport, Conn.: Greenwood Press.

Blau, Peter. 1987a. Contrasting theoretical perspectives. In *The micro-macro link,* edited by Jeffrey C. Alexander, Bernard Giesen, Richard Munch and Neil Smelser, 71–85. Berkeley and Los Angeles: University of California Press.

Blau, Peter. 1987b. Microprocess and macrostructure. In *Social exchange theory,* edited by Karen Cook, 83–100. Beverly Hills, Calif.: Sage.

Blau, Peter, Caroline Beeker, and Kevin Fitzpatrick. 1984. Crosscutting social circles and intermarriage. *Social Forces* 62: 585–606.

Blumer, Herbert. 1969. *Symbolic interaction: Perspective and method.* Englewood Cliffs, N.J.: Prentice-Hall.

Boden, Deirdre. 1990. The world as it happens: Ethnomethodology and conversation analysis. In *Frontiers of social theory: The new syntheses*, edited by George Ritzer, 185–213. New York: Columbia University Press.

Bosserman, Phillip. 1968. *Dialectical sociology: An analysis of the sociology of Georges Gurvitch*. Boston: Porter Sargent.

Bosworth, Susan Lovegren, and Gary A. Kreps. 1986. Structure as process: Organization and role. *American Sociological Review* 51: 699–716.

Bottomore, Tom, and David Frisby. 1978. Introduction to the translation. In Georg Simmel, *The philosophy of money*, 1–49. London: Routledge and Kegan Paul.

Boudon, Raymond. 1979/1981. *The logic of social action: Introduction to sociological analysis*. London: Routledge and Kegan Paul.

Boudon, Raymond. 1987. The individualistic tradition in sociology. In *The micro-macro link*, edited by Jeffrey Alexander, Bernard Giesen, Richard Munch, and Neil Smelser, 45–70. Berkeley and Los Angeles: University of California Press.

Bourdieu, Pierre. 1977. *Outline of a theory of practice*. Cambridge: Cambridge University Press.

Braverman, Harry. 1974. *Labor and monopoly capital: The degradation of work in the twentieth century*. New York: Monthly Review Press.

Brewer, John, and Albert Hunter. 1989. *Multimethod research: A synthesis of styles*. Newbury Park, Calif.: Sage.

Brown, Julia, and Brian G. Gilmartin. 1969. Sociology today: Lacunae, emphases, and surfeits. *American Sociologist* 4: 283–90.

Brown, Richard. 1987. *Society as text: Essays on rhetoric, reason, and reality*. Chicago: University of Chicago Press.

Brown, Richard. 1990. Social science and the poetics of public truth. *Sociological Forum*, 5: 55–74.

Brubaker, Rogers. 1984. *The limits of rationality*. London: George Allen and Unwin.

Bucher, Rue, and Anselm Strauss. 1961. Professions in process. *American Journal of Sociology* 66: 325–34.

Buckley, Walter. 1967. *Sociology and modern systems theory*. Englewood Cliffs, New Jersey: Prentice-Hall.

Bulmer, Martin. 1984. *The Chicago school of sociology: Institutionalization, diversity and the rise of sociological research*. Chicago: University of Chicago Press.

Bulmer, Martin. 1985. The Chicago school of sociology: What made it a school? *History of Sociology: An International Review* 5: 61–77.

Burawoy, Michael. 1979. *Manufacturing consent: Changes in the labor process under monopoly capitalism*. Chicago: University of Chicago Press.

Burgess, Robert, and Don Bushell. 1969. A behavioral view of some sociological concepts. In *Behavioral sociology*, edited by Robert Burgess and Don Bushell, 273–90. New York: Columbia University Press.

Burke, Peter. 1986. Strengths and weaknesses of the history of mentalities. *History of European Ideas* 7: 439–51.

Burns, Tom R. 1986. Actors, transactions, and social structure: An introduction to social rule system theory. In *Sociology: The aftermath of crisis*, edited by U. Himmelstrand, 8–37. London: Sage.

Burns, Tom R., and Helena Flam. 1986. *The shaping of social organization: Social rule system theory with applications.* Beverly Hills, Calif.: Sage.

Burt, Ronald. 1982. *Toward a structural theory of action: Network models of social structure.* New York: Academic Press.

Bushell, Don, and Robert Burgess. 1969. Some basic principles of behavior. In *Behavioral sociology,* edited by Robert Burgess and Don Bushell, 27–48. New York: Columbia University Press.

Butterfield, Herbert. 1931. *The Whig interpretation of history.* New York: Scribner's.

Calhoun, Craig. 1988. Populist politics, communications media, and large-scale societal integration. *Sociological Theory* 6:219–41.

Camic, Charles. 1987. The making of a model: A historical reinterpretation of the early Parsons. *American Sociological Review* 52: 421–39.

Carr, David. 1987. Review essay on *Futures Past,* by Reinhart Koselleck. *History and Theory* 26: 197–204.

Cicourel, Aaron. 1981. Notes on the integration of micro- and macro-levels of analysis. In *Advances in social theory and methodology,* edited by Karin Knorr-Cetina and Aaron Cicourel, 51–79. New York: Methuen.

Clawson, Dan, Alan Neustadtl, and James Bearden. 1986. The logic of business unity: Corporate contributions to the 1980 congressional elections. *American Sociological Review* 51: 797–811.

Cohen, Ira J. 1981. Introduction to the transaction edition: Max Weber on modern Western capitalism. In Max Weber, *General economic history,* xv–lxxxiii. New Brunswick, N.J.: Transaction Books.

Cohen, Jere, Lawrence Hazelrigg, and Whitney Pope. 1975. DeParsonizing Weber: A critique of Parsons' interpretation of Weber's sociology. *American Sociological Review* 40: 229–41.

Colclough, Glenna, and Patrick Horan. 1983. The status attainment paradigm: An application of a Kuhnian perspective. *Sociological Quarterly* 24: 25–42.

Cole, Jonathan R., and Stephen Cole. 1973. *Social stratification in science.* Chicago: University of Chicago Press.

Coleman, James. 1968. Review of Harold Garfinkel, *Studies in ethnomethodology. American Sociological Review* 33: 126–30.

Coleman, James. 1970. Relational analysis: The study of social organizations with survey methods. In *Sociological methods,* edited by Norman Denzin, 115–26. Chicago: Aldine.

Coleman, James. 1986a. *Individual interests and collective action: Selected essays.* Cambridge: Cambridge University Press.

Coleman, James. 1986b. Social theory, social research, and a theory of action. *American Journal of Sociology* 91: 1309–35.

Coleman, James. 1987. Microfoundations and macrosocial behavior. In *The micro-macro link,* edited by Jeffrey C. Alexander, Bernard Giesen, Richard Munch, and Neil Smelser, 153–73. Berkeley and Los Angeles: University of California Press.

Collingwood, R. G. 1956. *The idea of history.* New York: Oxford University Press.

Collins, Randall. 1975. *Conflict sociology: Toward an explanatory science.* New York: Academic Press.

Collins, Randall. 1981a. Introduction to *Sociology since midcentury: Essays in theory cumulation,* 1–9. New York: Academic Press.

Collins, Randall. 1981b. Micro-translation as a theory-building strategy. In *Advances in social theory and methodology,* edited by Karin Knorr-Cetina and Aaron Cicourel, 81–108. New York: Methuen.

Collins, Randall. 1981c. On the microfoundations of macrosociology. *American Journal of Sociology* 86: 984–1014.

Collins, Randall. 1985. *Weberian sociological theory.* Cambridge: Cambridge University Press.

Collins, Randall. 1986a. Is 1980s sociology in the doldrums? *American Journal of Sociology* 91: 1336–55.

Collins, Randall. 1986b. *Max Weber: A skeleton key.* Beverly Hills, Calif.: Sage.

Collins, Randall. 1986c. The passing of intellectual generations: Reflections on the death of Erving Goffman. *Sociological Theory* 4: 106–13.

Collins, Randall. 1987a. A micro-macro theory of intellectual creativity: The case of German idealistic philosophy. *Sociological Theory* 5: 47–69.

Collins, Randall. 1987b. Interaction ritual chains, power, and property: The micro-macro connection as an empirically based theoretical problem. In *The micro-macro link,* edited by Jeffrey C. Alexander, Bernard Giesen, Richard Munch, and Neil Smelser, 193–206. Berkeley and Los Angeles: University of California Press.

Collins, Randall. 1988. The micro contribution to macro sociology. *Sociological Theory* 6: 242–53.

Collins, Randall. 1989a. Sociology: Proscience or antiscience? *American Sociological Review* 54: 124–39.

Collins, Randall. 1989b. Toward a neo-Meadian sociology of mind. *Symbolic Interaction* 12: 1–32.

Collins, Randall. 1990. Conflict theory and the advance of macro-historical sociology. In *Frontiers of social theory: The new syntheses,* edited by George Ritzer, 68–87. New York: Columbia University Press.

Colomy, Paul. 1986. Recent developments in the functionalist approach to change. *Sociological Focus* 19:139–58.

Connolly, William E. 1973. Theoretical self-consciousness. *Polity* 6: 5–35.

Cook, Karen S. 1987a. Emerson's contribution to social exchange theory. In *Social exchange theory,* edited by Karen S. Cook, 209–22. Beverly Hills, Calif.: Sage.

Cook, Karen S., ed. 1987b. *Social exchange theory.* Beverly Hills, Calif.: Sage.

Cook, Karen S., and Richard M. Emerson. 1978. Power, equity and commitment in exchange networks. *American Sociological Review* 43: 721–39.

Cook, Karen S., Richard Emerson, Mary B. Gillmore, and Toshio Yamagishi. 1983. The distribution of power in exchange networks: Theory and experimental results. *American Journal of Sociology* 89: 275–305.

Cook, Karen S., Jodi O'Brien, and Peter Kollock. 1990. Exchange theory: A blueprint for structure and process. In *Frontiers of social theory: The new syntheses,* edited by George Ritzer, 158–81. New York: Columbia University Press.

Coser, Lewis, ed. 1965. *Georg Simmel.* Englewood Cliffs, N.J.: Prentice-Hall.

Coser, Lewis. 1975. Two methods in search of a substance. *American Sociological Review* 40: 691–700.

Couch, Carl. 1987. Objectivity: A crutch and club for lost bureaucrats/Subjectivity: A haven for lost souls. *Sociological Quarterly* 26: 105–18.

Cozzens, Susan E. 1985. Comparing the sciences: Citation context analysis of papers from neuropharmacology and the sociology of science. *Social Studies of science* 15: 127–54.

Cozzens, Susan E. 1986. Editor's introduction: Funding and knowledge growth. *Social Studies of Science* 16: 9–22.

Crane, Diana. 1969. Social Structure in a group of scientists: A test of the "invisible college" hypothesis. *American Sociological Review* 34: 335–51.

Crane, Diana. 1980. An exploratory study of Kuhnian paradigms in theoretical high energy physics. *Social Studies of Science* 10: 23–54.

Crombie, A. C. 1986. What is the history of science? *History of European Ideas* 7: 21–31.

Crozier, Michel, and Erhard Friedberg. 1980. *Actors and systems: The politics of collective action.* Chicago: University of Chicago Press.

Dahrendorf, Ralf. 1959. *Class and class conflict in industrial society.* Stanford, Calif.: Stanford University Press.

Dawe, Alan. 1978. Theories of social action. In *A history of sociological analysis,* edited by Tom Bottomore and Robert Nisbet, 362–417. New York: Basic Books.

Denzin, Norman. 1986. Postmodern social theory. *Sociological Theory* 4:194–204.

Derber, Charles, ed. 1982. *Professionals as workers: Mental labor in advanced capitalism.* Boston: G. K. Hall and Co.

DeVille, Phillippe. 1989. Human agency and social structure in economic theory: The general equilibrium theory and beyond. Paper presented at conference, Social Theory and Human Agency, The Swedish Collegium for Advanced Study in the Social Sciences, Uppsala, Sweden, 29 September–1 October 1989.

De Vos, George A. 1975. Apprenticeship and paternalism. In *Modern Japanese organization and decision making,* edited by Ezra Vogel, 210–77. Berkeley and Los Angeles: University of California Press.

Diggins, John Patrick. 1984. The oyster and the pearl: The problem of contextualism in intellectual history. *History and Theory* 23:151–69.

Dingwall, Robert. 1976. Accomplishing professions. *Sociological Review* 24: 331–49.

Dolman, Han, and Henk Bodewitz. 1985. Sedimentation of a scientific concept: The use of citation data. *Social Studies of Science* 15: 507–24.

Douglas, Jack. 1980. Introduction to *The sociologies of everyday life,* edited by Jack Douglas, Patricia A. Adler, Peter Adler, Andrea Fontana, C. Robert Freeman and Joseph Kotarba. Boston: Allyn and Bacon.

Duncan, O. D., and L. F. Schnore. 1959. Cultural, behavioral, and ecological perspectives in the study of social organization. *American Journal of Sociology* 65: 132–46.

Dunn, John. 1972. The identity of the history of ideas. In *Philosophy, politics, and society,* edited by Peter Laslett, W. G. Runciman, and Quentin Skinner, 158–73. New York: Barnes and Noble.

Durkheim, Emile. 1893/1960. Montesquieu's contribution to the rise of social science. In *Montesquieu and Rousseau: Forerunners of sociology,* 1–64. Ann Arbor: University of Michigan Press.

Durkheim, Emile. 1893/1964. *The division of labor in society.* New York: Free Press.

Durkheim, Emile. 1895/1964. *The rules of sociological method.* New York: Free Press.

Emile Durkheim. 1897/1951. *Suicide.* New York: Free Press.

Durkheim, Emile. 1912/1965. *The elementary forms of religious life.* New York: Free Press.

Durkheim, Emile. 1918/1960. Rousseau's social contract. In *Montesquieu and Rousseau: Forerunners of sociology,* 65–138. Ann Arbor: University of Michigan Press.

Durkheim, Emile. 1922/1956. *Education and sociology.* New York: Free Press.

Durkheim, Emile. 1928/1962. *Socialism.* New York: Collier Books.

Durkheim, Emile, and Marcel Mauss. 1903/1963. *Primitive classification.* Chicago: University of Chicago Press.

Eckberg, Douglas, and Lester Hill. 1979. The paradigm concept in sociology: A critical review. *American Sociological Review* 44: 925–37.

Edel, Abraham. 1959. The concept of levels in sociological theory. In *Symposium on sociological theory,* edited by L. Gross, 167–95. Evanston, Ill.: Row Peterson.

Effrat, Andrew. 1972. Power to the paradigms. *Sociological Inquiry* 42: 3–33.

Eisenstadt, S. N., and M. Curelaru. 1976. *The form of sociology: Paradigms and crises.* New York: John Wiley.

Eisenstadt, S. N., and H. J. Helle. 1985a. General introduction to perspectives on sociological theory. In *Macro-sociological theory: Perspectives on sociological theory,* edited by S. N. Eisenstadt and H. J. Helle, 1:1–3. London: Sage.

Eisenstadt, S. N., and H. J. Helle, eds. 1985b. *Macro-sociological theory: Perspectives on sociological theory.* Vol. 1. London: Sage.

Elster, Jon. 1982. Marxism, functionalism, and game theory: The case for methodological individualism. *Theory and Society* 11: 453–82.

Elster, Jon. 1985. *Making sense of Marx.* Cambridge: Cambridge University Press.

Emerson, Richard M. 1972a. Exchange theory, part I: A psychological basis for social exchange. In *Sociological theories in progress,* vol. 2, edited by Joseph Berger, Morris Zelditch, and Bo Anderson, 38–57. Boston: Houghton-Mifflin.

Emerson, Richard M. 1972b. Exchange theory, part II: Exchange relations and networks. In *Sociological theories in progress,* vol. 2, edited by Joseph Berger, Morris Zelditch, and Bo Anderson, 58–87. Boston: Houghton-Mifflin.

Emerson, Richard M. 1976. Social exchange theory. In *Social psychology: Sociological perspectives,* edited by Morris Rosenberg and Ralph H. Turner, 30–65. New York: Basic Books.

Emerson, Richard M. 1981. Social exchange theory. In *Social psychology: Sociological perspectives,* edited by Morris Rosenberg and Ralph H. Turner, 30–65. New York: Basic Books.

Engels, Friedrich. 1890/1972. Letter to Joseph Bloch. In *The Marx-Engels reader,* edited by Robert C. Tucker, 640–42. New York: Norton.

Etzioni, Amitai. 1968. *The active society: A theory of societal and political processes.* New York: Free Press.

Etzioni, Amitai. 1988. *The moral dimension: Toward a new economics.* New York: Free Press.

Falk, William, and Shanyang Zhao. 1989. Paradigms, theories, and methods in contemporary rural sociology: A partial replication. *Rural Sociology* 54: 587–600.

Falk, William, and Shanyang Zhao. 1990. Paradigms, theories, and methods revisited: We respond to our critics. *Rural Sociology* 55: 112–22.

Fararo, Thomas J. 1989. The spirit of unification in sociological theory. *Sociological Theory* 7: 175–90.

Fararo, Thomas J., and John Skvoretz. 1986. E-state structuralism: A theoretical method. *American Sociological Review* 51: 591–602.

Fendrich, Michael. 1984. Wives' employment and husbands' distress: A meta-analysis and a replication. *Journal of Marriage and the Family* 46: 871–79.

Fine, Gary. 1990. Symbolic interactionism in the post-Blumerian age. In *Frontiers of social theory: The new syntheses,* edited by George Ritzer, 117–57. New York: Columbia University Press.

Fiske, Donald W., and Richard A. Shweder, eds. 1986. *Metatheory in social sciences: Pluralisms and subjectivities.* Chicago: University of Chicago Press.

Ford, Ramona. 1988. *Work, organization, and power: Introduction to industrial sociology.* Boston: Allyn and Bacon.

Foucault, Michel. 1965. *Madness and civilization: A history of insanity in the age of reason.* New York: Vintage.

Foucault, Michel. 1966. *The order of things: An archaeology of the human sciences.* New York: Vintage.

Foucault, Michel. 1969. *The archaeology of knowledge and the discourse on language.* New York: Harper Colophon.

Foucault, Michel. 1975. *The birth of the clinic: An archaeology of medical perception.* New York: Vintage.

Foucault, Michel. 1979. *Discipline and punish: The birth of the prison.* New York: Vintage.

Foucault, Michel. 1980. *The history of sexuality.* Vol. 1, *An introduction.* New York: Vintage.

Freidson, Eliot. 1970. *The profession of medicine.* New York: Dodd, Mead.

Friedheim, Elizabeth. 1979. An empirical comparison of Ritzer's paradigms and similar metatheories. *Social Forces* 58: 59–66.

Friedman, Debra, and Michael Hechter. 1988. The contribution of rational choice theory to macrosociological research. *Sociological Theory* 6: 201–18.

Friedman, Debra, and Michael Hechter. 1990. The comparative advantages of rational choice theory. In *Frontiers of social theory: The new syntheses,* edited by George Ritzer, 214–29. New York: Columbia University Press.

Friedrichs, Robert. 1970. *A sociology of sociology.* New York: Free Press.

Friedrichs, Robert W. 1974. The potential impact of B.F. Skinner upon American sociology. *American Sociologist* 9: 3–8.

Fries, Sylvia. 1984. The ideology of science during the Nixon years: 1970–76. *Social Studies of Science* 14: 323–42.

Frisby, David. 1984. *Georg Simmel.* Chichester, England: Ellis Horwood.

Fuhrman, Ellsworth R., and William E. Snizek. 1987. Finnish and American sociology: A cross-cultural comparison. *Sociological Inquiry* 57: 204–21.

Fuhrman, Ellsworth R., and William Snizek. 1990. Neither proscience nor anti-science: Metasociology as dialogue. *Sociological Forum* 5: 17–31.

Furfey, Paul Hanly. 1953/1965. *The scope and method of sociology: A metasociological treatise.* New York: Cooper Square Publishers.

Gandy, D. Ross. 1979. *Marx and history: From primitive society to the communist future.* Austin: University of Texas Press.

Garfinkel, Harold. 1967. *Studies in ethnomethodology.* Englewood Cliffs, N.J.: Prentice-Hall.

Geison, Gerald L. 1981. Scientific change, emerging specialties, and research schools. *History of Science* 19:20–40.

Geras, Norman. 1983. *Marx and human nature: Refutation of a legend.* London: NLB.

Gergen, Kenneth J. 1973. Social psychology as history. *Journal of Personality and Social Psychology* 26: 309–20.

Gergen, Kenneth J. 1986. Correspondence versus autonomy in the language of understanding human action. In *Metatheory in social science: Pluralisms and subjectivities,* edited by Donald W. Fiske and Richard A. Shweder, 136–62. Chicago: University of Chicago Press.

Gergen, Kenneth J., and Mary M. Gergen. 1982. Explaining human conduct: Form and function. In *Explaining human behavior,* edited by Paul. F. Secord, 127–54. Beverly Hills, Calif.: Sage.

Gerstein, Dean. 1987. To unpack micro and macro: Link small with large and part with whole. In *The micro-macro link,* edited by Jeffrey C. Alexander, Bernard Giesen, Richard Munch, and Neil Smelser, 86–111. Berkeley and Los Angeles: University of California Press.

Gerth, Hans, and C. Wright Mills. 1953. *Character and social structure.* New York: Harcourt, Brace and World.

Gerth, Hans, and C. Wright Mills, eds. 1958. *From Max Weber.* New York: Oxford University Press.

Gibbs, Jack P. 1989. *Control: Sociology's central notion.* Urbana and Chicago: University of Illinois Press.

Gibney, Frank. 1982. *Miracle by design.* New York: Time Books.

Giddens, Anthony. 1971. *Capitalism and modern social theory.* Cambridge: Cambridge University Press.

Giddens, Anthony, ed. 1972. *Emile Durkheim: Selected writings.* Cambridge: Cambridge University Press.

Giddens, Anthony. 1976. *New rules of sociological method.* New York: Basic Books.

Giddens, Anthony. 1979. *Central problems in social theory: Action, structure, and contradiction in social analysis.* Berkeley and Los Angeles: University of California Press.

Giddens, Anthony. 1981. *A contemporary critique of historical materialism.* Berkeley and Los Angeles: University of California Press.

Giddens, Anthony. 1982. *Profiles and critiques in social theory.* Berkeley and Los Angeles: University of California Press.

Giddens, Anthony. 1984. *The constitution of society: Outline of the theory of structuration.* Berkeley and Los Angeles: University of California Press.

Giddens, Anthony. 1987. Erving Goffman as a systematic social theorist. In *Social theory and modern sociology,* edited by Anthony Giddens, 109–39. Cambridge, England: Polity Press.

Gieryn, Thomas F., and Richard F. Hirsh. 1983. Marginality and innovation in science. *Social Studies of Science* 13: 87–106.

Godelier, Maurice. 1972. *Rationality and irrationality in economics.* London: NLB.

Goffman, Erving. 1959. *The presentation of self in everyday life.* Garden City, N.Y.: Anchor.

Goffman, Erving. 1983. The interaction order. *American Sociological Review* 48: 1–17.

Gottdiener, Mark, and Joe R. Feagin. 1988. The paradigm shift in urban sociology. *Urban Affairs Quarterly* 24: 163–87.

Gould, Carol. 1978. *Marx's social ontology: Individuality and community in Marx's theory of social reality.* Cambridge: MIT Press.

Gouldner, Alvin. 1958. Introduction to *Socialism and Saint-Simon,* by Emile Durkheim. Yellow Springs, Ohio: Antioch Press.

Gouldner, Alvin. 1965. *Enter Plato: Classical Greece and the origins of social theory.* New York: Basic Books.

Gouldner, Alvin. 1970. *The coming crisis of Western sociology.* New York: Basic Books.

Gramsci, Antonio. 1971. *Selections from the prison notebooks.* New York: Basic Books.

Granovetter, Mark. 1973. The strength of weak ties. *American Journal of Sociology* 78:1360–80.

Granovetter, Mark. 1983. The strength of weak ties: A network theory revisited. In *Sociological theory—1983,* edited by Randall Collins, 201–33. San Francisco: Jossey-Bass.

Granovetter, Mark. 1985. Economic action and social structure: The problem of embeddedness. *American Journal of Sociology* 91:484–510.

Greenwood, Ernest. 1957. Attributes of a profession. *Social Work* 2: 45–55.

Gross, Llewellyn. 1961. Preface to a metatheoretical framework for sociology. *American Journal of Sociology* 67: 125–36.

Guillain, Robert. 1970. *The Japanese challenge.* Philadelphia and New York: J. B. Lippincott Company.

Gurvitch, Georges. 1964. *The spectrum of social time.* Dordrecht, The Netherlands: D. Reidel.

Habermas, Jurgen. 1984. *The theory of communicative action.* Vol. 1, *Reason and the rationalization of society.* Boston: Beacon Press.

Habermas, Jurgen. 1987. *The theory of communicative action.* Vol. 2, *Lifeworld and system: A critique of functionalist reason.* Boston: Beacon Press.

Haferkamp, Hans. 1987. Complexity and behavior structure, planned associations, and creation of structure. In *The micro-macro link,* edited by Jeffrey C. Alexander, Bernard Geisen, Richard Munch and Neil Smelser, 177–92. Berkeley and Los Angeles: University of California Press.

Hage, Jerald. 1980. *Theories of organization.* New York: John Wiley.

Haines, Valerie. 1985. From organicist to relational human ecology. *Sociological Theory* 3:65–74.

Hall, Richard. 1982. *Organizations: Structure and process.* 3d ed. Englewood Cliffs, N.J.: Prentice-Hall.

Hall, Richard. 1983. Theoretical trends in the sociology of occupations. *Sociological Quarterly* 24: 5–23.

Handberg, Roger. 1986. Practicing Western science inside the West: Psychological and institutional parallels between Western and Nonwestern academic cultures. *Social Studies of Science* 16: 529–33.

Hankins, Thomas L. 1979. In defence of biography: The use of biography in the history of science. *History of Science* 17: 1–16.

Harvey, Lee. 1982. The use and abuse of Kuhnian paradigms in the sociology of knowledge. *British Journal of Sociology* 16: 85–101.

Harvey, Lee. 1987. The nature of "schools" in the sociology of knowledge: The case of the "Chicago School." *Sociological Review* 35: 245–78.

Hayes, Adrian. 1985. Causal and interpretive analysis in sociology. *Sociological Theory* 3: 1–10.

Heberle, Rudolph. 1965. Simmel's methods. In *Georg Simmel,* edited by Lewis Coser, 116–21. Englewood Cliffs, N.J.: Prentice-Hall.

Hechter, Michael. 1983a. A theory of group solidarity. In *The microfoundations of macrosociology,* edited by Michael Hechter, 16–57. Philadelphia: Temple University Press.

Hechter, Michael. 1983b. Introduction to *The microfoundations of macrosociology,* edited by Michael Hechter, 3–15. Philadelphia: Temple University Press.

Hechter, Michael. 1987. *Principles of group solidarity.* Berkeley and Los Angeles: University of California Press.

Hekman, Susan. 1983. *Weber, the ideal type, and contemporary social theory.* Notre Dame, Ind.: University of Notre Dame Press.

Helle, H. J., and S. N. Eisenstadt, eds. 1985. *Micro-sociological theory: Perspectives on sociological theory.* Vol. 2. London: Sage.

Heller, Agnes. 1976. *The theory of need in Marx.* New York: St. Martin's.

Henry, Michel. 1983. *Marx: A philosophy of human reality.* Bloomington, Ind.: Indiana University Press.

Heritage, John. 1984. *Garfinkel and ethnomethodology.* Cambridge, England: Polity Press.

Heritage, John, and J. Maxwell Atkinson. 1984. Introduction to *Structures of social actions,* edited by John Heritage and J. Maxwell Atkinson, 1–15. Cambridge: Cambridge University Press.

Heritage, John, and David Greatbatch. 1986. Generating applause: A study of rhetoric and response in party political conferences. *American Journal of Sociology* 92:110–57.

Hilbert, Richard A. 1986. Anomie and moral regulation of reality: The Durkheimian tradition in modern relief. *Sociological Theory* 4: 1–19.

Hilbert, Richard A. 1987. Bureaucracy as belief, rationalization as repair: Max Weber in a post-functionalist age. *Sociological Theory* 5: 47–69.

Hill, Lester, Jr., and Douglas Lee Eckberg. 1981. Clarifying confusions about paradigms: A reply to Ritzer. *American Sociological Review* 46: 248–52.

Hindess, Barry. 1986. Actors and social relations. In *Sociological theory in transition,* edited by Mark L. Wardell and Stephen Turner, 113–26. Boston: Allen and Unwin.

Hinkle, Roscoe. 1963. Antecedents of the action orientation in American sociology before 1935. *American Sociological Review* 28: 705–15.

Hirsch, Paul, Stuart Michaels, and Ray Friedman. 1987. "Dirty hands" versus "clean models": Is sociology in danger of being seduced by economics? *Theory and Society* 16: 317–36.

Holmes, F. L. 1981. The fine structure of scientific creativity. *History of Science* 19: 60–70.

Holzner, Burkhart, and John H. Marx. 1979. *Knowledge application: The knowledge system in society.* Boston: Allyn and Bacon.

Homans, George. 1961/1974. *Social behavior: Its elementary forms.* New York: Harcourt Brace Jovanovich.

Homans, George. 1969. The sociological relevance of behaviorism. In *Behavioral sociology,* edited by Robert Burgess and Don Bushell, 1–24. New York: Columbia University Press.

Homans, George. 1971. Commentary. In *Institutions and social exchange,* edited by Herman Turk and Richard Simpson, 363–74. Indianapolis, Ind.: Bobbs-Merrill.

Homans, George. 1984. *Coming to my senses: The autobiography of a sociologist.* New Brunswick, N.J.: Transaction Books.

Horowitz, Irving Louis. 1983. *C. Wright Mills: An American utopian.* New York: Free Press.

Huaco, George. 1986. Ideology and general theory: The case of sociological functionalism. *Comparative Studies in Society and History* 28:34–54.

Huber, Joan. 1990. Macro-micro links in gender stratification. *American Sociological Review* 55: 1–10.

Hughes, Everett C. 1958. *Men and their work.* Glencoe, Ill.: Free Press.

Hunter, J. E., and F.L. Schmidt. 1989. *Methods of meta analysis: Correcting error and bias in research findings.* Newbury Park, Calif.: Sage.

Hunter, J.E., F.L. Schmidt, and G.B. Jackson. 1982. *Meta-analysis: Cumulating research findings across studies.* Beverly Hills, Calif.: Sage.

Israel, Joachim. 1971. *Alienation: From Marx to modern sociology.* Boston: Allyn and Bacon.

Iwata, Ryuahi. 1982. *Japanese-style management: Its foundations and prospects.* Tokyo: Asian Productivity Organization.

Jackman, M.R., and R.W. Jackman. 1973. An interpretation of the relation between objective and subjective social status. *American Sociological Review* 38: 569–82.

Jameson, Fredric. 1984. Postmodernism, or cultural logic of late capitalism. *New Left Review* 146: 53–93.

Jasanoff, Sheila S. 1987. Contested boundaries in policy-relevant science. *Social Studies of Science* 17: 195–230.

Johnson, Chalmers. 1982. *MITI and the Japanese miracle.* Stanford, Calif.: Stanford University Press.

Johnson, Terence. 1972. *The professions and power.* London: Macmillan.

Jones, Robert Alun. 1977. On understanding a sociological classic. *American Journal of Sociology* 83: 279–319.

Jones, Robert Alun. 1978. Subjectivity, objectivity, and historicity: A response to Johnson. *American Journal of Sociology* 84: 175–81.

Jones, Robert Alun. 1981. Review essay: On Quentin Skinner. *American Journal of Sociology* 87: 453–67.

Jones, Robert Alun. 1983a. The new history of sociology. *Annual Review of Sociology* 9: 447–69.

Jones, Robert Alun. 1983b. On Merton's "history" and "systematics" of sociological theory. In *Functions and uses of disciplinary histories,* edited by Loren Graham, Wolf Lepenies, and Peter Weingart, 8: 121–42. Dordrecht, The Netherlands: D. Reidel.

Jones, Robert Alun. 1985. Presentism, anachronism, and continuity in the history of sociology: A reply to Seidman. *History of Sociology* 6: 153–60.

Kalberg, Stephen. 1980. "Max Weber's types of rationality: Cornerstones for the analysis of rationalization processes in history. *American Journal of Sociology* 85: 1145–79.

Kalberg, Stephen. 1983. Max Weber's universal-historical architectonic of economically-oriented action: A preliminary construction. In *Current Perspectives in social theory,* edited by Scott McNall, 4:253–88. Greenwich, Conn.: JAI Press.

Karady, Victor. 1983. The Durkheimians in academe: A reconsideration. In *The sociological domain,* edited by Philippe Besnard, 71–89. Cambridge: Cambridge University Press.

Kautsky, Karl. 1927/1978. *The materialist conception of history.* New Haven: Yale University Press.

Kellner, Douglas. 1988. Postmodernism as social theory: Some challenges and problems. *Theory, Culture and Society* 5:239–69.

Kellner, Douglas. 1990. The postmodern turn: Positions, problems, and prospects. In *Frontiers of social theory: The new syntheses,* edited by George Ritzer, 255–86. New York: Columbia University Press.

Kemeny, Jim. 1976. Perspectives on the micro-macro distinction. *Sociological Review* 24: 731–52.

Kirk, Jerome, and Marc. L. Miller. 1986. *Reliability and validity in qualitative research.* Newbury Park, Calif.: Sage.

Klegon, Douglas. 1978. The sociology of professions: An emerging perspective. *Sociology of Work and Occupations* 5: 259–83.

Knorr-Cetina, Karin D. 1981a. Introduction: The micro-sociological challenge of macro-sociology: Towards a reconstruction of social theory and methodology. In *Advances in social theory and methodology,* edited by Karin Knorr-Cetina and Aaron Cicourel, 1–47. New York: Methuen.

Knorr-Cetina, Karin D. 1981b. *The manufacture of knowledge: An essay on the constructivist and contextual nature of science.* Oxford: Pergamon Press.

Knox, John. 1963. The concept of exchange in sociological theory: 1884 and 1961. *Social Forces* 41: 341–46.

Korenbaum, Mildred. 1964. Translator's preface to *The spectrum of social time,* by George Gurvitch. Dordrecht, The Netherlands: D. Reidel.

Koselleck, Reinhart. 1985. *Futures past: On the semantics of historical time.* Cambridge: MIT Press.

Kotarba, Joseph A., and Andrea Fontana, eds. 1984. *The existential self in society.* Chicago: University of Chicago Press.

Kreps, Gary A. 1985. Disaster and the social order. *Sociological Theory* 3: 49–64.

Kuhn, Thomas. 1962. *The structure of scientific revolutions.* Chicago: University of Chicago Press.

Kuhn, Thomas. 1970a. Reflections on my critics. In *Criticism and the growth of knowledge,* edited by Imre Lakatos and Alan Musgrave, 231–78. Cambridge: Cambridge University Press.

Kuhn, Thomas. 1970b. *The structure of scientific revolutions.* 2d ed. Chicago: University of Chicago Press.

Kurzweil, Edith. 1980. *The age of structuralism: Levi-Strauss to Foucault.* New York: Columbia University Press.

Kurzweil, Edith. 1987. Psychoanalysis as the macro-micro link. In *The micro-macro link,* edited by Jeffrey C. Alexander, Bernard Giesen, Richard Munch, and Neil Smelser, 237–54. Berkeley and Los Angeles: University of California Press.

Kyle, David. 1989. Beyond seduction: Sociology, economics, and development. Paper presented at the Conference on Socio-Economics at the Harvard Business School, 31 March–2 April 1989.

Lakatos, Imre. 1978. *The methodology of scientific research programs.* Cambridge: Cambridge University Press.

Lamont, Michelle. 1987. How to become a dominant French philosopher: The case of Jacques Derrida. *American Journal of Sociology* 93: 584–622.

Lamont, Michelle, and Robert Wuthnow. 1990. Betwixt and between: Recent cultural sociology in Europe and the United States. In *Frontiers of social theory: The new syntheses,* edited by George Ritzer, 287–315. New York: Columbia University Press.

Laudan, Larry. 1977. *Progress and its problems: Toward a theory of scientific growth.* Berkeley and Los Angeles: University of California Press.

Layder, Derek. 1985. Power, structure, and agency. *Journal for the Theory of Social Behaviour* 15: 131–49.

Lefebvre, Henri. 1968. *The sociology of Marx.* New York: Vintage.

Lehman, Edward W. 1988. The theory of the state versus the state of theory. *American Sociological Review* 53: 807–23.

Leinhart, Samuel. 1977. *Social networks: A developing paradigm.* New York: Academic Press.

Lemert, Charles. 1990. The uses of French structuralisms in sociology. In *Frontiers of social theory: The new syntheses,* edited by George Ritzer, 230–54. New York: Columbia University Press.

Lengermann, Patricia Madoo. 1979. The founding of the *American Sociological Review. American Sociological Review* 4: 185–98.

Lengermann, Patricia Madoo, and Jill-Niebrugge Brantley. 1988. Contemporary feminist theory. In *Sociological theory,* edited by George Ritzer, 400–443. New York: Alfred A. Knopf.

Lengermann, Patricia Madoo, and Jill-Niebrugge Brantley. 1990. Feminist sociological theory: The near-term prospects. In *Frontiers of social theory: The new syntheses,* edited by George Ritzer, 316–44. New York: Columbia University Press.

Levine, Donald. 1981. Rationality and freedom: Weber and beyond. *Sociological Inquiry* 51: 5–25.

Levine, Donald. 1989. Simmel as a resource for sociological metatheory. *Sociological Theory* 7: 161–74.

Lindenberg, Siegwart, James S. Coleman, and Stefan Nowak, eds. 1986. *Approaches to social theory.* New York: Russell Sage Foundation.

Lodahl, Janice B., and Gerald Gordon. 1972. The structure of scientific fields and the functioning of university graduate departments. *American Sociological Review* 37: 57–72.

Lomnitz, Larissa Adler, Martha W. Rees, and Leon Cameo. 1987. Publication and referencing patterns in a Mexican research institute. *Social Studies of Science* 17: 115–34.

Lovejoy, Arthur. 1936/1960. *The great chain of being: A study of the history of an idea.* New York: Harper Torchbooks.

Lovejoy, Arthur. 1948. *Essays in the history of ideas.* Baltimore: Johns Hopkins University Press.

Luhmann, Niklas. 1987. The evolutionary differentiation between society and interaction. In *The micro-macro link,* edited by Jeffrey C. Alexander, Bernard Giesen, Richard Munch, and Neil Smelser, 112–31. Berkeley and Los Angeles: University of California Press.

Lukacs, Georg. 1922/1968. *History and class consciousness.* Cambridge: MIT Press.

Lukes, Steven. 1973. *Emile Durkheim: His life and work.* New York: Harper & Row.

Lukes, Steven. 1977. Power and structure. In *Essays in social theory,* edited by Steven Lukes, 3–29. London: Macmillan.

Lyotard, Jean-François. 1984. *The postmodern condition.* Minneapolis: University of Minnesota Press.

Macdonald, Keith, and George Ritzer. 1988. The sociology of the professions: Dead or alive? *Work and Occupations* 15: 251–72.

Mackay, Robert W. 1974. Words, utterances, and activities. In *Ethnomethodology: Selected readings,* edited by Roy Turner, 197–215. Harmondsworth, England: Penguin.

MacLeod, Roy, and Kay MacLeod. 1979. The contradictions of professionalism: Scientists, trade unionism; and the First World War. *Social Studies of Science* 9: 1–32.

McMahon, A. M. 1984. The two social psychologies: Postcrises directions. In *Annual review of sociology,* edited by Ralph H. Turner and James F. Short, 10: 121–40. Palo Alto, Calif.: Annual Reviews.

McMillan, Charles J. 1984. *The Japanese industrial system.* Berlin: Walter de Gruyter.

McMurty, John. 1978. *The structure of Marx's world-view.* Princeton, N.J.: Princeton University Press.

McPhail, Clark, and Cynthia Rexroat. 1979. Mead vs. Blumer. *American Sociological Review* 45: 449–67.

McPhail, Clark, and Cynthia Rexroat. 1980. Rejoinder: Ex cathedra Blumer or ex libris Mead? *American Sociological Review* 45: 420–30.

Maines, David. 1982. In search of mesostructure: Studies in the negotiated order. *Urban Life* 11: 267–79.

Mandel, Ernest. 1983. *Introduction to Marxist economic theory.* 2d ed. New York: Pathfinder Press.

Mandelbaum, Maurice. 1965. The history of ideas, intellectual history, and the history of philosophy. In The historiography of the history of philosophy, Beiheft 5. *History and Theory:* 33–66.

Mann, Michael. 1986. *The sources of social power.* Vol. 1. New York: Cambridge University Press.

Mannheim, Karl. 1936. *Ideology and utopia: An introduction to the sociology of knowledge.* New York: Harvest Books.

Marini, Margaret M. 1988. Sociology of gender. In *The future of sociology,* edited by Edgar F. Borgatta and Karen S. Cook, 374–93. Beverly Hills, Calif.: Sage.

Markovsky, Barry. 1985. Multilevel justice theory. *American Sociological Review* 50: 822–39.

Markovsky, Barry. 1987. Toward multilevel sociological theories: Simulations of actor and network effects. *Sociological Theory* 5: 101–17.

Marks, S. R. 1974. Durkheim's theory of anomie. *American Journal of Sociology* 82: 329–63.

Marske, Charles E. 1987. Durkheim's "cult of the individual" and the moral reconstitution of society. *Sociological Theory* 5: 1–14.

Martindale, Don. 1960. *The nature and types of sociological theory.* Boston: Houghton Mifflin.

Martindale, Don. 1979. Ideologies, paradigms, and theories. In *Contemporary issues in theory and research,* edited by William Snizek, Ellsworth Fuhrman, and Michael K. Miller, 7–24. Westport, Conn.: Greenwood Press.

Marx, Karl. 1857–58/1964. *Pre-capitalist economic formations.* New York: International Publishers.

Marx, Karl. 1857–58/1973. *The Grundrisse: Foundations of the critique of political economy.* New York: Random House.

Marx, Karl. 1859/1970. *A contribution to the critique of political economy.* Vol. 1. New York: International Publishers.

Marx, Karl. 1862–63/1963. *Theories of surplus value.* Part 1. Moscow: Progress Publishers.

Marx, Karl. 1862–63/1968. *Theories of surplus value.* Part 2. Moscow: Progress Publishers.

Marx, Karl. 1867/1967. *Capital: A critique of political economy.* Vol. 1. New York: International Publishers.

Marx, Karl. 1932/1964. *The economic and philosophic manuscripts of 1844.* Edited by Dirk J. Struik. New York: International Publishers.

Marx, Karl, and Friedrich Engels. 1845/1956. *The holy family: Or critique of critical critique.* Moscow: Foreign Languages Publishing House.

Marx, Karl, and Friedrich Engels. 1845–46/1970. *The German ideology.* Part 1. Edited by C. J. Arthur. New York: International Publishers.

Masterman, Margaret. 1970. The nature of a paradigm. In *Criticism and the growth of knowledge,* edited by Imre Lakatos and Alan Musgrove, 59–80. Cambridge: Cambridge University Press.

Mauss, Marcel. 1954. *The gift*. London: Cohen and West.

Mayhew, Bruce H. 1980. Structuralism versus individualism: Part 1, Shadowboxing in the dark. *Social Forces* 59: 335–75.

Mayhew, Bruce H. 1981. Structuralism versus individualism: Part 2, Ideological and other obfuscations. *Social Forces* 59: 627–48.

Mazlish, Bruce. 1984. *The meaning of Karl Marx*. New York: Oxford University Press.

Mehan, Hugh, and Houston Wood. 1975. *The reality of ethnomethodology*. New York: John Wiley.

Merton, Robert. 1957. *Social theory and social structure*. Rev. ed. New York: Free Press.

Merton, Robert. 1965. *On the shoulders of giants: A Shandean postscript*. New York: Free Press.

Merton, Robert. 1967. On the "history" and "systematics" of sociological theory. In *On theoretical sociology*, edited by Robert Merton, 1–37. New York: Free Press.

Merton, Robert. 1968. *Social theory and social structure*. Enlarged ed. New York: Free Press.

Merton, Robert. 1985. The historicist/presentism dilemma: A composite imputation and a foreknowing response. *History of Sociology* 6: 137–51.

Merton, Robert. 1986. Comments. In *Approaches to social theory*, edited by Siegwart Lindenberg, James S. Coleman, and Stefan Nowak, 61–62. New York: Russell Sage Foundation.

Messner, Steven F. 1986. Modernization, structural characteristics, and societal rates of crime: An application of Blau's macrosociological theory. *Sociological Quarterly* 27: 27–41.

Meszaros, Istvan. 1970. *Marx's theory of alienation*. New York: Harper Torchbooks.

Missner, Marshall. 1985. Why Einstein became famous in America. *Social Studies of Science* 15: 267–92.

Mitroff, Ian. 1974. Norms and counter-norms in a select group of Apollo moon scientists: A case study of the ambivalence of scientists. *American Sociological Review* 39: 579–95.

Mitzman, Arthur. 1969. *The iron cage: An historical interpretation of Max Weber*. New York: Grosset and Dunlap.

Mizruchi, Mark S., and Koenig, Thomas. 1986. Economic sources of corporate political consensus: An examination of interindustry relations. *American Sociological Review* 51: 482–91.

Mommsen, Wolfgang J. 1974. *The age of bureaucracy: Perspectives on the political sociology of Max Weber*. New York: Harper and Row.

Monk, Richard, ed. 1986. *Structures of knowing*. Lanham, Md.: University Press of America.

Morris, Monica. 1977. *Excursion into creative sociology*. New York: Columbia University Press.

Mulkay, Michael, and G. Nigel Gilbert. 1982. Joking apart: Some recommendations concerning the analysis of scientific culture. *Social Studies of Science* 12: 585–614.

Mulligan, G., and B. Lederman. 1977. Social facts and rules of practice. *American Journal of Sociology* 83: 539–50.

Mullins, Nicholas. 1973. *Theories and theory groups in contemporary American sociology.* New York: Harper and Row.

Mullins, Nicholas. 1983. Theories and theory groups revisited. In *Sociological theory—1983,* edited by Randall Collins, 319–37. San Francisco: Jossey-Bass.

Munch, Richard. 1987. The interpenetration of microinteraction and macrostructures in a complex and contingent institutional order. In *The micro-macro link,* edited by Jeffrey C. Alexander, Bernard Giesen, Richard Munch, and Neil Smelser, 319–36. Berkeley and Los Angeles: University of California Press.

Munch, Richard. 1989. Code, structure, and action: Building a theory of structuration from a Parsonsian point of view. In *Theory building in sociology,* edited by Jonathan Turner, 101–18. Newbury Park, Calif.: Sage.

Munch, Richard, and Neil Smelser. 1987. Relating the micro and macro. In *The micro-macro link,* edited by Jeffrey C. Alexander et al., 356–87. Berkeley and Los Angeles: University of California Press.

Needham, Rodney. 1963. Introduction to *Primitive classification,* by Emile Durkheim and Marcel Mauss. Chicago: University of Chicago Press.

Nicolaus, Martin. 1973. Foreword to *The Grundrisse: Foundations of the critique of political economy,* by Karl Marx. New York: Random House.

Nisbet, Robert. 1967. *The sociological tradition.* New York: Basic Books.

Nisbet, Robert. 1974. *The sociology of Emile Durkheim.* New York: Oxford University Press.

Noblit, George W., and R. Dwight Hare. 1988. *Meta-ethnography: Synthesizing qualitative studies.* Newbury Park, Calif.: Sage.

Oakes, Guy. 1975. Introductory essay to *Roscher and Knies: The logical problems of historical economics,* by Max Weber. New York: Free Press.

Oakes, Guy. 1984. The problem of women in Simmel's theory of culture. In *On women, sexuality, and love,* by Georg Simmel, 3–62. New Haven, Conn.: Yale University Press.

Oldroyd, David R. 1986. Grid/group analysis for historians of science? *History of Science* 24: 145–71.

Ollman, Bertell. 1971. *Alienation.* Cambridge: Cambridge University Press.

Ollman, Bertell. 1976. *Alienation.* 2d ed. Cambridge: Cambridge University Press.

Osterberg, Dag. 1988. *Metasociology: An inquiry into the origins and validity of social thought.* Oslo, Norway: Norwegian University Press.

Overington, Michael A. 1979. Doing what comes rationally: Some developments in metatheory. *American Sociologist* 14: 2–12.

Parsons, Talcott. 1937/1949. *The structure of social action.* 2d ed. New York: Free Press.

Parsons, Talcott. 1954a. The present position and prospects of systematic theory in sociology. In *Essays in sociological theory,* by Talcott Parsons, 212–37. New York: Free Press.

Parsons, Talcott. 1954b. The prospects of sociological theory. In *Essays in sociological theory,* by Talcott Parsons, 348–69. New York: Free Press.

Parsons, Talcott. 1961a. Comment. *American Journal of Sociology* 47: 136–40.

Parsons, Talcott. 1961b. Some considerations on the theory of social change. *Rural Sociology* 26: 219–39.

Parsons, Talcott. 1964. Levels of organization and the mediation of social inter-action. *Sociological Inquiry* 34: 207–20.

Parsons, Talcott. 1966. *Societies.* Englewood Cliffs, N.J.: Prentice-Hall.

Parsons, Talcott. 1971. *The system of modern societies.* Englewood Cliffs, N.J.: Prentice-Hall.

Parsons, Talcott. 1979. On theory and metatheory. *Humboldt Journal of Social Relations* 7: 5–16.

Parsons, Talcott, and Edward A. Shils, eds. 1951. *Toward a general theory of action.* Cambridge: Harvard University Press.

Pegels, Carl C. 1984. *Japan vs. the West: Implications for management.* Boston: Kluwer-Nijhoff.

Phillips, Derek. 1973. Paradigms, falsifications, and sociology. *Acta Sociologica* 16: 13–31.

Picou, J. Steven, Evans W. Lurry, and Richard Wells. 1990. Partial paradigm shifts and the social sciences: Twenty years of research in rural sociology. *Rural Sociology* 55: 101–11.

Picou, J. Steven, Richard H. Wells, and Kenneth L. Nyberg. 1978. Paradigms, theories, and methods in contemporary rural sociology. *Rural Sociology* 43: 559–83.

Platt, Jennifer. 1986. Functionalism and the survey: The relation of theory and method. *Sociological Review* 34:501–36.

Podgorecki, Adam, and Maria Los. 1979. *Multi-dimensional sociology.* London: Routledge and Kegan Paul.

Polit, Denise F., and Toni Falbo. 1987. Only children and personality develop-ment: A quantitative review. *Journal of Marriage and the Family* 49:309–25.

Pope, Whitney. 1973. Classic on classic: Parsons' interpretation of Durkheim. *American Sociological Review* 38: 399–415.

Pope, Whitney. 1975. Durkheim as functionalist. *Sociological Quarterly* 16: 361–79.

Pope, Whitney. 1976. *Durkheim's "Suicide": A classic analyzed.* Chicago: University of Chicago Press.

Pope, Whitney, and Jere Cohen. 1978. On R. Stephen Warner's "Toward a re-definition of action theory": Paying the cognitive element its due. *American Journal of Sociology* 83: 1359–67.

Pope, Whitney, Jere Cohen, and Lawrence Hazelrigg. 1975. On the divergence of Weber and Durkheim: A critique of Parsons' convergence thesis. *American Sociological Review* 40: 417–27.

Porpora, Douglas. 1989. Four concepts of social structure. *Journal for the Theory of Social Behaviour* 19: 195–211.

Price, Derek J. De Solla. 1963. *Little science, big science.* New York: Columbia University Press.

Radnitzky, Gerard. 1973. *Contemporary schools of metascience.* Chicago: Henry Regnery.

Rattansi, Ali. 1982. *Marx and the division of labour.* London: Macmillan.

Ritzer, George. 1975a. The emerging power perspective in the sociological study of the professions. Paper presented at the meetings of the American Socio-logical Association, San Francisco, Calif., 1975.

Ritzer, George. 1975b. Professionalization, bureaucratization, and rationalization: The views of Max Weber. *Social Forces* 53: 627–34.

Ritzer, George. 1975c. *Sociology: A multiple paradigm science.* Boston: Allyn and Bacon.

Ritzer, George. 1975d. Sociology: A multiple paradigm science. *American Sociologist* 10: 156–67.

Ritzer, George. 1979. Toward an integrated sociological paradigm. In *Contemporary issues in theory and research,* edited by William Snizek, Ellsworth Fuhrman, and Michael K. Miller, 24–46. Westport, Conn.: Greenwood Press.

Ritzer, George. 1980. *Sociology: A multiple paradigm science,* Rev. ed. Boston: Allyn and Bacon.

Ritzer, George. 1981a. Paradigm analysis in sociology: Clarifying the issues. *American Sociological Review* 46: 245–48.

Ritzer, George. 1981b. *Toward an integrated paradigm: The search for an exemplar and an image of the subject matter.* Boston: Allyn and Bacon.

Ritzer, George. 1983. The McDonaldization of society. *Journal of American Culture* 6: 100–107.

Ritzer, George. 1985. The rise of micro-sociological theory. *Sociological Theory* 3: 88–98.

Ritzer, George. 1987. The current state of metatheory. *Sociological Perspectives: The Theory Section Newsletter* 10: 1–6.

Ritzer, George. 1988a. The micro-macro link: Problems and prospects. *Contemporary Sociology* 17: 703–6.

Ritzer, George. 1988b. Sociological metatheory: Defending a subfield by delineating its parameters. *Sociological Theory* 6: 187–200.

Ritzer, George. 1988c. *Sociological theory.* New York: Alfred A. Knopf.

Ritzer, George. 1989a. Metatheorizing as a prelude to theory development. Paper presented at the meetings of the American Sociological Association, San Francisco, Calif.

Ritzer, George. 1989b. The new economy? The perpetually new economy: The case for the resuscitation of economic sociology. *Work and Occupations* 16: 243–72.

Ritzer, George. 1989c. Of levels and "intellectual amnesia." *Sociological Theory* 7: 226–229.

Ritzer, George. 1989d. The sociology of work: A metatheoretical analysis. *Social Forces* 67: 593–604.

Ritzer, George. 1990a. The current status of sociological theory: The new syntheses. In *Frontiers of social theory: The new syntheses,* edited by George Ritzer, 1–30. New York: Columbia University Press.

Ritzer, George. 1990b. Micro-macro linkage in sociological theory: Applying a metatheoretical tool. In *Frontiers of social theory, The new syntheses,* edited by George Ritzer, 347–70. New York: Columbia University Press.

Ritzer, George, ed. 1990c. Symposium: Metatheory its uses and abuses in contemporary sociology. *Sociological Forum* 5: 1–74.

Ritzer, George. 1990d. "Metatheorizing in sociology." *Sociological Forum* 5: 3–15.

Ritzer, George. 1991a. The recent history and the emerging reality of American sociological theory. *Sociological Forum,* forthcoming.

Ritzer, George. 1991b. *Studies in sociological metatheorizing.* Newbury Park: Calif.: Sage, forthcoming.

Ritzer, George, and Richard Bell. 1981. Emile Durkheim: Exemplar for an integrated sociological paradigm. *Social Forces* 59: 966–95.

Ritzer, George, and David Walczak. 1986. *Working: Conflict and change*. 3d ed. Englewood Cliffs, N.J.: Prentice-Hall.

Ritzer, George, and David Walczak. 1988. Rationalization and the deprofessionalization of physicians. *Social Forces* 67: 1–22.

Ritzer, George, and Terri LeMoyne. 1990. Hyperrationality and the rise of Japanese industry: An application of neo-Weberian theory. Paper presented at the meetings of the International Sociological Association, Madrid, Spain, 1990.

Rock, Paul. 1979. *The making of symbolic interactionism*. Totowa, N.J.: Rowman and Littlefield.

Roemer, John. 1982. Methodological individualism and deductive Marxism. *Theory and Society* 11: 513–20.

Roemer, John. 1986. *Analytical Marxism*. Cambridge: Cambridge University Press.

Rohlen, Thomas P. 1975. The company work group. In *Modern Japanese organization and decision making*, edited by Ezra Vogel, 185–209. Berkeley and Los Angeles: University of California Press.

Rosenberg, Alexander. 1988. *Philosophy of social science*. Boulder, Colo.: Westview Press.

Rosenberg, Morris. 1989. Self-concept research: A historical review. *Social Forces* 68: 34–44.

Rossi, Ino. 1983. *From the sociology of symbols to the sociology of signs*. New York: Columbia University Press.

Rothenberg, Albert. 1987. Einstein, Bohr, and Creative Thinking in Science. *History of Science* 25: 147–66.

Rubenstein, David. 1986. The concept of structure in sociology. In *Sociological theory in transition*, edited by Mark L. Wardell and Stephen P. Turner, 80–94. Boston: Allen and Unwin.

Salas, Charles G. 1987. Collingwood's historical principles at work. *History and Theory* 26: 53–71.

Schegloff, Emanuel. 1987. Between macro and micro: Contexts and other connections. In *The micro-macro link*, edited by Jeffrey C. Alexander, Bernard Giesen, Richard Munch, and Neil Smelser, 207–34. Berkeley and Los Angeles: University of California Press.

Schluchter, Wolfgang. 1981. *The rise of western rationalism: Max Weber's developmental history*. Berkeley and Los Angeles: University of California Press.

Schmitt, Neal, Richard Z. Gooding, Raymond A. Noe, and Michael Kirsch. 1984. Meta-analyses of validity studies published between 1964 and 1982 and the investigation of study characteristics. *Personnel Psychology* 37: 407–22.

Schonberger, Richard J. 1982. *Japanese manufacturing techniques*. New York: Free Press.

Schulin, Ernst. 1981. German "Geistesgeschichte," American "intellectual history," and French "histoire des mentalites" since 1900: A comparison. *History of European Ideas* 1: 195–214.

Schutz, Alfred. 1932/1967. *The phenomonology of the social world*. Evanston, Ill.: Northwestern University Press.

Schutz, Alfred. 1962. *Collected papers 1: The problem of social reality*. The Hague: Martinus Nijhoff.

Schutz, Alfred. 1964. *Collected papers 2: Studies in social theory.* The Hague: Martinus Nijhoff.

Schutz, Alfred. 1966. *Collected papers 3: Studies in phenomenological philosophy.* The Hague: Martinus Nijhoff.

Sciulli, David. 1986. Voluntaristic action as a distinct concept: Theoretical foundations of societal constitutionalism. *American Sociological Review* 51: 743–66.

Secord, James A. 1986. The geological survey of Great Britain as a research school, 1839–1855. *History of Science* 24: 223–75.

Secord, Paul F., ed. 1982. *Explaining human behavior: Consciousness, human action, and social structure.* Beverly Hills, Calif.: Sage.

Seidman, Steven. 1983. *Liberalism and the origins of European social theory.* Berkeley and Los Angeles: University of California Press.

Seidman, Steven. 1985. Classics and contemporaries: The history and systematics of sociology revisited. *History of Sociology* 6: 121–35.

Shalin, Dimitri. 1986. Pragmatism and social interactionism. *American Sociological Review* 51: 9–29.

Shapin, Steven. 1982. History of science and its sociological reconstructions. *History of Science* 20: 157–211.

Sharrock, Wes, and Bob Anderson. 1986. *The ethnomethodologists.* Chichester, England: Ellis Horwood.

Sheridan, Alan. 1980. *Michel Foucault: The will to truth.* London: Tavistock.

Shils, Edward. 1970. Tradition, ecology, and institution in the history of sociology. *Daedalus* 99: 760–825.

Sica, Alan. 1983. Parsons, Jr. *American Journal of Sociology* 89: 200–219.

Simmel, Georg. 1907/1978. *The philosophy of money.* London: Routledge and Kegan Paul.

Simmel, Georg. 1908/1950. Subordination under a principle. In *The sociology of Georg Simmel,* edited by Kurt Wolff, 250–67. New York: Free Press.

Simmel, Georg. 1908/1959. The problem of sociology. In *Essays in sociology, philosophy, and aesthetics,* edited by Kurt Wolff, 310–36. New York: Harper Torchbooks.

Simmel, Georg. 1908/1971. Subjective culture. In *Georg Simmel,* edited by Donald Levine, 227–34. Chicago: University of Chicago Press.

Simmel, Georg. 1911/1968. On the concept and the tragedy of culture. In *Georg Simmel: The conflict in modern culture and other essays,* edited by K. Peter Etzkorn, 27–46. New York: Teachers College, Columbia University.

Simmel, Georg. 1921/1968. The conflict in modern culture. In *George Simmel: The conflict in modern culture and other essays,* edited by K. Peter Etzkorn, 11–25. New York: Teachers College, Columbia University.

Simpson, George. 1964. Introduction to *The rules of sociological method,* by Emile Durkheim. New York: Free Press.

Simpson, Ida Harper. 1989. Sociology of work: Where have the workers gone? *Social Forces* 67: 563–81.

Singelmann, Peter. 1972. Exchange as symbolic interaction. *American Sociological Review* 38: 414–24.

Skinner, B.F. 1971. *Beyond freedom and dignity.* New York: Alfred A. Knopf.

Skinner, Quentin. 1969. Meaning and understanding in the history of ideas. *History and Theory* 8: 3–53.

Skinner, Quentin. 1974. Some problems in the analysis of political thought and action. *Political Theory* 2: 277–303.

Skinner, Quentin. 1975–76. Hermeneutics and the role of history. *New Literary History* 7: 209–32.

Skinner, Quentin. 1978. *The foundations of modern political thought*. Vol. 1, *The Renaissance*. London: Cambridge University Press.

Skocpol, Theda. 1979. *States and social revolutions*. Cambridge: Cambridge University Press.

Skocpol, Theda. 1986. The dead end of metatheory. *Contemporary Sociology* 16: 10–12.

Smelser, Neil. 1987. Depth psychology and the social order. In *The micro-macro link*, edited by Jeffrey C. Alexander, Bernard Giesen, Richard Munch, and Neil Smelser, 267–86. Berkeley and Los Angeles: University of California Press.

Smelser, Neil. 1988. Sociological Theory: Looking forward. *Perspectives: The Theory Section Newsletter* 11: 1–3.

Smelser, Neil. 1989. External influences on sociology. *International Sociology* 4: 414–29.

Snizek, William. 1976. An empirical assessment of "sociology: A multiple paradigm science." *American Sociologist* 11: 217–19.

Snizek, William. 1979. Toward a clarification of the interrelationship between theory and research: Its form and implications. In *Contemporary issues in theory and research*, edited by William Snizek, Ellsworth Fuhrman, and Michael K. Miller, 197–209. Westport, Conn.: Greenwood Press.

Snizek, William, Ellsworth Fuhrman, and Michael K. Miller. 1979. Introduction to *Contemporary issues in theory and research*, edited by William Snizek, Ellsworth Fuhrman, and Michael K. Miller, vii–ix. Westport, Conn.: Greenwood Press.

Sorokin, Pitirim. 1928. *Contemporary sociological theories*. New York: Harper Brothers.

Sorokin, Pitirim. 1956. *Fads and foibles in modern sociology and related sciences*. Chicago: Regnery.

Spencer, Herbert. 1904. *An autobiography*. 2 vols. New York: D. Appleton and Co.

Staats, Arthur. 1976. Skinnerian behaviorism: Social behaviorism or radical behaviorism? *American Sociologist* 11: 59–60.

Stewart, David W. 1984. *Secondary research: Information, sources, and methods*. Beverly Hills, CA: Sage.

Stinchcombe, Arthur. 1986. The development of scholasticism. In *Approaches to social theory*, edited by Siegwart Lindenberg, James S. Coleman, and Stefan Nowak, 45–51. New York: Russell Sage Foundation.

Strasser, Hermann. 1976. *The normative structure of sociology*. London: Routledge and Kegan Paul.

Sutherland, Gillian, and Stephen Sharp. 1980. "The fust official psychologist in the wurrld." *History of Science* 18: 181–208.

Swartz, David. 1990. The reflexive sociologies of Pierre Bourdieu and Alvin Gouldner and metatheorizing in sociology. Paper presented at Miniconference on Metatheorizing in Sociology at the Meetings of the American Sociological Association, Washington, D.C., August 1990.

Swedberg, Richard. 1987. Economic sociology: Past and present. *Current Sociology* 35: 1–221.

Swedberg, Richard. 1989. Socioeconomics and the new methodenstreit: On the paradigmatic struggle in contemporary economics. Paper presented at the conference on Socio-Economics at the Harvard Business School, 31 March–2 April, 1989.

Swedberg, Richard, Ulf Himmelstrand, and Goran Brulin. 1987. The paradigm of economic sociology: Premises and promises. *Theory and Society* 16: 169–213.

Swidler, Ann. 1986. Culture in action: Symbols and strategies. *American Sociological Review* 51: 273–86.

Swingewood, Alan. 1975. *Marx and modern social theory.* New York: John Wiley and Sons.

Sztompka, Piotr. 1989. Human agency: The Marxian tradition and beyond. Paper presented at conference, Social Theory and Human Agency, The Swedish Collegium for Advanced Study in the Social Sciences, Uppsala, Sweden, 29 September–1 October 1989.

Tarter, Donald. 1973. Heeding Skinner's call: Toward the development of a social technology. *American Sociologist* 8: 153–58.

Taylor, Jared. 1983. *Shadows of the rising sun.* New York: Random House.

Tendzin, Takla, and Whitney Pope. 1985. The force imagery in Durkheim: The integration of theory, metatheory, and method. *Sociological Theory* 3: 74–88.

Thomason, Burke C. 1982. *Making sense of reification: Alfred Schutz and constructionist theory.* Atlantic Highlands, N.J.: Humanities Press.

Tilman, Rick. 1984. *C. Wright Mills: A native radical and his intellectual roots.* University Park: Pennsylvania State University Press.

Timasheff, Nicholas. 1967. *Sociological theory: Its nature and growth.* 2d ed. New York: Random House.

Tiryakian, Edward A. 1962. *Sociologism and existentialism: Two perspectives on the individual and society.* Englewood Cliffs, N.J.: Prentice-Hall.

Tiryakian, Edward A. 1979. The significance of schools in the development of sociology. In *Contemporary issues in theory and research,* edited by William Snizek, Ellsworth Fuhrman, and Michael K. Miller, 211–33. Westport, Conn.: Greenwood Press.

Tiryakian, Edward A. 1986. Hegemonic schools and the development of sociology: Rethinking the history of the discipline. In *Structures of knowing,* edited by Richard C. Monk, 417–41. Lanham, Md.: University Press of America.

Tiryakian, Edward A. 1988. Durkheim, Mathiez, and the French revolution: The political context of a sociological classic. *European Journal of Sociology* 29: 373–96.

Tominaga, Ken' ichi. 1989. Max Weber on Chinese and Japanese social structure. In *Cross-national research on sociology,* edited by Melvin L. Kohn, 125–146. Newbury Park, CA: Sage.

Touraine, Alain. 1977. *The self-production of society.* Chicago: University of Chicago Press.

Tribe, Keith. 1985. Translator's introduction to *Futures past: On the semantics of historical time,* by Reinhart Koselleck. Cambridge: MIT Press.

Turner, Jonathan H. 1984. *Societal stratification: A theoretical analysis.* New York: Columbia University Press.

Turner, Jonathan. 1985. In defense of positivism. *Sociological Theory* 3: 24–30.

Turner, Jonathan. 1987. Toward a sociological theory of motivation. *American Sociological Review* 52: 15–27.

Turner, Jonathan. 1989. Can sociology be a cumulative science? Introduction to *Theory building in sociology: Assessing theoretical cumulation,* edited by Jonathan Turner, 8–18. Newbury Park, Calif.: Sage.

Turner, Jonathan. 1990a. The misuse and use of metatheory. *Sociological Forum* 5: 37–53.

Turner, Jonathan. 1990b. The past, present, and future of theory in American Sociology. In *Frontiers of social theory: The new syntheses,* edited by George Ritzer, 371–91. New York: Columbia University Press.

Turner, Jonathan. 1991. *The structure of sociological theory.* 5th ed. Belmont, Calif.: Wadsworth.

Turner, Jonathan, and A. Z. Maryanski. 1978. *Functionalism: An intellectual portrait.* Palo Alto, Calif.: Cummings.

Turner, Jonathan, and A. Z. Maryanski. 1988a. Is "neofunctionalism" really functional? *Sociological Theory* 6: 110–21.

Turner, Jonathan, and A. Z. Maryanski. 1988b. Sociology's lost human relations area files. *Sociological Perspectives* 31: 19–34.

Turner, R. Steven. 1987. Paradigms and productivity: The case of physiological optics, 1840–94. *Social Studies of Science* 7: 35–68.

Udehn, Lars. 1981. The conflict between methodology and rationalization in the work of Max Weber. *Acta Sociologica* 24: 131–47.

Venable, Vernon. 1945. *Human nature: The Marxian view.* New York: Alfred A. Knopf.

Vidich, Arthur J., and Stanford M. Lyman. 1985. *American sociology: Worldly rejections of religion and their directions.* New Haven: Yale University Press.

Vogel, Ezra F. 1979. *Japan as number one: Lessons for America.* New York: Harper and Row.

Wagner, David. 1984. *The growth of sociological theories.* Beverly Hills, Calif.: Sage.

Wagner, David, and Joseph Berger. 1985. Do sociological theories grow? *American Journal of Sociology* 90: 697–728.

Wagner, Helmut. 1964. Displacement of scope: A problem of the relationship between small-scale and large-scale sociological theories. *American Journal of Sociology* 69: 571–84.

Wallace, Walter. 1969. Overview of contemporary sociological theory. In *Sociological theory,* edited by Walter Wallace, 1–59. Chicago: Aldine.

Wallace, Walter. 1988. Toward a disciplinary matrix in sociology. In *Handbook of sociology,* edited by Neil Smelser, 23–76. Newbury Park, Calif.: Sage.

Wallerstein, Immanuel. 1974. *The modern world-system: Capitalist agriculture and the origins of the European world-economy in the 16th century.* New York: Academic Press.

Wallerstein, Immanuel. 1980. *The modern world-system 2: Mercantilism and the consolidation of the European world-economy, 1600–1750.* New York: Academic Press.

Wallerstein, Immanuel. 1989. *The modern world-system 3: The second era of great expansion of the capitalist world-economy, 1730–1840.* New York: Academic Press.

Walliman, Isidor. 1981. *Estrangement: Marx's conception of human nature and the division of labor.* Westport, Conn.: Greenwood Press.

Wallwork, Ernest. 1972. *Durkheim: Morality and milieu.* Cambridge: Harvard University Press.

Warriner, K. Charles. 1956. Groups are real: A reaffirmation. *American Sociological Review* 21: 549–54.

Warriner, K. Charles. 1970. *The emergence of society.* Homewood, Ill.: Dorsey.

Weber, Max. 1903–6/1975. *Roscher and Knies: The logical problems of historical economics.* New York: Free Press.

Weber, Max. 1903–17/1949. *The methodology of the social sciences.* New York: Free Press.

Weber, Max. 1904–5/1958. *The Protestant ethic and the spirit of capitalism.* New York: Scribner's.

Weber, Max. 1916/1964. *The religions of China: Confucianism and Taoism.* New York: Macmillan.

Weber, Max. 1916–17/1958. *The religion of India: The sociology of Hinduism and Buddhism.* Glencoe, Ill.: Free Press.

Weber, Max. 1920/1952. *Ancient Judaism.* Edited by Hans H. Gerth and Don Martindale. New York: Free Press.

Weber, Max. 1921/1962. *Basic concepts in sociology.* New York: Philosophical Library.

Weber, Max. 1921/1968. *Economy and society.* 3 vols. Totowa, N.J.: Bedminster Press.

Weber, Max. 1921/1978. *Economy and Society: An outline of interpretive sociology.* 2 vols. Edited by Guenther Roth and Claus Wittich. Berkeley and Los Angeles: University of California Press.

Weber, Max. 1927/1984. *General economic history.* New Brunswick: Transaction Books.

Weber, Max. 1947. *The theory of social and economic organization.* New York: Free Press.

Weber, Max. 1958. *From Max Weber: Essays in sociology.* Edited by H.H. Gerth and C. Wright Mills. New York: Oxford University Press.

Weingartner, Rudolph. 1959. Form and content in Simmel's philosophy of life. In *Essays on sociology, philosophy, and aesthetics,* edited by Kurt Wolff, 33–60. New York: Harper Torchbooks.

Weinstein, Deena, and Michael A. Weinstein. 1990. The postmodern discourse of metatheory. Paper presented at Miniconference on Metatheorizing in Sociology at the Meetings of the American Sociological Association, Washington, D.C., August 1990.

Wellman, Barry. 1983. Network analysis: Some basic principles. In *Sociological theory—1983,* edited by Randall Collins, 155–200. San Francisco: Jossey-Bass.

Whitaker, M. A. B. 1984. Science, scientists, and history of science. *History of Science* 22: 421–24.

White. H.C., S. A. Boorman, and R.L. Breiger. 1976. Social structure from multiple networks: Parts 1 and 2. *American Journal of Sociology* 81: 730–80; 1384–1446.

White, Hayden. 1973. *The historical imagination in nineteenth-century Europe.* Baltimore: Johns Hopkins University Press.

Wilensky, Harold. 1964. The professionalization of everyone? *American Journal of Sociology* 70: 137–58.

Wiley, Norbert. 1979. The rise and fall of dominating theories in American sociology. In *Contemporary issues in theory and research,* edited by William Snizek, Ellsworth Fuhrman, and Michael K. Miller, 47–79. Westport Conn.: Greenwood Press.

Wiley, Norbert. 1985. The current interegnum in American sociology. *Social Research* 52: 179–207.

Wiley, Norbert. 1986. Early American sociology and the Polish peasant. *Sociological Theory* 4: 20–40.

Wiley, Norbert. 1988. The micro-macro problem in social theory. *Sociological Theory* 6: 254–61.

Wiley, Norbert. 1989. Response to Ritzer. *Sociological Theory* 7: 230–31.

Wilke, Arthur S., and Raj P. Mohan. 1979. Units of analysis and paradigms in contemporary sociological theory. *Social Science* Winter: 28–34.

Wippler, Reinhard, and Siegwart Lindenberg. 1987. Collective phenomena and rational choice. In *The micro-macro link,* edited by Jeffrey C. Alexander, Bernard Giesen, Richard Munch, and Neil Smelser, 135–52. Berkeley and Los Angeles: University of California Press.

Wolf, Frederick M. 1986. *Meta-analysis: Quantitative methods for research synthesis.* Beverly Hills, Calif.: Sage.

Worsley, Peter. 1982. *Marx and Marxism.* Chichester, England: Ellis Harwood.

Wright, Susan. 1986. Molecular biology or molecular politics? The production of scientific consensus on the hazards of recombinant DNA technology. *Social Studies of Science* 16: 593–620.

Wrong, Dennis. 1961. The oversocialized conception of man. *American Sociological Review* 26: 183–193.

Zimmerman, Don, and Melvin Pollner. 1970. The everyday world as a phenomenon. In *Introduction to the sociologies of everyday life,* edited by Jack Douglas, Patricia A. Adler, Peter Adler, Andrea Fontana, C. Robert Freeman, and Joseph Kotarba, 80–113. Boston: Allyn and Bacon.

Author Index

Subject Index

About the Author

For George Ritzer, professor of sociology at the University of Maryland, this book constitutes both an addition to, and a culmination of, almost two decades of work on metatheoretical issues. This body of work includes *Sociology: A Multiple Paradigm Science* (1975, 1980), *Toward an Integrated Sociological Paradigm* (1981), as well as a number of essays that have appeared in such journals as the *American Sociological Review, Social Forces,* and *Sociological Theory.* He has also edited a special issue of *Sociological Forum* (March, 1990) and an anthology (forthcoming) devoted to metatheoretical concerns. Professor Ritzer is immediate past-chair of the Section on Theoretical Sociology of the American Sociological Association and his textbook, *Sociological Theory,* 2nd edition (1988) is the most widely used theory textbook in the world. His non-metatheoretical passions include his wife, his two sons, long walks with books-on-tape, and his yellow labrador, Brandy.